MODERNIZING WOMEN

SECOND EDITION

MODERNIZING WOMEN

Gender and Social Change in the Middle East

Valentine M. Moghadam

LYNNE
RIENNER
PUBLISHERS

BOULDER
LONDON

Published in the United States of America in 2003 by
Lynne Rienner Publishers, Inc.
1800 30th Street, Boulder, Colorado 80301
www.rienner.com

and in the United Kingdom by
Lynne Rienner Publishers, Inc.
3 Henrietta Street, Covent Garden, London WC2E 8LU

Library of Congress Cataloging-in-Publication Data
Moghadam, Valentine M.
   Modernizing women : gender and social change in the Middle East / Valentine M.
Moghadam.—2nd ed.
      p.   cm.
   Includes bibliographical references and index.
   ISBN 1-58826-195-6 (alk. paper) — ISBN 1-58826-171-9 (pbk. : alk. paper)
      1. Women—Middle East—Social conditions.   2. Muslim women—Middle East—Social
conditions.   3. Women—Middle East—Economic conditions.   4. Muslim women—Middle
East—Economic conditions.   I. Title.

HQ1726.5.M64   2003
305.42'0956—dc21

                                                                                2003041423

British Cataloging in Publication Data
A Cataloguing in Publication record for this book
is available from the British Library.

Printed and bound in the United States of America

The paper used in this publication meets the requirements
of the American National Standard for Permanence of
Paper for Printed Library Materials Z39.48-1992.

5 4 3 2 1

Contents

Illustrations

Tables

Figures

Photographs

Preface

When the first edition of this book was nearing completion in 1992, Afghanistan had fallen to the U.S.-backed Mujahidin rebels after a fourteen-year experiment in modern, socialistic governance whose defining features were policies and laws to enhance women's positions in the family and society. I thus dedicated the book to Afghan women, whose aspirations for equality and empowerment had been deferred. Much has happened since then, in Afghanistan and throughout the Middle East and North Africa (MENA). Globalization, sociodemographic changes, violent civil war in Algeria, more internationalized conflict in Afghanistan, the second Palestinian intifada (uprising), the reform movement and Islamic feminism in Iran, and the women's movement in MENA are but some of the new developments that required analysis and explanation. The decision to update and revise the book for a second edition was made prior to the tragedy of September 11, 2001, but that event imparted some urgency to the project.

The subject of this study is social change in the Middle East, North Africa, and Afghanistan; its impact on women's legal status and social positions; and women's varied responses to, and involvement in, change processes. It also deals with constructions of gender during periods of social and political change. Social change is usually described in terms of modernization, revolution, cultural challenges, and social movements. Much of the standard literature on these topics does not examine women or gender, and thus I hope this study will contribute to an appreciation of the significance of gender in the midst of change. Neither are there many sociological studies on MENA and Afghanistan or studies on women in MENA and Afghanistan from a sociological perspective. Myths and stereotypes abound regarding women, Islam, and the region, and the events of September 11 and since have only compounded them. This book is intended in part to "normalize" the Middle

East by underscoring the salience of structural determinants other than religion. It focuses on the major social-change processes in the region to show how women's lives are shaped not only by "Islam" and "culture," but also by economic development, the state, class location, and the world system. Why the focus on women? It is my contention that middle-class women are consciously and unconsciously major agents of social change in the region, at the vanguard of movements for modernity, democratization, and citizenship.

This book is written for a wide audience: those who study gender and social change, students of MENA and Afghanistan, gender-and-development researchers, and those bureaucrats and policymakers with time to read. Thus the book is descriptive, explanatory, and at times policy oriented. Policy implications are especially noticeable in the chapters on employment (Chapter 2), the changing family (Chapter 4), and Afghanistan (Chapter 7).

The idea for the first edition of the book originated in April 1990 over a delicious Moroccan meal at a restaurant in Paris with Moroccan sociologist and feminist Fatima Mernissi, author of the classic study *Beyond the Veil: Male-Female Dynamics in Modern Muslim Society.* She asked me why, despite all the journal articles I had published, I had not yet written a book on the subject of women and Islam. She then pushed aside plates, bowls, and glasses, brought out a notepad and pen, and proceeded to list the subjects of my various articles in one column and suggestions for chapter headings in another. Fatima even proposed a title for my future book; all I can recall of it now is that it included the word "Islam" and that I balked at that. But I did promise a sociological approach to women in the Middle East.

The next source of inspiration was Kumari Jayawardena, Sri Lankan political scientist, historian, and feminist. At the time, I was with the United Nations University and based in Helsinki, Finland, and had been asked by the Institute of Development Studies of the University of Helsinki to conduct a seminar series for the fall of 1990. Kumari wisely suggested that I organize the lectures around chapter themes for the book, adding that her own famous book, *Feminism and Nationalism in the Third World,* took shape in just this manner. I took her advice and began to write lectures with the book in mind, continuing to work on the project during 1991.

That year I received an announcement from Lynne Rienner Publishers that Mary Moran, whom I had met when I was a postdoctoral fellow at Brown University's Pembroke Center for Teaching and Research on Women, would be editing a series called "Women and Change in the Developing World." Coincidentally, my book's working title at that time was *Women and Social Change in the Middle East.* I took this coincidence to be a good sign, wrote to Mary, and sent her the first draft of the manuscript. After I received a challenging and very helpful external review, I was off and running with the second draft. The first edition appeared in 1993.

Research for this updated and revised edition began in the summer of 2001 and most of the writing was done during the academic year 2001–2002, while I was a Public Policy Fellow at the Woodrow Wilson International Center for Scholars, in Washington, D.C. I am enormously grateful to my institution, Illinois State University (ISU), for the sabbatical leave that enabled me to complete this project. Many thanks are due the Woodrow Wilson Center for its generous resources and an incredibly stimulating environment. I owe special thanks to my colleagues and graduate assistants at the Women's Studies Program at ISU for their support over the years. Last but by no means least, I dedicate this book to the memory of my father, from whom I learned so much.

—Valentine M. Moghadam

Note on Transliteration and the Iranian Calendar

The system of transliteration adopted in this book is a (very) modified version of that recommended by the *International Journal of Middle East Studies*. All the diacritical marks are deleted, with the exception of the ayn and the hamza when they appear in the middle of a word. It is difficult to be consistent when transliteration involves standard Arabic, North African Arabic, Dari, Persian, and Pashtu, but I finally settled on the following spellings: ayatollah, burqa, gharbzadegi, hezbollah, hijab, jihad, Khomeini, moudjahidate, Mujahidin, Mutahhari, Pashtunwali, Quran, Shari'a, Taliban, walwar.

The Iranian solar *(shamsi)* calendar year starts on March 21. An Iranian year may be converted to the international year by adding 621. Thus the Iranian year 1367 refers to the period March 21, 1988, to March 20, 1989, or, as a shorthand, 1988. In 2002 the Iranian year was 1381.

1

Recasting the Middle East, North Africa, and Afghanistan

> *Men are the managers of the affairs of women*
> *for that God has preferred in bounty*
> *one of them over another. . . .*
> *And those you fear may be rebellious*
> *admonish; banish them to their couches, and beat them.*
> —Quran, Sura 4, verse 38

> *[I]nsofar as all texts are polysemic, they are open to variant readings. We*
> *cannot therefore look to a text alone to explain why people have read it in*
> *a particular mode or why they tend to favor one reading of it over another.*
> *This is especially true of a sacred text like the Qur'an which "has been*
> *ripped from its historical, linguistic, literary, and psychological contexts*
> *and then been continually recontextualized in various cultures and accord-*
> *ing to the ideological needs of various actors" (Arkoun 1994, 5). . . . In*
> *particular, we need to examine the roles of Muslim interpretive communi-*
> *ties and states (the realm of sexual politics) in shaping religious knowledge*
> *and authority in ways that enabled patriarchal readings of the Qur'an.*
> —Asma Barlas

The study of social change has tended to regard certain societal institutions and structures as central and then to examine how these change. Family structure, the organization of markets, the state, religious hierarchies, schools, the ways elites have exploited masses to extract surpluses from them, and the general set of values that governs society's cultural outlook are part of the long list of key institutions. In societies everywhere, cultural institutions and practices, economic processes, and political structures are interactive and relatively autonomous. In the Marxist framework, infrastructures and superstructures are made up of multiple levels, and there are various types of transformations from one level to another. There is also an interactive relationship between structure and agency, inasmuch as structural changes are linked to "consciousness"—whether this be class consciousness (of interest to Marxists) or gender consciousness (of interest to feminists).

Social change and societal development come about principally through technological advancements, class conflict, and political action. Each social formation is located within and subject to the influences of a national class structure, a regional context, and a global system of states and markets. The world-system perspective regards states and national economies as situated within an international capitalist nexus with a division of labor corresponding to its constituent parts—core, periphery, and semiperiphery. As such, no major social change occurs outside of the world context.[1] Thus, to understand the roles and status of women or changes in the structure of the family, for example, it is necessary to examine economic development and political change—which in turn are affected by regional and global developments. As we shall see in the discussion of women's employment, the structural determinants of class location, state legal policy, development strategy, and world-market fluctuations come together to shape the pace and rhythm of women's integration in the labor force and their access to economic resources. Figure 1.1 illustrates the institutions and structures that affect and are affected by social changes in a Marxist-informed world-system perspective. The institutions are embedded within a class structure (the system of production, accumulation, and surplus distribution), a set of gender arrangements and norms (ascribed roles to men and women through custom or law; cultural understandings of feminine and masculine), a regional context (e.g., the Middle East, Europe, Latin America), and a world system of states and markets characterized by asymmetries between core, periphery, and semiperiphery countries.

The study of social change is also often done comparatively. Although it cannot be said that social scientists have a single, universally recognized "comparative method," some of our deepest insights into society and culture are reached in and through comparison. In this book, comparisons among women within the region will be made, and some comparisons will be made between Middle East/North African women and women of other third world regions. Indeed, as a major objective of this book is to show the changing and variable status of women in the Middle East, the most effective method is to study the subject comparatively, emphasizing the factors that best explain the differences in women's status across the region and over time.

Yet such an approach is rarely applied to the Middle East, and even less so to women in Muslim societies in general.[2] Indeed, in the wake of the terrorist assaults on the World Trade Center in New York on September 11, 2001, a new wave of commentary appeared, especially in the United States, that questioned the capacity of Muslim and especially Middle Eastern countries to establish modern, democratic, secular, and gender-egalitarian social systems. One article claimed that Muslim societies have fallen behind Western societies because of the "slow evolution of Islamic societies' treatment of women."[3] Even a disinterested academic study on religion, secularization, and

Figure 1.1   Social Structures and Principal Institutions in Contemporary Societies; Their Embeddedness Within Class, Gender, and Regional and Global Relations

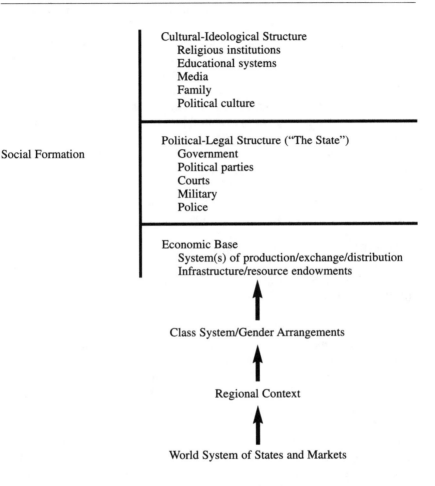

gender equality asserted that countries in the Islamic world are most resistant to the achievement of equality between women and men.[4]

Debating the Status of Muslim Women

That women's legal status and social positions are worse in Muslim countries than anywhere else is a common view. The prescribed role of women in Islamic theology and law is often argued to be a major determinant of women's status. Women are perceived as wives and mothers, and gender segregation is customary, and sometimes legally required. Whereas economic provision is the responsibility of men, women must marry and reproduce to earn status. Men, unlike women, have the unilateral right of divorce; a woman can work and travel only with the written permission of her male guardian; family honor and good reputation, or the negative consequence of shame, rest most heavily upon the conduct of women. Through the Shari'a, Islam dictates the legal and institutional safeguards of honor, thereby justifying and reinforcing the segregation of society according to sex. Muslim societies are characterized by higher-than-average fertility, higher-than-average mortality, and rapid rates of population growth. It is well known that age at marriage affects fertility. As recently as the late 1980s, an average of 34 percent of all brides in Muslim countries were under twenty years of age, and women in Muslim nations bore an average of six children.

The Muslim countries of the Middle East, North Africa, and South Asia also have a distinct gender disparity in literacy and education, as well as low rates of female labor force participation and labor force shares. In 1980 women's share of the labor force was lowest in the Middle East and North Africa (MENA, 23 percent) and highest in the communist economies of Eastern Europe and the Soviet Union (including Central Asia). In 1997 women's share of the labor force in MENA had increased to about 27 percent, but it was still the lowest of any region in the world economy, including South Asia, where the female share was 33 percent.[5]

High fertility, low literacy, and low labor force participation are commonly linked to the low status of women, which in turn is often attributed to the prevalence of Islamic law and norms in Middle Eastern societies. It is said that because of the continuing importance of values such as family honor and modesty, women's participation in nonagricultural or paid labor carries with it a social stigma, and gainful employment is not perceived as part of their role.[6]

Muslim societies, like many others, harbor illusions about immutable gender differences. There is a very strong contention that women are different beings—*different* often meaning *inferior* in legal status and rights—which strengthens social barriers to women's achievement. In the realm of education and employment, not only is it believed that women do not have the same interests as men and will therefore avoid men's activities, but also care is exercised to make sure they cannot prepare for roles considered inappropriate. Women's reproductive function or religious norms have been used to justify their segregation in public, their restriction to the home, and their lack of civil and legal rights. As both a reflection of this state of affairs and a contributing factor, those governments of Muslim countries that have signed or ratified the United Nations Convention on the Elimination of All Forms of Discrimination Against Women (CEDAW) have done so with religiously based reservations that counteract both the spirit and the letter of the convention.[7]

Is the Middle East, then, so different from other regions? Can we understand women's roles and status only in terms of the ubiquity of deference to Islam in the region? In fact, such conceptions are too facile. It is my contention that the position of women in the Middle East cannot be attributed to the presumed intrinsic properties of Islam. It is also my position that Islam is neither more nor less patriarchal than other major religions, especially Hinduism and the other two Abrahamic religions, Judaism and Christianity, all of which share the view of woman as wife and mother. Within Christianity, religious women continue to struggle for a position equal with men, as the ongoing debate over women priests in Catholicism attests. As late as 1998, the Southern Baptist Convention in the United States passed a resolution calling on wives to follow and obey their husbands. In Hinduism a potent female symbol is that of the *sati,* the self-immolating widow. And the Orthodox Jewish law of personal status bears many similarities to the fundamentals of Islamic law, especially with respect to marriage and divorce.[8] The gender configurations that draw heavily from religion and cultural norms to govern women's work, political praxis, family status, and other aspects of their lives in the Middle East are not unique to Muslim or Middle Eastern countries.

Religious-based law exists in the Middle East, but not exclusively in Muslim countries; it is also present in the Jewish state of Israel. Rabbinical judges are reluctant to grant women divorces, and, as in Saudi Arabia, Israeli women cannot hold public prayer services. The sexual division of labor in the home and in the society is largely shaped by the Halacha, or Jewish law, and by traditions that continue to discriminate against women. Marital relations in Israel, governed by Jewish law, determine that the husband should pay for his wife's maintenance, while she should provide household services. According to one account, "The structure of the arrangement is such that the woman is sheltered from the outside world by her husband and in return she adequately runs the home. The obligations one has toward the other are not equal but rather based on clear gender differentiation."[9]

Neither are the marriage and fertility patterns mentioned above unique to Muslim countries; high fertility rates are found in sub-Saharan African countries today and were common in Western countries in the early stage of industrialization and the demographic transition. The low status accorded women is found in non-Muslim areas as well. In the most patriarchal regions of West and South Asia, especially India, there are marked gender disparities in the delivery of healthcare and access to food, resulting in an excessive mortality rate for women.[10] In northern India and parts of rural China, the preference for boys leads to neglect of baby girls to such extent that infant and child mortality is greater among females; moreover, female feticide has been well documented. As recently as 2002, the female/male sex ratio in China and India was 94:100. The low status of women and girls, therefore, should be understood not in terms of the intrinsic properties of any one religion but of kin-ordered patriarchal and agrarian structures.

Finally, it should be recalled that in all Western societies women as a group were disadvantaged until relatively recently.[11] Indeed, Islam provided women with property rights for centuries while women in Europe were denied the same rights. In India, Muslim property codes were more progressive than English law until the mid–nineteenth century. It should be stressed, too, that even in the West today there are marked variations in the legal status, economic conditions, and social positions of women. The United States, for example, lags behind northern Europe in terms of social policies and overall security for women. Why Muslim women lag behind Western women in legal rights, mobility, autonomy, and so forth, has more to do with developmental issues—the extent of urbanization, industrialization, and proletarianization, as well as the political ploys of state managers—than with religious and cultural factors.

Gender asymmetry and the status of women in the Muslim world cannot be solely attributed to Islam, because adherence to Islamic precepts and the applications of Islamic legal codes differ throughout the Muslim world. For example, Tunisia and Turkey are secular states, and only Iran has direct clerical rule. Consequently, women's legal and social positions are quite varied, as this book will detail. And within the same Muslim society, social class largely determines the degrees of sex segregation, female autonomy, and mobility. Today upper-class women have more mobility than lower-class women, although in the past it was the reverse: veiling and seclusion were upper-class phenomena. By examining changes over time and variations within societies and by comparing Muslim and non-Muslim gender patterns, one recognizes that the status of women in Muslim societies is neither uniform nor unchanging nor unique.

Assessing Women's Status

Since the 1980s, the subject of women in the Middle East has been tied to the larger issue of Islamic revival, also known as fundamentalism or Islamism, in the region. The rise of Islamist movements in the Middle East has reinforced stereotypes about the region, in particular the idea that Islam is ubiquitous in the culture and politics of the region, that tradition is tenacious, that the clergy have the highest authority, and that women's status is everywhere low. How do we begin to assess the status of women in Islam or in the Middle East? Critics and advocates of Islam hold sharply divergent views on the matter. One author sardonically classified much of the literature on the status of women as representing either "misery research" or "dignity research." The former focuses on the utterly oppressive aspects of Muslim women's lives, while the latter seeks to show the strength of women's positions in their families and communities. In either case, it is the status of women *in Islam* that is being scrutinized. In some of their writings, secular feminists Juliette Minces, Mai Ghoussoub, Haideh Moghissi, and Haleh Afshar describe adherence to Islamic norms and laws as the main impediment to women's advancement. Leila Ahmed once concluded that Islam is incompatible with feminism—even with the more mainstream/modernist notion of women's rights—because Islam regards women as the weak and inferior sex.[12] Fatima Mernissi, although critical of the existing inequalities, has stressed that the idea of an inferior sex is alien to Islam; it was because of their "strengths" that women had to be subdued and kept under control.[13] Freda Hussein raised counterarguments based on the concept of "complementarity of the sexes" in Islam. Azizah al-Hibri, Riffat Hassan, Asma Barlas, and other Western-based Islamic or Muslim feminists seek to show the genuinely egalitarian and emancipatory content of the Quran, which they maintain has been hijacked by patriarchal interpretations since the early Middle Ages.[14] Finally, those who identify most closely with Islamic law are convinced that Islam provides all the rights necessary for humankind and womankind, and that Islamic states go the furthest in establishing these rights (see Chapter 5 for a discussion of Islamist women activists).

As noted by the Turkish sociologist Yakin Ertürk, these arguments draw attention to interesting and controversial aspects of the problem, but many of them neither provide us with consistent theoretical tools with which to grasp the problem of women's status nor guide us in formulating effective policy for strategy and action. They are either ethnocentric in their critique of Islam or relativistic in stressing cultural specificity. The former approach attributes a conservative role to Islam, assuming that it is an obstacle to progress— whether it be material progress or progress with respect to the status of women. Ertürk argues that overemphasizing the role of Islam not only prevents us from looking at the more fundamental social contradictions that often foster religious requirements but also implies little hope for change, because Islam is regarded by its followers as the literal word of God and therefore absolute. For the Muslim thinkers, a relativist stand is essentially a defensive response and imprisons its advocates in a pseudonationalistic and religious pride. The cultural relativist approach produces a circular argument by uncritically relying on the concept of cultural variability/specificity in justifying Islamic principles.[15] Many Western observers who resort to relativism in their approach to Islam hold liberal worldviews and treat Islamic practices within the context of individual freedom to worship; any interference with that freedom is seen as a violation of human rights. During the 1980s and 1990s, this view underpinned policies of "multiculturalism," "diversity," and "tolerance" in Western Europe and North America, which many feminists came to criticize, arguing that gender differences and inequalities are occluded by this preoccupation with the human rights of cultural groups.[16]

The focus on the status of women *in Islam* may be important to theologians and to believing women, but it does little to satisfy social science or feminist inquiry. For one thing, Islam is experienced, practiced, and interpreted quite differently over time and space. Tunisian sociologist Abdelwahab Bouhdiba convincingly shows that although the Islamic community may consider itself unified, Islam is fundamentally "plastic," inasmuch as there are various Islams—Tunisian, Iranian, Malay, Afghan, Saudia Arabian, Nigerian, and so on.[17] In order to understand the social implications of Islam, therefore, it is necessary to look at the broader sociopolitical and economic order within which it is exercised. Whether the content of the Quran is inherently conservative and hostile toward women or egalitarian and emancipatory is not irrelevant to social science or feminist inquiry, but it is less central or problematical than it is often made out to be.

Clearly, an alternative is needed to the conceptual trap and political problem created by the devil of ethnocentrism and the deep blue sea of cultural relativism. In this regard it is useful to refer to various "universal declarations" and conventions formulated within the United Nations and agreed upon by the world community. For example, the Universal Declaration on Human Rights (of 1948) provides for both equality between women and men and freedom of religion. The practical meaning of gender equality and means to achieve it have been reflected in the United Nations Convention on the Elimination of All Forms of Discrimination Against Women (CEDAW), adopted on December 10, 1979. The convention entered into force in 1981 and by April 2000 all but twenty-six countries had ratified or acceded to it. Similarly, with the Beijing Declaration and Platform for Action, adopted by the 1995 Fourth World Conference on Women, governments reached a consensus to "seek to promote and protect the full enjoyment of all human rights and the fundamental freedoms of all women throughout the life cycle." The Universal Declaration on Human Rights, CEDAW, and the Platform for Action are all intended to set out universally agreed-upon norms. They were framed by people from diverse cultures, religions, and nationalities and intended to take into account such factors as religion and cultural traditions of countries. For that reason, CEDAW makes no provision whatsoever for differential interpretation based on culture or religion. Instead, it states clearly in Article 2 that "States Parties . . . undertake . . . to take all appropriate measures, including legislation, to modify or abolish existing laws, regulations, customs and practices which constitute discrimination against women."[18] All three conventions are thus culturally neutral and universal in their applicability. They provide a solid and legitimate political point of departure for women's rights activists everywhere. In turn, women's rights activists throughout the Middle East seek implementation of CEDAW and the formulation of national action plans for women's advancement based on the Beijing Platform for Action, and are strong proponents of human rights, which they understand to encompass civil, political, and social rights. Many feminists, including Marxist-feminists, would agree with Abdullahi An-Na'im that "human rights are claims we make for the protection of our vital interests in bodily integrity, material well-being, and human dignity."[19]

As for social-scientific research to assess and compare the positions of women in different societies, a sixfold framework of dimensions of women's status adopted from Janet Giele—a framework that is quite consistent with the spirit of CEDAW and the Beijing Platform for Action—can usefully guide concrete investigations of women's positions within and across societies:

> *Political expression.* What rights do women possess, formally and otherwise? Can they own property in their own right? Can they express any dissatisfactions within their own political and social movements?
> *Work and mobility.* How do women fare in the formal labor force? How mobile are they, how well are they paid, how are their jobs ranked, and what leisure do they get?
> *Family* (formation, duration, and size). What is the age of marriage? Do women choose their own partners? Can they divorce them? What is the status of single women and widows? Do women have freedom of movement?
> *Education.* What access do women have, how much can they attain, and is the curriculum the same for them as for men?
> *Health and sexual control.* What is women's mortality, to what particular illnesses and stresses (physical and mental) are they exposed, and what control do they have over their own fertility?
> *Cultural expression.* What images of women and their "place" are prevalent, and how far do these reflect or determine reality? What can women do in the cultural field?[20]

This is a useful way of specifying and delineating changes and trends in women's social roles in the economy, the polity, and the cultural sphere. It enables the researcher (and activist) to move from generalities to specificities and to assess the strengths and weaknesses of women's positions. It focuses on women's betterment rather than on culture or religion, and it has wide applicability. At the same time, it draws attention to women as actors. Women are not only the passive targets of policies or the victims of distorted development; they are also shapers and makers of social change—especially Middle Eastern women in the new millennium.

Diversity in the Middle East

To study the Middle East and North Africa is to recognize the diversity within the region and within the female population. Contrary to popular opinion, the Middle East is not a uniform and homogeneous region. Women are themselves stratified by class, ethnicity, education, and age. There is no archetypal Middle Eastern Woman, but rather women inserted in quite diverse socioeconomic and cultural arrangements. The fertility behavior and needs of a poor peasant woman are quite different from those of a professional woman or a wealthy urbanite. The educated Saudi woman who has no need for employment and is chauffeured by a Sri Lankan migrant worker has little in common with the educated Moroccan woman who needs to work to augment the family income and also acquires status with a professional position. There is some overlap in cultural conceptions of gender in Morocco and Saudi Arabia, but there are also profound dissimilarities (and driving is only one of the more trivial ones). Saudi Arabia is far more conservative than Morocco in terms of what is considered appropriate for women.

Women are likewise divided ideologically and politically. Some women activists align themselves with liberal, social democratic, or communist organizations; others support Islamist/fundamentalist groups. Some women reject religion as patriarchal; others wish to reclaim religion for themselves or to identify feminine aspects of it. Some women reject traditions and time-honored customs; others find identity, solace, and strength in them. More research is needed to determine whether social background shapes and can predict political and ideological affiliation, but in general women's social positions have implications for their consciousness and activism.

The countries of the Middle East and North Africa differ in their historical evolution, social composition, economic structures, and state forms. All the countries are Arab except Afghanistan, Iran, Israel, and Turkey. All the countries are predominantly Muslim except Israel. All Muslim countries are predominantly Sunni except Iran, which is predominantly Shi'a, and Iraq, with equal parts Sunni and Shi'a. Some of the countries have Christian populations that were once sizable (Iraq, Egypt, Lebanon, the Palestinians, Syria); others are ethnically diverse (Afghanistan, Iran, Iraq); some have had strong working-class movements and trade unions (Iran, Egypt, Tunisia, Turkey) or large communist organizations (Iran, Egypt, the Palestinians, Sudan). A few still have nomadic and semi-sedentary populations (Afghanistan, Libya, Saudi Arabia). In almost all countries, a considerable part of the middle classes have received Western-style education.

Economically, the countries of the region comprise oil economies poor in other resources, including population (Kuwait, Libya, Oman, Qatar, Saudi Arabia, United Arab Emirates [UAE]); mixed oil economies (Algeria, Iraq, Iran, Egypt, Tunisia, Syria); and non-oil economies (Israel, Jordan, Morocco,

Sudan, Turkey, Yemen). The countries are further divided into the city-states (such as Qatar and the UAE); the "desert states" (for example, Libya and Saudi Arabia); and the "normal states" (Iran, Egypt, Syria, Turkey). The latter have a more diversified structure, and their resources include oil, agricultural land, and large populations. Some MENA countries are rich in capital and import labor (Kuwait, Libya, Saudi Arabia), while others are poor in capital or are middle-income countries that export labor (Algeria, Egypt, Morocco, Tunisia, Turkey, Yemen). Some countries have more-developed class structures than others; the size and significance of the industrial working class, for example, varies across the region. There is variance in the development of skills ("human capital formation"), in the depth and scope of industrialization, in the development of infrastructure, in standards of living and welfare, and in the size of the female labor force.

Politically, the state types range from theocratic monarchism (Saudi Arabia) to secular republicanism (Turkey). Several Gulf states have no constitutions; until 1992 the Kingdom of Saudi Arabia had no formal constitution apart from the Quran and the Shari'a, the Islamic legal code. Many of the states in the Middle East have experienced legitimacy problems, which became acute in the 1980s. Political scientists have used various terms to describe the states in the Middle East: "authoritarian-socialist" (for Algeria, Iraq, Syria), "radical Islamist" (for Iran and Libya), "patriarchal-conservative" (for Jordan, Morocco, Saudi Arabia), and "authoritarian-privatizing" (for Egypt, Tunisia, Turkey). Most of these states have strong capitalistic features, while some retain feudalistic features. In this book I use "neopatriarchal state," adopted from Hisham Sharabi, as an umbrella term for the various state types in the Middle East.[21] In the neopatriarchal state, unlike liberal or social democratic societies, religion is bound to power and state authority; moreover, the family, rather than the individual, constitutes the universal building block of the community. The neopatriarchal state and the patriarchal family reflect and reinforce each other. For Sharabi, "the most advanced and functional aspect of the neopatriarchal state . . . is its internal security apparatus, the *mukhabarat.* . . . In social practice ordinary citizens not only are arbitrarily deprived of some of their basic rights but are the virtual prisoners of the state, the objects of its capricious and ever-present violence. . . . It is in many ways no more than a modernized version of the traditional patriarchal sultanate."[22] Although the 1990s saw the beginnings of political liberalization and quasi-democratization, MENA states remain authoritarian and citizen participation limited.

In the Middle East there is a variable mix of religion and politics. Although Turkey is the only country in the region with a constitutional separation of religion and the state, Islam is not a state religion in Syria, whose constitution provides that "freedom of religion shall be preserved, and the state shall respect all religions and guarantee freedom of worship to all, provided that public order is not endangered." Syria's Muslim majority coexists with a Christian minority totaling about 12 percent of the population. Christian holidays are recognized in the same way as Muslim holidays. Syria observes Friday rest but also allows time off for Christian civil servants to attend Sunday religious services. The constitution also guarantees women "every opportunity to participate effectively and completely in political, social, economic, and cultural life." In Syria, as in many countries in the region, urban women, especially those who are educated and professional, enjoy a degree of freedom comparable to their counterparts in, for example, Latin American countries. But it is difficult to reconcile women's rights with Islamic law (Shari'a), which remains unfavorable to women with regard to marriage, divorce, and inheritance. Most of the countries of the Middle East and North Africa are governed to some degree by the Shari'a. This is especially the case in the area of family law, although in some countries the penal code is also based on Islamic law. In the Jewish state of Israel, family law is based on the Halacha and supervised by the rabbinate. Tunisia modernized its family law immediately after independence, and further reforms were adopted in 1993. Turkey's family law was not based on Islam but was quite conservative nonetheless, until the women's movement forced changes in 2001. Elsewhere, family laws based on Islamic texts continue to govern the personal and family status of women, and hence confer on them second-class citizenship.

This second-class citizenship is illustrated in Tables 1.1 and 1.2, which offer economic and political indicators relevant to an understanding of women's legal status and social standing in the region, and compared to other regions.

Table 1.1   Female Economic Activity Rates by Region, 2000

	Rate (%)	Index (1990 = 100)	As % of Male Rate
Arab states	32.9	117	41
East Asia and the Pacific	68.9	99	82
Latin America and the Caribbean	42.0	108	51
South Asia	43.3	106	51
Sub-Saharan Africa	62.3	99	73
Central and Eastern Europe and the CIS (former Soviet Union)	57.8	99	81

Source: UNDP, *Human Development Report 2002* (New York: Oxford University Press, 2002), tab. 25, p. 237.
    Note: The category "Arab states" excludes Iran and Turkey.

Table 1.2   Women's Political Participation, MENA in Comparative Perspective

| | % Parliamentary Seats in Single or Lower-Level Chamber Occupied by Women | | | % Women in Decisionmaking Positions in Government | | | |
| | | | | Ministerial Level | | Subministerial Level | |
	1987	1995	1999	1994	1998	1994	1998
MENA							
Algeria	2	7	3	4	0	8	10
Bahrain				0	0	0	1
Egypt	4	2	2	4	6	0	4
Iran	1	3	5	0	0	1	1
Iraq	13	11	6	0	0	0	0
Israel	8	9	12	4	0	5	9
Jordan	0	1	0	3	2	0	0
Kuwait	0	0	0	0	0	0	7
Lebanon		2	2	0	0	0	0
Libya				0	0	2	4
Morocco	0	1	1	0	0	0	8
Oman				0	0	2	4
Qatar				0	0	3	0
Saudi Arabia				0	0	0	0
Sudan	8	8	5	0	0	0	0
Syria	9	10	10	7	8	0	0
Tunisia	6	7	7	4	3	14	10
Turkey	1	2	4	5	5	0	17
UAE	0	0	0	0	0	0	0
Yemen		1	1	0	0	0	0
Other							
Argentina	5	22	28	0	8	3	9
Brazil	5	7	6	5	4	11	13
Chile		8	11	13	13	0	8
China	21	21	22	6		4	
Cuba	34	23	28	0	5	9	11
Malaysia	5	8	8	7	16	0	13
Mexico	11	14	17	5	5	5	7
Philippines	9	9	12	8	10	11	19
South Africa	2	25	30	6		2	
Venezuela	4	6	13	11	3	0	7
Vietnam	18	18	26	5	0	0	5

Source: United Nations, *The World's Women: Trends and Statistics 2000* (New York: United Nations), tab. 6A.

Note: Blank spaces indicate data not available.

Given the range of socioeconomic and political conditions, it follows that gender is not fixed and unchanging in the Middle East (and neither is culture). As this book will document, there exists intra-regional differentiation in gender norms, as measured by differences in women's legal status, education levels, fertility trends, employment patterns, and political participation. For example, gender segregation in public is the norm and the law in Saudi Arabia but not in Lebanon, Jordan, Morocco, Tunisia, or Syria. Following the Iranian Revolution, the new authorities prohibited abortion, discouraged contraception, and lowered the age of marriage for girls to puberty. Not surprisingly, fertility rates soared in the 1980s (though they dropped in the late 1990s after a policy change). But in Tunisia contraceptive use was widespread in the 1980s and the average age of marriage for women was, and remains, twenty-four. Afghanistan has the highest rate of female illiteracy among Muslim countries, but the state took important steps after the revolution of April 1978 to expand educational facilities and income-generating activities for women (although setbacks occurred when Islamists took power in the early 1990s). Turkish women were given the right to vote in 1930, and in the 1950s and 1960s women began to occupy a large share of high-status occupations such as law, medicine, and university appointments. And, as seen in Table 1.2, women's participation in government as key decisionmakers and as members of parliament varies across the region. In almost all MENA countries, women vote, run for parliament, and are appointed to governmental positions. About 25 percent of judges in Algeria and Tunisia are women, whereas some other MENA countries still ban women from judicial positions.

If all the countries we are studying are predominantly Muslim (save Israel), and if the legal status and social positions of women are variable, then logically Islam and culture are not the principal determinants of their status. Of course, Islam can be stronger in some cases than in others, but what I wish to show in this book is that women's roles and status are structurally determined by state ideology (regime orientation and juridical system), level and type of economic development (extent of industrialization, urbanization, proletarianization, and position in the world system), and class location. A sex/gender system informed by Islam may be identified, but to ascribe principal explanatory power to religion and culture is methodologically deficient, as it exaggerates their influence and renders them timeless and unchanging. Religions and cultural specificities do shape gender systems, but they are not the most significant determinants and are themselves subject to change. The content of gender systems is also subject to change.

A Framework for Analysis:
Gender, Class, the State, Development

The theoretical framework that informs this study rests on the premise that stability and change in the status of women are shaped by the following structural determinants: the sex/gender system, class, and economic development and state policies that operate within the capitalist world system.

The Gender System

Marxist-feminists first used the term "sexual division of labor" to refer to the ideological and material ordering of roles, rights, and values in the family, the workplace, and the society that have their origins in male-female sexual difference and especially in women's reproductive capacity. They pointed out that patriarchy, a system of male dominance over women, historically has coexisted with modes of production, and that women's status has been affected by both the sexual division of labor and class divisions corresponding to modes of production. Today the term "gender" is used more broadly to denote the meanings given to masculine and feminine, asymmetrical power relations between the sexes, and the ways that men and women are differently situated in and affected by social processes. Judith Lorber defines gender as "a process of social construction, a system of social stratification, and an institution that structures every aspect of our lives because of its embeddedness in the family, the workplace, and the state, as well as in sexuality, language, and culture."[23] Lorber and other feminists regard gender as a powerful source of social distinctions, while also recognizing that gender differences are elaborated by class and, where relevant, by race and ethnicity.

Combining the Marxist-feminist and sociological perspectives leads to an understanding of the sex/gender system as a cultural construct that is itself constituted by social structure. That is to say, gender systems are differently manifested in kinship-ordered, agrarian, developing, and advanced industrialized settings. Type of political regime and state ideology further influence the gender system. States that are Marxist (for example, Cuba or the former German Democratic Republic), liberal democratic (the United States), social democratic (the Nordic countries), or neopatriarchal (Islamic Republic of Iran) have had quite different laws about women and different policies on the family.[24]

The thesis that women's relative lack of economic power is the most important determinant of gender inequalities, including those of marriage, parenthood, and sexuality, is cogently demonstrated by Rae Blumberg and Janet Chafetz, among others. The division of labor by gender at the macro (societal) level reinforces that of the household. This dynamic is an important source of women's disadvantaged position and of the stability of the gender system. Another important source is juridical and ideological. In most contemporary societal arrangements, "masculine" and "feminine" are defined by law and custom; men and women have unequal access to political power and economic resources, and cultural images and representations of women are fundamentally distinct from those of men—even in societies formally committed to social (including gender) equality. Inequalities are learned and taught, and "the non-perception of disadvantages of a deprived group helps to perpetuate those disadvantages."[25] Many governments do not take an active interest in improving women's status and opportunities, and not all countries have active and autonomous women's organizations to protect and further women's interests and rights. High fertility rates limit women's roles and perpetuate gender inequality. Where official and popular discourses stress sexual differences rather than legal equality, an apparatus exists to create stratification based on gender. The legal system, educational system, and labor market are all sites of the construction and reproduction of gender inequality and the continuing subordination of women.

According to Hanna Papanek, "Gender differences, based on the social construction of biological sex distinctions, are one of the great 'fault lines' of societies—those marks of difference among categories of persons that govern the allocation of power, authority, and resources." Contemporary gender systems are often designed by ideologues and inscribed in law, justified by custom and enforced by policy, sustained by processes of socialization and reinforced through distinct institutions. But gender differences are not the only "fault lines"; they operate within a larger matrix of other socially constructed distinctions, such as class, ethnicity, religion, and age, that give them their specific dynamics in a given time and place. Gender is thus not a homogeneous category. To paraphrase Michael Mann, gender is stratified and stratification is gendered.[26] Nor is the gender system static. In the Middle East, the sex/gender system, while still patriarchal, has undergone change.

Class

Class constitutes a basic unit of social life and thus of social research. Class is here understood in the Marxist sense as determined by ownership or control of the means of production; social classes also have differential access to political power and the state. Class location shapes cultural practices, patterns of consumption, lifestyle, reproduction, and even worldview. As Ralph Miliband put it, class divisions "find expression in terms of power, income, wealth, responsibility, 'life chances,' style and quality of life, and everything else that makes up the texture of existence."[27] Class shapes women's roles in the sphere of production, and it shapes women's choices and behavior in reproduction.

In the highly stratified MENA societies, social-class location, along with state action and economic development, acts upon gender relations and women's social positions. Although state-sponsored education has resulted in a certain amount of upward social mobility and has increased the number of women seeking jobs, women's access to resources, including education, is largely determined by their class location. That a large percentage of urban employed women in the Middle East are found in the services sector or in professional positions can be understood by examining class. As in other third world regions where social disparities are great, upper-middle-class urban women in the Middle East can exercise a greater number of choices and thus become much more "emancipated" than lower-middle-class, working-class, urban poor, or peasant women. In 1971, Constantina Safilios-Rothschild wrote that women could fulfill conflicting professional and marital roles with the help of cheap domestic labor and the extended family network.[28] In 2002 this observation was still true for women from wealthy families, although middle-class women in most of the large Middle Eastern countries are less likely to be able to afford domestic help in these post-oil-boom days and more likely to rely on a mother or mother-in-law. As Margot Badran has noted, whereas some states are committed to women's participation in industrial production (e.g., Egypt, Morocco, Tunisia, Turkey), the system extracts the labor of women in economic need without giving them the social services to coordinate their productive roles in the family and workplace.[29]

Economic development has led to the growth of the middle class, especially the salaried middle class. The middle class in Middle Eastern countries is internally differentiated; there is a traditional middle class of shopkeepers, small bazaaris, and the self-employed—what Marxists call the traditional petty bourgeoisie. There is also a more modern salaried middle class, persons employed in the government sector or in the private sector as teachers, lawyers, engineers, administrators, secretaries, nurses, doctors, and so on. But this modern salaried middle class is itself differentiated culturally, for many of its members are children of the traditional petty bourgeoisie. The political implications are profound, for Islamist movements evidently have recruited from the more traditional sections of the contemporary middle class: the petty bourgeoisie and the most conservative elements of the professional middle class.

Economic Development and State Policies

Since the 1960s and 1970s the Middle East has been participant in a global process variously called the internationalization of capital, the new (or changing) international division of labor, global Fordism, and globalization. National development plans, domestic industrialization projects, and foreign investment led to significant changes in the structure of the labor force, including an expansion of nonagricultural employment. Oil revenues assisted industrial development projects, which also led to new employment opportunities and changes in the occupational structure. The Middle East has historically been a region with thriving cities, but increased urbanization and rural-urban migration since the 1950s occurred in tandem with changes in the economy and in property relations. Property ownership patterns changed concomitantly from being based almost exclusively on land or merchant capital to being based on the ownership of large-scale industrial units and more complex and international forms of commercial and financial capital. The process of structural transformation and the nearly universal shift toward the nonagrarian urban sector in economic and social terms produced new class actors and undermined (though it did not destroy) the old. Industrial workers, a salaried middle class, and large-scale capitalists are products of and participants in economic development. Mass education and bureaucratic expansion led to prodigious growth in the new middle class; the creation and absorption into the public sector of important productive, commercial, and banking assets spawned a new managerial state bourgeoisie.[30] Other classes and strata affected by economic development and state expansion have been the peasantry, rural landowning class, urban merchant class, and traditional petty bourgeoisie. High population growth rates, coupled with rural-urban migration, concentrated larger numbers of semiproletarians, informal workers, and the unemployed in major urban areas.

In the heyday of economic development, most of the large MENA countries, such as Algeria, Egypt, Iran, and Turkey, embarked on a development strategy of import-substitution industrialization (ISI), where machinery was imported to run local industries producing consumer goods. This strategy was associated with an economic system characterized by central planning and a large public sector. State expansion, economic development, oil wealth, and the region's increased integration within the world system combined to create educational and employment opportunities for women in the Middle East. For about ten years after the oil price increases of the early 1970s, a massive investment program by the oil-producing nations affected the structure of the labor force not only within the relevant countries but throughout the region as a result of labor migration. The urban areas saw an expansion of the female labor force, with women occupying paid positions as workers and professionals. The state played a central role in the development process.

Indeed, between the 1950s and 1980s, the third world state was a major actor in the realization of social and economic development. As such, the state had a principal part in the formulation of social policies, development strategies, and legislation that shaped opportunities for women. Family law; affirmative action-type policies; protective legislation regarding working mothers; policies on education, health, and population; and other components of social policy designed by state managers have affected women's status and gender arrangements. Strong states with the capacity to enforce laws may undermine customary discrimination and patriarchal structures—or they may reinforce them. The state can enable or impede the integration of women citizens in public life. As Jean Pyle found for the Republic of Ireland, state policy can have contradictory goals: development of the economy and expansion of services on one hand, maintenance of the "traditional family" on the other.[31] Such contradictory goals could create role conflicts for women, who may find themselves torn between the economic need or desire to work and the gender ideology that stresses family roles for women. Conversely, economic development and state-sponsored education could have unintended consequences: the ambivalence of neopatriarchal state managers notwithstanding, there is now a generation and stratum of educated women who actively pursue employment and political participation in defiance of cultural norms and gender ideologies.

The positive relationship between women's education and nonagricultural employment is marked throughout the Middle East. Census data reveal that each increase in the level of education is reflected in a corresponding increase in the level of women's nonagricultural employment and a decrease in fertility. Education seems to increase the aspirations of women in certain sectors of society for higher income and better standards of living.[32] Moreover, it has weakened the restrictive barriers of traditions and increased the propensity of women to join the labor force and public life. These social changes have had a positive effect in reducing traditional sex segregation and female seclusion and in producing a generation of middle-class women who have achieved economic independence and no longer depend on family or marriage for survival and status.

At the same time, it is necessary to recognize the limits to change—including those imposed by a country's or a region's location within the economic zones of the capitalist world system. Development strategies and state economic policies are not formulated in a vacuum; they are greatly influenced, for better or for worse, by world-systemic imperatives. Although most of the large MENA countries are semiperiphery countries, the function of the region within the world system thus far has been to guarantee a steady supply of oil for foreign, especially core-country, markets, and to import industrial goods, especially armaments, mainly from core countries. One result has been limited industrialization and manufacturing for export. Another result has been limited employment opportunities for women in the formal industrial sector, as capital-intensive industries and technologies tend to favor male labor. And since the 1980s, socioeconomic problems have bedeviled the region, with wide-ranging implications for women.

The section that follows examines in more detail the gender dynamics of social change in the region—and, by extension, the organization of this book.

Social Changes and Women in the Middle East

One of the ways societies influence each other economically, politically, and culturally is through international labor migration, which also has distinct gender-specific effects. In the Middle East and North Africa, oil-fueled development encouraged labor migration from labor-surplus and capital-poor economies to capital-rich and labor-deficit oil economies. For example, there was substantial Tunisian migrant labor in Libya, Egyptian and Palestinian migrant labor in the Gulf emirates, and Yemeni labor in Saudi Arabia. This migration affected, among other things, the structure of populations, the composition of the households, and the economies of both sending and receiving countries. Many of the oil-rich Gulf states came to have large populations of noncitizens, and female-headed households proliferated in the labor-sending countries. During the years of the oil boom, roughly until the mid-1980s, workers' remittances were an important factor in not only the welfare of families and households but also in the fortunes of economies such as Jordan's and Egypt's. Labor migration to areas outside the Middle East has been undertaken principally by North Africans and Turks. Historically, North Africans have migrated to the cities of France, although large populations of Moroccans have settled in Belgium, the Netherlands, and Spain as well. And in the late 1980s Italy became another destination for North African migrant workers. Turkish "guest workers" have been an important source of labor to (West) German capital since the 1950s.

Labor migration may be functional for the economies of the host country (in that it receives cheap labor) and the sending country (in that unemployment is reduced and capital inflows through workers' remittances are increased); emigration, especially of professionals (the so-called brain drain) also may be advantageous to receiving countries. Like exile, however, labor migration and emigration have other consequences, including social-psychological, cultural, and political effects. In the case of Iran—characterized by the brain drain of Iranian professionals following the 1953 Shah-CIA coup d'état, the massive exodus of students to the West in the 1960s and 1970s, a second wave of emigration and exile following Islamization, and the proliferation of draft-dodgers in the mid-1980s—the society became fractured and contentious. When, in 1978–1979, tens of thousands of Iranian students in the United States and Europe returned en masse to help construct the new Iran, they brought with them both organizational and leadership skills learned in the anti-Shah student movement *and* a secular, left-wing political-cultural orientation that put them at odds with the Islamists.[33]

Exile, emigration, and refugee status almost always result in changes in attitudes and behavior, but whether these changes improve or worsen women's lot depends on many intervening factors. In the refugee camps on the Algeria-Morocco border, where 160,000 Sahrawis have lived for some two decades, the women who make up three-quarters of the adult population have played a central role in running the camps from the time of their arrival. They set up committees for health, education, local production, social affairs, and provisions distribution.[34] Janet Bauer informs us that among Algerian Muslim immigrants in France, women have a strong role in maintaining religious rituals and symbolic meanings that are important in preserving cultural identity and adaptation. The same is true for many Turkish residents in Germany. The situation for Iranian refugees, exiles, and immigrants seems to differ, however, as they may be ambivalent about the very traditions and religious rituals from which individuals are said to seek comfort in times of crisis or change. Socioeconomic status and political ideology may also explain differences between Algerian, Turkish, and Iranian immigrants. In her study of Iranian immigrants in France, Vida Nassehy-Behnam states: "Since the initiation of 'theocracy,' Iranian emigration in general has been partly motivated by the pervasiveness of a religious ideology which impinges so dramatically upon individual lifestyles." She then offers two categories of emigrants: (1) political emigrants—that is, those whose exodus began in February 1979, including monarchists, nationalists, communists, and the Iranian Mujahidin; and (2) sociocultural emigrants, defined as those Iranians who were not politically active to any great extent but left the country out of fear over an uncertain future for their children or because of the morose atmosphere that prevailed in Iran, especially for women and youth. In their study of Iranian exiles and immigrants in Los Angeles, Mehdi Bozorgmehr and Georges Sabagh show that some 65 percent of immigrants and 49 percent of exiles had four or more years of college. These findings for Iranians stand in contrast to the figures for many other migration streams. Another difference between Iranian exiles, refugees, and immigrants and those of North Africa and Turkey is the greater preponderance of religious minorities—Christians, Jews, and Baha'is—among Iranians. Such minorities are especially prevalent within the Iranian exile group in Los Angeles. Bozorgmehr and Sabagh offer these religious patterns as an explanation for why the Iranian exiles they surveyed perceived less prejudice than other groups, which may contain a larger share of Muslims.[35]

These factors—socioeconomic status, education, and political ideology—shape the experience of women exiles, immigrants, and refugees. Bauer notes that although women in Middle Eastern Muslim societies are rarely described as migrating alone, many Iranian women do go into exile alone. The women she interviewed in Germany typically had been involved in secular-left political and feminist activities in Iran; many had high school or college educations. She elaborates: "Some married young in traditional marriages; others were single or divorced. Some were working class; others middle or upper middle class . . . but most of those I interviewed did come into exile with some ideas about increasing personal autonomy and choice."[36]

Can there be emancipation through emigration? Bauer notes the growing feminist consciousness of Iranian exiles and writes that among those she interviewed, there was a general feeling that the traumatic events of 1979–1982 had initiated cross-class feminist cooperation among women and rising consciousness among all Iranians on the issue of gender relations. She adds that larger political goals may be lost, however, as people put aside notions of socialist revolution, social transformation, and political activity and wrap themselves in introspection and their individual lives. Although this was true for the early 1990s, a repoliticization occurred in the latter part of the 1990s, in tandem with the emergence of a movement for political reform within Iran. Expatriate Iranians have regained their political identity and aspirations, with different perspectives on the reform movement, "Islamic feminism," prospects for "Islamic democracy," secularism, and other political alternatives.

The key elements of social change that are usually examined are economic structure and, tied to that, class and property relations. The major source of social change in the Middle East in the post–World War II period has been the dual process of economic development and state expansion. There can be no doubt that over the past fifty years, the economic systems of the region have undergone modernization and growth, with implications for social structure (including the stratification system), the nature and capacity of the state, and the position of women. Much of this economic modernization was based on income from oil, and some came from foreign investment and capital inflows. Economic development alters the status of women in different ways across nations and classes. How women have been involved in and affected by economic development is the subject of Chapter 2. As the state is the manager of economic development in almost all cases, and as state economic and legal policies shape women's access to employment and economic resources, this chapter underscores the government's role in directing development and its impact on women. It also examines shifting state policies in an era of globalization, and their effects on women's employment and economic status.

Another source of social change is revolution, whether large-scale social revolutions or more limited political revolutions. In some Middle Eastern countries, notably Saudi Arabia, change comes about slowly and is carefully orchestrated by the ruling elite. But where revolutions occur, change comes about rapidly and dramatically, with unintended consequences for the masses and the leadership alike. Revolutions have resulted in strong, centralized states whose programs may or may not be in accord with the spirit of the revolutionary coalition (as in the case of the Iranian Revolution). Still, modernizing revolutionary states have been crucial agents in the advancement of women by enacting changes in family law, providing education and employment, and encouraging women's participation in public life. For example, the Iraqi Ba'th regime in its radical phase (1960s and 1970s) undertook social transformation by introducing a land reform program that changed the conditions of the peasantry and by establishing a welfare state for the urban working classes and the poor. In its drive against illiteracy and for free education, the Ba'thist revolution produced one of the best-educated intelligentsias in the Arab world. Even a hostile study of Iraq credited the regime with giving women the right to have careers and participate in civic activities.[37] Such radical measures effected by states and legitimized in political ideologies have been important factors in weakening the hold of traditional kinship systems on women—even though the latter remain resilient. On the other hand, weak states may be unable to implement their ambitious programs for change. The case of Afghanistan is especially illustrative of the formidable social-structural and international hurdles that may confront a revolutionary state and of the implications of these constraints for gender and the status of women. The sociology of revolution has not considered changes in the status of women as a consequence of revolution and has so far been oblivious to the overriding importance of the "woman question" to revolutionaries and reformers. Chapter 3 examines the effect of radical reforms and revolutions in the Middle East on the legal status and social positions of women, including variations in family law. This chapter underscores the gender dynamics of reforms and revolutionary changes, with a view also to correcting an oversight in the sociology of revolution.

Political conflict or war can also bring about social change, including change in the economic and political status of women, a heightened sense of gender awareness, and political activism on the part of women. World War II has been extensively analyzed in terms of gender and social change. Wartime conditions radically transformed the position of women in the work force. Ruth Milkman notes that virtually overnight, the economic mobilization in the United States produced changes that advocates of gender equality both before and since have spent decades struggling for.[38] Postwar demobilization rapidly restored the prewar sexual division of labor, and American culture redefined woman's place in terms of the now famous "feminine mystique." But it is also true that in many Western countries involved in World War II, female labor force participation rose rapidly in the postwar decades. Some authors have begun exploring the complex relationship between gender, consciousness, and social change, suggesting a strong link between the wartime experience and the emergence, two decades later, of the second wave of feminism. The Middle East has encountered numerous wars and political conflicts since the 1950s, with varying implications for societies and for women. In some cases, an unexpected outcome of economic crisis caused by war could be higher education and employment opportunities for women. A study conducted by a professor of education at the Lebanese University suggests that Lebanese parents feel more strongly that educating their daughters is now a good investment, as higher education represents a financial asset. In addition to offering better work opportunities and qualifications for a "better" husband, a degree acts as a safety net should a woman's marriage fail or should she remain single.

In a study I undertook of women's employment patterns in postrevolutionary Iran in 1986, I was surprised to discover that, notwithstanding the exhortations of Islamist ideologues, women had not been driven out of the work force and their participation in government employment had slightly increased relative to 1976. This I attributed to the imperatives of the wartime economy, the manpower needs of the expanding state apparatus, and women's resistance to subordination.[39] A recent study by Maryam Poya confirmed my hypothesis. She found that the mobilization of men at the war front, and the requirements of gender segregation, had resulted in an increased need for female teachers and nurses.[40] In Iraq the mobilization of female labor accelerated during the war with Iran, though this was apparently coupled with the contradictory exhortation to produce more children.[41]

The most obvious case of the impact of political conflict is that of the Palestinians, whose expulsion by Zionists or flight from their villages during periods of strife caused changes in rural Palestinian life and the structure of the family.[42] The prolonged uprising, which has organized and mobilized so many Palestinians, had a positive impact on women's roles, inasmuch as women were able to participate politically in what was once the most secular and democratic movement in the Arab world. Internationally, the best-known Palestinian women have been the guerrilla fighter Leila Khaled and the negotiator and English professor Hanan Ashrawi—two contrasting examples of roles available to Palestinian women in their movement. In the 1970s Palestinian women's political activity and participation in resistance groups expanded, whether in Lebanon, the West Bank, Gaza, universities, or refugee camps. And during the first intifada, or uprising against occupation, which began in 1987, Palestinian women organized themselves into impressive independent political groups and economic cooperatives. A feminist consciousness became more visible among Palestinian women, and some Palestinian women writers, such as Samira Azzam and Fadwa Tuqan, combined a critique of patriarchal structures and a fervent nationalism to produce compelling work. Likewise, the long civil war in Lebanon produced not only suffering and destruction but a remarkable body of literature with strong themes of social and gender consciousness. Miriam Cooke's analysis of the war writings of the "Beirut Decentrists" in the late 1970s and early 1980s shows the emergence of a feminist school of women writers. Indeed, Cooke's argument is that what has been seen as the first Arab women's literary school is in fact feminist.[43]

At the same time, the Palestinian movement has exalted women as mothers and as mothers of martyrs. This emphasis on their reproductive role has created a tension on which a number of authors have commented. During the latter part of the 1980s, another trend emerged among the Palestinians, especially in the impoverished Gaza Strip: Islamist vigilantes who insisted that women cover themselves when appearing in public. The frustrations of daily life, the indignities of occupation, and the inability of the secular and democratic project to materialize may explain this shift. What began as a sophisticated women's movement in the early 1990s that sought feminist interventions in the areas of constitution-writing and social policy experienced setbacks toward the end of the decade, as the West Bank and Gaza faced Islamization and continued Israeli occupation.[44] As noted by Zahira Kamal, a leading figure in the women's movement, "Palestinian women are prisoners of a concept of 'women and the intifada.'"[45]

One important dimension of social change in the region has been the weakening of the patriarchal family and traditional kinship systems. Demographic changes, including patterns of marriage and fertility behavior, have followed from state-sponsored economic development, state-directed legal reforms, and women's educational attainment. Industrialization, urbanization, and proletarianization have disrupted kinship-based structures, with their gender and age hierarchies. In some cases, revolutionary states have undermined patriarchal structures, or attempted to do so, through legislation aimed at weakening traditional rural landlord structures or the power of tribes. Often this type of change comes about coercively. Whether changes to the patriarchal family structures come about gradually and nonviolently or rapidly and coercively, the implications for the status of women within the family and in the society are profound. Yet most MENA states have been ambivalent about transforming women and the family. They have sought the apparently contradictory goals of economic development and strengthening of the family. The latter objective is often a bargain struck with more conservative social elements, such as religious leaders or traditional local communities. Changes in the patriarchal social structure, the contradictory role of the neopatriarchal state, and the profound changes occurring to the structure of the family are examined in Chapter 4.

One of the most vexed issues of the region, with significant implications for the rise of Islamism and the question of women, is the nonresolution of the Palestinian-Israeli conflict. A deep sense of injustice directed at Zionist actions and U.S. imperialism pervades the region. In Iran the 1953 CIA-sponsored coup d'état against the government of Prime Minister Mohammad Mossadegh and subsequent U.S. support for the second Pahlavi monarch linger in collective memory. That the Shah gave Israel near-diplomatic status in Iran in the 1960s was also used against him during the Iranian Revolution. Significantly, one of the first acts of the new revolutionary regime in Iran in 1979 was to invite Palestine Liberation Organization (PLO) chairman Yasir Arafat to Tehran and hand over the former Israeli legation building to the PLO. Throughout the region—in Lebanon, Iraq, Syria, Algeria—large segments of the population find the displacement of fellow Arabs or Muslims (Palestinians) and the intrigues of Israel and the United States an enormous affront. Although this sense of moral outrage is common to liberals, leftists, and Islamists alike, it is typically strongest among Islamists, who make the elimination of Zionism, the liberation of Jerusalem, humiliation of the United States, and other such aspirations major goals and slogans of their movements—as we saw with Al-Qaida and the events of September 11, 2001.

The implications for women are significant, inasmuch as anti-Zionist, anti-imperialist, and especially Islamist movements are preoccupied with questions of cultural identity and authenticity. As women play a crucial role in the socialization of the next generation, they become symbols of cultural values and traditions. Some Muslim women regard this role as an exalted one, and they gladly assume it, becoming active participants, in some cases ideologues, in Islamist movements. Other women find it an onerous burden; they resent restrictions on their autonomy, individuality, mobility, and range of choices. In some countries, these nonconformist women pursue education, employment, and foreign travel to the extent that they can, joining women's associations or political organizations in opposition to Islamist movements. In Algeria, the Islamist movement spurred a militant feminist movement, something that did not exist before. In other, more authoritarian countries, nonconformist women face legal restrictions on dress, occupation, travel, and encounters with men outside their own families. Their response can take the form of resentful acquiescence, passive resistance, or self-exile. This response was especially strong among middle-class Iranian women during the 1980s, although in the 1990s women began to challenge the gender system and patriarchal Islamist norms more directly. The emergence of Islamist movements and women's varied responses, including feminist responses, is examined in Chapter 5.

To veil or not to veil has been a recurring issue in Muslim countries. Polemics surrounding hijab (modest Islamic dress for women) abound in every country. During the era of early modernization and nation building, national progress and the emancipation of women were considered synonymous. This viewpoint entailed discouragement of the veil and encouragement of schooling for girls. The veil was associated with national backwardness, as well as female illiteracy and subjugation. But a paradox of the 1980s was that more and more educated women, even working women (especially in Egypt), took to the veil. It is true that the veil has been convenient to militants and political activists. For example, in the Algerian war for independence against the French and the Iranian Revolution against the Shah, women used the *chador,* or all-encompassing veil, to hide political leaflets and arms. But is veiling always a matter of individual choice, or does social pressure also play a part? In the case of compulsory veiling in the Islamic Republic of Iran, Saudi Arabia, or Afghanistan under the Taliban, the answer is clear. But what of the expansion of veiling in Algeria, Egypt, Turkey, and among the Palestinians? Chapter 5 takes up this question as well.

Certainly there are Islamist women activists—as well as secular feminists and Islamic feminists. Much of feminist scholarship over the past twenty years has sought to show that women are not simply passive recipients of the effects of social change. They are agents, too; women as well as men are makers of history and builders of movements and societies. This holds equally true for the Middle East and North Africa. Women are actively involved in movements for social change—revolution, national liberation, human rights, women's rights, and democratization. Besides national groupings, there are regionwide organizations and networks within which women are active, such as the Arab Women's Solidarity Association, the Arab Human Rights Organization, and Women Living Under Muslim Laws, a transnational feminist network. Women are also actively involved in support of and against Islamist/fundamentalist movements. Islamist women are discernible by their dress, the Islamic hijab. Anti-fundamentalist women are likewise discernible by their dress, which is Western, and by their liberal or left-wing political views. In between are Muslim women who may veil but are also opposed to second-class citizenship for women. All in all, women in the Middle East, North Africa, and Afghanistan have participated in political organizations, social movements, and revolutions. Women also have been involved in productive processes and economic development. Whether as peasants, managers of households, factory workers, service workers, street vendors, teachers, nurses, or professionals, MENA women have contributed significantly to economic production and social reproduction—though their contributions are not always acknowledged, valued, or remunerated.

I have said that political conflicts and war are an important part of the process of social change in the Middle East, with implications for women and gender relations. Apart from the long-standing Arab-Israeli tensions, a conflict in the region that influenced women's positions was the Iran-Iraq War, which lasted eight long years (1980–1988). One result of the war in both countries was the ever-increasing allocation of central government expenditure to defense, at the expense of health, education, and services. Also, during the war women in Iran were constantly harassed by zealots if they did not adhere strictly to Islamic dress and manner. Those women who complained about hijab or resisted by showing a little hair or wearing bright-colored socks were admonished to "feel shame before the corpses of the martyrs of Karbala"—a reference to an incident in religious history as well as to the fallen soldiers in the battle with Iraq. However, as mentioned above, an unintended consequence of the war was to override early ideological objections to female employment in the civil service. As the state apparatus proliferated, and as a large proportion of the male population was concentrated at the war front, women found opportunities for employment in the government sector that Islamist ideologues had earlier denied them. Eventually, the war had a deteriorating effect on employment for both men and women. Yet today the Iranian authorities actively encourage women to take up fields of study and employment they deem both socially necessary and appropriate for women, especially medicine and teaching. Meanwhile, Iranian women themselves are making major demands for the modernization of family law and for greater political participation.

Iran constitutes one of the two case studies in this book. The Iranian case deserved further amplification because of its fascinating trajectory from a deeply patriarchal and very repressive theocracy to a parliamentary Islamic republic in which liberals and Islamic feminists are becoming increasingly vocal and visible. (It is also the case of women and social change with which I am most personally involved.) Thus Chapter 6 examines the contradictions of Islamization and the changing status of women in Iran. The subject of Chapter 7 is the prolonged battle over women's rights in Afghanistan. The Afghan case needed its own chapter, too, if only to place the Marxist-inspired reforms of 1978 in proper historical and social context and to show how the subversion of a modernizing state by an Islamist grouping financed by an international coalition of states led straight to the Taliban.[46] The elaboration of the Afghan case is necessary to demonstrate its gender dimension—occluded in almost all mainstream accounts—and to show its relevance to the study of social change.

This book, therefore, is an exploration of the causes, nature, and direction of change in the Middle East, North Africa, and Afghanistan, particularly as these have affected women's status and social positions. The economic, political, and cultural dimensions of change will be underscored, and the unintended consequences of state policies as they affect women will be highlighted. The chapters will reveal the contradictions and paradoxes of social change, as well as its more predictable patterns and trends. In particular, the chapters draw attention to the potentially revolutionary role of middle-class Middle Eastern women, especially secular feminists and Muslim feminists using the languages of socialism, liberalism, feminism, and an emancipatory Islam. These women are not simply acting out roles prescribed for them by religion, by culture, or by neopatriarchal states; they are questioning their roles and status, demanding social and political change, participating in movements, and taking sides in ideological battles. In particular, they are at the center of the new social movements for democratization, civil society, and citizenship.

Notes

The opening quote from Asma Barlas is from her book *Believing Women in Islam: Unreading Patriarchal Interpretations of the Qur'an* (Austin: University of Texas Press, 2002), chap. 1.

1. Daniel Chirot, *Social Change in the Modern Era* (San Diego: Harcourt Brace Jovanovich, 1983), p. 3. For an elaboration of the structuralist and Marxist approach, see Christopher Lloyd, *Explanation in Social History* (London: Basil Blackwell, 1986), especially pt. 3. On world-system theory, see Immanuel Wallerstein, *The Modern World-System,* vol. 3 (San Diego: Academic Press, 1989); and Christopher Chase-Dunn, *Global Formation: Structures of the World-Economy,* 2nd ed. (Lanham, Md.: Rowman and Littlefield, 1998).

2. But see Sami G. Hajjar, ed., *The Middle East: From Transition to Development* (Leiden: E. J. Brill, 1985). Although the collection is uneven, especially useful are the introduction by Hajjar, the chapter on demography by Basheer Nijim, and the essay on education and political development in the Middle East by Nancy and Joseph Jabbra. See also Nicholas S. Hopkins and Saad Eddin Ibrahim, eds., *Arab Society: Class, Gender, Power, and Development* (Cairo: American University in Cairo Press, 1997).

3. David S. Landes and Richard A. Landes, "Do Fundamentalists Fear Our Women?" *New Republic,* September 29, 2001. See also Samuel P. Huntington, "The Age of Muslim Wars," *Newsweek,* January 2002; and Francis Fukuyama, "Their Target: The Modern World," *Newsweek,* January 2002.

4. Pippa Norris and Robert Inglehart, "Religion, Secularization and Gender Equality," mimeo, John F. Kennedy School of Government, Harvard University. The paper was a preliminary draft from chap. 3 of their book, *Rising Tide: Gender Equality and Shifts in the Cultural Zeitgeist* (New York: Oxford University Press, 2003).

5. United Nations, *The World's Women 2000: Trends and Statistics* (New York: United Nations, 2000), chart 5.1, p. 110.

6. Nadia Youssef, "The Status and Fertility Patterns of Muslim Women," in Lois Beck and Nikki Keddie, eds., *Women in the Muslim World* (Cambridge: Harvard University Press, 1978), pp. 69–99; John Weeks, "The Demography of Islamic Nations," *Population Bulletin* 43 (4) (December 1988): Fatima Mernissi, *Beyond the Veil: Male-Female Dynamics in Modern Muslim Society,* rev. ed. (Bloomington: Indiana University Press, 1987); Ruth Leger Sivard, *Women . . . A World Survey* (Washington, D.C.: World Priorities, 1985); Julinda Abu Nasr, N. Khoury, and H. Azzam, eds., *Women, Employment, and Development in the Arab World* (The Hague: Mouton/ILO, 1985); and Ester Boserup, "Economic Change and the Roles of Women," in Irene Tinker, ed., *Persistent Inequalities: Women and World Development* (New York: Oxford University Press, 1990), pp. 14–24.

7. See *Al-Raida* (quarterly journal of the Institute for Women's Studies in the Arab World, Lebanese American University, Beirut) 15 (80–81) (Winter–Spring 1998), a special issue on Arab countries and CEDAW. See also Jane Connors, "The Women's Convention in the Muslim World," in Mai Yamani, ed., *Feminism and Islam: Legal and Literary Perspectives* (New York University Press, 1996), pp. 351–371.

8. See contributions in V. M. Moghadam, ed., *Identity Politics and Women: Cultural Reassertions and Feminisms in International Perspective* (Boulder: Westview Press, 1994).

9. Pnina Lahav, "Raising the Status of Women Through Law: The Case of Israel," in Wellesley Editorial Committee, ed., *Women and National Development: The Complexities of Change* (Chicago: University of Chicago Press, 1987), p. 199. See also Shulamit Aloni, "Up the Down Escalator," in Robin Morgan, ed., *Sisterhood Is Global* (New York: Anchor Books, 1984), pp. 360–364; and Madeleine Tress, "Halaka, Zionism, and Gender: The Case of Gush Emunim," in Moghadam, *Identity Politics and Women,* pp. 307–328.

10. Urvashi Boutalia, "Indian Women and the New Movement," *Women's Studies International Forum* 8 (2) (1985): 131–133; Barbara Miller, *The Endangered Sex* (Ithaca: Cornell University Press, 1981); and Jean Drèze and Amartya Sen, *Hunger and Public Action* (Oxford: Clarendon Press, 1989), esp. chap. 4.

11. See Vern Bullough, Brenda Shelton, and Sarah Slavin, *The Subordinated Sex: A History of Attitudes Toward Women* (Athens: University of Georgia Press, 1988).

12. Azar Tabari, "Islam and the Struggle for Emancipation of Iranian Women," and Haleh Afshar, "Khomeini's Teachings and Their Implications for Iranian Women," both in Azar Tabari and Nahid Yeganeh, eds., *In the Shadow of Islam: The Women's*

Movement in Iran (London: Zed Books, 1982), pp. 5–25 and 75–90; Mai Ghoussoub, "Feminism—or the Eternal Masculine—in the Arab World," *New Left Review* 161 (January–February 1987): 3–13; Juliette Minces, *The House of Obedience* (London: Zed Books, 1982); and Haideh Moghissi, *Feminism and Islamic Fundamentalism: The Limits of Postmodern Analysis* (London: Zed Books, 1999).

13. Mernissi, *Beyond the Veil;* and Fatna A. Sabbah, *Woman in the Muslim Unconscious* (New York: Pergamon Press, 1985).

14. Freda Hussein distinguishes "authentic Islam" from "pseudo-Islam" and believes that the former is emancipatory. See her introduction in Freda Hussein, ed., *Muslim Women* (London: Croom Helm, 1984). Leila Ahmed once poignantly wrote, "One can perhaps appreciate how excruciating is the plight of the Middle-Eastern feminist caught between those opposing loyalties [sexual and cultural identities] forced almost to choose between betrayal and betrayal." See her essay in Hussein, *Muslim Women.* See also Asma Barlas, *Believing Women in Islam: Unreading Patriarchal Interpretations of the Qur'an* (Austin: University of Texas Press, 2002); Riffat Hassan, "Rights of Women Within Islamic Communities," in John Witte Jr. and Johan D. van der Vyver, eds., *Religious Human Rights in Global Perspective: Religious Perspectives* (The Hague: Martinus Nijhoff, 1996), pp. 361–386; and Azizah al-Hibri, "Islam, Law and Custom: Redefining Muslim Women's Rights," *American University Journal of International Law & Policy* 12 (1) (1997): 1–43.

15. Yakin Ertürk, "Convergence and Divergence in the Status of Muslim Women: The Cases of Turkey and Saudi Arabia," *International Sociology* 6 (1) (September 1991): 307–320. For critiques of the cultural relativist approach, see also Mona Abaza and Georg Stauth, "Occidental Reason, Orientalism, and Islamic Fundamentalism," *International Sociology* 3 (4) (December 1988): 343–364.

16. Multicultural policies were first criticized in the early 1990s by feminists in the UK associated with Women Against Fundamentalism and Southall Black Sisters. See also Joshua Cohen, Matthew Howard, and Martha C. Nussbaum, eds., *Is Multiculturalism Bad for Women?* with Susan Moller Okin (Princeton: Princeton University Press, 1999).

17. Abdelwahab Bouhdiba, *Sexuality in Islam* (London: Routledge and Kegan Paul, 1985).

18. See Division for the Advancement of Women, United Nations Office at Vienna, "International Standards of Equality and Religious Freedom: Implications for the Status of Women," in Moghadam, *Identity Politics and Women,* pp. 425–438.

19. Abdullahi an-Na'im, "Promises We Should Keep in Common Cause," in Cohen, Howard, and Nussbaum, *Is Multiculturalism Bad for Women?* pp. 59–64.

20. Janet Z. Giele, "Introduction: The Status of Women in Comparative Perspective," in Janet Z. Giele and Audrey C. Smock, eds., *Women: Roles and Status in Eight Countries* (New York: John Wiley, 1977), pp. 3–31.

21. Hisham Sharabi, *Neopatriarchy: A Theory of Distorted Change in the Arab World* (New York: Oxford University Press, 1988). Another useful discussion of the state is contained in Alan Richards and John Waterbury, *A Political Economy of the Middle East,* 2nd ed. (Boulder: Westview Press, 1996). And still relevant is Michael Hudson, *Arab Politics: The Search for Legitimacy* (New Haven: Yale University Press, 1977).

22. Sharabi, *Neopatriarchy,* p. 145.

23. Judith Lorber, *Paradoxes of Gender* (New Haven: Yale University Press, 1994), p. 5.

24. For a comparative study of changing family law in Western countries (from patriarchal to egalitarian), see Mary Ann Glendon, *State, Law, and Family: Family Law in Transition in the United States and Western Europe* (Cambridge: Harvard Uni-

versity Press, 1977); and Mary Ann Glendon, *The Transformation of Family Law* (Chicago: University of Chicago Press, 1989).

25. Hanna Papanek, "Socialization for Inequality: Entitlements, the Value of Women, and Domestic Hierarchies," Center for Asian Studies, Boston University, 1989. See also Rae Lesser Blumberg, *Stratification: Socio-Economic and Sexual Inequality* (Dubuque, Iowa: W. C. Brown, 1978); and Janet Saltzman Chafetz, *Sex and Advantage* (Totowa, N.J.: Rowman and Allanheld, 1984).

26. Michael Mann, "A Crisis in Stratification Theory? Persons, Households/Family/Lineages, Genders, Classes, and Nations," in Rosemary Crompton and Michael Mann, eds., *Gender and Stratification* (Cambridge, UK: Polity Press, 1986), pp. 40–56. The quote by Papanek is from her paper "Socialization for Inequality." On patriarchy, see Chapter 4.

27. Ralph Miliband, *Divided Societies: Class Struggle in Contemporary Capitalism* (Oxford: Clarendon Press, 1989), p. 25.

28. Constantina Safilios-Rothschild, "A Cross-Cultural Examination of Women's Marital, Educational, and Occupational Options," in M. T. S. Mednick et al., eds., *Women and Achievement* (New York: John Wiley and Sons, 1971), pp. 96–113.

29. Margot Badran, "Women and Production in the Middle East and North Africa," *Trends in History* 2 (3) (1982): 80.

30. Richards and Waterbury, *A Political Economy of the Middle East;* and Massoud Karshenas, *Oil, State, and Industrialization in Iran* (Cambridge University Press, 1990).

31. Jean Pyle, "Export-Led Development and the Underdevelopment of Women: The Impact of Discriminatory Development Policy in the Republic of Ireland," in Kathryn Ward, ed., *Women Workers and Global Restructuring* (Ithaca: ILR Press, 1990), pp. 85–112.

32. Mary Chamie, *Women of the World: Near East and North Africa* (Washington, D.C.: U.S. Department of Commerce, Bureau of the Census, and U.S. Agency for International Development, Office of Women in Development, 1985); and H. Azzam, Julinda Abu Nasr, and I. Lorfing, "An Overview of Arab Women in Population, Employment, and Economic Development," in Julinda Abu Nasr, A. Khoury, and H. Azzam, eds., *Women, Employment, and Development in the Arab World,* p. 11.

33. The Iranian students abroad were organized in the Confederation of Iranian Students, one of the largest and best-organized student movements anywhere. See Afshin Matin Asgari, *Iranian Student Opposition to the Shah* (Costa Mesa, Calif.: Mazda, 2002). See also Val Moghadam, "Socialism or Anti-Imperialism? The Left and Revolution in Iran," *New Left Review* 166 (November–December 1987): 5–28.

34. Helen O'Connell, *Women and the Family* (London: Zed Books, 1993).

35. Mehdi Bozorgmehr and Georges Sabagh, "Iranian Exiles and Immigrants in Los Angeles," in Asghar Fathi, ed., *Iranian Refugees and Exiles Since Khomeini* (Costa Mesa, Calif.: Mazda, 1991), pp. 121–144. In the same volume, see also Janet Bauer, "A Long Way Home: Islam in the Adaptation of Iranian Women Refugees in Turkey and West Germany," pp. 77–101; and Vida Nassehy-Behnam, "Iranian Immigrants in France," pp. 102–119.

36. Bauer, "A Long Way Home," p. 93.

37. Samir al-Khalil, "Iraq and Its Future," *New York Review of Books,* April 11, 1991, p. 12. This does of course raise the question of the impact of the Gulf War and devastation of Iraq on women's status. The paucity of information makes a serious study impossible at this time, but the available evidence suggests that the combination of wars, international sanctions, and Saddam Hussein's own flawed policies and priorities have resulted in the deterioration of women's status and conditions.

38. Ruth Milkman, *Gender at Work: The Dynamics of Job Segregation by Sex During World War II* (Chicago: University of Illinois Press, 1987); and Karen Anderson, *Wartime Women: Sex Roles, Family Relations, and the Status of Women During World War II* (Westport, Conn.: Greenwood Press, 1981).

39. Aisha Harb Zureik, "The Effect of War on University Education," project discussed in *Al-Raida* (Beirut University College) 9 (52) (Winter 1991): 4–5. See also Val Moghadam, "Women, Work, and Ideology in the Islamic Republic," *International Journal of Middle East Studies* 20 (2) (May 1988): 221–243.

40. Maryam Poya, *Women, Work, and Islamism: Ideology and Resistance in Iran* (London: Zed Books, 1999).

41. Andrea W. Lorenz, "Ishtar Was a Woman," *Ms.,* May–June 1991, pp. 14–15.

42. See Khalil Nakhleh and Elia Zureik, eds., *The Sociology of the Palestinians* (New York: St. Martin's Press, 1980).

43. Miriam Cooke, *War's Other Voices: Women Writers on the Lebanese Civil War* (Cambridge: Cambridge University Press, 1986). See also Margot Badran and Miriam Cooke, eds., *Opening the Gates: A Century of Arab Feminist Writing* (Bloomington: Indiana University Press, 1990), esp. the book's introduction.

44. Julie Peteet, "Authenticity and Gender: The Presentation of Culture," in Judith Tucker, ed., *Arab Women: Old Boundaries, New Frontiers* (Bloomington: Indiana University Press, 1993); Cheryl Rubenberg, *Palestinian Women: Patriarchy and Resistance in the West Bank* (Boulder: Lynne Rienner, 2001); Rema Hammami and Penny Johnson, "Equality with a Difference: Gender and Citizenship in Transition Palestine," *Social Politics* 6 (3) (Fall 1999): 314–343; and Robin Morgan, "Women in the Intifada," in Suha Sabbagh, ed., *Palestinian Women of Gaza and the West Bank* (Bloomington: Indiana University Press, 1998), pp. 153–170.

45. Zahira Kamal, "The Development of the Palestinian Women's Movement in the Occupied Territories: Twenty Years after the Israeli Occupation," in Sabbagh, *Palestinian Women of Gaza and the West Bank,* pp. 78–88; quote appears on p. 88.

46. For a nongendered account, see John K. Cooley, *Unholy Wars: Afghanistan, America, and International Terrorism* (London: Pluto Press, 1999, new edition 2000).

2

Economic Development, State Policy, and Women's Employment

Let me explain this to you. If you want a position, something good, you have to pay a bribe. There is someone, like an agent, like the man you see to rent a house, and he is just for the small jobs in the government, like the police, or work cleaning an office, things like that. You give him money and he looks around for a position for you. Every job has its price, depending on how well it pays. You pay more for jobs that have a higher salary. But if you just want something normal, then you talk to people, you say hello to them everyday, get to know them, and see if they can find something for you. That is for the regular jobs, the ones that pay just 500 dirhams a month, things in a store or in a beauty shop. For a job with a good salary, you have to pay the agent. Maybe you will get something, and then he can have an offer for that job from someone else, and he can get you put out and he will put someone else there.

—Rabia, a twenty-four-year-old
working-class woman, Marrakech, 2001

Women have invaded the public space: the markets, the streets, public transport, even airplanes. Women are today fruit and vegetable vendors, run second-hand clothes stores, are hairdressers and photographers; there is even a female butcher and at least one taxi-driver. They operate in the open in an area where a decade ago the philosophy of religious extremists projecting the distorted image of women's role and place was rampant, and women largely confined to an "inside" role.

—Essma Ben Hamida,
ENDA Inter-Arabe, March 2000

The position of women within the labor market is frequently studied as an empirical measure of women's status. Access to remunerative work in the formal sector of the economy—as distinct from outwork, housework, or other types of informal-sector activities—is regarded by many feminists and researchers in the field of women-in-development (WID) and gender-and-development (GAD) as an important indicator of women's social positions and legal status. For those who argue that women's economic dependence on men is the root cause of their disadvantaged status, the gender composition of the labor force and change in the structure of labor force rewards are key targets. Employed women tend to have greater control over decisionmaking within the family. Households also benefit when women control income and spending, and the well-being of children is increasingly linked to female education and income. Many feminists regard women's involvement in paid employment as a pathway to social and gender consciousness, autonomy, and empowerment. Societal benefits of increased female employment include diminishing fertility rates and a more skilled and competitive human resource base. Investment in women's education and employment is increasingly understood as integral to building the national human resource base.[1]

At the same time, much feminist and WID/GAD scholarship has documented the adverse conditions under which many women work, particularly in developing countries with authoritarian regimes and weak labor protection laws. Marxist and feminist researchers have been especially critical of factory employment tied to multinational corporations (MNCs), and much ink has been spilled over the exploitation of women in export processing zones (EPZs) and free trade zones. Many studies argued that the changing international division of labor was predicated upon the globalization of production and the search for cheap labor, and that the feminization of labor, especially in textiles and electronics, was the latest strategy in that search. A major debate arose over whether this new utilization of female labor reduced women's economic status or improved it. Most of the case studies in the literature came from Latin America, especially Mexico, and from Southeast Asia, particularly South Korea and Malaysia.[2] Ester Boserup, whose landmark study *Women's Role in Economic Development* launched the field of women-in-development and argued that the process of industrialization marginalized female producers, noted later that economic development has opposing effects on different groups of women: "Whereas young women are drawn into industrial employment and increasing numbers of educated women obtain white-collar jobs in social and other services, the situation of older, uneducated women may deteriorate because the family enterprises in which they work may suffer from competition with the growing modern sector."[3]

Are MENA women solely the victims of patriarchal gender arrangements, or does political economy, including the vagaries of the global economy, play a role? The Middle East has not figured prominently in the WID/GAD literature, partly because of the difficulty of obtaining data and partly because of a common view that cultural and religious factors influence women's lives more than do economic factors. In the same essay cited above, Boserup states that rapid development inevitably creates tension between sexes and generations and spawns pressure groups that seek to preserve or reintroduce the traditional hierarchical cultural pattern. She cites the "oil rich countries in the Arab world, which have attempted to preserve the family system of domesticated and secluded women by mass importation of foreign male labor, and in which mass movements of Muslim revival pursue the same aim."[4] A reader in women, gender, and development includes two chapters on the Middle East (out of thirty-five), but both are about veiling and oppressive family laws rather than women and development issues per se.[5]

As was discussed in Chapter 1, myths and stereotypes abound regarding women's social positions in Muslim countries. A common view has held that traditional gender relations are entrenched and women's economic roles are insignificant, especially in the modern sector. What are some of the patterns, or comparative indicators, that support such a view? In 1975 the percentage of economically active females among those of working age in Muslim countries (which would include those of Africa, South Asia, and Southeast Asia as well as the Middle East) was less than half of that in non-Muslim countries.[6] Because of their industrialization strategies, Indonesia and Malaysia began to develop relatively large female labor forces, but the Muslim countries of South Asia, the Middle East, and North Africa lagged behind. By 1980 the female share of the paid labor force was smaller in MENA countries than in the Southeast Asian newly industrialized countries and, of course, smaller than in the advanced industrialized countries, though not substantially different from that of Latin America or South Asia, with their huge informal sectors. But the ratio of women to men in the labor force was lowest in the Middle East (29 percent) and highest in Eastern Europe and the Soviet Union, where the ratio was 90 percent.[7] In 1990, women's share of the labor force in the MENA countries was 18.7 percent, compared with 22.0 percent in South Asia, 26.3 percent in Latin America and the Caribbean, 37.8 percent in sub-Saharan Africa, and 41.2 percent in East and Southeast Asia.[8] And as recently as 2000, women's activity rates were lowest in the Arab countries, when compared with other developing or middle-income regions, as we saw in Table 1.1. Such comparative data cannot be contested. But what explains the differences? According to a UN survey, "the level of women's work [is] consistently low in countries with a predominantly Muslim population, such as Bangladesh, Egypt, Jordan, Pakistan, and the Syrian Arab Republic, where cultural restrictions that discourage women from doing most types of work are common."[9] Richard Anker of the International Labour Organisation (ILO) has written of MENA that "a key feature of this region is the predominance of Islam, an influence that undoubtedly plays a major role in affecting occupational segregation by sex, as well as female labor force participation."[10] Note that only "culture" is provided as an explanation.

Following from the premise that an important indicator of women's status is the extent of their integration into the formal labor force, this chapter examines women's employment opportunities and describes the specific characteristics of the paid female labor force in the Middle East and North Africa. The chapter also identifies the structural determinants of women's access to remunerative work in the formal sector of the economy and explains the variations in the region. Attention to this region is important because (1) it is underresearched outside of Middle East studies; (2) it is frequently left out of book volumes on women workers in the world economy; and (3) it is a good test of assumptions and propositions about capital's global quest for cheap labor and about the relationship between women's employment and women's empowerment.

This chapter will show that women's employment patterns are largely shaped by the political economy of the region and that female employment has been constrained by overall limited industrialization. At the same time, there is considerable variation within the region in terms of women's economic status and employment opportunities. To explain these differences, we need to examine specific development strategies, state policies, the nature of political elites, and women's class location. I will also show how the post-oil-boom era of economic liberalization and the challenges of globalization have affected or are likely to affect women's employment and economic status.

The Internationalization of Capital and the Middle East

In the 1960s and 1970s the Middle East was part of the global process of the internationalization of productive and financial capital—now better known as (economic) globalization. Relationships between countries and regions changed as the old colonial division of labor—whereby the periphery provided raw materials and the core countries provided manufactured goods (at very unequal pricing schemes)—underwent some modification. Increasingly, countries on the periphery (also known as third world countries, developing countries, or less-developed countries) established an industrial base, sought to diversify their products, and aspired to export manufactures and industrial goods to the core. The term "newly industrialized country," or NIC, was coined to describe countries making a significant shift in the composition of their labor force, the source of the national product, and the direction of trade. Major changes occurred in the structure of national economies and the labor force.

During the 1970s and 1980s the trends included the following: a regional and global decline in agriculture; an increase in the service sector; and a shift toward industrial employment, especially in the developing countries, many of which had embarked upon rapid industrialization as a key factor in their development. Significant factors influencing these trends were the changing structure of world labor markets, involving massive rural and international migration; the relocation of labor-intensive industries; and the spread of new technologies, changing the nature of work. Particularly important for women was the relocation of labor-intensive industries from industrially developed to developing countries in search of cheap labor; the laborers were mostly young, unmarried, and inexperienced women. Textiles and clothing were the first industries relocated, followed by food processing, electronics, and in some cases pharmaceuticals. In this process, various forms of subcontracting arrangements were made to relocate production or set up subsidiaries with foreign or partly foreign capital.[11]

During this period the large MENA countries, such as Iran, Egypt, Turkey, and Algeria, were pursuing import-substitution industrialization, where machinery was imported to run local industries producing consumer goods. This strategy was associated with an economic system characterized by central planning and a large public sector, and it opened up some employment opportunities for women, mainly in the expanded civil service but also in state-run factories or industrial plants in the private sector receiving state support and foreign investment. The rise of oil prices in the early 1970s led to a proliferation of development projects in the OPEC countries, massive intraregional male labor flows from capital-poor to oil-rich countries, and considerable intraregional investment and development assistance. In the MENA region as a whole, the augmentation in the activities of capital was followed by increased male employment and an increase in the portion of the labor force involved in industry and services. These changes also affected women, who were increasingly brought into the labor force.

Among those developing countries where female employment grew significantly during the 1970s, especially high increases were reported in Tunisia and South Yemen. In a 1982 special economic report on South Yemen (the People's Democratic Republic of Yemen [PDRY]), the World Bank estimated women's employment at more than 20 percent. Between 1976 and 1984 the number of women working in the public and mixed sectors doubled in South Yemen. Massive intraregional migration of men from the labor surplus countries of Jordan, Egypt, Lebanon, Syria, and Yemen to better-paying jobs in the oil-rich states of the region (such as Libya, Saudi Arabia, Kuwait, and the UAE) also affected female employment patterns. The migratory trend created shortages in the labor markets of the sending countries, resulting in some cases in the agricultural sector's dependence on female workers.[12] At least one of the labor-receiving countries also experienced a dramatic rise in female labor force participation. In Kuwait the number of economically active women doubled between 1970 and 1980, by which time women represented 18.8 percent of total salaried employees. Women's employment grew in Iran during the 1970s, as well.

As new jobs were created in the service and industrial sectors, many came to be filled by women. For relatively well-educated women, jobs in teaching, health, and welfare offered the greatest possibilities, while in countries such as Turkey and Egypt women's participation increased in commercial and industrial enterprises and public administration. During the period of rapid growth, governments instituted social security programs, and protective legislation for working mothers—such as paid maternity leave and workplace nurseries—was in place in all MENA countries.[13]

The degree of occupational choice that women had within the structure of employment was linked to the type of industrialization the country was undergoing, the extent of state intervention, the size of the public sector, and the class background of women entering the labor force. In some places, development and state expansion afforded women a wider range of professional work opportunities than was available in the most industrialized societies of the West. This breadth of options was particularly striking in Turkey, where in the 1970s the female share of teaching, banking, and medical positions reached one-third, and where one in every five practicing lawyers was female.[14] A similar pattern was found for other third world countries, such as Mexico, Argentina, and India. Cross-national studies conducted in the 1970s indicated that in societies undergoing capitalist development, there was a curvilinear relationship between the level of development and the range of professional careers open to women. At intermediate levels there were higher proportions of women in professional schools and the professional labor market than at either extreme. Thus, law, medicine, dentistry, and even engineering constituted a cluster of occupations open to women.[15] But class was another explanatory variable. A kind of "positive discrimination" or quota system was operating for the upper class, limiting the social mobility of the lower classes. Ayse Oncü explained that under conditions of rapid expansion, the elite recruitment patterns into the most prestigious and highly remunerated professions were maintained by the admission of women from the upper reaches of the social hierarchy.[16]

In the Middle East, as elsewhere, the formal economy could not absorb all the entrants to the labor force, and the urban population grew rapidly because of natural population growth and high in-migration rates. By the 1990s, a combination of declining oil prices, mismanagement of economic resources, and expensive and destructive conflicts led to economic stagnation and indebtedness in many countries. There was less foreign direct investment (FDI) in the Middle East than in any other region in the world economy. This period also saw rising unemployment (including very high rates of women's unemployment), the expansion of the urban informal sector, and an increase in female-headed households resulting from male migration, divorce, and widowhood.

Oil, Liberalization, and Women's Employment

Chapter 1 noted the social structural diversity of the Middle East, which has implications for gender relations generally and for women's roles and status more specifically. We now examine the political economy of the region and its implications for women's employment. In particular I will try to show the connection between patterns of industrialization and patterns of female employment. It may be helpful to begin with two complementary typologies of the region. In his discussion of industrialization in the Middle East, Robert Mabro has offered the following classification:

- Oil economies poor in other resources, including population (Kuwait, Libya, Oman, Qatar, Saudi Arabia, UAE).
- Mixed oil economies (Algeria, Egypt, Iran, Iraq, Syria, Tunisia).
- Non-oil economies (Israel, Jordan, Morocco, Sudan, Turkey, Yemen).

In their 1990 study of the political economy of the region, Alan Richards and John Waterbury offer the following taxonomy:

- The Coupon Clippers: Libya, Kuwait, Oman, UAE, Bahrain, and Qatar. These states have much oil and little of anything else, including people. They have been and will continue to be almost entirely dependent upon oil and any money earned from overseas investments.
- The Oil Industrializers: Iraq, Iran, Algeria, and Saudi Arabia. The first three states share the main features of large oil exports, a substantial population, other natural resources, and a chance to create industrial and agricultural sectors that will be sustainable over the long run. Saudi Arabia lacks the non-oil resources of the first three countries.
- The Watchmakers: Israel, Jordan, Tunisia, and Syria. These four small countries have limited natural resources and must therefore concentrate on investing in human capital and exporting skill-intensive manufactures. In the early 1990s, manufactured goods accounted for 84 percent of Israeli, 52 percent of Jordanian, and 42 percent of Tunisian exports.
- The NICs: Turkey, Egypt, and Morocco. These countries have relatively large populations, relatively good agricultural land or potential, and a long experience with industrial production.
- The Agro-Poor: Sudan and Yemen. These are the poorest countries of the region and ones where the agricultural-development-led strategy of industrial growth seems to offer the best hope.[17]

The two classifications differ somewhat, but the essential point I make here is that patterns of women's employment generally follow from the given political economy. Unlike Latin America and Southeast Asia, the Middle East has seen fairly limited industrialization, which has served, among other things, to limit female labor force participation. But, as we shall see below, there are interesting variations in women's labor force participation.

Concerted industrialization began in Latin America and Southeast Asia earlier than it did in the Middle East. In the case of South Korea, first Japan and then the United States played a role in expanding agricultural and industrial production as well as education. In Brazil and Mexico, foreign investment played an important role in propelling industrialization, although import-substitution industrialization remained the main development strategy. In the early 1960s, Southeast Asian countries embarked upon a state-directed export industrialization strategy, which, along with the rapid expansion of world trade in the 1960s, contributed to their dramatic economic growth.[18] In the Caribbean, where plantation agriculture and the demands of colonialism had already created a supply of female labor, foreign investment relied on female labor for export manufacturing.[19] In the Middle East, the industrialization drive gained momentum when revolutionary regimes took over in Egypt, Iraq, and Syria and the Shah of Iran decided to divert oil revenues to finance industrialization. Between 1955 and 1975 the industrialization of the Middle East (with the notable exception of Israel) followed a classic pattern of import-substitution industrialization.

Those countries rich in oil and poor in other resources (Mabro's first category) chose an industrial strategy based on petroleum products and petrochemicals. A strategy relying on oil, gas, and finance, which is heavily capital-intensive and minimizes the use of labor, is not conducive to female employment. The industrialization of other countries (Mabro's second and third groups) followed a typical pattern of ISI, although Algeria, Iran, and Iraq remained dependent on oil revenues for foreign exchange and to finance imports and development projects. In the Middle East, unlike Latin America, ISI did not evolve into manufacturing for export. Because of oil revenues, governments chose to extend the import-substitution process, moving into capital-intensive sectors involving sophisticated technology. For the OPEC countries in MENA, foreign exchange from oil revenues constituted the accumulation of capital, although an industrial labor force in the manufacturing sector was also created. In both the oil and mixed oil economies, the contribution of petroleum to the national income was such as to make the apparent share of other sectors appear insignificant. Oil revenues certainly were used for domestic investment purposes. But investment in iron and steel plants, petrochemicals, car assembly plants, and similar industries turned out to be not only costly and inefficient but also not especially conducive to increased female employment.

If oil-based growth and capital-intensive production did not lead to a huge demand for female labor, another factor in the relatively low levels of female employment during the oil-boom era pertained to the high wages that accrued to workers in the region. An analysis of wage trends by economist Massoud Karshenas shows that workers' wages were higher in most of the countries of the Middle East and North Africa than they were in Asian countries such as Indonesia, Korea, and Malaysia. Higher wages earned by men served to limit the supply of job-seeking women during the oil-boom years.[20] This reinforced what we may call the patriarchal gender contract—the implicit and often explicit agreement that men are the breadwinners and are responsible for financially maintaining wives, children, and elderly parents, and that women are wives, homemakers, mothers, and caregivers. The patriarchal gender contract also has justified men's domination within the public sphere of markets and the state and women's concentration in the private sphere of the family.

In the 1980s, in line with the changing global economy and as a result of rising indebtedness, the non-oil MENA countries turned to an export-oriented growth strategy in manufacturing and agriculture. For example, although Tunisia exports oil, as a share of exports oil was a smaller commodity in Tunisia than in OPEC countries—42 percent in 1985 compared to Saudi Arabia's 97 percent or Iran's 85 percent. In 1990 its manufactured exports constituted 69 percent of total exports, and in 2000 that figure increased to 77 percent. Turkey provides another example. Following the 1980 military coup, Turkey began to liberalize its economy and shift from ISI to export-oriented industrialization (EOI). By 1990 its manufactured exports constituted 68 percent of total exports, and in 2000 that figure grew to 81 percent. Morocco and Jordan similarly expanded their manufacturing sectors.[21] Egypt under Sadat tried to follow the Turkish model and liberalize its economic system to promote industrial exports, but since then it has been less successful than Turkey. It should be noted that the non-oil industrializing economies (the Watchmakers and NICs) have tended to employ more women than the oil economies, and in some of those countries policymakers have actively encouraged women's economic participation.

Industrialization and Female Proletarianization

By 1990, global trends in female employment included the following: the proletarianization of women and their sectoral distribution in services and industry; the globalization of female labor via MNCs and female labor migration; and the feminization of poverty, with the interrelated phenomena of high unemployment rates, growth of the urban informal sector, and the proliferation of female-headed households. MNC relocation initially mainly affected women in Latin America, the Caribbean, and Southeast Asia, where the most important areas of activity for foreign investors in the export manufacturing sector were the textile, clothing, and electronics industries. In the 1990s, China saw a growing share of foreign direct investment and MNC activity, combined with high levels of female employment in the export manufacturing sector.

Turkish women's involvement in export manufacturing, especially of ready-made garments, has increased. Photo by Val Moghadam.

Compared to other regions in the world economy, the Middle East has received relatively low levels of foreign direct investment. Despite the role played by petrodollars in global finance, the Arab world and Iran remain comparatively cut off from financial globalization, for better or for worse. Considering just the Arab region, the share of total FDI barely came to 1 percent over the period 1976–1998, with a steady downward trend.[22] Along with the factors mentioned above (the oil economy and high wages), this has served to limit female proletarianization and overall participation in paid employment. In Iran a world-market factory, commencing operations in 1974 with U.S. and West German capital investment, produced shoes, leather goods, textiles, and garments.[23] However, most of the workers were male. The high concentrations of female labor in MNCs characteristic of Southeast Asian and some Latin American countries are rarely found in the Middle East, partly because EOI has not been pursued by all the countries of the region and partly because of reliance on revenue and foreign exchange from oil exports. Mabro has written that Iran probably would have embarked upon an export-oriented strategy if the 1979 revolution and the war with Iraq had not arrested the process of industrial development.[24] This proposition would help explain the decline in female industrial employment in the years immediately following the 1979 revolution and the stagnation in overall female employment in the Islamic Republic. (See Chapter 6 for details.)

Despite some industrialization and growth in manufacturing exports, industry in MENA countries has failed to make progress comparable to that achieved in India, Brazil, South Korea, or China. Richards and Waterbury note that total manufacturing value-added (MVA) in the region is slightly less than that of South Korea, and that it is instructive "to compare MVA for Turkey and Iran with that of Italy, which has roughly the same number of people: Italy's MVA is ten and one-half times that of Turkey and roughly sixteen times that of Iran."[25] This ratio has implications for patterns of female employment: lower levels of industrialization or manufacturing for export mean less female proletarianization and activity in the productive sectors.

However, countries that embarked on export-led industrialization report higher proportions of women involved in the manufacturing sector. For example, Tunisia and Morocco have seen considerable amounts of foreign direct investment from France, Italy, and Spain in telecommunications, metals, textiles and garments, and food processing. Data from the ILO show that by the early 1990s, the female share of manufacturing workers was 43 percent in Tunisia and 37 percent in Morocco; in each country, a high proportion of all working women were involved in manufacturing.[26] Evidence from the MENA region would therefore confirm the view in the WID/GAD literature that export-led industrialization and female employment are positively related. The region also provides evidence that oil-centered industrialization inhibits female employment. Algeria, Iran, and Saudi Arabia have relied heavily on oil extraction and revenues, and in all three countries only a small proportion of the female economically active population is gainfully employed.

We should discuss the special case of Turkey, because although it is the most industrialized MENA country, it does not have the high levels of female industrial employment or even the high female share of formal-sector employment that one would expect. In fact, Turkish women remain concentrated in agricultural work rather than in the modern industrial sector. Although Turkey's proximity to Europe and its greater participation in the international division of labor have drawn more women into world-market activities, most of these activities are in the informal sector—unwaged, family-based production of agricultural goods or carpets or textiles, as has been documented by Mine Cinar and others. Agriculture, light manufacturing industry (tobacco, textiles/apparel, food/beverages, packaging of chemicals), and certain subdivisions of service industries are typically "feminine" occupations, but they constitute a relatively small percentage of Turkey's female labor force. In 1980 fully 88 percent of all economically active Turkish women were in agriculture. During the 1990s this figure declined to 65 percent and more women became involved in manufacturing employment with the shift from import-substitution to export-oriented industrialization; in fact, one survey showed that women's share of manufacturing reached a high of 25 percent in the mid-1990s.[27] Turkish feminist economists have conducted studies that confirm a positive relationship between export orientation and share of female employment. They have also found that marital status is an important determinant of women's participation in manufacturing; "wives and mothers" are less likely to be found in formal manufacturing firms and more likely to be found working in subcontracting arrangements at home, where they are not always captured in official statistics.[28] Employment in the formal manufacturing sector therefore remains a predominantly male phenomenon in Turkey.

Another special case is that of Palestine, where refugee and nonrefugee women were drawn into the textile industry, often as part of subcontracting arrangements with Israeli firms under exploitative conditions. Hanan Aruri of the Palestinian Working Women Society (PWWS) wrote in 1998 that the textile workshops in the West Bank and Gaza employed about 30,000 workers, of whom 70 percent were women. The majority of the workshops were subcontracting for Israeli companies that supplied the cloth, designs, and patterns. The majority of the women were from rural areas and refugee camps and worked out of economic need, but they lacked education and literacy and were often unskilled. A PWWS survey found that 80 percent of the women workers surveyed were the head of their household; the health conditions in the factories ranged from poor to moderate; and the salaries of the women workers were 25–30 percent of the salaries of men with the same working hours and years of service. Suha Hindiyeh-Mani studied married women homeworkers and found that the husband was the one who received his wife's salary. Jennifer Olmsted, who studied nonrefugee women in Bethlehem, found that acceptance of women working in the wage labor force was growing, but there was still a perception that women should not work in certain types of work, particularly manual labor.[29] Palestine is a special case in that the gender division of labor changed after the expropriation of Palestinian land with the creation of the state of Israel in 1948 and the occupation of the West Bank in 1967, and changed again as a result of new economic arrangements in the 1990s. In any event, the limited access to paid labor that Palestinian women were beginning to have was disrupted by the second intifada, the reoccupation of the West Bank, and the Israeli military incursions of 2002.

A Methodological Note

It is important to establish at the outset the problems entailed in studying women's economic activities in the Middle East. First, the region suffers from a paucity of data on women's productive activities and contributions to national development. A major problem involves definitions of work and employment; much of what women perform in the urban informal sector or household is not recognized as a contribution to the national income or development but is rather perceived to be a private service to the family. Women's agricultural work also has tended to be underreported in national accounts. This nonrecognition lies not only with statisticians and policymakers but also with ordinary men and women, who may be motivated by prevailing attitudes and modesty codes to refrain from providing an accurate description of women's productive activities. As a result, census data in many countries frequently report an extremely small economically active female population. A second problem: inconsistency in data collection across government agencies. The census bureau may report a very small female agricultural work force, but a manpower or labor force survey, or an agricultural census, will account for women more properly and indicate a much larger female work force. There is also inconsistency in data collection across countries, making comparisons difficult. Some countries count persons over the age of fifteen as part of the labor force, other countries count persons aged ten and above, still others include persons aged six and over. A third problem lies with the informal sector. Small workshops, such as textile enterprises, that rely on female labor may avoid taxation through nonregistration. Not only does this result in a further underestimation of women's industrial participation, but it entails more exploitative work conditions.[30]

Because of such problems, which make time-series and comparative analysis difficult, care must be exercised in reviewing and interpreting available data. However, this chapter is concerned principally with examining women's access to the formal sector of the economy and to salaried employment, where the data presented are more reliable. Women's employment data in public services and large-scale industry are virtually free from gaps in coverage.

Table 2.1 provides data on the female share of employment in all nonagricultural economic activities (that is, manufacturing and services). The table shows the diversity across countries in the region, but it also illustrates the limited nature of women's involvement in the nonagricultural labor force and in paid employment, especially when compared with Asian countries. Because of the methodological problems discussed above, it is difficult to discern a pattern of women's involvement in manufacturing; in some countries the female share of manufacturing declined between the 1960s and 1980s (e.g., Jordan, Iran) while in others the female share steadily increased (e.g., Egypt, Morocco, Syria, Tunisia). It is not clear why women's manufacturing employment declined between 1961 and 1979 in Jordan's case; one can speculate about enumeration issues, rising wages, or the impact of the 1967 war and the influx of Palestinian refugees. In Iran's case, the dramatic decline between 1976 and 1986 is certainly a function of the revolution and the new

Table 2.1   Female Share of Employment in Nonagricultural Activities (%), MENA and East Asian Countries

MENA	All Workers		Paid Employment	
	Manufacturing	Nonagriculture	Manufacturing	Nonagriculture
Egypt				
1960	4	11	3	12
1966	5	10	4	13
1976	7	14	7	12
1989	—	—	9	18
Iran				
1956	34	23	30	24
1966	40	21	33	22
1976	38	22	20	17
1986	15	11	7	11
Jordan				
1961	16	11	3	10
1979	6	10	5	12
1984	11	23	11	23
Morocco				
1960	30	16	22	22
1982	36	26	—	—
Syria				
1960	7	10	7	12
1981	11	12	9	13
Tunisia				
1956	22	17	8	12
1975	52	29	29	21
1984	56	30	34	24
Turkey				
1965	8	8	—	—
1970	23	13	14	12
1980	15	13	14	15
1985	15	13	15	16

Sources: ILO, *Yearbook of Labour Statistics 1990, 1995* (Geneva: ILO, 1990, 1995); and for Sri Lanka, Guy Standing, "Global Feminization Through Flexible Labour: A Theme Revisited," *World Development* 27 (3) (1999): 583–602.

Note: Some of the data are based on enterprise surveys, others on census data.

regime's emphasis on family roles for women. The table also provides figures on paid employment. It shows that in some countries the majority of women in manufacturing are not salaried workers but rather home-based workers. This seems especially to be the case with Iran in 1976, Turkey in 1970, and Tunisia in all years.

But what is most striking about Table 2.1—apart from the way that Morocco and Tunisia stand out among MENA countries in terms of women's involvement in manufacturing—is the contrast with the Asian countries. Dur-

Table 2.1   continued

East Asia	All Workers		Paid Employment	
	Manufacturing	Nonagriculture	Manufacturing	Nonagriculture
China				
1980	39	35	39	35
1991	45	39	45	39
Hong Kong				
1961	33	30	35	32
1976	46	37	48	39
1986	46	40	47	42
S. Korea				
1960	27	27	26	26
1975	38	34	38	33
1980	36	34	38	34
Indonesia				
1961	38	30	—	—
1971	43	35	35	25
1980	45	35	36	24
Malaysia				
1957	17	14	14	14
1980	41	31	42	32
Thailand				
1960	38	39	27	23
1980	47	44	43	37
Sri Lanka				
1975	32	18	32	18
1985	39	25	39	25
1988	47	35	47	35
1991	58	39	58	39

ing the period under consideration, women in the Asian countries had a far larger share of manufacturing employment—and larger shares of paid employment in manufacturing and other nonagricultural sectors—than did women in the Middle East and North Africa.

Thus, Susan Joekes's argument that industrialization in parts of the third world "has been as much female-led as export led" must be qualified for the Middle East. And Guy Standing's contention that "women are being substituted for men in various occupational categories, including manufacturing and production work" also does not quite apply in the Middle East, where men predominate in the industrial sector, except for Morocco and Tunisia.[31] To be sure, in nearly all the large countries women are engaged in light manufacturing—clothing, woven goods, shoes, food processing, confectioneries. But in the cities of the Middle East, most women are marginalized from production and especially from the formal-sector productive process, and are concentrated in community, social, and personal services. There does seem to be a widespread Middle Eastern attitude that factory work is not suitable for women, although this belief may be tied to the limited demand for female labor given the type of industrialization path the MENA countries chose in the past. Economic development has led to the creation of a female labor force, but that labor force is small in part because industrialization, an important stage of economic development, has been fairly limited in the region. From a world-system perspective, because the region has functioned as a source of oil and petrodollars, international capital and Middle East states alike have not aggressively pursued foreign investment in the kinds of industry likely to enhance female employment. As Mabro has observed: "The Arab countries, Iran, and, to a lesser extent, Turkey have still a long way to go on the road to industrialization."[32]

Characteristics of the Female Labor Force

I have argued above that oil-based industrialization served to limit the demand for and supply of women workers, hence the low involvement of MENA women in manufacturing (except for Morocco and Tunisia) when compared to Asian countries and those Latin American countries that saw increasing levels of investment by multinational corporations in the 1960s and 1970s. In the 1980s and 1990s, as MENA countries shifted from a state-directed development strategy with large public sectors to a neoliberal growth strategy favoring the expansion of the private sector, women encountered new employment problems. I will discuss these employment problems at the end of this section. What will be highlighted now are some of the distinctive characteristics of the female labor force in the MENA region.

Since the 1970s, many researchers have noted that to the extent that women are employed in MENA countries, they tend to be concentrated in professional occupations, mainly in what are known as community, social, and public services. The high incidence of women workers in the "professional, technical, and related workers" group in most countries could have been the outcome of occupational stereotyping prevalent in the region, where women cluster around specific jobs such as teaching and nursing. It could also have been a function of the relationship between class, income, and work participation, whereby women from elite families were most likely to be those who were employed. Researchers also have commented on an apparent disinclination by women to enter sales work and service occupations in the private sector. Ghazy Mujahid explained women's avoidance of such jobs in terms of cultural norms, as these are occupations with the highest likelihood of indiscriminate contact with outsiders.[33] One likely explanation is that the merchant class has been typically male, and the traditional urban markets—bazaars and souks—have been the province of men. Thus, until recently, the largest percentages of employed women in MENA countries were in the teaching professions. Some of these observations remain true even today, but there have been some changes. Variations should also be mentioned. Nursing has not been considered an appropriate occupation for women in the Gulf countries, including Saudi Arabia, and these countries import nurses from abroad. Clerical work is common among women in Egypt and Turkey, but not in the Islamic Republic of Iran. Working women tend to be unmarried in Jordan and Syria, but in Egypt a higher proportion of women in the work force are married.

One characteristic of the female labor force in MENA countries pertains to the very low rates of participation. The labor force participation rate—or the economic activity rate—refers to the proportion of the economically active population in relation to the working-age population. As can be seen in Table 2.2, the female rates were extremely low between the 1960s and 1980s. During the 1970s, economic activity rates of women were exceeding 20 percent in most regions of the developing world; by the 1980s, about 40 percent of the population of working-age women were employed in most countries. The highest rates of economic activity for women were found in East Asia (59 percent) and the Soviet Union (60 percent). The very low rates for the MENA region seen in Table 2.2 may be partly related to some methodological flaws (e.g., undercounting of women in agriculture and in the urban informal sector), although it is not clear why the undercounting of women should be so much more severe in the MENA region than elsewhere. But even assuming some undercounting, the fact remains that labor force participation has been a largely male activity. Women's activity rates rose during the 1990s, partly the result of an increase in the supply of job-seeking women due to economic difficulties in the post-oil-boom era, and partly due to better enumeration techniques. In 1997, women's labor force participation rates averaged 31 percent for the Middle East and North Africa. This was still low compared to other regions in the developing world, where women's economic activity rates were between 45 and 62 percent. But some MENA countries reported higher rates than the average—Turkey 50 percent, Tunisia 37 percent, and Morocco 41 percent in 2000.[34]

Another characteristic is the small female share of the total labor force, again compared to other regions. According to one UN database, the female share of the total labor force in 1995 in various regions was as follows: 37 percent in sub-Saharan Africa, 25 percent in South Asia, 43 percent in East Asia, 37 percent in Southeast Asia, 27 percent in Latin America and the Caribbean—and 17 percent in the Arab region (which would exclude Iran and

Table 2.2 Evolution of Labor Force Participation (%), Selected Countries

Country	Year	Male	Female	Total
Algeria	1966	42.2	1.8	21.7
	1975	43.4	1.9	22.3
	1982	38.9	2.9	21.1
	1987	42.4	4.4	23.6
	1995	76.1	24.3	50.4
Egypt	1966	51.2	4.2	27.9
	1975	50.4	4.1	27.9
	1982	48.2	5.8	27.3
	1986	48.1	6.2	27.7
	1995	67.3	21.6	47.9
Iran	1966	50.7	8.3	30.2
	1976	48.1	8.9	29.1
	1982[a]	46.3	7.0	27.6
	1986	45.5	5.4	25.9
	1995	79.2	25.2	52.5
Jordan	1961	42.4	2.6	22.9
	1971	43.1	2.6	23.1
	1979	38.0	3.3	21.3
	1990	75.6	17.4	47.4
Kuwait	1965	61.3	4.8	39.4
	1970	53.0	5.2	32.4
	1975	49.5	7.8	30.6
	1980	55.1	10.9	36.2
	1985	55.8	18.1	39.5
	1995	78.8	59.8	39.0
Libya	1964	46.6	2.7	25.6
	1975	47.4	2.7	25.9
	1990	80.6	20.6	52.8
	1995	78.2	22.9	52.3
Morocco	1960	50.1	5.9	28.0
	1971	44.5	8.0	26.3
	1975	44.4	7.9	26.1
	1982	47.9	11.6	29.6
	1990	80.0	38.8	59.2
	1995	79.3	59.5	40.0
Syria	1960	46.0	5.4	26.3
	1970	42.7	5.5	24.8
	1981	42.2	4.1	23.6
	1984	40.3	6.8	23.9
	1990	78.3	23.6	51.2
	1995	78.1	26.1	52.3
Tunisia	1966	44.4	3.0	24.1
	1975	48.9	12.6	31.0
	1984	47.4	13.3	30.6
	1990	79.6	32.9	56.3
	1995	79.4	35.0	57.3
Turkey	1985	50.1	21.9	36.2
	1990	79.7	34.2	56.6
	1997	74.4	27.8	50.8

Sources: ILO, *Yearbook of Labour Statistics, Retrospective Edition, 1945–1989* (Geneva: ILO, 1990), tab. 1, p. 60; ILO, *Yearbook of Labour Statistics 1981, 1985, 1991* (Geneva: ILO, 1981, 1985, 1991), tab. 1. Figures for the 1990s are from ILO, *Key Indicators of the Labour Market, 1999 ed.* (Geneva: ILO, 1999).

Notes: The labor force participation rate refers to the proportion of the population of working years involved in some form of economy activity.

a. The 1982 figures for Iran are for urban areas only.

Turkey). The average for all developing countries was 35 percent.[35] A different UN database shows that whereas in 1980 women composed about 20 percent of the total labor force in Western Asia (which would include Iran and Turkey), that figure increased to 26 percent in 1997. But again, the female share was relatively small, compared to South America (38 percent), the Caribbean, East Asia, and Southeast Asia (43 percent), and Central Asia (46 percent).[36]

A third characteristic of the female labor force, again relative to other regions and to men, has been the limited access of women to wage employment. Women generally constitute a small percentage of the total salaried work force in the MENA countries.[37] Between 1970 and 1990, the female share of total employees increased, but it remained small. This is illustrated in Table 2.3. A fourth feature is that women have been conspicuously absent from certain occupations, especially in private sales and services and in the sector of hotels, restaurants, and wholesale and retail trade, at least according to official statistics for wage employment. Lebanon may be an exception to this rule, given its traditionally large private sector and small public sector.[38] This particular characteristic of female labor in MENA countries is illustrated in Table 2.4.

A fifth distinctive feature is that female nonagricultural employment in MENA countries has been concentrated in public-sector professional jobs, a function of the correlation between educational attainment and female labor force participation. Indeed, according to one analyst, "women's share of employment in [the professional and technical group] is two and a half times

Table 2.3   Female Share of Total Employees (%), Selected MENA Countries

	1970	1980	1990	Other Years
Algeria	5	8	10	
Egypt	9	9	16	17.7 (1995)
Iran	15	12	10	12 (1996)
Iraq	—	8	11	
Jordan	—	9	10	11 (1993)
Kuwait	8	14	21	
Morocco	—	18	25	22 (1992)
Syria	10	9	15	17 (1991)
Tunisia	6	15	17	23 (1994)
Turkey	14	15	18	

Sources: UN, *WISTAT* CD-ROM (Geneva: UN, 1994); ILO, *Yearbook of Labor Statistics 1996, 1997* (Geneva: ILO, 1996, 1997), tab. 2E; *Statistical Yearbook of Iran 1375/1996* (Tehran: Islamic Republic of Iran, 1997), tab. 3.4, p. 74, and tab. 3.9, p. 81.

Note: On Lebanon, see *Al-Raida* 15 (82) (Summer 1998), special issue: *Women in the Labor Force,* which reports that women's share of employment is 20 percent (p. 16).

Table 2.4 Female Service Employment by Subsectors (%), Selected MENA Countries

	Trade, Restaurants, and Hotels		Transport, Storage, and Communications		Finance, Insurance, Real Estate, and Business Services		Community, Social, and Personal Services	
	1980	1990–1994	1980	1990–1994	1980	1990–1994	1980	1990–1994
Algeria	2.7	3.7	3.4	4.2	16.4	12.4	19.4	19.9
Bahrain	4.1	6.9	9.9	11.9	27.1	12.3	21.9	31.4
Egypt	5.7	17.7	3.3	5.9	18.8	18.1	17.6	26.1
Iran, Islamic Republic	2.0	1.7	2.2	1.4	9.4	9.2	18.9	13.6
Jordan	2.1	2.1	0.6	0.6	15.9	15.9	13.8	13.8
Kuwait	3.2	4.6	4.9	5.8	14.2	16.2	25.1	36.1
Lebanon		4.4	0.0	3.4		10.8		20.3
Libya		1.4		0.8		8.3		10.5
Morocco	4.8	3.9	2.9	2.4	27.9	23.7		
Qatar		1.4		3.8		9.7		18.8
Saudi Arabia		0.7		0.5		0.6		9.7
Syria	2.7	2.9	2.4	2.6	14.7	12.3	16.8	21.2
Tunisia	6.0	8.1	5.3	21.9	24.6	24.6	21.0	21.0
Turkey	4.6	7.0	4.9	4.7	25.8	29.3	14.8	19.2
United Arab Emirates	2.8	4.0	2.3	3.3	11.0	11.2	11.3	20.5

Source: UN, Women's Indicator and Statistics Database (WISTAT), 1994.

their share in the non-agricultural labour force. Turkey, an OECD member, follows the typical pattern of Middle Eastern countries where a large proportion of working women are in a professional or technical occupation. . . . Social and cultural factors do ensure that most adult women in the Middle East and North Africa region do not work in the non-agricultural labour force, but for the relatively few who do, an unusually high percentage (by world standards) have a professional or technical job (often teacher or nurse)."[39] These features are illustrated in Table 2.4, which shows a consistent concentration of women in community, social, and personal services. But that table also shows another feature—the relatively large proportion of women obtaining professional jobs in finance, insurance, real estate, and business services, especially in Morocco, Tunisia, and Turkey. And as seen in Table 2.5, a growing proportion of public service jobs are held by women.

In examining occupational distribution, one finds that MENA countries have minimal female presence in administrative and managerial occupations.

Table 2.5   Women's Share of Public Service Employment, Selected MENA Countries

	% Female
Iran	
1986	30
1991	31
1996	38
Kuwait	
1983	31
1994	39
Morocco	
1989	29
1991	31
Qatar	
1988	9
Syria	
1980	19
1992	27
Turkey	
1994	35

Sources: Alachkar, Ahmad. 1996. "Economic Reform and Women in Syria." Pp. 99–114 in Khoury and Demetriades, eds., *Structural Adjustment, Economic Liberalization, Privatization, and Women's Employment in Selected Countries of the Middle East and North Africa;* UNDP-Ankara. 1996. *Human Development Report 1996 Turkey.* Ankara: UNDP; Islamic Republic of Iran [IRI]. 1995. *National Report on Women in the Islamic Republic of Iran: Prepared for the Fourth World Conference on Women.* Tehran: Bureau of Women's Affairs; IRI. 1997. *Statistical Yearbook 1375 [1996].* Tehran: Statistical Center of Iran; and Guy Standing, "Global Feminization Through Flexible Labor: Labour: A Theme Revisited," *World Development* 27 (3) (1999): 583–602.

In the late 1990s the percentages ranged from a low of under 6 percent in Algeria, Iran, Jordan, Kuwait, and Syria, to 10–13 percent in Egypt, Tunisia, and Turkey. Only Morocco, interestingly but inexplicably, reported a 25 percent female share of administrative and managerial positions.[40]

I have discussed the political economy of the region, the specificities of development strategies, the limited nature of industrialization, and the consequent patterns of female employment. In the 1980s all Middle Eastern countries were beset by economic and political difficulties, which also affected women's economic status and employment possibilities. The economic crisis in the Middle East occurred in the context of a worldwide crisis resulting in part from the drop in real prices of primary commodities, including oil. The global oil market became very unstable, leading to fluctuating and declining prices. The near-collapse of prices in 1986 (from $28 per barrel to $7 per barrel) had repercussions throughout the Middle East: austerity measures were introduced, availability of development aid decreased, and major development projects were reevaluated or suspended. The Iraqi invasion of Kuwait in August 1990 raised the price of oil again, but the damage already had been done. In the 1980s countries of the Middle East, and especially North Africa, experienced low or negative economic growth rates, declining state revenues, and high levels of indebtedness to foreign creditors. In some cases (Egypt, Morocco, Algeria), debts became truly enormous in relation to the country's economic capacities; Turkey was placed on the World Bank's list of "severely indebted middle-income countries." According to the UN, debt as a percentage of GNP for the Middle East and North Africa in 1989 rose to 70 percent; during the 1980s the region's debt increased from $4.4 billion to $118.8 billion.[41]

The most active Arab borrowers from the World Bank—Algeria, Egypt, Jordan, Morocco, Syria, Tunisia—had to impose austerity measures on their populations as a result of World Bank and International Monetary Fund (IMF) structural adjustment policy packages, and several experienced "IMF riots."[42] High population growth rates coupled with heavy rural-urban migration concentrated larger numbers of the unemployed in major cities. The livelihood of lower-middle-class and working-class women (and men) was adversely affected by the debt and the inflationary-recessionary cycles plaguing the region, especially in Morocco, Algeria, Iran, and Egypt. In Israel the serious economic plight was alleviated by massive U.S. aid. But elsewhere, tough economic reforms, along with poverty, unemployment, and debt servicing— as well as political repression—served to delegitimize "Western-style" systems and revive questions of cultural identity, including renewed calls for greater control over female mobility. It was in this context of economic failures and political delegitimation that Islamist movements began to present themselves as alternatives. (See Chapter 5 for a full discussion.)

One effect of this economic downturn on women's labor force participation was an increase in the supply of job-seeking women—but also a dramatic increase in women's unemployment during the 1990s. In Algeria, Egypt, Iran, Jordan, Morocco, and Tunisia, women's unemployment rates ranged from 20 to 25 percent; even in the ostensibly rich oil-producing shaikhdoms of Bahrain and Oman, job-seeking young women experienced rates of unemployment as high as 30 percent.[43] The frustration that working-class women in particular experienced in looking for meaningful jobs but not finding them is captured in the first quote at the beginning of this chapter. Given the low rates of female labor force participation and the small amount of female labor force shares, it is clear that women's unemployment rates have been disproportionately high. During the 1990s, therefore, the MENA countries produced yet another distinctive feature of the female labor force—the feminization of unemployment.

State Policies and Women's Status: Some Cases

If natural resource endowments, national development strategies, and international economic factors have largely shaped women's employment patterns, what distinct role has the national state played? What is the impact of state-directed legal measures, public campaigns, educational programs, and investment decisions? We find that (1) there are variations in state policies in the region, particularly with regard to the mobilization of female labor and women's integration into the formal economy and public life, and (2) in all cases the state has been a major determinant of women's legal and economic status. In some cases a regime's search for political legitimacy, a larger labor force, or an expanded social base led it to construct health, education, and welfare services conducive to greater work participation by women, and to encourage female activity in the public sphere. Examples are the Iraqi Baathists during the 1960s and 1970s, the Pahlavi state in Iran in the same period, Tunisia under the late president Habib Bourguiba, and Egypt under Gamal Abdul Nasser. In other cases state managers were wedded to the patriarchal gender contract and refrained from encouraging female participation in the paid labor force. Examples included Saudi Arabia, Algeria, and Jordan.

In most MENA countries, women have remained an underutilized human resource because of limited industrialization, the gender ideology stressing women's family roles, and ambivalence on the part of state managers toward the full participation of women in economic development and policy formulation. As a result, MENA women have not yet established labor force attachment, and they have a long way to go before they attain the participation rates and access to salaried employment of women in other semiperipheral countries, not to mention the advanced industrialized world. Nevertheless, economic development, the expansion of the state, legal reform, and educational attainment by women have had interesting consequences, some intended, others wholly unintended. Let us examine these on a country-by-country basis.

Turkey

Turkey provides a nearly unique example (the other being Tunisia) of a country that replaced the Islamic personal status laws with a civil law code regulating personal and family relations and equalizing the duties and responsibilities of the sexes. As we will see in Chapter 3, Kemalist reforms in the 1920s introduced secular legal codes based on Western models. Such legal codes provide an important basis for women to act as autonomous persons. In the late 1960s there were signs that women in one region of western Turkey were exercising their full legal right to sue for divorce to protect their personal reputations and their claims to property. Another result of the Kemalist reforms is that Turkey became unique among Middle Eastern or Muslim countries in having large numbers of women in the legal profession.[44] But during the 1980s there was a shift in state orientation, when the social democratic years of the 1970s were halted by the 1980 military coup. Between 1983 and 1990 some 700 Quranic schools were established throughout the country, and their graduates raised calls for Islamization. During this period Prime Minister Turgut Ozal, the architect of a tough stabilization and structural adjustment program, was also the most openly Islamic Turkish leader in modern times.

One area where the Turkish state has been deficient is in the provision of literacy and education, especially for girls. Between 1975 and 1985 the illiterate female population declined from 49 percent to 32 percent, but the reduction of male illiteracy was much steeper, from 24 percent to 13 percent. By the end of the 1990s, the illiteracy rate of women over age fifteen had declined to 25 percent—but this compared with a male illiteracy rate of just 7 percent. Discriminatory attitudes toward women persist in Turkey, especially in the rural areas, where most female illiteracy is found.

For the majority of Turkish women, wage work is elusive, primarily because of the structure of Turkey's agrarian sector, in which so many women are involved. Unlike many developing countries that have large commercialized farms or semifeudal landholdings, Turkey's countryside is characterized by what Caglar Keyder calls a system of "peasant proprietorships."[45] This system, along with Turkey's pursuit of agricultural production for export, has left most Turkish women as unwaged family workers, undereducated, and situated in rural patriarchal gender arrangements. Rural-urban migration did not lead to higher levels of female economic participation; to the contrary, research has shown that the earlier generation of migrant women withdrew from the labor force. Since then, migrant women have been more inclined to take in home-based work or to engage in domestic employment.[46]

There is evidence from Turkey that, in contrast to farm work or traditional manufacturing (monetized rural carpet weaving), wage work in the formal sector seems to improve women's standing in the household. Yildiz Ecevit's study of Turkish factory workers showed that "married women factory workers in Bursa have gained a considerable degree of power over decision-making in their families as a result of their employment. Over half the married women who were interviewed reported that they and their husbands took decisions together and often consulted each other." Hale Bolak's research on marital power dynamics within working-class households in Istanbul led her to conclude that "whether or not the woman's position as breadwinner has a critical effect on her financial autonomy and on the allocation of household responsibilities, the traditional basis of male authority *is* ideologically challenged through a discourse that includes intra- as well as extra-household roles in the definition of 'male responsibility.'"[47]

Egypt

In the late 1950s and during the administration of the late Gamal Abdul Nasser, Egypt's public sector expanded significantly through a series of Egyptianization decrees (1956–1959) that gave the government control of foreign-owned assets such as the Suez Canal. These decrees were followed in the early 1960s by the adoption of a highly centralized development policy approach and a massive wave of nationalizations of Egyptian-owned enterprises in industry, banking, trade, and transport. At the same time, the government embarked on an employment drive that required state-owned enterprises to include among their annual targets the creation of significant numbers of new jobs; the administrative apparatus of the state was also expanded rapidly at both the central and local government levels. Equally important was the objective of spreading health and education services, bringing a corresponding growth of government employment in these services. The state's guarantee of a job to all high school and university graduates encouraged women, including women from working-class and lower-middle-class families, to take advantage of the government's free education policy.

A distinctive feature of the Nasser government was its political support for the education of women and their integration into national development. Labor Law 91 of 1954 guaranteed equal rights and equal wages, and made special provisions for married women and mothers. As Homa Hoodfar notes, these provisions were expanded under Anwar Sadat to facilitate women's labor-market participation. "This law was applied primarily in the public sector, which made jobs in this area particularly attractive to women. As a result, the state became the single most important employer of women."[48]

The Nasser era ended when his successor, Sadat, introduced the policy of *infitah,* or economic opening. By the mid-1980s the Egyptian government was faced with the difficult issue of how to reduce its commitment to job creation in the face of severe recessionary conditions. These conditions included a record level of 15.5 percent overall (open) unemployment, according to the 1986 population census (up from 7 percent in the 1976 census), and with poor prospects for either the domestic productive sectors or the oil-rich Arab markets to create significant job opportunities for Egyptian workers. Moreover, high inflation effectively eroded the financial advantage of the white-collar work force. The recession fueled social tensions and led to a growth in Islamism, with its attendant ideological and social pressures on women. Employed women now felt compelled to appear in hijab at work, even though they would claim that the turn to Islamic dress was their own choice.

Since Nasser's time many women have entered previously male strongholds—universities, the administration, professions, industry, the business world, diplomacy, politics. But the economic crisis in Egypt and rapid population growth limit formal employment opportunities for women. As economic conditions worsened, more women sought work out of economic need, but found few job opportunities. When the government cut back on public-sector employment, the rate of unemployment among educated women increased dramatically—to 22 percent in 1995. For the vast majority of Egyptian women, life goes on as unpaid family workers on peasant plots, as street vendors and hawkers in the urban informal sector, as home-based seamstresses or beauticians, or in any one of a myriad of small-scale income-generating activities.

Poor women in southern Egypt augment the family budget by working in small clothing factories. Photo by Val Moghadam.

Tunisia

Government policy since independence has prioritized women's emancipation and integration into the economy, and the constitution and civil code have reflected and reinforced that position. Staunchly secular, President Bourguiba made the participation of women in public life a major policy goal. The constitution ensured all citizens the same rights and obligations. Polygamy and male repudiation were outlawed, allowing women the right to petition for divorce and custody of their children. The legacy of such legal reform has made Tunisia the most liberal country in the Arab world.

In 1960 a law gave the minority of women who were members of the social insurance service (mainly those employed in industry, handicrafts, and services, with the exception of housework) the right to pregnancy leave—six weeks before delivery and six weeks afterward. During this period 50 percent of monthly wages were to be paid.[49] Subsequently, the length of maternity leave was set at thirty days, apparently as part of government policy to lower the birthrate. Public employees were also entitled to childcare leaves. Law no. 81-6 of February 12, 1981, introduced a social security scheme for wage-earning agricultural workers and those engaged in cooperative undertakings. The following year this scheme was extended to cover small farmers and the self-employed—a law that would benefit women as well.

In the 1980s the distribution of the female labor force was more balanced in Tunisia than in many other Middle Eastern countries: 26 percent in agriculture, 48 percent in manufacturing, 21 percent in services. The female share of government employment was 24.5 percent in 1987; of the country's magistrates, 13.5 percent were women; of medical personnel, 20.6 percent; of paramedical personnel, 48 percent; of the country's teachers, 31.5 percent. Women's participation in formal politics matched the trends in employment. In 1981 there were seven female deputies in parliament; in 1983 there were 50,000 female members of the ruling social-democratic Neo-Destour Party and 57,000 members of the National Union of Tunisian Women; and in 1985 some 492 women were voted municipal councilors around the country.[50]

The following years saw economic problems that encouraged Islamist forces and threatened women's gains. In May 1989 Islamists competed openly in Tunisia's parliamentary elections, winning 14 percent of the total vote and 30 percent in Tunis and other cities to beat the main secular opposition party, the Movement of Democratic Socialists, into third place.[51] After the removal of Habib Bourguiba by Zein el-Abedin Ben Ali, more mosques were built and Quranic universities restored. However, the Tunisian state remained opposed to Islamist political aspirations and formally committed to the advancement of women and their full involvement in economic development. President Ben Ali, in particular, saw himself as a champion of women's rights. Tunisian women benefit from a favorable political-legal environment and enjoy an array of professional and occupational choices, although they face daunting unemployment rates. Tunisia also has developed a cadre of professional women—such as Essma Ben Hamida of ENDA Inter-Arabe, quoted at the beginning of this chapter—who work with low-income women on development projects that provide microcredit services, vocational training, job counseling, and environmental education, and "promote active exercise of citizenship."[52]

Iraq

During the 1960s and 1970s, the Ba'th Party had an interest both in recruiting women into the labor force to alleviate a continuing labor shortage and in wresting women's allegiance away from kin, family, or ethnic group and shifting it to the party-state. The Free Education Law of 1975 benefited women as well as men. The 1978 Personal Status Law, although limited in its objectives, aimed to reduce the control of extended families over women. In November 1977 the government conducted a census to determine the characteristics of the illiterate; of 2.2 million illiterates aged fifteen to forty-five, 70 percent were women. The government then passed laws requiring attendance at adult literacy classes, made extensive use of trade unions and other "popular organizations" and daily use of television and radio. Different textbooks were prepared for peasants, workers, and housewives.[53] Women were recruited into state-controlled agencies and put through public education as well as vocational training and political indoctrination.

By 1979, 51 percent of Baghdad University's first-year medical school class was female, as were 75 percent of students in the English translation department at Mustansiriyah University. The General Federation of Iraqi Women grew in importance, even organizing sports events for women athletes. The ruling Ba'th Party encouraged a wide range of employment for women, who by the late 1970s accounted for 29 percent of the country's medical doctors, 46 percent of dentists, 70 percent of pharmacists, 46 percent of teachers and university lecturers, 33 percent of the staff of government departments, 26 percent of workers in industry, and 45 percent of farm employees.[54] Maternity leave was generous, and jobs of pregnant women were protected. Many young Iraqi women traveled abroad and studied on scholarships.

The onset of the war with Iran brought about a toughening of the state's position on women, and progress stalled under Saddam Hussein. In April 1982 the government issued a regulation stating that married women were not allowed to travel unless accompanied by their husbands; unmarried women were required to have the written consent of their fathers or guardians. Women were told that it was their patriotic duty to fill jobs vacated by men now at the front; they also were told that they should bear five children to narrow the gap between Iraq's population (then 15 million people) and Iran's (47 million). In 1986 birth control devices disappeared from pharmacy shelves. According to one account, women's participation in the formal labor force more than doubled in the 1980s.[55] During the 1990s, Iraq's invasion of Kuwait led to the destructive coalition war against Iraq and a harsh sanctions regime that resulted in the deterioration of the country's physical and social infrastructure and a serious decline in the population's well-being. What began as a forward-looking program for socioeconomic development and women's rights in the 1960s and 1970s encountered setbacks in the 1980s and 1990s as a result of misguided state actions and punitive international measures.

Iran

The case of Iran elucidates the unintended consequences of development and state policies on women's gender consciousness. In 1962 the Pahlavi state granted women the vote and in 1967 introduced the Family Protection Act, which limited polygamy, allowed women to initiate divorce, and increased their child custody rights after divorce or widowhood. However, the Shah himself was opposed to "women's lib" and frequently derided the demands of Western feminists. Moreover, his reforms were in place for only ten years and did not have widespread impact. In 1979 the new Islamic state abrogated many of these liberal codes. Among other things, the new authorities adopted a pronatalist stance that deemed women, especially young mothers, inappropriate for full-time work. Significantly, the very first display of opposition to the Islamists—and this at the height of the new regime's popularity and support—came from educated middle-class women in early March 1979. These were the women who had been the principal beneficiaries of several decades of modernization. Development—however limited and skewed in its Iranian variant—combined with state reforms had allowed a segment of the female population upward social mobility through education and employment. There was a stratum and generation of women who opposed veiling and rejected Islamist exhortations that working women in the civil service return to the joys of domesticity. These women were subsequently silenced—and some were imprisoned, killed, or exiled—but their political activism must be regarded as nothing less than remarkable.

By the late 1980s a number of factors converged to modify and liberalize the Islamist state's position on women, education, and work. These factors included the expansion of the state apparatus, the dearth of male labor in a war situation, and women's own resistance to their second-class citizenship. Educated and employed secular and Islamic feminists in Iran—lawyers, publishers, members of parliament, university professors—have been demanding a modification of the rigid gender rules implemented in the early 1980s and pushing for changes in family law and labor legislation to increase women's rights. This activism is illustrative of both the interplay of structure, consciousness, and agency, and of unexpected outcomes of state policies. (See Chapter 6 for details on Iran.)

For the small percentage of women in the formal sector, government employment provides many advantages. Nearly all women who are waged and salaried are in the public sector, where they enjoy insurance, pensions, and other benefits. Labor legislation enacted in 1990 provides women with ninety days of maternity leave, at least half of which must be taken after childbirth. There is also a job-back guarantee with no loss of seniority and a half-hour break every three hours for breast-feeding, with a crèche provided at the workplace.[56] The private sector remains a largely male domain in Iran, although more women are beginning to work in the growing sector of voluntary or nongovernmental organizations. All working women, however, are required to appear in hijab, which is at minimum a large scarf covering all the hair and neck, and a long-sleeved and loose-fitting smock or manteau that covers the body's contours.

Algeria

Throughout the 1960s and 1970s the Algerian government promoted industrialization in tandem with the preservation of the close-knit family union. The state's attitude toward family law and personal status oscillated for over twenty years. Both the industrial strategy and the pronatalist Boumedienne social policy worked against female employment. By the 1980s, as a result of a galloping birthrate, nearly three-quarters of Algeria's population was under the age of thirty, and many were unemployed. According to the 1987 census, the employed population numbered 3.7 million men and a mere 365,000 women—out of a total population of 13 million people over the age of fifteen. The female share of the employed population was 8.8 percent. Still, these figures represented a steady increase in female employment since 1966.

Reasons for the low levels of female employment were Algeria's chronically high unemployment, a conservative cultural stance on the part of the leadership, and the specific development strategy pursued by the state. In Marnia Lazreg's pithy words, the state's attitude could be summed up as, "You don't have to work, sisters! This is socialism." Algeria's strategy emphasized heavy industrialization, partly on the assumption that this approach would eventually encourage mechanized agriculture. The new, large-scale factories such as steel works and petrochemical plants required skilled workers, and it was men who were trained for those jobs. The result was very low female labor participation in industry. Consequently, women became an underutilized source of labor, with implications for fertility, population growth rates, and overall societal development.

In the early 1980s the Algerian government began to make concessions to the growing Islamist movement and its supporters within the National Assembly. A family code was drafted, which alarmed many women and provoked protest demonstrations. In the midst of a privatization effort and faced with high rates of unemployment (on the order of 22 percent), a heavy debt-servicing burden, and other assorted economic ills, Algerian policymakers were unwilling to risk legislation that could potentially aggravate the situation and thus conceded to the Islamists in the National Assembly. The final bill, passed in 1984, gave women the legal right to work but rendered them economic dependents of men.[57] In the municipal elections of June 1990, the Islamist party won the most seats, a situation North African feminists and democrats felt was bound to adversely affect women's already fragile and limited rights. (See Chapter 5 for details.)

As a result of the Algerian state's cultural conservatism, women's participation in state and other social agencies was quite low compared to male participation. In the late 1980s women constituted only 11 percent of the employees of ministries, 34 percent of schoolteachers, 24 percent of higher education instructors, and 36 percent of public health workers. There were no women in the religious affairs and civil protection sectors. Still, Algerian women were more likely to work in the government sector than in the private sector. Indeed, 86 percent of employed Algerian women were employed in the public sector, as against 14 percent in the private sector. For Algerian men, the respective rates were 55 percent and 45 percent.[58] In the 1990s Algerian women faced a violent civil conflict pitting Islamists against the state, as well as serious economic problems that forced more women to seek jobs. Although their labor force participation increased, so did their unemployment rates. Algerian women's share of employment and income can be described only generously as inadequate. In 1995 women's share of earned income was 19 percent and their per capita income was $2,051, as compared with $7,467 for men.[59]

Jordan

In Jordan one finds a low overall participation rate, partly due to a very high rate of population growth, a large under-fifteen population, high out-migration, and low female economic activity. During the 1970s the state encouraged education and indeed made school compulsory for nine years. The result was an impressive increase in female education: by 1984–1985 girls accounted for some 48 percent of the total school enrollment. The area of women's employment, however, showed less impressive progress, despite the fact that social policy provided for generous benefits to employed women. In 1979 the percentage of economically active women in the total labor force was only about

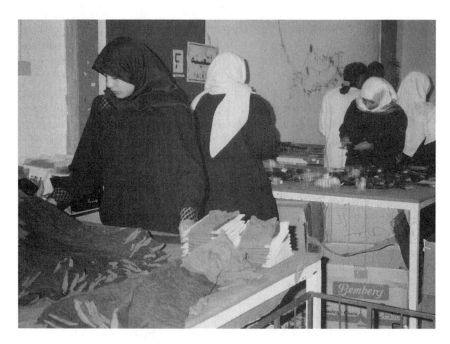

Although Jordan's female labor force remains small, both working-class and middle-class women participate: (above) hosiery factory employs women; (below) a personnel assistant at Hikma Pharmaceuticals in Amman. Photos by Val Moghadam.

4 percent, and the female share of employees was only 9 percent. Out-migration of Jordanian male labor did not cause an increasing number of women to enter the wage labor market; rather, their activities in the informal sector and as unpaid family workers increased. Labor shortages due to migration led to labor importation, mainly from Egypt, at all skill levels instead of the training of women in marketable skills.[60]

Jordan's five-year plan (1980–1985) ostensibly sought to further integrate women into the development process and predicted an increase in female labor force participation and a larger female share of the total labor force. But by 1984 the female participation rate was only 4.8 percent. Only 8.4 percent of women of working age (fifteen to sixty-five) were reported as economically active, constituting a mere 10.5 percent of the total work force. Nearly half of all women in the modern sector were in education, while textile workers represented about 30 percent of Jordan's female labor force. In an untoward economic situation characterized by a large external debt and growing male unemployment, government policy implicitly discouraged female employment, and women's unemployment rates soared during the 1990s. Although Jordanian women are among the most educated in the region, this has not led to greater female involvement in the paid labor force, partly due to continuing conservative attitudes within the state and society and partly due to the difficulties of the economy in the context of the continuing Israel-Palestine conflict.

In the November 1989 parliamentary elections, the first held since 1967, thirty-four out of eighty seats were won by members of the Muslim Brotherhood and like-minded Islamists. That political outcome did nothing to help the legal status, economic conditions, and social positions of Jordanian women. But it did help to spur a women's movement that is challenging the patriarchal gender contract. (See Chapter 8.)

Saudi Arabia

State personnel designed policy not only to promote economic growth and development but also to reproduce traditional familial relations and sex segregation in education and employment. In Saudi Arabia women's place is in the home, and their lives are more circumscribed than in any other MENA country: the percentage of Saudi women who worked outside the home, mainly in the teaching and health sectors, was about 5 percent in the 1980s and 10 percent in the late 1990s. Elements of Saudi culture—devotion to Islam, extended-family values, the segregated status of women, and the Al-Saud monarchic hegemony—have been formulated in an increasingly deliberate fashion into a new political culture that acts as a screen to ensure that technological and human progress remains within acceptable bounds.[61]

The first private school for girls was started in the late 1950s and was the initiative of a princess from the royal family. Fifteen private girls schools subsequently opened in four Saudi Arabian cities. In 1960 the female education system was placed under the auspices of the government, with supervision by the religious order. Expatriate teachers were employed to start with, then replaced progressively by Saudi women teachers. Educational facilities for girls became available nationwide and have provided for general, technical, vocational, and university-level education. In the 1980s, nearly a million female students were enrolled at various levels and constituted nearly 45 percent of the national student population. Professional education included medicine, pharmacy, teaching, commerce, and the social sciences.

By 1987 over 80,000 Saudi women were employed in the government, education, and health sectors.[62] Nursing, however, was seen as culturally inappropriate for Saudi women, hence the importation of nurses from Egypt, the Philippines, India, and elsewhere. More recently, and to minimize sensitivities concerning male physicians and female patients, a substantial number of Saudi women physicians have been trained to treat women patients. In the wake of the Gulf crisis following Iraq's invasion of Kuwait in August 1990, Saudi authorities called for wider participation of women in the labor force "in the area of human services and medical services within the context of fully preserving Islamic and social values."[63] In November 1990 a group of forty Saudi women, most of them university lecturers, took this opportunity to demonstrate their desire for change by driving their own cars through the streets of Riyadh, an extraordinary action that stunned the country.

Saudi Arabia is not a country that readily provides a statistical profile of its population dynamics or its labor force; thus we know very little about the exact patterns of women's employment. We know that rich Saudi women own businesses, although male kin or employees often run the businesses. What is clear is that despite the country's enormous oil wealth, 36 percent of Saudi women over the age of fifteen were illiterate as recently as 1998. World Bank figures show that in 1997, nine years of schooling was expected for females—compared with eleven years in the Islamic Republic of Iran and fourteen years in South Korea.[64] In the wake of the very expensive Gulf War and declining oil prices, Saudi Arabia has confronted indebtedness, rising unemployment, and growing relative poverty. In this context, popular calls for change—including more demands by women—can be expected.

The State and Women's Employment: Opportunities and Constraints

Women's entry into public life in the MENA region was facilitated by state-sponsored education and by job opportunities in the expanding government sector and public services. Formal/modern-sector employment, and especially opportunities in the civil service, became an important source of status and livelihood. The active role of the government in national development meant that many women no longer relied on a male guardian as provider, but rather the state. In this regard, the Middle East is not so different from other countries, for around the world the public sector and government employment have provided women with jobs, benefits, and security that may elude them in the private sphere.[65] As Fatima Mernissi once remarked, "The North African woman of today usually dreams of having a steady, wage-paying job with social security and health and retirement benefits, at a State institution; these women don't look to a man any longer for their survival, but to the State. While perhaps not ideal, this is nevertheless a breakthrough, an erosion of tradition. It also partly explains the Moroccan women's active participation in the urbanization process: they are leaving rural areas in numbers equaling men's migrations, for a 'better life' in the cities—and in European cities, as well."[66] In the latter part of the 1990s, Moroccan women's prospects for greater economic opportunity seemed poised to improve when a progressive government led by a socialist prime minister sought to implement a national action plan for women's development.

On the other hand, what the state gives the state can take away—as we have seen with the examples of Algeria, Iran, and Iraq in the 1980s. Moreover, the state is not always favorable to the advancement of women and their economic equality—especially when it is led by men holding patriarchal attitudes concerning women, work, and family. And some states are held hostage to international forces, such as the power wielded by the World Bank, the International Monetary Fund, and the World Trade Organization, not to mention the U.S. government. As a Moroccan woman activist rhetorically asked, "How can the state improve the status of women, children, and the poor when international financial institutions are in control?"[67]

Development, Work, and Women's Empowerment

"Integrating women in development" has come under attack by feminist researchers of Latin America, Asia, and Africa. They argue that women have indeed been integrated into development—much to their disadvantage, as they have become the latest group of exploited workers, a source of cheap and expendable labor. It has also been argued that capitalist development has everywhere reduced the economic status of women, resulting in marginalization and impoverishment. It is true that the term "development" obscures the relations of exploitation, unequal distribution of wealth, and other disparities (not to mention environmental degradation) that ensue. But it is also true that within a national economic framework there is room to improve working women's lot. Sex-segregated occupational distribution can be challenged and altered, as can gender-based wage differentials, inadequate support structures for working mothers, unfair labor legislation pertaining to women, unhealthy work environments, and so on. These issues typically are taken up by trade unions, social movements, and women's organizations. Moreover, although the proletarianization of women entails labor control (as it does for men), wage work also provides prospects for women's autonomy—not an insignificant consideration in patriarchal contexts.

Whether modernization and paid employment have resulted in an increase or a diminution of women's economic status continues to be a matter of debate for the Middle East as for other semiperipheral countries. Some have argued that men's work and women's work are complementary in nomadic communities, and that modernization reduces, marginalizes, and devalues women's work. Amal Rassam argued that women of rural backgrounds suffered a decline in status; they lost the productive role they traditionally played in the preindustrial economy as the goods they produced were replaced by imported or locally produced factory ones. Mernissi's research, however, suggests a link between the deterioration of women's position and their preexisting dependence on men. Her interviews with Moroccan women working in various craft industries (such as weaving textiles and rugs) show how dependent women are upon men as intermediaries, a situation that only increases their precarious economic position. She concludes that the increasing capitalist penetration of such industries has had the consequence of further degrading women's status.[68] Thus, patriarchal gender arrangements constitute an intervening factor in the impact of development on women's status.

The complex and contradictory nature of the relationship between development and women's status has been explored by a number of Turkish and Iranian researchers. Deniz Kandiyoti's research in the 1970s comparing the status of Turkish women in nomadic tribes, peasant villages, rural towns, and cities found that the influence of the patrilineal extended household—where the father dominates younger men and all women, and there is a hierarchy by age among the women—was pervasive in all sectors, but less so in the towns and cities because of neolocal residence and the diminished importance of elders. Compared to peasant and nomadic women, urban women played a sharply reduced role in the productive process. But peasant and nomadic women did not receive recognition for their own labor, not even for their offspring, as these belonged to the patrilineal extended family. In many parts of rural Turkey, women have been traditionally called the "enemy of the spoon," reflecting the perception that they share the food on the table without contributing economically to the household. Gunseli Berik's study of carpet weavers in rural Central Anatolia showed that male kin controlled the labor power and the wages of female weavers. This pattern has been found for Iran and Afghanistan as well. Nermin Abadan-Unat refers to the persistence of "archaic and patriarchal family structures," and Kandiyoti observes that "we cannot speak of a simple decline in women's status with the transition to an urban wage labor economy. Their diminished role in production may be offset by other factors, which are, however, increasingly specific to certain class sectors."[69]

In a patriarchal context, therefore, the effects of development on women's status have varied by class and by location. Women certainly have more options in an urban setting, whereas in rural areas patriarchal family arrangements limit their options. Moreover, the major beneficiaries of the development process have largely been middle-class and upper-middle-class women, even though national development, legal reforms, and especially public education have resulted in some social mobility for women of other classes. There can be no doubt that expanding education and employment opportunities have created a generation of Middle Eastern women who are accustomed to working in the formal sector and indeed expect it. It should not be surprising that middle-class educated and employed women are the ones agitating for more progressive social change—for women as women and for women as workers.

Development must be seen, therefore, to have had a differential impact on women's lives. Its effects have been positive as well as negative, depending on region, culture, and class. Positive effects of development, and especially of wage employment, on working-class women include their greater participation in decisionmaking in the household. Ecevit's study of Turkish factory workers, cited earlier in this chapter, is instructive. There is growing evidence from around the world that employed women, including working-class women with factory jobs, value their work for the economic independence and family support it provides and for the opportunity to delay marriage and childbearing. In many countries, young women in particular are able to escape restrictive family circumstances and enjoy horizon-broadening experiences and the companionship of other women. Even women in EPZs or world-market factories have been known to express satisfaction with their jobs, although their working conditions are usually poor. In one study of Mexican *maquila* workers, almost two-thirds of respondents declared that they would keep working even if they did not need the money. Fatima Mernissi's interviews with working women in a world-market electronics plant show the value these women place on their jobs and the satisfaction employment brings to them. During a visit I made to a large pharmaceutical plant (not an EPZ) outside Casablanca in early December 1990, women workers revealed that they enjoyed their jobs, were cognizant of the better conditions of work and higher wages at that plant, and would continue to work even if the household did not require their additional income. The work force was unionized (the result of a bitter labor dispute some ten years earlier), and several of the women with whom I spoke had been or were workers' representatives.[70]

Multinational corporations are not known for providing long-term stable jobs, and women's continued employment in the large-scale private sector depends to a great extent upon the vagaries of international trade and the world market. As is well known, there is no job security in the private sector. Moreover, the public-sector wage bill everywhere is in a state of contraction as a result of privatization, the structural adjustment policies that began in the 1980s, and the imperatives of neoliberal globalization that emerged in the 1990s. Reasons for the labor market difficulties that Middle Eastern women have encountered are certainly not to be found in religion or culture. Economic and political forces have shaped their employment opportunities and constraints to a far greater extent.

Conclusion

This chapter has surveyed patterns of female employment over the past four decades in the modernizing countries of the Middle East and North Africa. An essential point of the endeavor has been to underscore the diversity of women's positions within the region and to link women's status and work opportunities to their class location, as well as to state policies, development strategies, the region's political economy, and the global economy. Many studies on the Middle East and commentaries by Islamists themselves tend to understate the heterogeneity of the region; they project a uniform culture and exaggerate its importance, elevating culture or religion to the status of single explanatory variable. My alternative position is that there is an interactive relationship of economic processes, political dynamics, and cultural practices. Only through such an approach can variations within the region and changes over time be understood.

Since the 1960s state expansion, economic development, oil wealth, and increased integration within the world system have combined to create educational and employment opportunities for women in the Middle East. Although benefits have spread unevenly, female education and employment are undermining patriarchal attitudes and practices. It should be noted that just as women were making inroads into public life, including the work force, a cultural and political backlash in the form of conservative Islamist movements took shape and targeted them. Notwithstanding the challenges of Islamization, MENA women have pursued educational attainment and employment to the extent possible, and have indeed made demands on their governments for greater economic participation. (See Chapter 8 for details.)

Female labor force participation is still low in relation to that of other regions of the world and, of course, in relation to male labor force participation. Several explanatory factors have been discussed in this chapter. One factor is the ambivalence of state managers to equality and empowerment for women. Another is economic mismanagement and stagnation. A third factor is the general low level of industrialization and transnational capitalist activity in the region, and the correspondingly small percentage of women in industrial jobs. The oil economies chose a strategy that relied on oil, gas, and finance, thereby minimizing the use of labor and offering relatively few opportunities for women. Elsewhere, although ISI opened up some employment for women—for example, in state-run factories or industrial plants in the private sector receiving state support—the strategy tended to be capital-intensive and to favor male employment. In contrast, an export-led development approach accompanied by an influx of multinational corporations into a country seems to result in significant increases in female labor force participation, in particular increases in the female share of manufacturing, as we have seen with Morocco and Tunisia. The combination of petty commodity production, family farming, and oil production has worked to limit demand for female labor. In addition, women have been locked into a patriarchal family structure based on the traditional division of labor.

Equity and empowerment remain elusive for women when access to economic resources is reserved mainly for men. In the Middle East there continues to exist an exceedingly large population of underutilized labor—that is, women. Attention to the ways and means of integrating women in development therefore remains a pressing item on the national agenda of each country of the region. Policymakers must be persuaded of the positive payoff of investing in the education and employment of women: a more skilled work force, stabilized population growth, healthier children, more prosperous households, an expanding tax base. As countries have turned toward economic liberalization, encouraging manufacturing for export and increased trade, women's economic activity rates have increased. MENA women themselves are increasingly seeking paid employment, both to realize personal aspirations and because of economic need, as a Lebanese study found.[71] Paid employment, however, remains elusive for the majority of women, hence their high unemployment rates. At the beginning of the new millennium, working women in the MENA region have come a long way, and in many countries they have significantly contributed to national development and economic growth, but economic development and state policies should have served women better than they have to date.

Notes

The opening quote from Rabia is from an interview conducted in Moroccan Arabic and translated for me by Patricia Kelly Spurles; Rabia was responding to the question: "How do you find a job?" The quote from Essma Ben Hamida is from her paper "Empowering Women Through Micro-Credit: A Case Study from Tunisia," presented at the Civil Society Workshop of the MDF3 Conference, Cairo, March 2000.

1. The following list is by no means complete, but it is representative of the WID/GAD and sociology-of-gender perspective, which puts a premium on women's integration into the paid labor force of the formal economy: Rae Lesser Blumberg,

"Introduction: Engendering Wealth and Well-Being in an Era of Economic Transformation," in Rae Lesser Blumberg et al., eds., *Engendering Wealth and Well-Being: Empowerment for Global Change* (Boulder: Westview Press, 1995); Janet Saltzman Chafetz, *Sex and Advantage: A Comparative Macro-Structural Theory of Sex Stratification* (Totowa, N.J.: Rowman and Allanheld, 1984); Daisy Dwyer and Judith Bruce, eds., *A Home Divided: Women and Income in the Third World* (Stanford: Stanford University Press, 1988); Barbara Finlay, *The Women of Azua: Work and Family in the Rural Dominican Republic* (New York: Praeger, 1989); Janet Giele, "Women's Status in Comparative Perspective," in Janet Giele and Audrey Smock, eds., *Women's Roles and Status in Eight Countries* (New York: John Wiley, 1977), pp. 1–32; Susan Joekes, *Women in the World Economy: An INSTRAW Study* (New York: Oxford University Press, 1987); Linda Lim, "Capitalism, Imperialism, and Patriarchy," in June Nash and Maria Patricia Fernandez-Kelly, eds., *Women, Men, and the International Division of Labor* (Albany: State University of New York Press, 1983), pp. 70–92; Linda Lim, "Women's Work in Export Factories: The Politics of a Cause," in Irene Tinker, ed., *Persistent Inequalities: Women and World Development* (New York: Oxford University Press, 1990), pp. 101–122; Helen Safa, "Gender Inequality and Women's Wage Labour: A Theoretical and Empirical Analysis," in V. M. Moghadam, ed., *Patriarchy and Development: Women's Positions at the End of the Twentieth Century* (Oxford: Clarendon Press, 1996), pp. 184–219; and V. M. Moghadam, ed., *Women, Work, and Economic Reform in the Middle East and North Africa* (Boulder: Lynne Rienner, 1998).

2. Diane Elson and Ruth Pearson, "The Subordination of Women and the Internationalisation of Factory Production," in Kate Young et al., eds., *Of Marriage and the Market: Women's Subordination in International Perspective* (London: CSE Books, 1981), pp. 144–166; Kathryn Ward, ed., *Women Workers and Global Restructuring* (Ithaca: ILR Press, 1990); Nash and Fernandez-Kelly, *Women, Men, and the International Division of Labor;* Annette Fuentes and Barbara Ehrenreich, *Women in the Global Factory* (Boston: South End Press, 1983); and Gita Sen and Caren Grown, *Development, Crises, and Alternative Visions: Third World Women's Perspectives* (New York: Monthly Review Press, 1987). For overviews of the debate, see Susan Tiano, "Gender, Work, and World Capitalism: Third World Women's Role in Development," in Beth Hess and Myra Marx Feree, eds., *Analyzing Gender* (Beverly Hills: Sage, 1987), pp. 216–243; and Ruth Pearson, "Gender Issues in Industrialization," in T. Hewitt, H. Johnson, and D. Wield, eds., *Industrialization and Development* (Oxford: Oxford University Press, 1992), pp. 222–247.

3. Ester Boserup, "Economic Change and the Roles of Women," in Tinker, *Persistent Inequalities,* pp. 14–26. The quote appears on p. 24. Boserup's famous book is *Women's Role in Economic Development* (New York: St. Martin's Press, 1970).

4. Boserup, "Economic Change and the Roles of Women," p. 24.

5. Nalini Visvanathan et al., *The Women, Gender, and Development Reader* (London: Zed Books, 1997).

6. G. B. S. Mujahid, "Female Labour Force Participation in Jordan," in Julinda Abu Nasr, N. Khoury, and H. Azzam, eds., *Women, Employment, and Development in the Arab World* (The Hague: Mouton/ILO, 1985), p. 114.

7. Ruth Leger Sivard, *Women . . . A World Survey* (Washington, D.C.: World Priorities, 1985), p. 13.

8. Data from United Nations Development Programme (UNDP), *Human Development Report 1990* (New York: Oxford University Press, 1990), tab. 23, pp. 173–175.

9. Cited in Rae Lesser Blumberg, *Making the Case for the Gender Variable* (Washington, D.C.: USAID, 1989), p. 91.

10. Richard Anker, *Gender and Jobs: Sex Segregation of Occupations in the World* (Geneva: ILO, 1998), p. 145. Anker does concede that "the status of women varies greatly across Islamic countries."

11. ILO/INSTRAW, *Women in Economic Activity: A Global Statistical Survey, 1950–2000* (Santo Domingo: INSTRAW, 1985); Susan Joekes, *Women in the World Economy;* and Guy Standing, *Global Feminisation Through Flexible Labour,* WEP Labour Market Analysis Working Paper no. 31 (Geneva: ILO, 1989).

12. Mary Chamie, *Women of the World: Near East and North Africa* (Washington, D.C.: U.S. Department of Commerce and Agency for International Development, 1985), p. 3; H. Azzam, Julinda Abu Nasr, and I. Lorfing, "An Overview of Arab Women in Population, Employment, and Economic Development," in Julinda Abu Nasr, N. Khoury, and H. Azzam, eds., *Women, Employment, and Development in the Arab World,* pp. 5–38.

13. ILO, *Women at Work* (special issue) (Geneva: ILO, 1985); and Anne-Marie Brocas, Anne-Marie Cailloux, and Virginie Oget, *Women and Social Security: Progress Towards Equality of Treatment* (Geneva: ILO, 1990).

14. Gulten Kazgan, "Labour Participation, Occupational Distribution, Educational Attainment, and the Socio-Economic Status of Women in the Turkish Economy," in Nermin Abadan-Unat, ed., *Women in Turkish Society* (Leiden: E. J. Brill, 1981).

15. Constantina Safilios-Rothschild, "A Cross-Cultural Examination of Women's Marital, Educational, and Occupational Options," in M. T. S. Mednick et al., eds., *Women and Achievement* (New York: John Wiley and Sons, 1971), pp. 96–113.

16. Ayse Oncü, "Turkish Women in the Professions: Why So Many?" in Abadan-Unat, *Women in Turkish Society,* p. 189.

17. Robert Mabro, "Industrialization," in Michael Adams, ed., *The Middle East* (New York: Facts-on-File, 1988), p. 689; and Alan Richards and John Waterbury, *A Political Economy of the Middle East: State, Class, and Economic Development* (Boulder: Westview Press, 1990), pp. 78–79.

18. Rhys Jenkins, "The Political Economy of Industrialization: A Comparison of Latin American and East Asian Newly Industrializing Countries," *Development and Change* 22 (2) (April 1991): 197–232. See also Nigel Harris, *The End of the Third World: Newly Industrializing Countries and the Decline of an Ideology* (Harmondsworth: Penguin, 1986).

19. Mary Johnson Osirim, "We Toil All the Livelong Day: Women in the English-Speaking Caribbean," in Consuelo Lopez-Springfield, ed., *Daughters of Caliban: Women in the Twentieth Century Caribbean* (Bloomington: Indiana University Press, 1997), pp. 41–67.

20. See Massoud Karshenas and Valentine M. Moghadam, "Female Labor Force Participation and Economic Adjustment in the MENA Region," in Mine Cinar, ed., *The Economics of Women and Work in the Middle East and North Africa* (Amsterdam: JAI Press, 2001), pp. 51–74.

21. Data from UNDP, *Human Development Report 2002,* tab. 14, pp. 198–201.

22. UNDP, *Arab Human Development Report 2002* (New York: Oxford University Press, 2002). See also World Bank, *World Development Indicators 2000* (New York: Oxford University Press, 2000).

23. See F. J. Heinrichs Frobel and O. Kreye, *The New International Division of Labour* (Cambridge: Cambridge University Press, 1980), esp. the appendix's tab. III-17/18.

24. Mabro, "Industrialization," p. 692.

25. Richards and Waterbury, *A Political Economy of the Middle East,* 2nd ed. (Boulder: Westview Press, 1996), p. 65.

26. According to Laititia Cairoli, the garment industry in Fez is overwhelmingly female, although it attracts mainly young, unmarried women. See "Garment Factory Workers in the City of Fez," *Middle East Journal* 35 (1) (Winter 1999): 28–43.

27. Data from World Bank, *World Development Indicators 2000,* tab. 2.4, p. 52; and from ILO, *Yearbook of Labor Statistics 1997* (Geneva: ILO, 1997), tab. 2B. See also Mine Cinar, "Unskilled Urban Immigrant Women and Disguised Employment: Home Working Women in Contemporary Turkey," *World Development* 22 (3) (1994): 369–380.

28. Semsa Ozar and Gulay Gunluk-Senesen, "Determinants of Female (Non-) Participation in the Urban Labour Force in Turkey," *METU Studies in Development* 25 (2) (1998): 311–328. Their field survey also concluded that the high number of first-generation migrants in the big cities, who tend to be undereducated, affects labor force participation in the formal sector. See also Sule Ozler, "Export Orientation and Female Share of Employment: Evidence from Turkey," *World Development* 28 (7) (2000): 1239–1248.

29. Hanan Aruri, "The Palestinian Working Women Society," in *News From IRENE: International Restructuring Education Network Europe,* September 1998, p. 24; Jennifer Olmsted, "Women 'Manufacture' Economic Spaces in Bethlehem," *World Development* 24 (12) (1996): 1829–1840; and Suha Hindiyeh-Mani, "Women and Men Home-Based Workers in the Informal Sector in the West Bank Textile Industry," *Al-Raida* 15 (82) (Summer 1998): 24–27.

30. A very useful discussion of the methodological problems of Middle Eastern women's employment is Kailas C. Doctor and Nabil F. Khoury, "Arab Women's Education and Employment Profiles and Prospects: An Overview," in Nabil F. Khoury and Kailas C. Doctor, eds., *Education and Employment Issues of Women in Development in the Middle East* (Nicosia: Imprinta, 1991), esp. pp. 21–31.

31. Joekes, *Women in the World Economy,* p. 81; Standing, *Global Feminisation Through Flexible Labour,* p. 25.

32. Mabro, "Industrialization," p. 696.

33. Mujahid, "Female Labour Force Participation in Jordan," p. 115.

34. United Nations, *The World's Women: Trends and Statistics 2000* (New York: United Nations, 2000), chart 5.2, p. 110; UNDP, *Human Development Report 2002,* tab. 25. See also CAWTAR, *Globalization and Gender: Economic Participation of Arab Women* (Tunis: CAWTAR and UNDP, 2001), tab. A/27.

35. UNDP, *Human Development Report 1995,* tab. 39, p. 216.

36. United Nations, *The World's Women: Trends and Statistics 2000,* chart 5.1, p. 110.

37. However, because women's informal-sector, home-based, and agricultural work is generally undercounted, a higher proportion of the measured female labor force is gainfully employed, statistically.

38. See, for example, *Al-Raida* 15 (82) (Summer 1998), a special issue on Lebanese women in the labor force. See also Doctor and Khoury, *Education and Employment Issues,* p. 28; and Anker, *Gender and Jobs,* p. 166.

39. Anker, *Gender and Jobs,* p. 164.

40. UNDP, *Human Development Report 1998,* tab. 3, p. 134.

41. United Nations Department of Public Information (UNDPI), *Economic Development: The Debt Crisis* (New York: UNDPI, 1989).

42. See Tim Niblock and Emma Murphy, eds., *Economic and Political Liberalization in the Middle East* (London: British Academic Press, 1993); Ilya Harik and

Denis J. Sullivan, eds., *Privatization and Liberalization in the Middle East* (Bloomington: Indiana University Press, 1992); and John Walton and David Seddon, *Free Markets and Food Riots: The Politics of Global Adjustment* (Oxford: Blackwell, 1994).

43. See CAWTAR, *Globalization and Gender,* esp. chap. 6. See also V. M. Moghadam, "Enhancing Women's Economic Participation in the Middle East and North Africa," in Heba Handoussa and Zafiris Tzannatos, eds., *Employment Creation and Social Protection in the Middle East* (Cairo: American University of Cairo Press, 2002), pp. 237–279.

44. Nermin Abadan-Unat, "The Modernization of Turkish Women," *Middle East Journal* 32 (1978): 303. See also June Starr, "The Legal and Social Transformation of Rural Women in Aegean Turkey," in Renée Hirschon, ed., *Women and Property: Women as Property* (New York: St. Martin's Press, 1984), pp. 96–116.

45. Caglar Keyder, "Social Structure and the Labour Market in Turkish Agriculture," *International Labour Review* 128 (6) (1989): 731–744.

46. Tahire Erman, "The Meaning of City Living for Rural Migrant Women and Their Role in Migration: The Case of Turkey," *Women's Studies International Forum* 20 (2) (1997): 263–273; and Gul Ozyegin, *Untidy Gender: Domestic Service in Turkey* (Philadelphia: Temple University Press, 2001).

47. Yildiz Ecevit, "The Ideological Construction of Turkish Women Factory Workers," in Nanneke Redclift and M. Thea Sinclair, eds., *Working Women: International Perspectives on Labour and Gender Ideology* (London: Routledge, 1991), pp. 56–78; quote appears on p. 77. See also Hale Cihan Bolak, "Towards a Conceptualization of Power Dyanmics: Women Breadwinners and Working-Class Households in Turkey," in Sirin Tekeli, ed., *Women in Modern Turkish Society: A Reader* (London: Zed Books, 1995), pp. 112–127; quote appears on p. 195.

48. Homa Hoodfar, "Return to the Veil: Personal Strategy and Public Participation in Egypt," in Redclift and Sinclair, *Working Women,* p. 108.

49. Swedish International Development Authority, *Women in Developing Countries: Case Studies of Six Countries* (Stockholm: SIDA Research Division, 1974).

50. United Nations Fund for Population Activities and the Ministry of Planning, *La Femme et la Famille Tunisienne a Travers les Chiffres* (Tunis: United Nations Fund for Population Activities and the Ministry of Planning, 1984); Union Nationale des Femmes Tunisiennes (UNFT), *La Femme au Travail en Chiffres* (Tunis: UNFT, 1987).

51. *The Economist,* July 8, 1989, p. 48.

52. ENDA Inter-Arabe, "CRENDA: Micro-Credit Programme in the Poor Suburbs of Ettadhamen, Douar Hicher, Mnihla, Omrane Supérieur," handout distributed at the MDF3 Conference, Cairo, March 2000. ENDA Inter-Arabe is an international NGO founded in Tunis in 1990 as an autonomous, regional branch of ENDA Third World, based in Dakar, Senegal. The CRENDA microcredit program was launched in 1995.

53. Richards and Waterbury, *A Political Economy of the Middle East* (1990), p. 121.

54. ILO, *Women at Work,* p. 16. See also Ismail A. el Dulaimy, "Women, Human Resources, and National Development in Iraq," in Khoury and Doctor, *Education and Employment Issues,* pp. 91–105.

55. Andrea W. Lorenz, "Ishtar Was a Woman," *Ms.,* May–June 1991, pp. 14–15.

56. *Labour Law and Social Security of the Islamic Republic of Iran* (Tehran: Korshid, 1369/1990), pp. 41–43 (in Persian).

57. See Peter Knauss, *The Persistence of Patriarchy: Class, Gender, and Ideology in Twentieth Century Algeria* (New York: Praeger, 1987).

58. Nouredine Saadi, *La Femme et la Loi en Algérie* (Casablanca: Editions Fennec for UNU/WIDER, 1991), p. 74. See also Institut National du Travail, *Revue Algérienne du Travail: L'Emploi en Algérie—Réalités et Perspectives* (Algiers: Institute National du Travail, 1987).

59. CAWTAR, *Globalization and Gender,* tab. A/24, p. 198.

60. Nadia Hijab, *Womanpower: The Arab Debate on Women and Work* (Cambridge: Cambridge University Press, 1988), p. 96; and Mujahid, "Female Labour Force Participation in Jordan," p. 105. See also V. M. Moghadam, "Economic Restructuring and the Gender Contract: A Case Study of Jordan," in Marianne H. Marchand and Anne Sisson Runyan, eds., *Gender and Global Restructuring: Sightings, Sites, and Resistances* (London: Routledge, 2000), pp. 99–115.

61. See Eugene B. Gallagher and C. Maureen Searle, "Health Services and the Political Culture of Saudi Arabia," *Social Science Medical* (UK) 21 (3) (1985): 251–262; and Eleanor Abdella Doumato, "Women and Work in Saudi Arabia: How Flexible Are Islamic Margins?" *Middle East Journal* 53 (4) (Autumn 1999): 568–583.

62. Ghazy Mujahid, "Tradition, Women's Education, and National Development in Saudi Arabia," in Khoury and Doctor, *Education and Employment Issues,* pp. 75–89.

63. Youssef M. Ibrahim, "Saudis, Aroused by Iraqi Threat, Take Steps to Mobilize Population," *New York Times,* September 5, 1990, p. A1.

64. World Bank, *World Development Indicators 2000,* tab. 2.12.

65. In the United States, for example, the so-called glass ceiling blocking the advancement of women and minorities is more firmly in place in the private sector than in the public sector, where affirmative action goals are enforced. Around the world, not only are women's wages and employment conditions better on average in the public sector than in private wage employment, but also wage differentials between men and women are smaller in the public sector. See Wouter van Ginneken, ed., *Government and Its Employees: Case Studies of Development Countries* (Aldershort, UK: Avebury, 1991); and Standing, *Global Feminisation Through Flexible Labour,* p. 25.

66. Fatima Mernissi, "The Merchant's Daughter and the Son of the Sultan," in Robin Morgan, ed., *Sisterhood Is Global* (New York: Anchor Books, 1984), pp. 448–449.

67. Khadija al-Feddy, speaking at the annual meeting of the Association of Women of the Mediterranean Region, Larnaca, Cyprus, July 2000.

68. Fatima Mernissi, *Doing Daily Battle: Interviews with Moroccan Women,* trans. Mary Jo Lakeland (London: Woman's Press, 1988); Amal Rassam, "Introduction: Arab Women—The Status of Research in the Social Sciences and the Status of Women," in *Social Science Research and Women in the Arab World* (London: Francis Pinter/UNESCO, 1984), pp. 1–3.

69. Deniz Kandiyoti, "Sex Roles and Social Change: A Comparative Appraisal of Turkey's Women," in Wellesley Editorial Committee, ed., *Women and National Development* (Chicago: University of Chicago Press, 1977), pp. 57–73; Deniz Kandiyoti, "Urban Change and Women's Roles in Turkey: An Overview and Evaluation," in Cigdem Kagitcibasi, ed., *Sex Roles, Family, and Community in Turkey* (Bloomington: Indiana University Press, 1982); and Deniz Kandiyoti, "Bargaining with Patriarchy," *Gender and Society* 2 (3) (September 1988): 274–289. See also Gunseli Berik, *Women Carpet Weavers in Rural Turkey: Patterns of Employment, Earnings, and Status,* Women, Work, and Development Series no. 15 (Geneva: ILO, 1987); and Abadan-Unat, "The Modernization of Turkish Women," p. 127. On Iran, see Haleh Afshar, "The Position of Women in an Iranian Village," in Haleh Afshar, ed., *Women, Work, and Ide-*

ology in the Third World (London: Tavistock, 1985), pp. 63–82. On Afghanistan, see Chapter 7.

70. Author interviews at Polymedic/Hoechst/Maroc, Route de Rabat, Casablanca, December 3, 1990. I am grateful to the director-general, M. Abderrahim Chawki, for the opportunity to interview the women employees, and I am especially grateful to M. Abdelhay Bouzoubaa of the national staff of UNDP for arranging the site visit and the interviews. See also Fatima Mernissi, *Chahrzad N'est Pas Marocaine* (Casablanca: Editions le fennec, 1987); and Susan Tiano, "Maquiladora Women: A New Category of Workers?" in Ward, *Women Workers and Global Restructuring,* pp. 193–223.

71. *Al-Raida* 15 (82) (Summer 1998).

3

Reforms, Revolutions, and "the Woman Question"

The proletariat cannot achieve complete freedom unless it achieves complete freedom for women.

—Lenin

Woman was transformed in this society so that a revolution could occur.
—Iranian magazine editorial

Around the world, changes in women's status have come about through a combination of long-term macrolevel change processes (industrialization, urbanization, proletarianization, education, and employment) and collective action (social movements and revolutions). In the context of both socioeconomic development and political change, legal reforms have been pursued to improve the status of women in the family and in the society. The 1917 Bolshevik Revolution in Russia provides the first historical example of sweeping legal reform in favor of women. Here the leadership adopted an official discourse of sexual equality and enacted policies of affirmative action–type policies, including quotas, and political education that many countries subsequently emulated. In Scandinavia the welfare state plays an important role in relieving women of some of the responsibilities of childcare and other forms of caregiving, releasing them for employment and participation in formal politics. In the former German Democratic Republic, a policy of combating sex discrimination, indeed of discrimination in favor of women, was in place from 1949 until the demise of the republic in 1990. Elsewhere, revolutionary movements and developmentalist, welfarist states—both socialist and nonsocialist—have been crucial agents of the advancement of women, promoting reforms in family law, encouraging education and employment, and formulating social policies intended to facilitate women's participation in public life.[1]

In many third world countries, including Middle Eastern ones, concepts of the emancipation of women emerged in the context of national liberation, state building, and self-conscious attempts to achieve modernity in the early part of the century, as Kumari Jayawardena noted in her classic 1986 text on feminisms and nationalism in the third world. In many cases, male feminists were instrumental in highlighting the woman question. Among the earlier generation of male women's rights advocates are Egypt's Qassem Amin (author of the 1901 study *The New Woman*) and Muhammad Abduh (1849–1905); Iran's Malkum Khan (who in an 1890 issue of his journal, *Qanun* [Law], wrote an article advocating women's education) and Iraq's Jamal Sudki Azza Khawy (who in 1911 advocated doing away with the veil); Turkey's Ziya Gökalp and Mustafa Kemal Ataturk; Afghanistan's Mahmud Tarzi (1866–1935); and Tunisia's Taher Haddad (author of the 1930 text *Our Woman, Islamic Law, and Society*). Many other intellectuals, inspired by socialist or liberal political thought, advocated the emancipation of women through unveiling, elimination of seclusion, and formal education. In most cases, especially in the first half of the twentieth century, these ideas were used to call for revolt against corrupt, feudalistic governments. Anti-colonialism, nation building, and modernity constituted the frame within which calls for women's emancipation were made.

In the post–World War II period, integrating women into national development may have been an objective for many male reformers. In postindependence Tunisia, President Habib Bourguiba replaced Shari'a-based Islamic family law with a civil law code regulating personal and family relations and equalizing the responsibilities of the sexes. Polygamy and unilateral male divorce were abolished, and the state assumed a strong stance in favor of female emancipation. In Syria and Iraq following the Baathist "revolutions" of the 1950s, women were granted political and social rights and encouraged, especially in Iraq, to utilize state-sponsored educational facilities. Nasserism as a reformist and developmentalist philosophy created unprecedented educational and employment opportunities for women in Egypt. In Iran women were granted the right to vote in 1962, and in 1967 the Pahlavi state introduced the Family Protection Act, which limited polygamy, allowed women to initiate divorce, and increased their child custody rights after divorce or widowhood.

Although male reformers have been instrumental in changing laws pertaining to women, women activists have been crucial agents themselves of legal and political change. In the early modern period, well-known women activists included Iran's Qurratul Ayn, the famous Baha'i leader who fought in battles and caused a scandal in the 1840s by going unveiled; Sediqheh Dowlatabadi, who, like Qurratul Ayn, was a fierce nationalist opposed to concessions to the British and publisher of the short-lived periodical *Zaban-e Zanan* (Women's Tongue); Egypt's Huda Sharawi, who formed the Egyptian Feminist Union in 1923 and dramatically threw her veil into the sea; and

Turkey's Halide Edip (1883–1964), a nationalist who had served in Mustafa Kemal's forces. Since then, women in the Middle East, like women in other countries, have been engaged in all manner of political manifestations: revolutions, reform movements, national liberation movements, anti-imperialist struggles, religious movements, bread riots, street demonstrations, and so on. Their formal political participation has not been as extensive as that of men because they have been unfairly handicapped by existing custom and law. But precisely because of this handicap, their participation in political movements must be considered remarkable. In some cases, as a direct result of their involvement in a movement, women's legal status improved. In other cases, women's political activities had little or no bearing on their subsequent legal status and social positions; if anything, their legal status diminished. It is essential to recognize that women in the Middle East have been actors in political movements, that these movements have had a variable effect on their social positions, and that gender and "the woman question" have been central features of political movements, reforms, and revolutions.[2]

In their 1986 book *Female Revolt,* Janet Chafetz and Gary Dworkin stated that "independent women's movements are totally absent" in the Middle East.[3] Although independent organizations, feminist or otherwise, were not as numerous in Arab countries and Iran as they were in, for example, India, the authors seemed unaware of the strong opposition mounted by women against the Khomeini regime in 1979 and the many independent women's groups that emerged that year. More striking was the emergence of an independent women's movement in Algeria, first in the early 1980s in opposition to the state's draft bill on a Muslim family code, and then after the political opening of 1988 and in the wake of the growing influence of the Islamist organization Front Islamique du Salut.[4]

This chapter will not describe the many political movements in which Middle Eastern women have participated. The purpose of this chapter is to examine a number of revolutionary movements in which the woman question figured prominently and as a result of which women's legal status and social positions underwent considerable change. Two sets of cases are examined. In one, national progress and societal transformation were viewed by the leadership as inextricably bound up with equality and the emancipation of women. I call this the Woman's Emancipation or egalitarian model of revolution. Such movements occurred within the context of the struggle against feudalism and backwardness and were in some cases inspired by socialist ideals. Education, employment, and unveiling were encouraged as a way of integrating women into the development of the country and thereby accelerating the process of social change. The Middle Eastern cases considered here are the radical Kemalist reforms in Turkey during the 1920s; the 1967 revolution in South Yemen and reform of family law in what came to be called the People's

Democratic Republic of Yemen; and the April 1978 Saur Revolution in Afghanistan, which sought to implement a controversial decree pertaining to marriage and the family. In the second set of cases, the leadership regarded cultural identity, integrity, and cohesion as strongly dependent upon the proper behavior and comportment of women, in part as a reaction to colonialist or neocolonialist impositions. Veiling, modesty, and family roles were encouraged for women. I call this the Woman-in-the-Family or patriarchal model of revolution. The two Middle Eastern cases considered here are the Algerian Revolution and the period following independence in 1962; and the Iranian Revolution of 1979 and the subsequent issue of veiling.

Quite apart from what this examination tells us about the varied positions of women and the role played by states in legislating gender in the Middle East, this chapter underscores the centrality of gender and the strategic role of the woman question in sociopolitical change processes. As such it offers theoretical lessons of a wider relevance regarding political battles and the reproduction of state power.

Gendering Revolutions

Feminists and social scientists of gender from across the disciplines have examined some of the ways women affect and are affected by national, ethnic, and state processes.[5] Some scholars of the French Revolution have examined how gender was constructed in the political discourse and discovered the legal disempowerment and exclusion of women based on the "natural fact" of sexual difference.[6] Unlike standard studies on revolution, feminist scholarship has been especially attentive to the theme of women and revolution. Siân Reynolds makes the interesting point that the participation of women as mothers and food distributors has a profoundly legitimizing effect on revolution— at least in its early stages.[7] In social science studies of revolution, however, gender has not been treated systematically in the causes, course, or even outcomes of revolutions, despite the fact that the woman question has been so closely entangled with the entire course of revolutions. In the sociology of revolution, gender, unlike class or the state or the world system, has not been seen as a constitutive category—although a new generation of feminist scholarship may soon change that.

Let us begin this discussion of women and revolutionary change by defining the word *revolution*. The *Oxford English Dictionary* defines it as "a complete overthrow of the established government in any country or state by those who were previously subject to it; a forcible substitution of a new ruler or form of government." As Michael Kimmel notes, this definition implies that revolutions take place on the political level. Other definitions cite the use of violence, as in Samuel Huntington's description of revolution as "a rapid fundamental and violent domestic change in the dominant values and myths of a society, in its political institutions, social structure, leadership, government activity, and policies." More than anyone else, Theda Skocpol has insisted upon the structural features of revolutionary causes and outcomes. She has defined social (as distinct from the more limited political) revolutions as "rapid, basic transformations of a society's state and class structure; they are accompanied and in part carried through by class based revolts from below." The definition by John Dunn includes the purposive dimension of revolutions: "a form of massive, violent, and rapid social change. They are also attempts to embody a set of values in a new or at least renovated social order." Finally, Perez Zagorin's definition is perhaps most useful for our present study, as it combines political change, attempts at social transformation, and concepts of the ideal society:

> A revolution is any attempt by subordinate groups through the use of violence to bring about (1) a change of government or its policy, (2) a change of regime, or (3) a change of society, whether this attempt is justified by reference to past conditions or to an as yet unattained future ideal.[8]

Let us agree, then, that revolutions are attempts to rapidly and profoundly change political and social structures; they involve mass participation; they usually entail violence and the use of force; they include notions of the "ideal" society; and they have some cultural reference points. Let us also note that revolutions have thus far occurred in societies undergoing the transition to modernity. The major theories of revolution—Marxist class analysis, relative deprivation, and resource mobilization—link revolution to the dynamics and contradictions of modernization.[9] Certain conditions are necessary for the seizure of state power and the successful transformation of social structures, but these conditions vary, particularly over historical eras and types of societies. World-systemic openings, such as economic crises or world wars, may create opportunities for revolutionary movements, but national-level class and social factors determine the specificities of revolutionary movements. Thus, the causes of the Iranian Revolution are necessarily different from causes of the Bolshevik Revolution, and of course their outcomes completely diverge.

Revolutionary programs are not always fulfilled, and the intentions of the revolutionary leadership and state may be subject to various constraints, such as poor resource endowments, civil war, a hostile international environment, or external intervention. There is increasing consensus among students of revolution that in addition to the state, class conflict, resource bases, and the world system, cultural dynamics also should be investigated. That is, because of the complexity of causality, revolutions should be explained in terms of the interaction of economic, political, *and cultural* developments within national, regional, and global contexts.[10] However, what the study of revolution has yet to consider systematically is the prominent position assumed by gender—the position of women, family law, the prerogatives of men—in the discourse of revolutionaries and the laws of revolutionary states. After all, a separate body of prolific research on the position of women in revolutionary Russia, China, Vietnam, Cuba, Algeria, Afghanistan, Nicaragua, El Salvador, Iran, and elsewhere strongly suggests that gender relations constitute an important part of the culture, ideology, and politics of revolutionary societies.[11]

This chapter uses gender as a constitutive category of the analysis of revolution, to show how revolutions in the Middle East have affected women's legal status and social positions. But in order to avoid inferences that gender is politicized and that women are political and cultural signifiers only in Muslim societies or that concepts of liberty, equality, and solidarity in Western countries have always been extended to women, I have included in this chapter two Western revolutions to add to the comparative perspective: the French Revolution and the Bolshevik Revolution. I will try to show that the first exemplifies the Woman-in-the-Family model of revolution, whereas the second is the quintessential Woman's Emancipation model of revolution.

The French Revolution

That the French Revolution was an event of world historical significance is uncontestable. Even before the 1840s, Marx was well aware that the French Revolution had become a representative event destined to be played out not once, but again and again. Elements of its progressive discourse have recurred in many subsequent revolutions in Europe and in the third world. Popular sovereignty, civil liberty, equality before the law—these are among the rich legacy of the French Revolution, itself a product of the Enlightenment. But feminist scholars have argued that women were the marginalized Other in the development of the liberal democratic state. Bonds between men qua men were constituted in opposition to women. In Western societies the division between the public sphere of state and civil society was conceptualized in opposition to the family, which was constructed as a natural and private institution headed by a man.[12] Even champions of the Enlightenment and of the French Revolution must concede that the consequences for women represent a serious drawback. British Marxist historian Eric Hobsbawm once called the woman question "the Achilles heel of the Enlightenment."[13]

What were the gender dynamics of the French Revolution? Reynolds cites Mary Wollstonecraft to the effect that in the minds of many of the French revolutionaries, women were associated with weakness, corruption, frailty, and specifically with the court and the ancien régime. Indeed, under the ancien régime, certain privileged women of all three estates took part in the preliminary voting for the Estates General of 1789, which may explain in part why the French republicans did not extend the new liberties to women.[14] On the other hand, with the collapse of the church's authority, the revolutionaries sought a new moral basis for family life counterposed to that of the old regime. They made divorce possible, they accorded full legal status to illegitimate children, and they abolished primogeniture. They also abolished slavery and gave full civil rights to Protestants and Jews. But it is important to note that the emerging political culture of the French Revolution was rather biased in favor of men. Subsequently, Napoleon reversed the most democratic provisions of the laws on family life, restoring patriarchal authority.

Harriet Applewhite and Darlene Levy describe the crucial participation of women of the popular classes during the spring and summer of 1792, a period of acute military/political crisis in Paris and throughout France. Their participation in armed processions was tolerated, if not positively encouraged and protected, by Girondin authorities such as Jerôme Pétion, the mayor of Paris, for its potential to co-opt key elements of the armed force and to apply collective pressure on both the national legislature and the royal executive. The marches reached insurrectionary proportions on June 20, when the thousands of men and women hastened the erosion of the constitutional monarchy. Finally, on August 10, 1792, the monarchy was brought down and a republic established. Both supporters and opponents of these fully mobilized democratic forces were sensitive to the strategic significance of women's involvement in these armed marches. According to Applewhite and Levy: "Revolutionary leaders exploited women's presence to create a gendered image of a national alliance of comrades in arms, mothers, sisters, and children. Authorities on both sides argued that it was extraordinarily difficult if not impossible to exercise repressive force effectively; they strongly implied that these armed families of *sectionnaires* constituted an insuperable popular force."[15]

The women who participated in the armed processions of 1792—women who bore weapons, shouted slogans, displayed banners, forged ties with National Guard battalions, demonstrated their solidarity with the passive male citizenry of the sections, and identified themselves as the sovereign people in arms—contributed to mobilizing the forces that democratized principles of sovereignty and militant citizenship. Such acts were necessary to the struggle for democratization but not sufficient to break through gender-based limitations on the meaning of political democracy. Authorities such as Pétion, who honored, tolerated, or even orchestrated women's involvement in the ceremonial and insurrectionary movements of 1792, never intended to grant women the expanded political rights under the republic. In the autumn of the following year, Jacobin leaders who, during their struggle against the Girondins, had encouraged the organized militancy of the Society of Revolutionary Republican Women, did not hesitate to outlaw women's political clubs when women's activism began to threaten their power base.

Robert Darnton notes that at the height of the French Revolution, virtue was the central ingredient of the new political culture. But to the revolutionaries, virtue was virile. At the same time, the cult of virtue produced a revalorization of family life. Darnton explains that the revolutionaries took their text from Rousseau and sermonized on the sanctity of motherhood and the importance of breast-feeding. "They treated reproduction as a civic duty and excoriated bachelors as unpatriotic."[16] Banners and slogans proclaimed: "Citizenesses! Give the Fatherland Children!" and "Now is the time to make a baby." Mothers had a certain legitimacy that unmarried *citoyennes* did not. Robespierre's Reign of Virtue involved an ideal of women as passive nurturers: women should bear children for the revolution and sacrifice them for France. He abhorred the active women from the revolutionary club, describing them as "unnatural" and "sterile as vice." Sheila Rowbotham writes that the action of women in the crowd over prices or in pushing for a part in popular sovereignty hinted at an active creation of women's roles, while Claire Lacombe attempted to appropriate revolutionary virtue for an extension of the power of the left-wing women. The deputation of the Society of Revolutionary Republican Women that came to the National Convention to protest the ban on their organization described the society as "composed in large part of mothers of families."[17]

Although Lynn Hunt's study does not focus on gender, she argues that in the French Revolution the radical break with the justification of authority by reference to historical origins implied the rejection of patriarchal models of authority. On the republic's official seal, in engravings and prints, and in the tableaux vivants of the festivals, feminine allegorizations of classical derivation replaced representations of the king. These female figures, whether living women or statues, always sat or stood alone, surrounded most often by abstract emblems of authority and power. The republic might have her children and even her masculine defenders, but there was never a father present. In the early years of the French Revolution, the symbol of the republic was Marianne.

Eventually Marianne was replaced by Hercules, a distinctly virile representation of sovereignty and an image with connotations of domination and supremacy. The introduction of Hercules served to distance the deputies from the growing mobilization of women. For both the Jacobin leaders and their *sans culottes* followers, politics was a quarrel between men.[18] On the grounds that women's active participation would lead to "the kinds of disruption and disorder that hysteria can produce," the convention outlawed all women's clubs at the end of October 1793. The Jacobin Chaumette said, "The *sans-culotte* had a right to expect his wife to run the home while he attended public meetings: hers was the care of the family, this was the full extent of her civic duties."[19] If the revolution had been female, the republic was to be male. The founding of the republic legitimized male power and banned women from the political stage.

What was to be the place of women in the new society? According to the Jacobin deputy André Amar: "Morality and nature itself have assigned her functions to her: to begin the education of men, to prepare the minds and hearts of children for the exercise of public virtues, to direct them early in life towards the good, to elevate their souls, to educate them in the cult of liberty—such are their functions after household cares. . . . When they have carried out these duties they will have deserved well of the fatherland."[20] In other words, the French woman was not a citizen but the chief source of civic education, responsible for the socialization of children in republican virtues. As we shall see, the Iranian case is very similar.

"O my poor sex," wrote feminist playwright Olympe de Gouges. "O women who have gained nothing from the Revolution!" Her cri de coeur that the advancement of men in the French Revolution had been accomplished at the expense of women suggests interesting theoretical possibilities, including an analogy with André Gunder Frank's development/underdevelopment thesis (whereby the two processes are symbiotic) or, perhaps more aptly, with Hegel's master/slave template.

The exclusion of women from the construction of the republic, their relegation to the sphere of the family, and their education in Catholic schools (until the 1850s) made them especially vulnerable in the anticlerical politics of the Second and Third Republics. The association of women with cultural and political conservatism led to their exclusion from the "universal suffrage" of 1848. As Michelet put it, giving women the vote would mean "giving thousands of votes to the priests."[21] This argument peaked under the Third Republic (1870–1940) and was shared by all anticlerical parties. Not until after World War II did women in France obtain the right to vote.

The Bolshevik Revolution

In contrast to the Woman-in-the-Family model of revolution as represented by the French Revolution, the Woman's Emancipation model constructs women as part of the productive forces, to be liberated from patriarchal controls expressly for economic and political purposes. Here the discourse more strongly stresses sexual equality than sexual difference. The first example historically of such a movement is the Bolshevik Revolution in Russia, which remains the avant-garde revolution par excellence, more audacious in its approach to gender than any revolution before or since.

With the onset of World War I, women had entered production in large numbers, and by 1917 one-third of Petrograd's factory workers were women. The Bolsheviks published a paper for women workers, *Rabonitsa,* and encouraged women to join factory committees and unions. Split over the question of organizing women, the party moved steadily in 1917 toward a policy of separate organizations for them. Support for the Bolsheviks, in turn, grew among laundresses, domestic servants, restaurant and textile workers, and soldiers' wives. Although the party was theoretically opposed to separate organizations for women, in practice *Rabonitsa*'s success resulted in the organization of the Petrograd Conference of Working Women in November 1917 and the formation of the Zhenotdel, or women's department, within the party in 1919.[22]

Under Alexandra Kollantai, people's commissar for social welfare, labor legislation was passed to give women an eight-hour day, social insurance, pregnancy leave for two months before and after childbirth, and time at work to breast-feed. It also prohibited child labor and night work for women. The early months of the revolution also saw legislation to establish equality between husband and wife, civil registration of marriage, easy divorce, abolition of illegitimacy, and the wife's right not to take her husband's name or share his domicile. Under Kollantai's directorship in particular, the Zhenotdel saw itself as a force for women's interests and the transformation of society. In Central Asia and the Caucasus it organized mass unveilings of Muslim women, ran literacy classes, and helped to promote a new and more egalitarian family code that was adopted from the audacious but unsuccessful reforms of King Amanullah in Afghanistan. All these developments followed from the view that the emancipation of women was an essential part of the socialist revolution, something to be accomplished through "the participation of women in general productive labor" and the socialization of domestic duties. Lenin sometimes expressed his views on the subject of women, revolution, and equality in rather forceful terms:

> Woman continues to be a domestic slave, because petty housework crushes, strangles, stultifies and degrades her, chains her to the kitchen and to the nursery, and wastes her labor on barbarously unproductive, petty, nerve-racking, stultifying and crushing drudgery.
>
> Enlightenment, culture, civilization, liberty—in all capitalist, bourgeois republics of the world all these fine words are combined with extremely infamous, disgustingly filthy and brutally coarse laws in which woman is treated as an inferior being, laws dealing with marriage rights and divorce, with the inferior status of a child born out of wedlock as compared with that of a "legitimate" child, laws granting privileges to men, laws that are humiliating and insulting to women.

The Bolsheviks also stressed the need for political participation of women, as the following quote from Lenin reveals: "We want women workers to achieve equality with men workers not only in law, but in life as well. For this, it is essential that women workers take an ever increasing part in the administration of public enterprises and in the administration of the state."[23]

The Bolsheviks took the initiative in calling the First Communist Women's Conference in 1920, and prepared the position paper for the occasion, *Theses of the Communist Women's Movement.* Apart from its commitment to the political equality of women and the guarantee of their social rights, the *Theses* included an attack on housewifery and "the domestic hearth." The document reflected the Engelsian view that female emancipation would be a twofold process, incorporating both the entry of women into the national labor force and the socialization of domestic labor.[24] The document also reflected the views of the outstanding communist women who contributed to its formulation, among them Alexandra Kollantai, Inessa Armand, and Clara Zetkin.

Like the French revolutionaries before them, the Bolsheviks strongly supported "free union" and therefore legalized divorce. But in other matters they parted company with the French revolutionaries. Debates on sexuality reflected the Bolsheviks' commitment to gender equality and their critique of the family. The liberation of peasant women could only come about through a massive change in the mode of production, as well as a revolutionary transformation of social values and practices. The implementation in the 1920s of the Land Code and the Family Code, with their emphasis on individual rights and freedoms—including women's rights to land and for maintenance—was an extremely audacious act that challenged centuries of patriarchal control. It also undermined the collective principle of the household, the very basis of peasant production, and was thus strongly resisted. In Soviet Central Asia in the 1920s, where there was virtually no industrial working class, Bolshevik strategists directed their campaigns at women because they were considered the most oppressed social category.[25]

Despite the Zhenotdel's best efforts, material scarcity crippled the Bolshevik vision of liberation, although jurists and party officials maintained their commitment to the "withering away" of the family, and convocations such as the Women's Congress in 1927 showed the potential of an active socialist women's organization. This potential was cut short in the 1930s with the consolidation of the power of Stalin and his associates, who ushered in a more culturally conservative and politically repressive era, disbanded the Zhenotdel, ended open discussions of women's liberation, and resurrected the family. The earlier critique of the family was replaced by a strong emphasis on the "socialist family" as the proper model of gender relations. Although family responsibilities were extolled for men as well as for women, economic, political, and ideological factors had converged to undermine the early libertarian views. Yet it cannot be denied that gender relations were altered, and significantly so, by conscious deed and were an integral part of the construction of the new social order, the new socialist economy, and the new political culture of the Soviet Union.

Let us now turn to reforms, revolutions, and the woman question in the modern Middle East. As will be evident, they follow the two models described above. The revolutionary experiences are listed in chronological order.

The Kemalist Revolution in Turkey

Kemalism was a transformative project but attention to the historical background is helpful. At the end of the nineteenth century, the Ottoman Empire was in the process of disintegration. It faced external pressure from the European powers who wished to expand their influence into the Middle East. Internally, the pressure came from two sources: growing feelings of nationalism among the non-Turkish population of the empire (Greeks, Arabs, Armenians, and people of the Balkans) and a desire for modernization and democratic institutions on the part of the Turks themselves. Among the latter, the strongest influence came from the ideals of the French Revolution.[26] The process of modernization along European lines had already begun in the late eighteenth century. During the first half of the nineteenth century, military officers were sent to France for training, and in Turkey two schools were established to produce civil servants.

The wide-ranging reforms known as the *Tanzimat* (reorganization) began in 1839 under the rule of Abdul Majid and inaugurated Turkey's shift from theocratic sultanate to modern state. The security of the subject's life, honor, and property was guaranteed, and fair public trials and a new penal code were instituted. The principle of equality of all persons of all religions before the law was considered a very bold move for the times. The tax structure was reformed, and a new provincial administration based on the centralized French system was set up. Primary and secondary state schools were established alongside the religious schools, and in 1847 the creation of a Ministry of Education effectively took away the ulamas' power of sole jurisdiction over education. The reforms continued during the sultanate of Abdul Aziz and included the introduction of a new civil code in 1876, which, however, was based on the Shari'a. In 1871 the American College for Girls was started, although for two decades it was restricted to Christians. (The first Muslim girl to complete her studies there was Halide Edip, a future women's leader.) But the trend had started, and many women educated in this manner were to make their mark as novelists and writers on women's emancipation.[27]

Toward the end of the nineteenth century, opposition to the sultan was manifested in the Young Turks movement, officially called the Committee of Union and Progress (CUP). One of the principal tenets of the Young Turks was the need for modernization; they were also unabashedly for Westernization. Closely linked to the need for modernization through Westernization was the emancipation of women. Kumari Jayawardena reminds us that the process of Europeanization was not only ideological; it also entailed the forging of economic links with the capitalist countries of Europe. Around this time, writer and sociologist Ziya Gökalp, who was often referred to as the theoretician of Turkish nationalism and was strongly influenced by the Comtean and Durkheimian tradition in French sociology, advocated equality in marriage and divorce and succession rights for women.[28]

World War I hastened the breakup of the Ottoman Empire and the emergence of a new group from among the Young Turks. This faction advocated the building of a modern Turkish national state that was "republican, secular, and nonimperialist." Mustafa Kemal, an army captain, set up a revolutionary government in Ankara in 1920, oversaw a peace treaty with the British, and established the Turkish Republic in 1923, with himself as president and leader of the Republican People's Party. The Kemalist reforms were the most far-reaching in both intent and effect. Ataturk, as he came to be known, furthered the process of Westernization through economic development, separation of religion from state affairs, an attack on tradition, Latinization of the alphabet, promotion of European dress, adoption of the Western calendar, and the replacement of Islamic family law by a secular civil code. The influence of the French Enlightenment and anticlericalism is clear in these reforms. By 1926 the Shari'a was abolished and the civil and penal codes were thoroughly secularized. Ziya Gökalp urged the Turks, "Belong to the Turkish nation, the Muslim religion and European civilization." Ataturk distanced himself from Islam much further than Gökalp did.[29]

Where the Turkish reformers diverged from their French predecessors was on the woman question. Turkish women obtained the legal right to vote in 1930, many years before French women did. Unlike the French, for whom the emancipation of women was not on the agenda, a central element of the conceptualization of Turkish nationalism, progress, and civilization was "Turkish feminism"—the exact words of Gökalp. Not only Ataturk and Gökalp but also Kemalist feminists such as nationalist fighter and writer Halide Edip and Ataturk's adopted daughter, Afet Inan (author of *The Emancipation of the Turkish Woman*), played major roles in creating images of the new Turkish woman. According to Deniz Kandiyoti, the new Turkish woman was a self-sacrificing "comrade-woman" who shared in the struggles of her male peers. She was depicted in the literature as an asexual sister-in-arms whose public activities never cast any doubt on her virtue and chastity. Turkish national identity was "deemed to have a practically built-in sexual egalitarianist component."[30] In this sense the image of the emancipated Turkish woman was in line with the emerging identity of the collectivity—the new Turkish nation.

Why was the question of women's rights so strategic to the self-definition of the Turkish reformers? It appears that Mustafa Kemal had been highly impressed by the courage and militancy of Turkish women during the Balkan wars and World War I. As Jayawardena notes, Turkish women had taken up new avenues of public employment as nurses on the war fronts and had worked in ammunition, food, and textile factories, as well as in banks, hospitals, and the administrative services. Political events caused their involvement in militant activities, and as early as 1908 a women's association formed alongside the CUP. The occupation of various parts of Turkey by European troops in 1919 aroused protests in which women joined, and women in Anatolia were part of Kemal's army, which had launched a war against the invaders. In his speeches in later years, Kemal constantly referred to the role played by Anatolian women in the nationalist struggle. In a speech at Izmir in 1923 he said, "A civilization where one sex is supreme can be condemned, there and then, as crippled. A people which has decided to go forward and progress must realize this as quickly as possible. The failures in our past are due to the fact that we remained passive to the fate of women."[31] On another occasion, also in 1923, he said, "Our enemies are claiming that Turkey cannot be considered as a civilized nation because this country consists of two separate parts: men and women. Can we close our eyes to one portion of a group, while advancing the other, and still bring progress to the whole group? The road of progress must be trodden by both sexes together, marching arm in arm."[32]

This sentiment has parallels with one shared by a number of Turkish writers who stressed the harmful individual and national effects of the subordination of women. Various stories and essays depicted individual women who suffered from subjugation, children who suffered because of their mother's ignorance, households that suffered because women could not manage money properly. The solution to these individual and household problems was education for women. Other writings depicted women who descended into abject poverty when their husbands or fathers died. The solution to that particular problem was work for women. Other stories sought to show that society and progress suffered when women were kept illiterate and subordinated to men.[33] Ziya Gökalp in particular linked education and employment of women with the development of the country. One of his poems reads:

> Women are also human beings, and as human beings
> They are equally entitled to the basic rights of human beings:
> education and enlightenment.
> So long as she does not work, she will remain unenlightened,
> Which means, the country will suffer.
> If she does not rise, the country will decline.
> No progress is complete without her contribution.[34]

In answer to Kandiyoti's question in the title of an essay, "Women and the Turkish State: Political Actors or Symbolic Pawns?" one may conclude that to the Turkish reformers, the women of Turkey were both participants in the political struggles *and* symbols of the new Turkey. The Kemalists' antipathy toward the traditional order became the source of the processes leading to the initiation of the Turkish Enlightenment. Women's rights and women's emancipation were integral parts of Turkey's transformation plan. Kemal Ataturk viewed women's equality to men as part of Turkey's commitment to Westernization, secularization, and republicanism.

National Liberation, Revolution, and Gender in Algeria

The French took over Algeria in June 1830. In contrast to their colonial policy in Morocco after 1912 and Tunisia after 1882, the French made an attempt in Algeria to dismantle Islam, its economic infrastructure, and its cultural network of mosques and schools. By the turn of the century, there were upwards of half a million French-speaking settlers in Algeria. European competition ruined most of the old artisan class by 1930. Small shopkeepers such as grocers and spice merchants survived, but others suffered severely from the competition of the *petits colons.* Industrialization in Algeria was given a low priority by Paris during the interwar period. Local development and employment generation were severely hampered, and there was considerable unemployment and male migration. Fierce economic competition, cultural disrespect, and residential segregation characterized the French administration. In this context, many Algerians regarded Islam and the Muslim family law as sanctuaries from French cultural imperialism.[35]

To many Algerian men, the unveiled woman represented a capitulation to the European and his culture; she was a person who had opened herself up to the prurient stares of the foreigners, a person more vulnerable to rape. The popular reaction to the *mission civilisatrice* was a return to the land and to religion, the foundations of the old community. Islamic norms were emphasized, the patriarchal family grew in importance, and the protection and seclusion of women were seen by Algerians as increasingly necessary.

When the Front de Libération Nationale (FLN) was formed, there was no provision for women to enjoy any political or military responsibilities. Nonetheless, military exigencies soon forced the officers of the Armée de Liberation Nationale (ALN) to use some women combatants. Upwards of 10,000 women participated in the Algerian Revolution. The overwhelming majority of those who served in the war were nurses, cooks, and laundresses.[36] But many women played an indispensable role as couriers, and because the French rarely searched them, women were often used to carry bombs. This practice recalls the function of women in the street processions of Paris in 1792. Among the heroines of the Algerian Revolution were Djamila Bouhired (the first woman sentenced to death), Djamila Bouazza, Jacqueline Guerroudj, Zahia Khalfallah, Baya Hocine, and Djoher Akrour.

Women who fought and did not survive the war of liberation included twenty-year-old Hassiba Ben Bouali, killed in the Casbah, and Djennet Hamidou, who was shot and killed as she tried to escape arrest. She was seventeen. Yamina Abed, who was wounded in battle, suffered amputation of both legs. She was twenty.[37] These Algerian women, like the women of Vietnam after them, are the stuff of legends.

One emancipatory development during the national liberation struggle was the admittance of unmarried women into the ranks of the FLN and ALN and the emergence by default of voluntary unions, or marriage without family arrangement, presided over by an FLN officer. (This was poignantly depicted in a scene in Pontecorvo's brilliant film *Battle of Algiers*.) Alya Baffoun notes that during this "rather exceptional period of struggle for national liberation," the marriage of Djamila Bouhired to an "infidel" non-Muslim foreigner, a French lawyer, was easily accepted by her community.[38]

After independence the September 1962 constitution guaranteed equality between the sexes and granted women the right to vote. It also made Islam the official state religion. Ten women were elected deputies of the new National Assembly and one of them, Fatima Khemisti, drafted the only significant legislation to affect the status of women passed after independence. In this optimistic time, when heroines of the revolution were being hailed throughout the country, the Union Nationale des Femmes Algériennes (UNFA) was formed. Indeed, one consequence of the Algerian Revolution and of women's role in it was the emergence of the *Moudjahidates* model of Algerian womanhood. The heroic woman fighter was an inspiration to the 1960s and 1970s generation of Algerians, particularly Algerian university women.[39]

But another, more patriarchal tendency was at work during and after the Algerian Revolution. One expression of this tendency was the pressure on women fighters during the liberation struggle to get married and thus prevent spurious talk about their behavior. Moreover, despite the incredible sacrifices of Algerian women, and although the female militants "acceded to the ranks of subjects of history," the Algerian Revolution has tended to be cast in terms of male exploits, and the heroic female feats have not received as much attention.[40]

Following independence, and in a display of authoritarianism, President Ben Bella proceeded to ban all political parties; the Federation of the FLN in France, which had advocated a secular state, had been dissolved; the new FLN general secretary, Mohammed Khider, had purged the radicals—who had insisted on the right of workers to strike—from the union's leadership. And of women, Khider said: "The way of life of European women is incompatible with our traditions and our culture. . . . We can only live by the Islamic morality. European women have no other preoccupations than the twist and Hollywood stars, and don't even know the name of the president of their republic."[41] In a reversal of the political and cultural atmosphere of the national liberation struggle, exaggerated patriarchal values became hegemonic in independent Algeria. In this context, the marriage of another Algerian heroine, Dalila, to a foreigner was deemed unacceptable. Alya Baffoun reports that Dalila's brother abducted and confined her "with the approving and silent consent of the enlightened elite and the politically powerful."[42]

Thus, notwithstanding the participation of upwards of 10,000 women in the Algerian Revolution, their future status was already shaped by "the imperative needs of the male revolutionaries to restore Arabic as the primary language, Islam as the religion of the state, Algeria as a fully free and independent nation, and themselves as sovereigns of the family."[43] This is why, pace the optimistic vision of Frantz Fanon, the country's independence did not signify the emancipation of women. Indeed, the FLN organ, *El Moudjahid,* opposed the term "emancipation" (identified with the French colonizers) and preferred "Muslim Woman"—although Doria Cherifati-Merabtine writes that "in this context [it] had a political rather than a religious meaning."[44] Juliette Minces and Souad Khodja both wrote of the patriarchal forces limiting Algerian women's public roles, especially in employment. Or, in Marnia Lazreg's pithy phrase, the message of the new revolutionary state to women was, "You don't have to work, sisters! This is socialism."[45]

In the 1960s Algerian marriage rates soared. In 1967 some 10 percent of Algerian girls were married at fifteen years of age; at twenty years of age, 73 percent were married. The crude fertility rate was 6.5 children per woman. The Boumedienne government's policy on demographic growth was predicated on the assumption that a large population is necessary for national power. It was therefore opposed to all forms of birth control unless the mother had already produced at least four children.[46] By the end of the Boumedienne years in 1979, 97.5 percent of Algerian women were without paid work. (Some 45 percent of Algerian men were unemployed or underemployed.) The UNFA had become the women's auxiliary of the FLN, devoid of feminist objectives.

On the positive side, state-sponsored education had created a generation of Algerian women who became a restive force for progressive social change in Algeria. These women protested the Chedli Bendjedid government's conservative family code in the early 1980s and confronted the violent Islamist movement in the 1990s. (See Chapter 5 for an elaboration.)

The People's Democratic Republic of Yemen

In November 1967 the National Liberation Front came to power after five years of guerrilla fighting and terminated 128 years of British colonial rule in South Yemen. The People's Democratic Republic of Yemen (PDRY) was born. In June 1969 the revolutionary government took a more radical turn that aimed at "the destruction of the old state apparatus," the creation of a unified, state-administered legal system, and rapid social structural transformation. Tribal segmentation and the local autonomy of ruling shaikhs, sultans, and emirs had resulted in a country devoid of a unified national economy, political structure, and legal system. Such a social order was seen by the revolutionaries as an obstacle to economic development and social reform. At the same time, it was clear that development and change required the active participation of women. Kin control over women, and the practice of seclusion, consequently had to be transformed. In this context the constitution of 1970 outlined the government's policies toward women, and a new family law was proposed in 1971 and passed in 1974. The PDRY came to be known as the "Cuba of the Middle East."

Quite unlike the Algerian FLN, the National Liberation Front of Yemen described itself as "the vanguard of the Yemen working class," and its official doctrine was inspired by the writings of Marx, Engels, and Lenin. Article 7 of the constitution, which described the political basis of the revolution as an "alliance between the working class, the peasants, intelligentsia and petty-bourgeoisie," went on to add that "soldiers, women, and students are regarded as part of this alliance by virtue of their membership in the productive forces of the people."[47] The constitution recognized women as both "mothers" and "producers," consequently as forming part of the "working people." In addition to giving all citizens the right to work and regarding work as "an obligation in the case of all able-bodied citizens," the constitution called upon women not yet involved in "productive work" to do so.

According to the preamble of the family law, the "traditional" or "feudal" family was deemed "incompatible with the principles and programme of the National Democratic Revolution . . . because its old relationships prevent it from playing a positive role in the building up of society." As Maxine Molyneux explains, the law began by denouncing "the vicious state of affairs which prevails in the family" and proclaimed that "marriage is a contract between a man and a woman who are equal in rights and duties, and is based on mutual understanding and respect." It established the principle of free-choice marriage; raised the minimum legal age of marriage to sixteen for girls and eighteen for boys; abolished polygamy except in exceptional circumstances such as barrenness or incurable disease; reduced the dower *(mahr);* stipulated that both spouses must bear the cost of supporting the family; ended unilateral divorce; and increased divorced women's rights to custody of their children.[48]

As in Soviet Russia, family reform was seen as necessary to mobilize women into economic and political activity and to effect economic change and social stability. What was distinctive and especially problematic about the process in the PDRY was that improvements in women's social and legal status involved reforming codes that were derived from Islam and considered to be of divine inspiration. The introduction of the new family law in the PDRY, as elsewhere (see the discussion of Afghanistan below), involved challenging both the power of the Muslim clergy and orthodox interpretations of Islam. After 1969 the government sought to curb the institutional and economic base of the traditional clergy and transferred its responsibilities to agencies of the state. Religious education in schools was made the responsibility of lay teachers. Kin, class, and tribal control over women were outlawed and to some degree delegitimized. Women came to be known as workers, national subjects, and political actors. The rearticulation of gender was an integral part of the restructuring of state and society. Gender redefinition was both a reflection of the new regime's political agenda *and* the means by which it could establish its authority and carry out its revolution.

As with the Bolsheviks, the Yemeni revolutionaries encouraged women's entry into the political realm, and women were given the vote in 1970 when universal suffrage was implemented. By 1977 women candidates were competing for electoral office, as well as working in factories, handicraft cooperatives, and local defense militias. Women were drawn into political activity through such organizations as the General Union of Yemeni Women, the party, neighborhood associations, and other mass organizations. In 1977 the women's union had a membership of 14,296, which included 915 women workers employed in factories and workshops; 528 agricultural workers and members of co-ops and state farms; 253 employees of various government agencies; secondary school and university students; and housewives. The women's union became especially active in the literacy campaign and in the campaign to gain support for the family law.[49]

As mentioned above, the Yemeni family law was passed in 1974 following extensive debate in what was a very conservative society. The law restricted polygamy but did not ban it. Men and women had equal rights when it came to divorce, and indeed there was a rise in the number of divorces immediately after the law was passed because it had become easier for women. The family law also required both spouses' consent to the marriage; set a limit to the dower; stipulated that the cost of running the household must be shared between husband and wife; and favored the mother for custody of the children even if she remarried, although the court had to decide in the child's best interests. A women's conference was held in April 1984, a decade after the family law had been passed, to see whether it needed any changes. The conference concluded that while there was nothing wrong with the law as it stood, there were still some problems in implementation.[50]

The government, party, and women's union retained a commitment to integrate Yemeni women into public life. Here is how one activist described it:

> We cannot speak of liberating women without making them participate in social life to convince them of their role in society. In our constitution we have included a commitment to the principle of women's liberation. It is

women's right now to work in factories. By encouraging women to work in factories and to go to school we will achieve the right orientation. The state has also abolished the existence of women as a special stratum. No text in the laws or constitution discriminates against women. If a woman wants to work in any sphere no one will stop her.[51]

In fact, not all women were able to enter public life. Notwithstanding some socioeconomic development and expansion of state authority, the PDRY government could not achieve its vision of a literate and productive society and emancipated women citizens. South Yemen remained poor, and there was still a cultural stigma attached to women performing income-generating activities outside the home. Disagreements within the party and pressures from surrounding countries forced a change in the PDRY. In 1990 the PDRY merged with its northern half, the Republic of Yemen, which was conservative and tribal-dominated. A retreat on the woman question was inevitable. With unification, the women of the south lost many of the legal rights they had gained under the PDRY.

Revolution, Islamization, and Women in Iran

The Iranian Revolution against the Shah, which unfolded between spring 1977 and February 1979, was joined by countless women. Like other social groups, their reasons for opposing the Shah were varied: economic deprivation, political repression, identification with Islamism. The large street demonstrations included huge contingents of women wearing the veil as a symbol of opposition to Pahlavi bourgeois or Westernized decadence. As in Algeria and revolutionary France, the massive participation of women was vital to the success of the insurrection. Many women who wore the veil as a protest symbol did not expect hijab (veiling) to become mandatory. Thus when the first calls were made in February 1979 to enforce hijab and Ayatollah Khomeini was quoted as saying that he preferred to see women in modest Islamic dress, many women were alarmed. Spirited protests and sit-ins were led by middle-class leftist and liberal women, most of them members of political organizations or recently formed women's associations. Limited support for the women's protests came from the main political groups. As a result of the women's protests, the ruling on hijab was rescinded—but only temporarily. With the defeat of the left and the liberals in 1980 and their elimination from the political terrain in 1981, the Islamists were able to make veiling compulsory and to enforce it strictly.[52]

The idea that women had "lost honor" during the Pahlavi era was a widespread one. Anti-Shah oppositionists decried the overly made-up "bourgeois dolls"—television announcers, singers, upper-class women in the professions—of the Pahlavi era. As in Algeria, the Islamists in Iran felt that "genuine Iranian cultural identity" had been distorted by Westernization, or what they called *gharbzadegi*. The unveiled, publicly visible woman was both a reflection of Western attacks on indigenous culture and the medium by which they were effected. The growing number of educated and employed women frightened and offended men of certain social groups, who came to regard the modern woman as the manifestation of Westernization and imperialist culture and a threat to their own manhood. Islamists projected the image of the noble, militant, and selfless Fatemeh—daughter of the Prophet Muhammad, earlier popularized by the late radical Islamic sociologist Ali Shariati—as the most appropriate model for the new Iranian womanhood.[53]

It is necessary to point out that in the 1979–1980 period, the women's movement, then quite dynamic, was bifurcated; there were pro-Khomeini and anti-Khomeini women, and even among Islamist women there were different perspectives on women's rights issues, including the veil. Moreover, many women were comfortable with the veil because of the prevalence of male harassment of women in Western dress. During the 1960s and 1970s, when I was growing up in Tehran, just waiting for a taxi or shopping downtown entailed major battles with men, who variously leered, touched, made sexual remarks, or cursed at women. Women were fair game, and it is understandable that many would want to withdraw to the protective veil when in public. But the legal imposition of hijab was not about protecting women, and it was certainly not part of any struggle against male sexism: it was about negating female sexuality and therefore protecting men. More profoundly, compulsory veiling signaled the (re)definition of gender rules, and the veiled woman came to symbolize the moral and cultural transformation of society.

The full implications of the Islamic dress code are spelled out in a booklet titled *On the Islamic Hijab* by a leading Iranian cleric, Murteza Mutahhari, who was assassinated in May 1979. In the preface by the International Relations Department of the Islamic Propagation Organization, it is argued that Western society "looks at women merely through the windows of sexual passion and regards woman as a little being who just satisfies sexual desires. . . . Therefore, such a way of thinking results in nothing other than the woman becoming a propaganda and commercial commodity in all aspects of Western life, ranging from those in the mass media to streets and shops." Mutahhari himself writes:

> If a boy and a girl study in a separate environment or in an environment where the girl covers her body and wears no make-up, do they not study better? . . . Will men work better in an environment where the streets, offices, factories, etc., are continuously filled with women who are wearing make-up and are not fully dressed, or in an environment where these scenes do not exist? . . .
> The truth is that the disgraceful lack of *hijab* in Iran before the Revolution . . . is a product of the corrupt western capitalist societies. It is one of

the results of the worship of money and the pursuance of sexual fulfilment that is prevalent amongst western capitalists.[54]

The idea that women had lost their modesty and men had lost their honor during the Pahlavi era was a widespread one. Kaveh Afrasiabi recounts a conversation he had in early February 1979 with a striking worker named Alimorad, who had just returned from Shahr-e Now (the red-light district in downtown Tehran), which had been destroyed by a fire set by Islamist militants:

> We burnt it all. Cleansed the city, he said.
> And women? I asked.
> Many were incinerated *[jozghaleh shodand].*
> Who are you? Where do you come from? I asked him.
> I am a worker from Rezaieh, married with children.
> What is your business in Tehran?
> To take part in the revolution!
> What is happening in Rezaieh?
> In Rezaieh there is just a movement *[jombesh],* but here there is a revolution.
> Why do you support the revolution?
> Islam, freedom, poverty, *zolm [oppression],* he answered without hesitation.
> What else? I insisted.
> Dignity *[heisiat].*
> Dignity?
> Yes brother. Shah took our dignity. He took man's right from him. My wife
>   is now working. What is left of family when the wife works?
> And what is your expectation of Islam?
> Islam is our dignity. I want to bring bread on my own—to have a wife at
>   home to cook and nurse the children, God and Islam willing.[55]

Such attitudes were behind the early legislation pertaining to women. The 1979 constitution spelled out the place of women in the ideal Islamic society the new leadership was trying to establish: within the family, through the "precious foundation of motherhood," rearing committed Muslims. Motherhood and domesticity were described as socially valuable, and the age of marriage for girls was lowered to puberty. Legislation was enacted to alter gender relations and make them as different as possible from gender norms in the West. In particular, the Islamic Republic emphasized the distinctiveness of male and female roles, a preference for the privatization of female roles (although public activity by women was never barred, and they retained the vote), the desirability of sex segregation in public places, and the necessity of modesty in dress and demeanor and in media images. Yet the Iranian Islamists were aware of modern sensibilities. The introduction to the constitution mentions women's "active and massive presence in all stages of this great struggle" and states that men and women are equal before the law. But this stated equality is belied by differential treatment before the law, particularly in the area of personal status or family law, based on the Shari'a. Women and men, and Muslims and non-Muslims, also are treated differently in the Islamic Republic's penal code.

The significance of the woman question to the Islamist revolutionaries and state-builders is captured in the following passage from an editorial in *Zan-e Rouz,* discussed by Afsaneh Najmabadi:

> Colonialism was fully aware of the sensitive and vital role of woman in the formation of the individual and of human society. They considered her the best tool for subjugation of the nations. . . . In the underdeveloped countries . . . women serve as the unconscious accomplices of the powers-that-be in the destruction of indigenous culture. So long as indigenous culture persists in the personality and thought of people in a society, it is not easy to find a political, military, economic or social presence in society. . . . And woman is the best means of destroying the indigenous culture to the benefit of imperialists. . . .
>
> In Islamic countries . . . Islamic belief and culture provide people of these societies with faith and ideals. . . . Woman in these societies is armed with a shield that protects her against the conspiracies aimed at her humanity, honor and chastity. This shield verily is her veil. For this reason, in societies like ours, the most immediate and urgent task was seen to be her unveiling, that is, disarming woman in the face of all calamities against her personality and chastity. . . . It is here that we realize the glory and depth of Iran's Islamic Revolution. This revolution transformed everyone, all personalities, all relations and all values. *Woman was transformed in this society so that a revolution could occur* [emphasis added].[56]

There can be no doubt that gender relations and the question of women were among the central components of the political culture and ideological discourse of the Islamic Republic of Iran.

Afghanistan: The Saur Revolution and Women's Rights

The Afghan Revolution represents an extreme case illustrating the problems of implementing modernizing and socialist reforms in the face of poverty and underdevelopment, precapitalist structures, counterrevolution, and external intervention. This revolution, and the extremely hostile international environment, had profound implications for the woman question.

In April 1978 the People's Democratic Party of Afghanistan (PDPA) seized power in what came to be called the Saur (April) Revolution and established the Democratic Republic of Afghanistan (DRA). Soon afterward the DRA introduced rapid reforms to change the political and social structure of Afghan society, including patterns of land tenure and gender relations—and this in one of the poorest and least developed countries in the world. The government of President Noor Mohammad Taraki targeted the structures and relations of "tribal-feudalism" and enacted legislation to raise women's status through changes in family law (including marriage customs) and policies to encourage female education and employment. As in other modernizing and socialist experiments, the woman question constituted an essential part of the political project. The Afghan state was motivated by a modernizing outlook and socialist ideology that linked Afghan backwardness to feudalism, widespread female illiteracy, forced marriages, and the exchange of girls. The leadership resolved that women's rights to education, employment, mobility, and choice of spouse would be a major objective of the "national democratic revolution." The model of revolution and of women's emancipation was Soviet Russia, and the Saur Revolution was considered to belong to the family of revolutions that also included Vietnam, Cuba, Algeria, the People's Democratic Republic of Yemen, and Ethiopia.

In addition to redistributing land, canceling peasants' debts and mortgages, and taking other measures to wrest power from traditional leaders, the government promulgated Decree no. 7, meant to fundamentally change the institution of marriage. A prime concern of the designers of the decree, which also mandated other reforms, was to reduce material indebtedness throughout the country; they further meant to ensure equal rights of women with men. In a speech on November 4, 1978, President Taraki declared: "Through the issuance of Decrees No. 6 and 7, the hard-working peasants were freed from bonds of oppressors and money-lenders, ending the sale of girls for good as hereafter nobody would be entitled to sell any girl or woman in this country."[57]

The first two articles in Decree no. 7 forbade the exchange of a woman in marriage for cash or kind customarily due from a bridegroom on festive occasions; the third article set an upper limit of 300 afghanis (afs.), the equivalent of $10 at that time, on the *mahr*. President Taraki explained, "We are always taking into consideration and respect the basic principles of Islam. Therefore, we decided that an equivalent of the sum to be paid in advance by the husband to his wife upon the nuptial amounting to ten 'dirhams' [traditional ritual payment] according to shariat be converted into local currency which is afs. 300. We also decided that marriageable boys and girls should freely choose their future spouses in line with the rules of shariat."[58]

The legislation aimed to change marriage customs so as to give young women and men independence from their marriage guardians. Articles 4 to 6 of the decree set the ages of first engagement and marriage at sixteen for women and eighteen for men (in contrast to what happened in the Iranian case). The decree further stipulated that no one could be compelled to marry against his or her will, including widows. This last provision referred to the customary control of a married woman (and the honor she represents) by her husband and his agnates, who retained residual rights in the case of her widowhood. The decree also stipulated that no one who wanted to get married could be prevented from doing so.

Along with the promulgation of Decree no. 7, the PDPA government embarked upon an aggressive literacy campaign. This was led by the Democratic Organization of Afghan Women (DOAW), whose function was to educate women, bring them out of seclusion, and initiate social programs. Throughout the countryside, PDPA cadres established literacy classes for men, women, and children in villages. By August 1979 the government had established 600 new schools. The PDPA's rationale for pursuing the rural literacy campaign with some zeal was that all previous reformers had made literacy a matter of choice; male guardians had chosen not to allow their females to be educated, and thus 98 percent of all Afghan women were illiterate. It was therefore decided not to allow literacy to remain a matter of (men's) choice, but rather a matter of principle and law.

This was an audacious program for social change, one aimed at the rapid transformation of a patriarchal society with a decentralized power structure based on tribal and landlord authority. For the DRA, revolutionary change, state building, and women's rights subsequently went hand in hand. The emphasis on women's rights on the part of the PDPA reflected (1) its socialist/Marxist ideology; (2) its modernizing and egalitarian outlook; (3) its social base and origins—the urban middle class, professionals, and those educated in the United States, the USSR, India, and Europe; and (4) the number and position of women within the PDPA.

The PDPA was attempting to accomplish what reformers and revolutionaries had done in Turkey, Soviet Central Asia, and South Yemen and to carry out what earlier Afghan reformers and modernizers had tried to do. (See Chapter 7 for a full exposition.) But PDPA attempts to change marriage laws, expand literacy, and educate rural girls met with strong opposition. Decrees 6 and 7 deeply angered rural tribesmen and the traditional power structure. In the summer of 1978, refugees began pouring into Pakistan, giving as their major reason the forceful implementation of the literacy program among their women. There was also universal resistance to the new marriage regulations, which, coupled with compulsory education for girls, raised the threat of women refusing to obey and submit to patriarchal authority. The attempt to impose a minimum age for marriage, prohibit forced marriage, limit divorce payments, and send girls to school deeply offended what one scholar referred to as the "massive male chauvinism" of Afghan men.[59] An Islamist opposition began organizing and conducted several armed actions against the government in the spring of 1979. In July 1979 the CIA began covert operations in support of the uprising. By December 1979 the situation had deteriorated to such an extent that the Soviet army intervened. The 1980s saw an internationalized civil conflict and serious setbacks to the DRA's revolutionary program.

In 1980 the PDPA slowed down its reform program and announced its intention to eliminate illiteracy in cities in seven years and in provinces in ten.

Unlike Soviet Russia, Turkey, or Iran, the Afghan state was not a strong one, able to impose its will through an extensive administrative and military apparatus. As a result, it was far less successful than other revolutionary regimes in carrying out its program—in Afghanistan's case, land redistribution and women's rights. Nor did twelve years of civil war and a hostile international climate provide conditions propitious for progressive social change. In 1987 the name Democratic Republic of Afghanistan was changed to the Republic of Afghanistan and the liberation of women took a backseat to national reconciliation. In 1990 the PDPA changed its name to the Homeland Party, or Hizb-e Watan. Similarly, the party made constitutional changes, dropping clauses that expressed the equality of men and women and reinstating Muslim family law. In 1992 the whole experiment collapsed, and the U.S.-supported Mujahidin set up an Islamic regime. Their very first act was to make veiling compulsory. The Mujahidin movement imploded from within and was eventually defeated and replaced in 1996 by the strangely medieval Taliban, who intensified the Mujahidin gender regime.

In large measure, then, the failure of the Saur Revolution in Afghanistan was linked to its gender dynamics and the DRA's audacious attempt to enhance the status of women—as well as to international hostility.

Revolution, State Building, and Women

Revolutions are a special case of social change that attempts to rapidly transform political and economic structures, social and gender relations, and societal institutions to conform to an ideology. The twentieth century has been called the century of revolutions, and many third world countries, including countries in the Middle East, have experienced revolutionary change. Where revolutions result in the emergence of strong, centralized states, as in Turkey, Iran, and Algeria, revolutionaries or state-builders are more successful in implementing their vision of the ideal society. But where revolutions occur in underdeveloped areas, states are not strong enough to carry out their program for rapid and radical social change, as was the case in Afghanistan and South Yemen. In all cases, however, gender plays a role in the course of revolution and in the programs of state-builders. Changes in gender relations, practices, and laws should be part of the explanation of the causes, preconditions, and outcomes of revolutions. The nature of gender discourse (for example, the radical language of the Bolsheviks versus the moralist rhetoric of the Islamists in Iran—i.e., gender equality versus gender difference) reveals a great deal about the nature of the revolution and the regime. During periods of revolutionary transformation, changes in societal values and ideologies affect gender relations and vice versa. Laws about women are closely bound to the power of the state. That is why, to paraphrase Hanna

Papanek, states and movements raise the woman question even when it creates so much trouble.[60]

Beginning at least as early as Marianne in the French Revolution, the idealized woman has historically played a major role as a national or cultural symbol. During transitional periods in a nation's history, women may be linked to either modernity or tradition. The woman question may be framed in the context of modernizing projects or in tandem with religious and moral movements; it may be raised to legitimize women or to mobilize them toward specific ends. At times of regime consolidation and state-building, questions of gender, family, and male-female relations come to the fore. The state becomes the manager of gender. Cultural representations of women, and of course legislation on family law and women's rights, reflect the importance of gender in politics and ideology and signal the political agenda of revolutionaries and regimes. Whether political discourses support women's emancipation and equality or whether they glorify tradition, morality, the family, and difference, the point remains that political ideologies and practices are gendered and that social transformation and state building entail changes in gender relations as well as new class configurations and property rights.

The twentieth century has seen two models of womanhood emerge in the context of societal reform and revolutionary change. One model, which I have called the Woman's Emancipation model, draws its inspiration from the Enlightenment, the socialist tradition, and the Bolshevik Revolution. This model emerges when revolutionaries target feudalism, tribalism, or backwardness and recognize the need to integrate women into programs for development and progress. The other archetype I called the Woman-in-the-Family model, and it occurs in cases of opposition to colonialist or neocolonialist modes of control, where revolutionaries draw from their own cultural repertoire. The historical precursor of this model of gender outcomes is, ironically, the French Revolution.

As Jayawardena observes in her study of feminism and nationalism in the third world, for modernizing states and revolutionary regimes of the first half of the twentieth century the image of the modern woman, unveiled, educated, and working in the public sphere, provided a potent symbol. Nationalism, state-building projects, and the emancipation of women were of a piece. The modern woman who cut her hair, worked outside the home, and was accepted, at least on paper, as a full citizen was associated with progress and modernity, as in Russia and Turkey (and later in China). As I have shown in this chapter, more recent extensions of the earlier model of societal transformation and women's emancipation were the revolutionary aims of the People's Democratic Republic of Yemen and the Democratic Republic of Afghanistan.

A second pattern of revolution and gender emerged in the second half of the twentieth century. With the rise of anti-colonialist and anti-imperialist movements, the modern woman came to be viewed with ambivalence, especially if she was associated with the culture of the colonialists and imperialists. We have seen in this chapter that in the Algerian and Iranian revolutions, the modern, unveiled woman was associated with social danger, moral decay, and imperialist culture. For "freedom fighters" who are staunchly opposed to modernizing projects, such as the Afghan Mujahidin in the 1980s or the Taliban in the 1990s, the image of the modern woman is anathema. Elsewhere, at a time of economic difficulties, social uncertainties, and confrontations with the West, the image of the traditional woman seems to promise a return to a comforting, stable, and idyllic past; she is seen as the repository of old values and ways of life and is linked to a more "genuine" cultural identity. The modern woman is taken to be representative of everything that appears threatening in the new and quickly changing world, of alien cultures and external subterfuge. This perception explains why not all revolutions in the latter half of the twentieth century have had favorable outcomes for the status of women. With some caveats, these comments apply equally well to the 1989 revolutions in Eastern Europe and the end of communism in the former Soviet Union, where the new leaderships and elites initially evinced an "allergy to women's rights," in Barbara Einhorn's words.[61] This demonstrates that a reactionary position on gender and on women's role within the society and the family in the late twentieth century has not been limited to Muslim countries.

Maxine Molyneux has argued that when revolutionary governments set about reforming the position of women in the first period of social and economic transformation, they tend to focus on three goals: (1) extending the base of the government's political support; (2) increasing the size or quality of the active labor force; and (3) helping harness the family more securely to the process of social reproduction. She has also discussed how revolutions can meet women's practical needs or strategic gender interests or both. In all the cases examined here, Molyneux's third factor was present. In addition, most revolutions did seek to meet the basic needs of men, women, and children. But the first and second factors are present only in the cases of modernizing, developmentalist states—those following what I have called the Woman's Emancipation model of revolution—whether guided by socialist ideology (as in the cases of South Yemen and Afghanistan) or bourgeois ideology (as in the case of Turkey). Here, too, revolutionary outcomes are far more likely to be conducive to women's longer-term and strategic interests in the areas of equality, autonomy, and empowerment. However, for the revolutionary leaders in Algeria or Iran, integrating women into the labor force to increase its size (which was not a goal in these labor-surplus countries) or its quality (which should have been a goal but was not) was clearly not an objective. Rather, their keen desire to restore cultural authenticity, religious integrity, and national traditions, which they felt colonialism or imperialism had distorted, led to the policy of family attachment rather than labor attachment for women.

In all the cases reviewed—Turkey, Algeria, South Yemen, Iran, and Afghanistan, and of course the French and Russian revolutions—the woman question figured prominently in political discourses, state ideologies, and legal policies. Gender relations and the position of women have figured prominently in other revolutionary movements as well, as Table 3.1 shows. The outcome of the woman question is determined by both structure and agency, as well as by economic, political, and ideological factors: the prevailing material conditions of social life, the international environment, the nature of the revolutionary leadership and its social program, the extent of women's participation in the revolution, the degree to which women are organized and capable of articulating their interests, and the ability of the revolutionary state to realize its vision of liberation and social transformation. Concepts of the ideal society invariably entail concepts of the ideal woman. The formation of national identity is both a political and a cultural exercise; as such, constructions of gender are an integral part of the process of identity and state formation. Political-cultural projects, and the position of women, are inextricably linked. Transforming society and transforming women are consequently two sides of the same coin.

Table 3.1   Gender Dynamics of Revolutions: A Typology

Type of Revolution	Bourgeois Revolutions	Socialist and Populist Revolutions
Women's emancipation a major goal or outcome	Kemalism in Turkey	France (1848) Russia (1917) China Cuba Vietnam Democratic Yemen Ethiopia Democratic Afghanistan Nicaragua El Salvador
Family roles for women a major goal or outcome	French Revolution Perestroika in the Soviet Union "1989 Revolutions" of Eastern Europe	Mexico Algeria Iran

Notes: "Revolutions" are defined as attempts at rapid economic, political, and ideological transformation. I have been unable to locate sufficient information on the gender dynamics of African revolutions.

Notes

1. See the collection of essays in Sonia Kruks, Rayna Rapp, and Marilyn Young, eds., *Promissory Notes: Women in the Transition to Socialism* (New York: Monthly Review Press, 1989). See also Val Moghadam, "Development and Women's Emancipation: Is There a Connection?" *Development and Change* 23 (3) (July 1992): 215–256. See also Kumari Jayawardena, *Feminism and Nationalism in the Third World* (London: Zed Books, 1986).

2. On the history of the Egyptian women's movement, see Margot Badran, "Independent Women: More Than a Century of Feminism in Egypt," in Judith Tucker, ed., *Old Boundaries, New Frontiers: Women in the Arab World* (Bloomington: Indiana University Press, 1993), pp. 59–88; Jayawardena, *Feminism and Nationalism in the Third World,* chap. 3; and Afaf Lutfi al-Sayyid Marsot, "The Revolutionary Gentlewomen in Egypt," in Lois Beck and Nikki R. Keddie, eds., *Women in the Muslim World* (Cambridge: Harvard University Press, 1978), pp. 261–276. On Iran, see Janet Afary, *The Iranian Constitutional Revolution, 1906–1911: Grassroots Democracy, Social Democracy, and the Origins of Feminism* (New York: Columbia University Press, 1996).

3. Janet Salzman Chafetz and Gary Dworkin, *Female Revolt: Women's Movements in World and Historical Perspective* (Totowa, N.J.: Rowman and Allanheld, 1986), p. 191.

4. For an elaboration, see V. M. Moghadam, "Organizing Women: The New Women's Movement in Algeria," *Cultural Dynamics* 13 (2) (2001): 131–154.

5. Mounira Charrad, *States and Women's Rights: The Making of Postcolonial Tunisia, Algeria, and Morocco* (Berkeley: University of California Press, 2001); Nira Yuval-Davis and Floya Anthias, eds., *Women-Nation-State* (London: Macmillan, 1989); Nira Yuval-Davis, *Gender and the Nation* (Thousand Oaks, Calif.: Sage, 1997); and Deniz Kandiyoti, ed., *Women, Islam, and the State* (London: Macmillan, 1991).

6. On women and the French Revolution, see Ruth Graham, "Loaves and Liberty: Women in the French Revolution," in Renate Bridenthal and Claudia Koonz, eds., *Becoming Visible: Women in European History* (Boston: Houghton Mifflin, 1977), pp. 1–10; Lynn Hunt, *Politics, Culture, and Class in the French Revolution* (Berkeley: University of California Press, 1984); Siân Reynolds, "Marianne's Citizens? Women, the Republic, and Universal Suffrage in France," in Siân Reynolds, ed., *Women, State and Revolution: Essays on Power and Gender in Europe Since 1789* (Amherst: University of Massachusetts Press, 1987), pp. 101–122; Jane Abray, "Feminism in the French Revolution," *American Historical Review* 80 (1975); Darline Gay Levy, Harriet Branson Applewhite, and Mary Durham Johnson, *Women in Revolutionary Paris, 1789–1795* (Urbana: University of Illinois Press, 1979); and Joan Landes, *Women and the Public Sphere in the Age of the French Revolution* (Ithaca: Cornell University Press, 1988).

7. Siân Reynolds, introduction to Reynolds, *Women, State and Revolution,* p. xiv.

8. Samuel Huntington, *Political Order in Changing Societies* (New Haven: Yale University Press, 1968), p. 264; Theda Skocpol, *States and Social Revolutions: A Comparative Analysis of France, Russia, and China* (Cambridge: Cambridge University Press, 1978), p. 4; John Dunn, *Modern Revolutions* (New York: Cambridge University Press, 1972), p. 12; and Perez Zagorin, *Rebels and Rulers,* vol. 1 (Cambridge: Cambridge University Press, 1982), p. 17, cited in Michael S. Kimmel, *Revolution: A Sociological Interpretation* (Cambridge, UK: Polity Press, 1990), p. 6. Kimmel's synthesis of the structural and purposive dimensions of revolution accords well with the analysis in the present chapter.

9. Terry Boswell, "World Revolutions and Revolutions in the World-System," in Terry Boswell, ed., *Revolution in the World-System* (Westport, CT: Greenwood Press, 1989), pp. 1–18. I refer, of course, to twentieth-century revolutions, most of which have taken place in developing or modernizing countries. As regards the changes in Eastern Europe and the former Soviet Union, whether or not these countries experienced a revolution in the sociological sense, and the nature of that revolution, remain matters of debate and require further research. It is likely that our definition of revolution may need to be revised to account for the changes in the former state socialist societies, particularly with regard to the generally nonviolent nature of the collapse of the communist states. And although these societies were not "modernizing" societies, they seem to have been rather hard hit by the vagaries of the world system, which would suggest that class conflict and world-systemic imperatives may explain the causes of the "1989 revolutions." But certainly what they have in common with earlier revolutions and with the discussion in this chapter is a gender dimension distinctly similar to the Woman-in-the-Family model of revolution.

10. See Kimmel, *Revolution;* Val Moghadam, "Populist Revolution and the Islamic State in Iran," in Boswell, *Revolution in the World-System,* pp. 147–163; John Foran, "Discourses and Social Forces: The Role of Culture and Cultural Studies in Understanding Revolutions," in John Foran, ed., *Theorizing Revolutions* (London: Routledge, 1997); and Eric Selbin, "Revolution in the Real World: Bringing Agency Back In," in Foran, *Theorizing Revolutions,* pp. 123–136.

11. On women and revolutions in the twentieth century, see Sheila Rowbotham, *Women, Resistance, and Revolution* (London: Allen Lane, 1972); Guity Nashat, ed., *Women and Revolution in Iran* (Boulder: Westview Press, 1983); Judith Stacey, *Patriarchy and Socialist Revolution in China* (Berkeley: University of California Press, 1983); Maxine Molyneux, "Socialist Societies Old and New: Progress Toward Women's Emancipation?" *Monthly Review* 34 (3) (July–August 1982): 56–100; Maxine Molyneux, "Mobilization Without Emancipation? Women's Interests, State, and Revolution," in Richard Fagen, Carmen Diana Deere, and José Luis Corragio, eds., *Transition and Development: Problems of Third World Socialism* (New York: Monthly Review Press, 1986), pp. 280–302; Johnetta Cole, "Women in Cuba: The Revolution Within the Revolution," in J. Goldstone, ed., *Revolutions: Theoretical, Comparative, and Historical Studies* (San Diego: Harcourt Brace Jovanovich, 1986), pp. 307–318; Linda Lobao, "Women in Revolutionary Movements: Changing Patterns of Latin American Guerrilla Struggles," in Guida West and Rhoda Lois Blumberg, eds., *Women and Social Protest* (New York: Oxford University Press, 1990), pp. 180–204; and Kruks, Rapp, and Young, *Promissory Notes.*

Much of this scholarship is concerned with assessing the extent of female emancipation in socialist societies, or describing patterns of women's participation in revolutionary movements, rather than theorizing the role of gender in revolutionary processes. A notable exception is Molyneux's essay, which introduced the concepts of women's practical needs and strategic gender interests in revolutionary processes. More recent studies that theorize gender dynamics in revolutions are Valentine M. Moghadam, "Gender and Revolutions," in Foran, *Theorizing Revolutions,* pp. 137–167, which grew out of this chapter in the 1993 edition; Karen Kampwirth, *Women and Guerrilla Movements: Nicaragua, El Salvador, Chiapas, Cuba* (University Park: Pennsylvania State University Press, 2002); and Julia Shayne, "The Revolution Question: Feminism in Cuba, Chile, and El Salvador Compared (1952–1999)," doctoral diss. in sociology, University of California–Santa Barbara, 2000. Works by Iranian feminist scholars have contributed much to our understanding of the centrality of gender, sexuality, and women's bodies in the Iranian Revolution. See, for example,

Afsaneh Najmabadi, "Power, Morality, and the New Muslim Womanhood," in Myron Weiner and Ali Banuazizi, eds., *The Politics of Social Transformation in Afghanistan, Iran, and Pakistan* (Syracuse, N.Y.: Syracuse University Press, 1994), pp. 366–389; Farideh Farhi, "Sexuality and the Politics of Revolution in Iran," in Mary Ann Tetreault, ed., *Women and Revolution in Africa, Asia, and the New World* (Columbia: South Carolina University Press, 1994), pp. 252–271; and Parvin Paidar, *Women and the Political Process in Twentieth Century Iran* (Cambridge: Cambridge University Press, 1995).

12. Carol Pateman, *The Sexual Contract* (Cambridge, UK: Polity Press, 1988). See also Susan Okin, *Women in Western Political Thought* (Princeton: Princeton University Press, 1979).

13. Personal communication with Eric Hobsbawm, Helsinki, Finland, August 9, 1990.

14. Reynolds, "Marianne's Citizens?" p. 110.

15. Harriet B. Applewhite and Darlene G. Levy, introduction to Harriet B. Applewhite and Darlene G. Levy, eds., *Women and Politics in the Age of the Democratic Revolution* (Ann Arbor: University of Michigan Press, 1990), p. 6.

16. Robert Darnton, "What Was Revolutionary About the French Revolution?" *New York Review of Books,* January 19, 1989, p. 4.

17. It is Rowbotham's contention that women's role in the French Revolution, and in particular left-wing women such as Claire Lacombe and the sans culottes women in the club and society, were the precursors of the socialist women of 1830–1848. Conversations with Sheila Rowbotham, Helsinki, Finland, August 1991. See also Rowbotham, *Women, Resistance, and Revolution,* chap. 5; and Rowbotham, *Women in Movement* (London: Routledge, 1993).

18. Hunt, *Politics, Culture, and Class,* pp. 31, 104, 109.

19. Quoted in Reynolds, "Marianne's Citizens?" p. 3.

20. Quoted in Linda Kelly, *Women of the French Revolution* (London: Hamish Hamilton, 1987), p. 127.

21. Quoted in Reynolds, "Marianne's Citizens?" p. 105.

22. Wendy Zeva Goldman, "Women, the Family, and the New Revolutionary Order in the Soviet Union," in Kruks, Rapp, and Young, *Promissory Notes,* pp. 59–81.

23. All three quotes by Lenin from *The Woman Question: Selections from the Writings of Karl Marx, Frederick Engels, V. I. Lenin, Clara Zetkin, Joseph Stalin* (New York: International Publishers, 1977), pp. 56, 59, 61.

24. Elizabeth Waters, "In the Shadow of the Comintern: The Communist Women's Movement, 1920–1943," in Kruks, Rapp, and Young, *Promissory Notes,* pp. 29–56. As Engels himself put it in *Origin of the Family,* "The supremacy of the man in marriage is the simple consequence of his economic supremacy, and with the abolition of the latter will disappear of itself" (p. 88).

25. On Bolshevik strategies in Central Asia, see Gregory Massell, *The Surrogate Proletariat* (Princeton: Princeton University Press, 1974).

26. Jayawardena, *Feminism and Nationalism in the Third World,* p. 25.

27. Ibid., p. 29; and Bernard Lewis, *The Emergence of Modern Turkey* (Oxford: Oxford University Press, 1965), p. 105.

28. Nermin Abadan-Unat, "Social Change and Turkish Women," in Nermin Abadan-Unat, ed., *Women in Turkish Society* (Leiden: E. J. Brill, 1981), p. 9.

29. Caglar Keyder, "The Political Economy of Turkish Democracy," *New Left Review* 115 (May–June 1979): 9; Jayawardena, *Feminism and Nationalism in the Third World,* p. 34; and Deniz Kandiyoti, "Women and the Turkish State: Political

Actors or Symbolic Pawns?" in Yuval-Davis and Anthias, *Women-Nation-State*, p. 141.

30. Kandiyoti, "Women and the Turkish State," pp. 141–142.

31. Quoted in Jayawardena, *Feminism and Nationalism in the Third World*, p. 36.

32. Suna Kili, "Modernity and Tradition: Dilemma Concerning Women's Rights in Turkey," paper presented to the annual meeting of the International Society of Political Psychology, Helsinki, Finland, July 1–5, 1991, p. 7.

33. See Emel Dogramaci, *The Status of Women in Turkey* (Ankara: Meteksan, 1984), esp. chap. 3, "The Status of Women as Reflected in the Works of Namik Kemal, Huseyin Rahmi Gürpinar, Halide Edip Adirar, and Ziya Gökalp."

34. Ibid., p. 127.

35. Peter Knauss, *The Persistence of Patriarchy: Class, Gender, and Ideology in Twentieth Century Algeria* (New York: Praeger, 1987), p. 49.

36. Ibid., p. 75.

37. Doria Cherifati-Merabtine, "Algeria at a Crossroads: National Liberation, Islamization, and Women," in V. M. Moghadam, ed., *Gender and National Identity: Women and Politics in Muslim Societies* (London: Zed Books, 1995), pp. 40–62.

38. Alya Baffoun, "Women and Social Change in the Muslim Arab World," *Women's Studies International Forum* 5 (2) (1982): 234.

39. Knauss, *The Persistence of Patriarchy*, p. 98. See also Cherifa Bouatta and Doria Cherifati-Merabtine, "The Social Representation of Women in Algeria's Islamist Movement," in V. M. Moghadam, ed., *Identity Politics and Women: Cultural Reassertions and Feminisms in International Perspective* (Boulder: Westview Press, 1994), pp. 183–201.

40. Cherifa Bouatta, "Feminine Militancy: Algerian *Moudjahidates* During and After the War," in Moghadam, ed., *Gender and National Identity*, pp. 18–39.

41. Quoted in Knauss, *The Persistence of Patriarchy*, p. 99.

42. Baffoun, "Women and Social Change in the Muslim Arab World," p. 234.

43. Knauss, *The Persistence of Patriarchy*, p. xiii.

44. Cherifati-Merabtine, "Algeria at a Crossroads," p. 48.

45. See Juliette Minces, "Women in Algeria," in Lois Beck and Nikki R. Keddie, eds., *Women in the Muslim World* (Cambridge: Harvard University Press, 1978), pp. 159–171; and Souad Khodja, "Women's Work as Viewed in Present-Day Algerian Society," *International Labour Review* 121 (4) (July–August 1982): 481–487.

46. Knauss, *The Persistence of Patriarchy*, p. 111.

47. Maxine Molyneux, "Legal Reform and Socialist Revolution in Democratic Yemen: Women and the Family," *International Journal of Sociology of Law* 13 (1985): 147–172.

48. Ibid., pp. 161–162.

49. "Building a New Life for Women in South Yemen" (interviews with Aisha Moshen and Noor Ba'abad by Maxine Molyneux), in Miranda Davies, ed., *Third World/Second Sex* (London: Zed Books, 1987), pp. 135–142. See also Richard Lobban, introduction to Richard A. Lobban, ed., *Middle Eastern Women and the Invisible Economy* (Gainesville: University of Florida Press, 1998), esp. pp. 34–35.

50. Nadia Hijab, *Womanpower: The Arab Debate on Women at Work* (Cambridge: Cambridge University Press, 1988), p. 24.

51. Noor Ba'abad, in Davies, *Third World/Second Sex*, p. 142.

52. See Azar Tabari and Nahid Yeganeh, eds., *In the Shadow of Islam: The Women's Movement in Iran* (London: Zed Books, 1982); and Nashat, *Women and Revolution in Iran*.

53. Nayereh Tohidi, "Modernity, Islamization, and Women in Iran," in Moghadam, *Gender and National Identity,* pp. 110–147; and Najmabadi, "Power, Morality, and the New Muslim Womanhood."

54. Murteza Mutahhari, *On the Islamic Hijab* (Tehran: Islamic Propagation Organization, 1987).

55. Kaveh Afrasiabi, "The State and Populism in Iran," Ph.D. diss., Department of Political Science, Boston University, 1987, p. 307.

56. Najmabadi, "Power, Morality, and the New Muslim Womanhood," p. 370.

57. Quoted in Nancy Tapper, "Causes and Consequences of the Abolition of Bride-Price in Afghanistan," in Nazif Shahrani and Robert Canfield, eds., *Revolutions and Rebellions in Afghanistan* (Berkeley: University of California International Studies Institute, 1984), p. 292.

58. Ibid.

59. Thomas Hammond, *Red Flag over Afghanistan* (Boulder: Westview Press, 1984), p. 71.

60. Hanna Papanek, paper prepared for the workshop "Women and the State in Afghanistan, Iran, and Pakistan," MIT Center for International Studies, March 1989.

61. Barbara Einhorn, comments at the Conference on Women and Post-Socialism, Helsinki, Finland, September 1991. See Barbara Einhorn, *Cinderella Goes to Market: Citizenship, Gender, and Women's Movements in East Central Europe* (London: Verso, 1993). See also V. M. Moghadam, ed., *Democratic Reform and the Position of Women in Transitional Economies* (Oxford: Clarendon Press, 1993).

4

Patriarchy and the Changing Family

> *The social institutions under which men [and women] of a definite histori-*
> *cal epoch and of a definite country live are conditioned by . . . the stage of*
> *development of labor, on the one hand, and of the family, on the other. . . .*
> *The less the development of labor, and the more limited its volume of pro-*
> *duction, . . . the more preponderatingly does the social order appear to be*
> *dominated by ties of sex.*
>
> —Frederick Engels

This chapter examines the impact of social change, especially education, on the family and patterns of marriage and reproduction. The "Middle Eastern Muslim family" has long been described as a patriarchal unit, and it has been noted that Muslim family laws have served to reinforce patriarchal gender relations and women's subordinate position within the family. The persistence of patriarchy is a matter of debate, and some feminist theorists argue that industrialized societies are also patriarchal. Sylvia Walby, for example, distinguishes between the "private patriarchy" of the premodern family and social order and the "public patriarchy" of the state and labor market in industrial societies.[1] In this chapter the term "patriarchy" is used in its strict rather than liberal sense—that is, in terms of Caldwell's "patriarchal belt" and Kandiyoti's "classic patriarchy," based on kinship systems in agrarian settings. I have also adopted Hisham Sharabi's concept of "neopatriarchal society," the result of the collision of tradition and modernity in the context of oil-based dependent capitalism and, as I argued in Chapter 2, limited industrialization.[2] Here I describe the contradictions and challenges that patriarchy and the family have encountered from economic development, the demographic transition, legal reform, and women's increasing educational attainment.

The family is perhaps the only societal institution that is conceptualized as "essential" and "natural." The biological basis of kin ties and women's reproductive capacities historically have conferred such a status on the family. This emphasis on biology has led to reductionist and functionalist accounts of the family, accounts that transcend cultural barriers and unite Muslim and Western conservatives. Consider sociologist Talcott Parsons's functionalist perspective. He argued that the modern family has two main functions: to socialize children into society's normative system of values and inculcate appropriate status expectations, and to provide a stable emotional environment that will cushion the (male) worker from the psychological damage of the alienating occupational world. These functions are carried out by the wife and mother. It is she who plays the affective, "expressive" role of nurturance and support, and it is the husband who plays the "instrumental" role of earning the family's keep and maintaining discipline. The Parsonian view is very similar to a contemporary Muslim view, which sees the family as the fundamental unit of society and stresses the mother's role in the socialization of children—particularly in raising "committed Muslims" and transmitting cultural values. These two similar accounts of the family and women are not only descriptive but also prescriptive.

Proponents of the family as a natural unit or a haven in a heartless world frequently warn of its impending death. Throughout the world, the alarm tends to be sounded by persons and groups of the right: Christian fundamentalists and Orthodox Jews in the United States, anticommunists in Eastern Europe and the former Soviet Union in the late 1980s, Islamists in the Middle East. What are some of the indicators of the weakening of the family? According to Kingsley Davis, the state of marriage has become severely weakened in Western nations over the past forty years. He cites easy divorce, the postponement of marriage, a rise in the proportion of the never-married, an increase in nonmarital cohabitation, and the ready availability of contraception as forces that have eroded the family and compromised its ultimate function—the licensing of reproduction. In the former Soviet Union and Eastern Europe, high divorce rates and low birthrates led demographers to warn that these societies may not be able to reproduce themselves.[3]

Laments about the current condition of the family imply that at an earlier time in history the family was more stable and harmonious than it is today. Yet despite massive research, historians have not located a "golden age of the family." One historian lists as causes for the small family size in fourteenth-century England, "birth control, infanticide, high infant mortality, late marriages, infertility due to poor diet, high female mortality, and economic limitations on nuptiality."[4] The marriages of seventeenth-century Europe were based on family and property needs, not on choice or affection. In one of the most famous historical observations, Thomas Hobbes described life in the mid-seventeenth-century as "solitary, poore, nasty, brutish, and short." Two in ten children died in infancy; another two died before reaching puberty; and more either died before reaching marrying age or simply never married. Those who did survive and marry spent most of their adult lives reproducing and raising the next generation.[5] Loveless marriages, tyrannical husbands, high death rates, and the beating, abuse, and abandonment of children add up to a grim image.[6] John Caldwell notes that many writers have tended to romanticize the peasant family, even though A. V. Chayanov calculated that Russian peasant women and girls worked 1.21 times as many hours as men and boys. Teodor Shanin writes that despite their heavy burden of labor (both housework and fieldwork) and their functional importance in the Russian peasant household, women were considered second-class members of it and were nearly always placed under the authority of males. Quarrels and tensions seem to be endemic to the extended household and family everywhere. Amartya Sen's model of "cooperative conflicts" within households and Hanna Papanek's concepts of "unequal entitlements to resource shares" and "socialization for inequality" contradict idealized notions of harmony.[7]

But myths about golden ages are easy to construct, especially during times of rapid social change, socioeconomic difficulty, or political crisis, as Stephanie Coontz found for the United States.[8] At times like this, the family question and its correlate, the woman question, come to the fore. These questions are tackled and answered quite differently by different social groups and political forces. For example, many conservatives feel that a major source of family dissolution is female employment. In the former Soviet Union during perestroika in the late 1980s, social problems were blamed on the "overemployment" of women and their "forced detachment" from the family under communism. The solution, according to this view, was to reduce female labor force attachment and increase women's family attachment. In Eastern Europe, too, a romanticization of the family, of domesticity, and of the private sphere, combined with an emphasis on women's maternal roles, followed the end of communist rule. Somewhat inconsistently, many writings and speeches presented the family as having been the site of resistance to the monolithic state *and* as having been destroyed by the communist policy of imposing public activity on women and substituting institutionalized childcare for mother's care. Barbara Einhorn explains that postcommunist ideology included the frequently voiced opinion that politics is men's prerogative in a return to a "natural order" in which women have privacy in the home and men in the public sphere.[9] There are parallels with the ideology of the conservative movement in the United States, as described by Rebecca Klatch:

> The ideal society, then, is one in which individuals are integrated into a moral community, bound together by faith, by common moral values, and by obeying the dictates of the family and religion. . . .
> While male and female roles are each respected and essential and complementary components of God's plan, men are the spiritual leaders and decision-makers in the family. It is women's role to support men in their position of higher authority through altruism and self-sacrifice.[10]

The parallels with modern Middle Eastern ideals of the role of women and the family are striking. According to the late Murteza Mutahhari, one of the major Iranian Islamist thinkers, "For Muslims, the institution of marriage based on mutuality of natural interest and cordiality between spouses represents a sublime manifestation of the Divine Will and Purpose." He continues:

> Marriage and family living are very significant aspects of a society. They are responsible institutional aspects for the benefit of posterity. Family upbringing of children determines the quality of successive generations. . . .
>
> Mutual affection and sincerity, as well as humane compassion and tenderness, are highly desirable attributes in married couples, in the context of their mutual and social interactions. These are often in evidence in societies governed by Islamic moral and legal checks and balances. In the others, such as those in the West, these qualities are seldom noticeable.[11]

In similar fashion, the late Egyptian Islamist Seyid Qutb placed far more significance on the role of marriage and the family than did historical Islam, which considered both as down-to-earth civil contracts, according to one account of Qutb's work. In accordance with conservative theories of motherhood and education, Qutb spoke in glowing terms of the family as "the nursery of the future," breeding "precious human products" under the guardianship of women. Qutb further celebrated the holy bond of pure love between a man and a woman, who both voluntarily enter into a relationship of marriage as two equal partners, each discharging functions assigned by nature and biology. A woman fulfills her functions by being a wife and mother, while a man is to be the undisputed authority, the breadwinner, and the active member in public life.[12]

To the Islamist intellectual, the Muslim family is by no means the site of oppression or subjugation. Consider the views of the Iranian woman writer Fereshteh Hashemi, who in 1981 wrote that in the context of marriage and the family,

> women have the heavy responsibility of procreation and rearing a generation: this is a divine art, because it creates, it gives birth; and it is a prophetic art, because it guides, it educates. God, therefore, absolves the woman from all economic responsibilities so that she can engage herself in this prophetic and divine act with peace in mind. Therefore, He makes it the duty of the man to provide all economic means for this woman, so as there shall not be an economic vacuum in her life. . . .
>
> And in the exchange for this heavy responsibility, that is, the financial burden of the woman and the family, what is he entitled to expect of the woman? Except for expecting her companionship and courtship, he cannot demand anything else from the woman. According to theological sources, he cannot even demand that she bring him a glass of water, much less expect her to clean and cook.[13]

In the Islamic Republic of Iran, a 1990 study by the Research Group for Muslim Women's Studies tried to explain low female employment by suggesting that Iranian women were by choice more attached to maternal and family roles:

> After the victory of the Islamic Revolution, in order to guarantee the implementation of the legal right of *nafaghe* (a continual allowance being paid by husband to his wife and children), many women who are not specialized in a particular field have chosen to limit their activities to their homes by taking care of their families. They have also realized that the real place for them is their homes, where they are able to raise and train Muslim children and disseminate revolutionary culture, a woman's effective role in the success of Islamic Revolution.[14]

The notion of the family as a woman-tended haven against a heartless world seems to be universal—or at least universal among middle classes in modern societies—rather than specific to any culture or religion. Some have argued that in the West, this concept of the family emerged in the course of real struggles against the market and the state.[15] But the haven ideology is deficient on a number of counts. It obfuscates the extent to which this ideal is socially limited; for example, it most obviously is not experienced in households maintained by women alone, a phenomenon that is becoming statistically significant throughout the world, especially in regions with considerable male out-migration. In the United States, 26 percent of all households are female-headed, up from 12 percent in 1970.[16] In Iran tens of thousands of women became widows during the Iran-Iraq War, and a far larger number of Afghan women were widowed in the 1980s and 1990s. Of what use to them is the ideology that their "real place" is at home rearing children while their husbands are earning the family's daily bread? The haven ideology obscures the very different opportunity structures available to men and women in the society and the economy; it occludes power differentials and inequality within the family; and it suggests a public/private dichotomy and separation of family and state that do not exist.

The relationship between the family and the state illustrates the fine line between the public and private spheres. Nowhere is the family free of state regulation. This intervention takes various forms. Apart from marriage registration (and defining what is acceptable and unacceptable), there is family law, the content of which differs across societies. There are also laws pertaining to reproductive rights, contraception, and abortion. There may or may not be legal codes regarding the provision of care within families and the responsibilities of family members to each other. In many cases female family members are understood, if not legally required, to be care providers (to children, to in-laws, and to parents). In other cases, a father is legally required to provide for his family. In yet other cases there are social policies creating extra-family supports: daycare, homes for the aged or infirm, nursing help, and so on. There may or may not be legal codes pertaining to domestic violence, child abuse, wife battering, or spousal rape. There are invariably laws pertaining to family disintegration (which may come about through divorce, death, abandonment, or migration). Far from being an enclave, the family is vulnerable to the state, and the laws and social policies that impinge upon it undermine the notion of separate spheres. Yet the haven ideology persists and is often strategically deployed by state authorities and dissidents alike.

Moreover, and notwithstanding Mutahhari's swipe at the presumed lack of family values in the West, the 1990s saw the formation of a coalition of conservative Muslim, Catholic, and Protestant governments and nongovernmental organizations over family values. It first formed around what it saw as objectionable recommendations pertaining to women's sexual rights in connection with the UN's International Conference on Population and Development (ICPD), which took place in Cairo in 1994, and the Fourth World Conference on Women (FWCW), in Beijing in 1995. The alliance regrouped in June 2001 at the special session of the UN General Assembly on AIDS in New York, to halt what it saw as the expansion of sexual and political protections and rights for gays being pushed by the European Union.[17]

There are some similarities and some differences between the trajectory of the Arab-Islamic family and that of the family in Western countries. They share a patriarchal structure that undergoes change as a result of economic and political developments. The timing, pace, and extent of the changes differ. In the contemporary Middle East, the family is a powerful signifier, and there is a strong conservative trend to strengthen it and reinforce women's maternal roles, albeit within a nuclear family setting. This trend seems to have arisen in the context of two parallel developments: (1) the erosion of classic patriarchy and the extended household unit, and (2) the rise of middle-class movements, mainly Islamist, that evince values and attitudes reminiscent of the moral discourse of the European bourgeoisie. Let us examine patriarchal social structures and gender relations in order to place in proper context changes in the family, fertility, and the status of women in Middle Eastern countries.

Patriarchal Society and Family

Patriarchal society is a precapitalist social formation that has historically existed in varying forms in Europe and Asia in which property, residence, and descent proceed through the male line. In classic patriarchy, the senior man has authority over everyone else in the family, including younger men, and women are subject to distinct forms of control and subordination. As noted by Deniz Kandiyoti, the key to the reproduction of classic patriarchy lies in the operations of the patrilocally extended household, which is also commonly associated with the reproduction of the peasantry in agrarian societies. The subordination of women in kinship-ordered or agrarian societies is linked to the reproduction of the kin group or the peasantry, as well as to the sexual division of labor. Childbearing is the central (though not exclusive) female labor activity. But just as in capitalism what a worker produces is not considered the property of the worker, so in a patriarchal context a woman's products—be they children or rugs—are not considered her property but those of the patriarchal family and especially the male kin. There is a predisposition to male dominance inherent in the relation between the precapitalist peasant household and the world of landlords and the state and in the reproduction of kinship-ordered groups, wherein women are exchanged and men transact what Gayle Rubin called "the traffic in women." In the context of classic patriarchy, women are considered a form of property. Their honor—and by extension the honor of their family—depends in great measure on their virginity and good conduct.[18] One classic study of "the values of Mediterranean society" described the importance of manliness, woman's sexual purity, and defense of family honor in Andalucia, Spain, villages in Greece and Cyprus, and among the Kabyle in Algeria and the Bedouins of Egypt. Pierre Bourdieu referred to honor killings among the Kabyle while J. G. Peristiany described honor and shame among Cypriots thus:

> Woman's foremost duty to self and family is to safeguard herself against all critical allusions to her sexual modesty. In dress, looks, attitudes, speech, a woman, when men are present, should be virginal as a maiden and matronly as a wife. . . . For an unmarried woman, shame reflects directly on parents and brothers, especially unmarried ones, who did not protect or avenge her honour.[19]

In *The Origin of the Family, Private Property, and the State,* Frederick Engels wrote of the "world-historical defeat of the female sex" in the wake of the agricultural revolution and the advent of civilization and class society. Gerda Lerner reversed Engels's narrative by arguing that the subordination of women—the creation of patriarchy enforced by legal codes in the ancient Near East—enabled the development of private property and state power there and elsewhere. Similarly, Michael Mann has described the trajectory of patriarchy historically and cross-culturally. He has identified and traced the interrelations of five principal stratification nuclei—five collective actors that have affected gender-stratification relations over recent history. They are: the atomized person (more pertinent to liberal, bourgeois society); the networks of household/family/lineage; genders; social classes; and nations and nation-states. According to Mann, the patriarchal society is one in which power is held by male heads of households. There is also clear separation between the public and private spheres of life. In the private sphere of the household, the patriarch enjoys arbitrary power over all junior males, all females, and all children. In the public sphere, power is shared between male patriarchs according to whatever other principles of stratification operate. Whereas many, perhaps most, men expect to be patriarchs at some point in their life cycle, no female holds any formal public position of economic, ideological, military, or political power. Indeed, females are not allowed into this public realm of power. (It goes without saying that men have the monopoly on the means of violence.) Within the household women may influence their male patriarch informally, but this is their only access to power.[20]

Mann's framework accords well with what we know about the legacy of *patria potestas,* the Roman paternal authority. Roman women citizens could inherit, own, and dispose of property, and they could divorce their husbands too. But otherwise the paterfamilias—the family patriarch—had total authority over all members of his household and could sell his children into slavery or prostitution. Roman law and custom also allowed parents to kill deformed children. The Christians of the first five centuries were not unaffected by these aspects of Roman culture, and the abandonment of children was practiced until a church decree banned it.[21]

Patriarchal societies distinguished the public arena from the private. In the public sphere, power relations overwhelmingly involved male household-heads (patriarchs), and the private sphere was usually ruled formally by a patriarch. This arrangement left no basis for collective action by women. If women sought public influence, they had to go through patriarchs. Social stratification was thus two-dimensional. One dimension comprised the two nuclei of household/family/lineage and male dominance. The second dimension comprised whatever combination of public stratification nuclei (classes, military elites, etc.) existed in a particular society. The latter dimension was connected to the former in that public power-groupings were predominantly aggregates of household/family/lineage heads. But apart from this connection, the two dimensions were segregated from each other.

As agrarian societies gave way to modern society, stratification became gendered internally with the entry of women into the public sphere. Mann notes that in Western Europe, from about the sixteenth to the eighteenth centuries, the stratification system changed under the pressure of emerging capitalism, first in agriculture and then in industry, as more of economic life became part of the public realm. Louise Tilly and Joan Scott have explored the effects of this change on women in terms of work and family relations.[22] Mann goes on to note that the particularist distinction between the public and the private was eroded first by employment trends and the emergence of more universal classes, second by universal citizenship, and third by the nation-state's welfare interventions in the private household/family. Thus Mann presents a model of the trajectory from patriarchy to neopatriarchy to a stratification system based on gendered classes, personhood, and the nation. It should be noted that women's rights movements have emerged in the latter part of this trajectory and have contributed to the elimination of some of the more egregious aspects of the patriarchal legacy.[23]

Like Judaism and Christianity before it, Islam came into being in a patriarchal society. The French ethnologist Germaine Tillion argued that the origin of women's oppression in Muslim societies had to be traced to ancient times and the beginnings of patrilineal society. She identified endogamy, the practice of marrying within the lineage, as setting the stage for the oppression of women in patrilineal society, long before the rise of Islam. Endogamy kept property (land and animals) within the lineage and protected the economic and political interests of the men. Quranic reforms provided women with certain legal rights absent in Judaism and Christianity and also corrected some injustices in pre-Islamic Arabian society. For example, Islam banned female infanticide, entitled women to contract their marriage, receive dower, retain control of wealth, and receive maintenance and shares in inheritance. In the early centuries of Islam, various legal schools of thought were established, and within the framework of the Shari'a, norms and laws were formulated to meet a woman's needs in a society where her largely domestic, childbearing roles rendered her sheltered and dependent upon her father, her husband, and her close male relations. Eleanor Doumato suggests that pre-existing Christian customs and Roman laws, as well as customary practices in Arabia, influenced early Muslim views on women and the family.[24] When family laws were codified and modernized much later, they were based on a combination of the Islamic legal schools (Hanafi, Maleki, Hanbali, Shafii), pre-Islamic or tribal customs, and Western (French, Swiss, Belgian) legal systems. Muslim family law gave male members of the kin group control over key decisions affecting "their" women's lives.

Despite the Muslim woman's legal and religious rights to inherit, own, and dispose of property, this right was often circumvented by more powerful male relatives, including her brothers, uncles, or husband's agnates. In the Shari'a, the custody of children is first accorded to mothers, but ultimately the children of Muslim marriage are taken into the formal custody of the father's patrilineal kin group, generally at the age of seven for boys and nine for girls, or puberty for the boy and the time of marriage for the girl, depending upon interpretation.[25] Alya Baffoun has noted that although men and women are in theory equal before religious law, "an imbalance is introduced through sexual and economic inequality—polygamy, unequal inheritance rights and male monopoly of the production of commodities."[26] Mounira Charrad has explained that Islamic law, especially in its Maleki version (which has historically predominated in North Africa), "encourages kin control of marriage ties and thus facilitates both marriages within the lineage and collectively useful outside alliances." She continues, "By favoring males and kin on the male side, inheritance laws solidify ties within the extended patrilineal kin group.

The message of the Maleki family law is that the conjugal unit may be short-lived, whereas the ties with the male kin may be enduring. Maleki law defines the kin group rather than the nuclear family as the significant locus of solidarity. It facilitates—and reflects—the maintenance of tribal communities."[27]

As Caldwell and Kandiyoti have described it, the "belt of classic patriarchy" includes areas in North Africa, the Muslim Middle East (including Turkey and Iran), and South and East Asia (Pakistan, Afghanistan, northern India, and rural China). Today, the tribal structure is the pristine type of patriarchal organization and can still be found in Afghanistan, Pakistan, and in parts of the Arab world and eastern Turkey. The social organization of the tribe *(qabila)* or the communal group *(qawm,* especially in Afghanistan) is based on blood ties and is patriarchal in the classic sense. Tribal identity, such as that of the Arab Bedouin or the Afghan Pashtuns, is generally based on notions of common patrilineal descent. Quite unlike the "primitive" groups studied by Lévi-Strauss, who were exogamous, the Arab-Islamic tribes are endogamous and favor cousin marriage, as noted also by Jack Goody. Germaine Tillion, Alya Baffoun, and Nikki Keddie all pointed out that endogamy increases the tendency to maintain property within families through the control of women in tightly interrelated lineages. Keddie writes that nomadic tribal groups "have special reasons to want to control women and to favor cousin marriage." Pastoral nomadic tribes, the most common type in the Middle East, trade animal products for agricultural and urban ones. Tribal cohesion is necessary to their economy, which requires frequent group decisions about migration. Groups closely tied by kin are desirable because they make decisions amicably. The practical benefits of close kinship, Keddie argued, are surely one reason cousin marriage has long been preferred among Middle Eastern people: it encourages family integration and cooperation. Keddie explained that continuing "controls on women are connected to the pervasiveness of tribal structures in the Middle East," or what Tillion called "the republic of cousins," and noted that "even though most nomadic women are not veiled and secluded, they are controlled."[28] Erika Friedl has made a similar observation with respect to village women in Iran, calling their apparent autonomy and mobility "a brittle freedom" that is "not grounded anywhere in ideology or practice." Of the Bedouins in Israel, Alean al-Krenawi writes that "the main goal is to keep women within the extended family and tribe."[29] Patriarchy is thus strongest in rural areas, within peasant as well as tribal communities.

In many parts of the patriarchal belt, and certainly in the Muslim regions, restrictive codes of behavior exist for women, along with the association of family honor with female virtue and a preoccupation with virginity in unmarried women. As Naila Kabeer notes, "Men are entrusted with safeguarding family honor through their control over female members; they are backed by complex social arrangements that ensure the protection—and dependence—

of women." A family's honor and reputation rest most heavily on the conduct of women. Real or perceived sexual misconduct by women result in honor killings. Sex segregation and veiling, legitimated on the basis of the Shari'a, is part of the Islamic gender system. In South Asian Muslim societies in particular, purdah (literally "curtain," also meaning "covering," "seclusion," and "segregation") remains common and is also strongly linked to men's honor. As David Mandelbaum put it, "Honor is the key good for these men, and their honor is balanced on the heads of the women."[30] Women's life options are severely circumscribed in the patriarchal belt. One typically finds an adverse sex ratio, low female literacy and educational attainment, high fertility rates, high maternal mortality rates, and low female labor force participation in the formal sector. Some analysts, noting these demographic facts, have characterized Afghanistan, Pakistan, Bangladesh, and northern India as having "a culture against women," in which women are socialized to sacrifice their health, survival chances, and life options.[31]

Patriarchy, therefore, should not be conflated with Islam but rather should be understood in social-structural and developmental terms. The emergence of a modern middle class tied to the capitalist economy or the state bureaucracy would seem to represent a weakening of the patriarchal order. The persistence of classic patriarchy would be tied in part to the structure of rural life and the nature of production relations. The largest MENA countries, for example, contain sizable rural populations or populations only recently settled or urbanized. Precapitalist forms of social organization, including tribes and nomadic groups, may be found in Afghanistan, Sudan, and Yemen. Turkey provides an apposite example of the split between a highly patriarchal countryside and an urban context where gender and family relations are more egalitarian. In Turkey as in other large MENA countries with agrarian sectors, women have always worked and engaged in productive activity. Their participation in rural production, while considerable, has been historically devalued by the pervasive patriarchal ideology that sees women as "lacking in mind and religion."[32] This ideology is so strong in the rural areas that even the rise of female-headed households in some of the poorer countries, such as Yemen, caused by male out-migration to the oil-rich countries did not significantly change women's position in the family or vis-à-vis men. Women themselves seem to be aware of urban-rural differences, as one Palestinian refugee's comment suggests:

> I think women who live in the cities are better off than the ones who live in villages. They are very different. In the villages, women don't even have basic rights. They don't have a life. For example, in the villages, men never take into consideration women's opinions. Women aren't even allowed to sit with their husbands or speak with them. They exist just to produce children. That's all. There are no discussions about or understanding of women on the part of men. I'm certain the situation of women in the cities is better.[33]

Patriarchy can be intensified as a result of political and economic changes. An example is provided by the experience of the Palestinians. Zionism left them landless and proletarianized, disrupting the traditional structure of the extended peasant family. Endogamous marriage was gradually replaced with exogamous marriage. But the proletarianization of Palestinian men, which was very unstable and insecure, was not accompanied by a similar process for women. As a result, family size did not decrease, fertility rates did not decline, and women's status did not improve. According to Nahla Abdo-Zubi, "The family in this period was transformed from a productive and reproductive unit—producing agricultural goods as well as a new generation of workers—into an almost exclusively reproductive unit. Whereas production took place outside the family, and was done by males, reproduction became centered in the family, as the women's main task." In this modern context, a new form of the patriarchal family was strengthened. Cheryl Rubenberg concludes that "Palestinian patriarchy, especially as it has developed in West Bank villages and the refugee camps, has been highly deleterious to women."[34]

Family Structure in the Middle East

Family structure in the Middle East has been described as extended, patrilineal, patrilocal, patriarchal, endogamous, and occasionally polygynous.[35] The concept of sanctity and privacy of family life remains strong and a high premium is placed on the good sexual conduct of its female members. In the past, such conduct was guaranteed via segregation of women in the "forbidden" sectors of the house—the hareem, or harem. Although hareems have disappeared, women are still more closely associated with the domestic chores and living arrangements of the household. Outside the home, good conduct and family honor are managed by segregating men and women in educational institutions, occupations, and workplaces, although physical segregation has given way to more interaction. The preferred marriage among Arabs and Muslims of the Middle East has been cousin marriage, particularly between children of two brothers (parallel patrilateral cousins), but it is of course not the exclusive form of marriage. Among Arabs and Iranians, ties to the natal family are hardly ever broken, even in out-marrying situations, and so the daughter has recourse to her own family in the event of repudiation, widowhood, or domestic problems. The situation in South Asia, Afghanistan, prerevolutionary China, and rural Turkey may be different; there, a girl's ties to her natal family tend to be weakened after marriage, making her more vulnerable before her husband's agnates. One reason for these differences may be the different kinds of "bridewealth," or "endowments of the bride."[36]

Among Arabs and Muslims there are different, and direct and indirect, forms of bridewealth: (1) endowing of the bride by her father *(jahaz)* or her in-laws *(mahr);* (2) in Iran and Afghanistan, indirect dower consisting partly of the *shirbaha* (literally, "milk price"), which is cash provided by the groom and given to the bride's father to buy a *jahaz,* to which he is expected to add at least the equivalent cash amount; and (3) direct *mahr,* which may be immediate or deferred but is intended as a sort of social insurance and financial protection for the wife in the event of repudiation or widowhood.[37] These marriage transactions are elaborated by class. A woman from a wealthy family may control relatively large amounts of wealth, which enhances her standing within her new family. In nonelite cases, however, the bride does not receive the dower directly; or the wife may forfeit it if she seeks a divorce; or the amount is too small to provide any financial security.

Some scholars argue that in a rural setting, the payment of brideprice to a woman's kinsmen symbolizes men's control over a woman and over the transfer of her productive and reproductive capacities to her husband's kin group. But a woman's natal ties are maintained throughout her life, and she may utilize the support of her kin in production and to bring pressure against her husband and his family. The support of kinsmen, however, is subject to variation. A woman may count on the aid of her brother. But a woman may also be beaten by her brother or father and sent back to her husband's household when she turns to kinsmen of limited resources with complaints of illness or maltreatment. In fact, the woman's own relatives may condone the husband's action and blame his fury on her bad attitude or her "long tongue."[38]

The early years of marriage in patriarchal settings are usually stressful for young brides. They are subjected to orders from older sisters-in-law and are clearly subservient to the authority of their husband's mother. In this extended family setting, the products of new brides' domestic and agricultural labor, like those of other members of the household, are under the control of the senior male and senior female (mother- and father-in-law in extended family households, older brother and wife in fraternal joint family households). Senior males and females are the center of authority. Soheir Morsy notes that quarrels between women in domestic groups reflect the conflicts and tensions between the men upon whom they are dependent.[39]

The pattern of cousin marriage is one strategy for keeping property within the lineage; it also seems to mitigate the view of women as property, argues Goody, rejecting the Lévi-Straussian view of women as pawns who embody transaction and exchange. But the exchange of women does seem to take place and has been discussed with respect to Afghanistan. There, brideprice is more customary, especially in out-marrying situations. Based on her fieldwork in the 1970s, Nancy Tapper has described the mobility and migration patterns that revolved around brideprice. Men from one region would travel to another to find inexpensive wives, while fathers would travel elsewhere in search of a higher price for their daughters. Patriarchy, therefore, persists where precapitalist social formations remain in place. Goody notes that pastoralists (such as the Bedouins) are closer to the exclusively patrilineal and patriarchal model. Jamal Nasir explains that in rural and bedouin areas, girls are married at ages below the required minimum age and frequently at thirteen.[40]

Whereas the patrilineal extended household is characteristic of rural areas in many Middle Eastern countries, it is less typical in cities, especially in large metropolitan areas. There, neolocal residence is assumed upon marriage, and the nuclear family form prevails. Some of the most extensive studies on changes in household or family types and the impact of economic changes on women's status have been undertaken in Turkey. In the 1970s Kandiyoti delineated six socioeconomic categories of women: nomadic, traditional rural, changing rural, small town, newly urbanized squatter *(gecekondu),* and urban, middle-class professionals and housewives. Family form and household composition varied across these groups, as did the gender division of labor. An interesting discovery was that although patriarchal attitudes and practices remained strongest in the countryside, the patrilocal extended household was being undermined by market incorporation, migration, and poverty. The wealthier landed households were in a better position to sustain extended families. In general, postmarital residence was linked to class, mode of production, resources, and bridewealth.[41]

State policy, including the legal system, exerts a further influence on the persistence, modernization, or weakening of patriarchy and, by extension, on women and the family. Let us examine the contribution of Middle Eastern states to the position of women, gender relations, and the fate of the patriarchal family.

Neopatriarchal States and Personal Status Laws

In her important book *Beyond the Veil,* Fatima Mernissi drew attention to the specific forms of the sexual division of labor in Muslim societies, especially as it occurs within the family. Islam privileges patrilineal bonds and enjoins men to take responsibility for the support of their wives and children. In the Arab-Islamic family, the wife's main obligations are to maintain a home, care for her children, and obey her husband. He is entitled to exercise his marital authority by restraining his wife's movements and preventing her from showing herself in public. I have referred to this as the patriarchal gender contract, and Kandiyoti has described how women "bargain with patriarchy" to maneuver within its confines.[42] The patriarchal contract is realized within the family and codified by the state. Thus, outside of the household, the source of patriarchal control is political-juridical: the state and legislation.

John Esposito has explained that in the tenth century A.D. the elaboration of Islamic law was considered complete, and for the next nine centuries family law remained intact and unchanging.[43] Toward the end of the nineteenth century, Muslim family law became subject to challenges from reformers and modernizers who sought changes in marriage, divorce, polygamy, child custody, and inheritance. This was part of the process of nation building, but concerns about women's position also motivated reforms. The first codification of Islamic Family Law was the Ottoman Law of Family Rights of 1917, which was also applied to the Arab provinces of the Ottoman Empire.[44] In 1926, Kemal Ataturk abolished it and replaced it with a secular civil code adopted from Switzerland. At the same time, King Amanullah of Afghanistan tried, but failed, to raise the status of Afghan women in the family and society by introducing a modern family code and encouraging girls' education. Egypt's reform movement took place in the early twentieth century, and gains were made by women in the Nasser period, although family law retained male privilege. Other countries formulated family laws that were extremely controlling of women; these included Jordan, Morocco, and Saudi Arabia, where tribal customs and the most patriarchal interpretations of Islamic law shaped the family law and therefore the legal status of women and girls. As Amira Sonbol notes, a new form of patriarchy based on the concept of the "family" became the basis of the law, and the state became an effective participant in enforcing personal matters that were not its business before.[45]

In the postcolonial period, the first comprehensive legal change in the status of women in the family came with the Bourguiba reforms in Tunisia in the 1950s, which abolished polygamy and unilateral male divorce. Similar, though less radical, reforms occurred in socialist Syria and Iraq. In Iran, the Pahlavi state's Family Protection Act (1967 and 1973) gave women more rights in family matters and raised the legal age of marriage. Significant reforms to bolster women's position in the family were also undertaken in the People's Democratic Republic of Yemen in the late 1960s and early 1970s, and in the Democratic Republic of Afghanistan in the late 1970s. Nasir reports that modern family laws raised the legal age of marriage for girls to fifteen, and in some countries it was even higher. Courts could deny permission to marry if the age gap between an adolescent bride and her prospective spouse was too wide.[46]

Some of the stronger critics of Muslim family law have complained that there is heavy resistance in the Arab world to changing anything having to do with the family.[47] Yet some states have challenged local and communal patriarchal interests, with important consequences for family legislation and more general policies affecting women. Modernizing, developmentalist elites—

particularly but not exclusively those with a socialist orientation—saw the emancipation of women as part of their program for change. These states were more inclined to curb the power of traditional and rural elites, which would entail an attack on forms of patriarchal control over women and young men, as was the case in Soviet Central Asia.[48] As discussed in Chapter 3, states in the patriarchal belt that undertook such actions were Turkey under Kemal Ataturk, the PDRY in the late 1960s and the 1970s, and the DRA in the late 1970s and early 1980s. The Iraqi Ba'th Party had an interest both in recruiting women into the labor force in the context of a continuing labor shortage and in wresting women's allegiance away from kin, family, or ethnic group and shifting it to the party-state. Women were recruited into state-controlled agencies and put through public education, vocational training, and political indoctrination. The 1978 personal status law, although limited in its objectives, aimed at reducing the control of extended families over women.[49] These were largely pre–Saddam Hussein advances.

In the late 1970s and early 1980s, the growing political power of Islamist movements led to conservative revisions of family laws in Algeria, Egypt, and Iran. In the early 1990s, revisions were enacted in Yemen (following the reunification of the conservative north and the socialist south) and in Afghanistan (following the fall of the left-wing government and the coming to power of Islamists). In response, women's organizations mobilized to call for more egalitarian laws. By the turn of the new century, family law had become the battleground upon which feminist organizations, Islamists, and neopatriarchal states vied for influence.

Despite some differences in the Muslim family laws across the countries of the region, some common patterns may be identified. Everywhere except for Turkey, religious law is elevated to civil status, and religious affiliation is a requirement of citizenship. Although Islamic law gives women the right to own and dispose of property, they inherit less property than men do. Women are required to obtain permission of father, husband, or other male guardian to marry, seek employment, start a business, or travel. The highly formal Islamic marriage contract does require the consent of the wife, and in some countries women may insert stipulations into the contract, such as the condition that she be the only wife. Marriage, however, remains largely an agreement between two families rather than two individuals with equal rights and obligations. Moreover, marriage gives the husband the right of access to his wife's body, and marital rape is not recognized.[50] Only men can divorce unilaterally and without cause. Children acquire citizenship and religious status through their fathers, not their mothers. Muslim women may not marry non-Muslim men. In many countries, the criminal code provides for acquittal or a reduction of sentence for men who commit honor crimes.

Change in family law is a significant index of social change in the Middle East, a barometer of the internal debate within Islam, and an illustration of the capacity for Islamic reform. It is also highly indicative of the role of the state and of state legal policy in matters of gender and the family. As Charrad has argued, legislation is a key element in the strategies available to the state in its efforts to produce social changes or to maintain the status quo. Through the law, and especially through family law, the state can maintain existing gender arrangements; it can alter social policies and laws in the direction of greater restrictions on women; or it can introduce new legislation to foster more equality within the family and raise women's social and economic status. "Family law regulates marriage, divorce, individual rights and responsibilities, and the transmission of property through inheritance; it is thus a prime example of state policy affecting women."[51] For this reason, women's organizations in the Middle East and North Africa have prioritized the modernization of family laws as a key demand of their movement for women's rights and citizenship. (See Chapter 8.)

The nature of the political system, objectives of state managers, and orientation of ruling elites constitute crucial factors in the equation that determines the legal status and social positions of women. Variations in the application of Muslim family law and in its patriarchal content depend principally on the type of political regime and the strength of modern social classes. In some cases, state legal policies have worked to undermine the patriarchal Arab-Islamic family; in other cases, policies foster and perpetuate family structure and the authority of male members in a more modernized form of patriarchy, or what Sharabi calls neopatriarchy. Thus, three parallel and sometimes conflicting developments may be discerned in recent MENA history: (1) the expansion of industrialization, urbanization, proletarianization, and state-sponsored education, which undermine tribes, the extended family unit, and patriarchal family authority; (2) the retention of Muslim family law, which legitimates the prerogatives of male family members over female family members; and (3) women's demands for greater civil, political, and social rights. Polemics surrounding women and the family are responses to the contradictions of social change and emerge in the context of patriarchal societies undergoing modernization and demographic transition.

"Neopatriarchal state" is useful as an umbrella term for the various types of political regime in the Middle East, as I argued in Chapter 1. Whether the regimes be monarchies or republics, radical or conservative, socialist or populist, they share the essential features of neopatriarchy. Sharabi applies the term even more broadly to describe discourses, relations, and institutions in the Arab world. For Sharabi, the concept refers equally to macrostructures (society, the state, the economy) and microstructures (the family or the individual). Neopatriarchy is the product of the encounter between modernity and tradition in the context of dependent capitalism; it is modernized patriarchy. Whatever the outward (modern) forms of the contemporary neopatriarchal family, society, or state, their internal structures remain rooted in the patriarchal values and social relations of kinship, clan, and religious and ethnic groups. A central feature of this system is the dominance of the father within the household and at the level of the state.[52]

Neopatriarchal state practices build upon and reinforce normative views of women and the family, often but not exclusively through the law. States that legitimize their own power on patriarchal structures such as the extended family foster its perpetuation through legislation that subordinates women to the control of men. Examples are laws about women's dress and behavior passed in the 1980s by the Islamist state in Iran and long in existence in Saudi Arabia, the sexual conduct laws of the Zia ul-Haq regime in Pakistan in the 1980s, the sanctioning of honor killings in Jordan and elsewhere (until recently), and the restrictive laws passed by Afghanistan's Mujahidin and Taliban rulers in the 1990s. Muslim family laws that render women legal minors and dependents of men reflect and perpetuate a modernized form of patriarchy.

The control of women is central to the reproduction of the patriarchal unit—the extended family, the community, and the state—but it may also be a political strategy. Constructions of gender and discourses about women and the family are sometimes a convenient weapon between contending political groups. Political elites or neopatriarchal states may raise the woman question to divert attention from economic problems or political corruption—this has been a common device utilized by Islamists in Iran. Another reason states may find it useful to foster patriarchal structures is that the extended family performs vital welfare functions. The joint household system and intergenerational wealth flows that are characteristics of patriarchal structures provide welfare and security for individuals. This, of course, is incumbent upon an adequate supply of household members, especially sons. The material consequences of reproductive failure are disastrous, as Mead Cain observed for Bangladesh.[53] It is especially dire for women, who attain status and old-age security through their sons. In all cases, the persistence of patriarchy relieves the state of the responsibility to provide welfare to citizens.[54]

The patriarchal family and patriarchal ideology persist, therefore, despite challenges from a number of quarters. It is true that the family and ideology mirror the larger social structure; but it is equally true that culture, or the superstructure, often lags behind changes in the economic structure. Turkish feminist scholars have noted that after seventy years of Kemalist secular republicanism, the preoccupation with virginity remains.[55] One might take a cue from Marx and note that the traditions of dead generations weigh heavily on the minds of the living.[56] An equally important reason for the persistence of patriarchy is that most neopatriarchal states in the Middle East have an instrumentalist approach toward women, gender, and the family: policies and laws that strengthen the position of the state itself are the ones that will be enacted.

The Demographic Transition and
Changes in Fertility Behavior

Given the persistence of the patriarchal society, family, and state, it was not surprising that the World Fertility Survey (WFS), conducted in forty-one countries between 1977 and 1982, found that high fertility persisted in the Middle East and sub-Saharan Africa, compared with other regions, as well as in South Asia, where the crude fertility rate was six children per woman in Bangladesh, Nepal, and Pakistan. In Iran, fertility increased between the 1976 census and the 1986 census due mainly to the pronatalism of the Islamic government in the early 1980s. The 1990s, however, saw a reversal of the Islamic state's policy on the family, widespread use of contraception, and a dramatic decline in fertility. Elsewhere, too, the demographic transition is in place and fertility rates are declining—a sign, perhaps, of the crisis of patriarchy in the Middle East.

The demographic transition is a process as far-reaching and important for the history and structure of populations as is industrialization. It involves a change from the high mortality and high fertility characteristic of preindustrial societies to patterns of low mortality and low fertility. Demographer John Caldwell argued that in Western Europe the economic and demographic transitions co-evolved: the transition from the traditional peasant (family-based) economy to the capitalist economy entailed changes in decisions about and need for reproduction. Large families became less rational as the cost of each additional child increased. But the process of change took place in two steps. First, mortality declined while fertility remained high or even increased, thus accelerating population growth. Harris explains that in the transition from peasant to commodity production, the stage of protoindustrialization entailed whole families working as a labor collective. Wages were so low that an adult male could not support himself, let alone a wife and family. As a result, the number of children increased. David Levine cites Michel Foucault to explain why: "The accumulation of men and the accumulation of capital . . . cannot be separated."[57] Then, as mortality continued to drop and as child and then infant mortality fell sharply, fertility began to decline as well, slowing rates of population growth.

In England and France, the rate of population growth increased by 1780, then slowed down after 1820 for France and 1879 for England. Although lower fertility came about in Western societies in the course of industrialization and urbanization, another important source of instability in the family-based system of production and reproduction, according to Caldwell, was "the egalitarian strain in the modern European ideology, powerfully augmented by the spread of education." The following trends, therefore, were significant in lowering the rates of fertility further: the enforcement of universal, compulsory education; an intensification of the movement for women's suffrage and more equal rights for women; and an increase in the availability of the wares of the consumption society and their advertisement.[58] These trends are consistent with Mann's trajectory of patriarchy to neopatriarchy to gendered societies.

Marriage patterns changed, too, in the course of the demographic transition in Western Europe. The age at which couples married fell (from twenty-six to under twenty-four for women in France) and the number of people who married increased. Marriage and employment became compatible, and proletarian women continued to work after marriage. During the nineteenth century people still delayed marriage in both rural and urban areas in England and France, and fertility was higher in urban industrial than in rural areas. In the twentieth century, birthrates continued their downward trend because of the practice of birth control, though there were periodic increases. Tilly and Scott stress that mortality, marriage, and fertility patterns differed by class and region.[59]

Demographers studying global fertility decline since the 1960s offer eight explanations for the fertility transition: mortality reduction; reduced economic contributions from children; opportunity costs of childbearing, especially for mothers; family transformation; vanishing cultural props for childbearing; improved access to effective fertility regulation; marriage delay; and diffusion of ideas and practices.[60] These are plausible and pertinent variables, but the role of socioeconomic development, as argued by John Caldwell, may provide the most robust explanation. Caldwell does not deny the salience of access to efficient contraceptives and the diffusion of concern about population growth ("ideologies, attitudes, and the mechanisms of fertility control"), but he stresses that inadequate socioeconomic change may explain why some countries or some social groups within countries have been excluded from the global fertility decline.[61] Karen Oppenheim Mason adds gender to the equation, arguing that the status of women and the family determine some of the explanations offered above.[62] The status of women is thus both an independent and a dependent variable in the demographic transition. In this respect she echoes Caldwell's earlier work.

Socioeconomic development, gender, class, and the state certainly play a role in fertility. Many comparative studies on the causes of high fertility have tended to concentrate on the cost of children and the status of women as key explanatory variables. Lower status means restricted access to education and employment and hence higher fertility. As women from elite families are generally those with the most access to education and employment, fertility is also variable by class. There are exceptions, however; in some countries (for example, Saudi Arabia) elite women will receive private, Western-style education but will not seek employment or will abandon it after marriage, often due to conservative social norms. Poor women who are economically dependent and who are not the beneficiaries of a social security system need adult sons in order to survive. Thus the cost of children and the status of women are themselves shaped by social class; reproductive behavior and fertility patterns, therefore, are class-differentiated. And as reproduction is so closely linked to production, the economic system within which families live and work will also explain and predict fertility patterns.[63] Simply put, there are rational reasons why the fertility behavior and needs of peasants, proletarians, professionals, and the poor differ. It should come as no surprise that salaried middle-class women are the ones having the fewest children.

High fertility persists in those areas with the traditional rural extended family, and in the 1970s and 1980s those areas were sub-Saharan Africa, North Africa, and Southwest and South Asia. Indeed, the World Fertility Survey found that fertility was highest in the Middle East and sub-Saharan Africa. But it also found that "substantial fertility declines have been observed over recent years in all regions except sub-Saharan Africa."[64] As previously noted, many countries in the patriarchal belt have large populations dependent upon agriculture. High fertility is advantageous to the peasant family and its most powerful members; it is also justified on cultural-religious grounds. However, though the familial mode of production is typically found in circumstances of subsistence production, it can adapt for at least a time to urban life and the market economy without fully succumbing to the rules of the market. Where the process of proletarianization is not yet complete, large segments of the urban population are informal workers rather than formal-sector wage workers. When households are engaged in cottage industries, it is rational for them to increase the number of "workers," as was the case in Europe during the protoindustrial stage. For capital, large supplies of cheap labor are functional and profitable. Poor rural-urban migrants need their children to secure a purchase on town life and enable them to stay. The traditional elite, the merchants, organize their families much as do farmers and feel few, if any, ill effects from high fertility.[65] By contrast, the fully developed labor-market mode of production offers no rewards for high fertility.

These explanations help us to understand the demographic transition in the Middle East, and its implications for the status of women, gender relations, and the family. As in other developing regions in the twentieth century, the demographic transition occurred more rapidly in MENA than it occurred in Europe. But MENA began its transition later than other countries with comparable levels of income, in part because of a slower pace of educational attainment and lower employment among women. The result of lowered mortality and high fertility in the second half of the twentieth century was accelerated population growth. MENA's annual population growth reached a peak of 3 percent around 1980, while the growth rate for the world as a whole reached its peak of 2 percent annually more than a decade earlier. On average, fertility in MENA declined from 7 children per woman around 1960 to 3.6 children in 2001. The total fertility rate (average number of births per woman) is less than 3 in Bahrain, Iran, Lebanon, Tunisia, and Turkey, and is more than 5 in Iraq, Oman, Palestine, and Saudi Arabia. There have been impressive fertility declines in Morocco and Egypt since the 1980s, but only a slight decline in Saudi Arabia and none at all in Yemen, where the average number of births per woman is close to 8.[66]

The declines in fertility have been accompanied by declines in infant mortality and under-5 child mortality, quite dramatically in some countries. For example, in 1960 Tunisia had an infant mortality rate (per 1,000 live births) of 159, and its under-5 child mortality rate was 255. In the 1980s this declined to 58 and 83, respectively. By 2000 the rate of infant mortality had dropped to just 30. Iran similarly saw impressive achievements in the health of children as well as of mothers during the 1990s. Indeed, maternal mortality rates have dropped throughout the region, though they remain highest in Afghanistan, Yemen, and Sudan, the poorest and most rural countries. Life expectancy varies; it is highest in the oil-rich Gulf states (72 years) and Israel (80 years), lowest in Afghanistan (45 years), Sudan (55 years), and Yemen (56 years).

As noted earlier, state policy, including population or family planning policies, affect women's productive and reproductive choices. For many newly independent third world states, at least until recently, a large population was associated with national strength. This idea was stated quite explicitly by leaders of Algeria, Kenya, India, and China, to name a few. A pronatalist policy was adopted in 1979 by the authorities in the Islamic Republic of Iran, which also banned abortion and prohibited the importation of contraceptives. In 1988 the total fertility rate in Iran was 5.6 births per woman and in Algeria it was 5.4 births per woman.

MENA countries have exhibited a variety of population policies and concerns. "Population policy" is understood to be an intention to improve the overall well-being of the nation's citizens. Definitions of "well-being" vary and are certainly debatable, as are prescriptions of how to reach objectives. In the 1990s, countries that were concerned about the rate of population growth (e.g., Iran and Egypt), faced the dual goal of improving health facilities, thus reducing natal and infant mortality, and of decreasing the birthrate. Other countries seek to reduce mortality rates and improve the population's health but do not actively seek to reduce birthrates (e.g., Israel, Saudi Arabia). At the level of state policymaking, the approach to population growth ranges from pronatalist to laissez-faire to pro–family planning. In several of the countries—notably Iran, Lebanon, Tunisia, and Turkey—the combined effects of socioeconomic development, women's educational attainment, and state-sponsored family planning programs have produced the lowest fertility rates of the region. Indeed, the average of about 2.5 children per woman in these MENA countries is even lower than the fertility rate of many Latin American countries.

In Iran, rural health workers, known as behvarzes, are local women with two years' training who monitor maternal and child health and family planning. Photo courtesy of Farzaneh Roudy-Fahimi.

Education and Women's Empowerment

Higher levels of education tend to result in more knowledge and use of contraceptives, although the availability of family planning programs is also an important variable. Research on Egypt showed that whereas on average women desired 4 children in Egypt, the mean jumped to 4.4 among illiterate mothers and dropped to 2.1 for women with secondary school education. The mean number of children born to university-educated women was 1.8. Contraceptive use among the more educated was clearly a factor here, and remains so. But although fertility and education are negatively correlated, small increases in education—for example, a few years of primary education—are insufficient for fertility decline. There is also much evidence that the work status of the wife, especially if she works in the modern sector of the economy (nonagricultural cash economy), is an important determinant of marital fertility.[67]

The Syrian Fertility Survey of 1978 found that "while those with no schooling have a rate of 8.6 children, those with incomplete primary and those with complete primary schooling or above have rates of 4.3 and 3.2, respectively." And this despite the fact that "Syria has no organized family planning programme." The report concluded, "The very large differences in recent fertility between women of varying educational background and between rural and urban sectors suggest the likelihood of further decline in the national level of fertility as the Syrian population becomes more educated and urbanized." Similarly, the Turkish Fertility Survey of 1978 found that "women with high socio-economic status tend to have higher age at marriage and may have lower fertility." The survey found pronounced sociocultural and demographic differences between urban and rural, eastern and western, and educated and uneducated people in Turkey.[68] The more recent Demographic and Health Surveys—conducted in the early 1990s in Egypt, Jordan, Morocco, Tunisia, Turkey, and Yemen, along with many other developing countries—similarly found that rural-urban residence, education, and socioeconomic status determined the number of children, as well as the health of the mother and child. In general, the surveys found declining fertility rates and rising age of marriage in the Middle Eastern countries surveyed.[69]

Thus we see that urbanization, industrialization, proletarianization, and mass schooling—so important to the demographic transition and the decline of classic patriarchy in the West—are present in the Middle East and have altered the social structure and gender relations. Developmentalist, welfarist, or revolutionary states also have helped to bring about societal changes, including legal reforms to bolster women's position in the family, as discussed above and in Chapter 3. Such legal reforms are an important basis for women to act as autonomous persons. But perhaps most important has been the expansion of schooling for girls. As Mernissi has stated: "Access to education seems to have an immediate, tremendous impact on women's perception of themselves, their reproductive and sex roles, and their social mobility expectations."[70]

The social changes just mentioned have led to differentiation among the female population and an expansion of the range of options available to women, including the right to make informed choices about marriage and childbearing. As Caldwell explained, a greater female role in reproductive decisionmaking would imply an important transition—a move toward a greater belief in female participation in work or social activities—and perhaps reflect and accelerate a decline in strong moral views on the separate roles of the sexes and the sanctity of maternity.[71] These trends are relevant to a growing proportion of the urban female population, and they have been visible enough to result in opposition by conservative forces. The relative rise in the position of women is seen by conservative forces as having the greatest potential of any factor to destroy the patriarchal family and its political, economic, and demographic structure.

Caldwell has argued that mass schooling probably has had a greater impact on the family in developing countries than it had even in the West. First, mass schooling has come in many countries at an earlier stage of economic and occupational structure development than it did in the West. Second, schooling frequently means Westernization, including Western concepts of family and gender. According to Caldwell, "Schools destroy the corporate identity of the family, especially for those members previously most submissive and most wholly contained by the family: children and women."[72] Mernissi similarly has emphasized the role of state-sponsored education in creating two generations of independent women. Her thesis is worth quoting at length:

> As corrupt and inefficient as it proved to be, the national state did nevertheless carry out a mass educational programme (limited to males only in the rural area) after independence, and fostered the emergence of a new class: *educated youth of both sexes*. This class is the result of the interplay of three factors: (1) the demographic factor, the "youthification" of the population; (2) a political factor, the emergence of the welfare state; (3) a cultural factor, the change in women's self-perception as actors in society. . . .
>
> Centuries of women's exclusion from knowledge have resulted in femininity being confused with illiteracy until a few decades ago. But things have progressed so rapidly in our Muslim countries that we women take literacy and access to schools and universities for granted.[73]

Educational attainment by parents seems to have some effect on their children's aspirations. A study of female education in Egypt in the early 1980s found that all the students whose father had a university education saw nothing less for themselves than a comparable education. Similar aspirations were also noticed among students whose mother completed a university education. Girls whose mothers were illiterate were more likely to see secondary education as their ultimate goal. The great majority of daughters whose mothers could read and write or had completed primary, preparatory, or secondary education intended to seek a university degree. Further analysis of students' aspirations in relation to fathers' occupations showed a high correlation between a student's level of aspiration for university or postgraduate studies and her father's employment in a professional field. Fully 100 percent of the daughters of fathers who worked in professional jobs aimed for a university or postgraduate education. Similarly, 96 percent of the daughters of fathers working in semiprofessional jobs expressed the same desire. The percentage of students aiming at only a secondary education was higher among girls whose fathers worked as small-business entrepreneurs (10 percent); religious functionaries, guards, and policemen (12 percent); skilled laborers (20 percent); and unskilled laborers (23 percent). The mother's employment status also showed a relationship to her daughter's hopes for higher education. The great majority (98 percent) of the daughters of working mothers expressed a desire to pursue a university education; the other 2 percent were satisfied with a secondary education as their goal. A higher proportion (12 percent) of the daughters of nonworking mothers did not intend to go beyond secondary school. When education was related to employment, the girls' responses were more positive regarding the employment of educated women. The overwhelming majority (93 percent) believed that once a young woman completes her education, she must work. They further asserted that the ultimate goal of education for women was future employment.[74] Indeed, many MENA women recognize the importance of education, and studies find that women associate education with higher status, income, and economic freedom, and express a desire to be able to earn an income.[75]

Algeria and Iran, two large MENA countries, are representative of the profound family changes under way in the region. Whereas a few decades ago the majority of women married before the age of twenty, today only 10 percent of that age group in Algeria and 18 percent in Iran are married.[76] As Mernissi remarked, "To get an idea of how perturbing it is for Iranian society to deal with an army of unmarried adolescents one has only to remember that the legal age for marriage for females in Iran is thirteen and for males fifteen." The legal age was lowered—in fact to puberty for girls—following the establishment of Islamic rule, but it is interesting that this did not translate into a higher rate of marriage for girls under twenty—another example of the gap between laws and social reality. In Turkey 14 percent, in Morocco 13 percent, and in Tunisia only 3 percent of young women aged fifteen to nineteen were ever married in the 1990s. Mernissi has argued that the idea of a young unmarried woman is completely novel in the Muslim world, for the whole concept of patriarchal honor is built around the idea of virginity, which reduces a woman's role to its sexual dimension: reproduction within an early marriage.[77] The concept of a menstruating and unmarried woman is so alien to the entire Muslim family system, Mernissi adds, that it is either unimaginable or necessarily linked with *fitna,* or moral and social disorder. The unimaginable is now a reality. Young men, faced with job insecurity or lacking a diploma to guarantee access to desired jobs, postpone marriage. Women, faced with the pragmatic necessity to count on themselves instead of relying on a rich husband, further their formal education.

As a result, the average age of marriage for women and men in most MENA countries has registered a noticeable increase. In Algeria, Jordan, and Tunisia, young women marry at age twenty-four or twenty-five; in Egypt, Iran, Morocco, and Turkey, it is twenty-one or twenty-two. Even the oil countries, known for their conservatism, have witnessed an increase of unmarried young women: age at marriage for women is twenty-two in Saudi Arabia, twenty-three in Qatar and the UAE, and as high as twenty-five in Kuwait. The ages for young men are usually three to five years higher than those of young women. The lowest age of marriage for girls is probably Afghanistan and Yemen, the poorest countries, where the fertility rates also are high. Of course, the patterns of nuptiality are influenced by urbanization: the more urbanized youth marry later in all countries. And it should be noted that in all cases the average age of marriage is considerably higher than the legal minimum.

The single most important determinant in the age of marriage has been education. More women are completing secondary school, and a growing proportion of university students are women. Educational statistics for MENA countries are not the most consistent or reliable, and it is sometimes difficult to discern patterns or trends over time. The figures in Table 4.1 have been gleaned from a number of sources, some of which contradict each other. Still, in comparing various data sets we can observe that women's share of university enrollments is nearly half in most of the large MENA countries. During the academic year 1999–2000, Lebanese women represented 53.2 percent of students enrolled in universities and institutions of higher learning, and 52.4 percent of these establishments' graduates.[78] And what are women studying? The fields of concentration—social sciences, humanities, natural sciences, medicine, law—vary from country to country. Women's share of education and the humanities has been high since at least 1980 in Egypt, Jordan, Lebanon, and Syria. But a noticeable trend in those countries, and in Algeria, Morocco, and Tunisia, is the feminization of enrollments in the medical sciences.[79]

There is some consensus that the dramatic increase in education among U.S. women in the postwar era was a major cause of the women's movement. The baby boomers, even more than those born a few years earlier, went to college in massive and unprecedented numbers. College education in turn increased women's labor force participation; at the same time there was an expansion of married women's labor force participation.[80] A similar pattern may be discerned in MENA countries—activist women, married and unmarried, emerge from the ranks of the educated and employed. This rapid social change—the impact of industrialization, urbanization, and education on marriage, the family, and gender roles—has caused a conservative backlash in the form of the Islamist movement. According to Mernissi, fundamentalism is a "defense mechanism against profound changes in both sex roles and the touchy subject of sexual identity."[81] Fundamentalists are concerned that education for women has dissolved traditional arrangements of space segregation, family ethics, and gender roles.

Although Mernissi underscores the revolutionary impact of the education of women in Muslim societies, she failed to consider the phenomenon of the educated Islamist woman. Islamist movements have been recruiting in the universities, and throughout the Middle East one sees veiled university women who are also active participants in Islamist movements. This, too, can be explained in terms of both the contradictions of social change and class

Table 4.1 Sociodemographic Features in MENA, 1990s

	% Females Literate 15+, 2000	% Female Enrollments in Secondary School, 1993–1997	Female Share of Tertiary Enrollment, mid-1990s*	Age at First Marriage (women) 1990s**	% Female-Headed Households	% Married Women Using Contraception (total)	Total Fertility Rate
Afghanistan	22	12	—	—	—	—	6.0
Algeria	57	62	—	24	11	52	3.1
Bahrain	83	97	58	23	—	62	2.8
Egypt	44	73	—	22	13	56	3.5
Iran	70	73	36[a]	21	6	73	2.6
Iraq	46	32	—	22	—	—	5.3
Israel	94	87	—	24	—	—	3.0
Jordan	84	—	47	25	— (9.6)	56	3.6
Kuwait	80	66	62	25	5	50	4.2
Lebanon	80	84	49	—	— (14.2)	61	2.5
Libya	68	—	17	—	—	49	3.9
Morocco	36	34	41[b]	22	15 (17.3)	58	3.4
Oman	62	66	46	19	— (12.5)	24	6.1
Palestine	—	—	44	—	— (7.7)	—	—
Qatar	83	79	73	23	—	43	3.9
Saudi Arabia	67	57	47	22	—	32	5.7
Sudan	46	20	41	26	13	10	4.9
Syria	61	40	45	—	— (9.3)	49	4.1
Tunisia	61	63	38	25	11	60	2.3
Turkey	77	48	—	22	10	64	2.5
UAE	79	82	—	23	—	28	3.5
Yemen	25	14	13	19 (YAR)	12	21	7.2

Sources: Population Reference Bureau, *Women of the World 2002* poster, except for * from CAWTAR, *Globalization and Gender: Economic Participation of Arab Women* (Tunis: CAWTAR, 2002), tab. A/33, p. 229, and UN, *The World's Women 2000: Trends and Statistics* (New York: UN, 2000), tab. 4.A; ** from UN, *The World's Women 2000: Trends and Statistics* (New York: UN, 2000); numbers in parentheses from ESCWA, *Women and Men in the Arab Region: A Statistical Portrait 2000* (Beirut: ESCWA, 2000), annex 10.

Notes: a. The figure for Iran did not include private universities. In 2002, the female share of university enrollments rose to over 50 percent.
b. The CAWTAR report cites a figure of 21 percent female share of university enrollment in Morocco.

factors: Islamists, whether they be male or female, are typically lower-middle-class and of recent rural or small-town background, "experiencing for the first time life in huge metropolitan areas where foreign influence is most apparent and where impersonal forces are at maximum strength."[82] In Algeria, Iran, Egypt, and Turkey, Islamist movements have women supporters drawn from the traditional or lower middle class. Such women continue to see the family unit as essential and natural. At the same time, many Islamist women have had to face second-class citizenship and subjection to patriarchal gender relations within their movements and communities, and many have rebelled against it. Often these educated—and sometimes employed—Islamist women raise questions about male domination, polygyny, and unequal norms and laws governing divorce and child custody. These women, who challenge their subordinate status within the family and the society, partly by engaging in a more woman-centered re-reading of the Quran and early Islamic history, have come to be known as Islamic feminists.

Women's employment has been almost as important as women's education in changing the position and self-perception of women, and in altering the patriarchal gender contract. This seems to be equally true of working-class and middle-class women. Sociologist Tahire Erman has shown how Turkish migrant women's involvement in paid employment has led them to question patriarchy, although she finds that other factors—such as affiliation with the Alevi sect, adherence to leftist ideology, and having strong mothers—also shape the extent to which women question patriarchy. In describing her entry into the world of paid employment, one woman told Erman:

> When I wanted to work, my husband objected to it. He said, "Who will take care of the children if you are not home all day?" (Another woman joins in, saying, "Our husbands didn't want us to work. They said they wouldn't live on women's money. This is the influence of the village.") But we needed money. We needed it for our children. Through a relative I found a job as a maid. First I didn't tell my husband (laughing). After a couple of days, I said to him, "Look, I started working for a nice lady. She pays me well. We need the money." This is how I started working.[83]

Around the world, educated and employed women have formed women's rights organizations, have become involved in trade unions and professional associations, and have helped change family relations from patriarchal to egalitarian. A similar pattern is emerging in the Middle East, where educated and employed women are pushing for the modernization of family law, greater participation, and more equality (see Chapter 8). A "critical mass" of educated and employed MENA women, with fewer children and more time for civic activities and collective action, have formed women's movements that are challenging patriarchal gender relations, the neopatriarchal state, and patriarchal family laws.

In this, they have the support of some men who share their values and goals of egalitarian family relations. In 1999–2000, Mansoor Moaddel and his associates undertook a comparative study of value orientations in Egypt, Jordan, and Iran concerning religion, gender, and politics. Their findings confirm the arguments I have made regarding significant social changes in the region as a whole but also variations across the MENA countries. For example, while the respondents in all three countries attached great value to the institution of marriage, a rather significant number of Iranians (17 percent) agreed with the statement that marriage had become an outdated institution. On the issue of wife obedience, only 47 percent of Egyptians, 42 percent of Jordanians, and 24 percent of Iranians strongly agreed with the statement that a wife must always obey her husband. Interestingly, the overwhelming majority of respondents in all three countries disagreed with the institution of polygamy.

Moaddel and his colleagues found, too, that the ideal number of children varied in the three countries. Most respondents in Egypt considered two or three to be the ideal number, in Jordan four or more, and in Iran, two. It should be noted that this corresponds almost exactly to the total fertility rate in each country. In response to a question asking if women needed to have children in order to feel satisfied, about 89 percent of Egyptians and Jordanians agreed, but only 47 percent of Iranians. Correspondingly, a far larger percentage of the Iranian respondents (40 percent) agreed that a working mother could develop intimate relations with her children, just like a nonworking mother, compared with 23 percent in Jordan and only 19 percent in Egypt. On the question of whether men should be favored over women in jobs, given high unemployment rates in the region, a considerable majority of respondents in all three countries said that men should be given preference. But the younger age group displayed less gender bias than the older age groups. And finally, in measuring the strength of family ties, the researchers found that 86 percent of Jordanians, 78 percent of Egyptians, and 53 percent of Iranians surveyed agreed with the statement that "making my parents proud of me is one of my main goals in life."[84] Family ties still matter.

Conclusion

As Esposito and others have shown, Islamic law was formulated in the early years from the victory of conservative jurists over those who wished to retain interpretation and contingency in Islamic jurisprudence. Muslim family law certainly determines women's legal status and shapes their social positions and options. But to explain the persistence of patriarchy and the preoccupation with women and the family, one must also look at the social structure: forms of economic organization, property relations, social classes, forms of stratification and segmentation, and the state. Since the 1960s, social structures in the Middle East have undergone rapid change through industrialization and modernizing state systems. The material bases of classic patriarchy crumble under the impact of capital penetration, infrastructural development, legal reform, mass education, and employment. In this context, women and the family have experienced change, and Muslim family law has become a field of contestation among feminists, fundamentalists, and the state. Particularly in urban areas, there has been a shift from the extended household unit characteristic of classic patriarchy to a more modernized version, or neopatriarchy. Some family forms in the contemporary Middle East are remarkably similar to those of the classic bourgeois nuclear family. Others reveal signs of a shift from patriarchal to more egalitarian gender dynamics. In general, the patriarchal gender contract remains in place, but economic changes and women's collective action may undermine it in the years to come.

It was also in this context of social change, and especially changes in the structure of the family, that legal conservatives and Islamist ideologues sought in the 1980s and 1990s to stem the tide by insisting on returning to or strengthening patriarchal family laws. (See Chapter 5.) In some countries, the conservatives made gains. But in countries like Algeria, Iran, Turkey, and Tunisia, conservative Islamic forces have had to face strong resistance from what I call modernizing women. It is clear that women do not represent a homogeneous social category in the Middle East. They are differentiated by region, class, and education; educated women are further divided politically and ideologically. Yet the available evidence shows that socioeconomic development and increasing rates of female education and employment have affected the structure and size of the family, as well as women's gender consciousness. During the region's long twentieth century, therefore, the Arab-Islamic family and its concomitants—rigid sex roles, women's legal status as minors, the prerogatives of fathers and husbands, high fertility—have been challenged by socioeconomic developments (industrialization, the expansion of the urban labor market, and education) and political action (state legal reform and women's movements).

Michael Mann has suggested an evolution, in the West, from classic patriarchy to neopatriarchy and a gendered class structure. The capitalist market and liberal bourgeois ideology worked in concert to break down the private/public and male/female dichotomies, while the growth of education "provided women with one of their furthest points of entry into the public sphere and into economic stratification."[85] Parallel to these socioeconomic changes were ideological, cultural, and discursive developments around women's equality, autonomy, and liberation. In the Western world, socioeconomic changes—including mass education and mass employment—have resulted in a dramatically different female relationship to the family, as well as in the proliferation of family or household forms. Rather than being limited by the family, "women's prospects are that around two-thirds of their adult lives will be spent without children in the household, and possibly half to two-thirds without a husband."[86] In the last 100 years, it has become increasingly possible for the individual to live without the insurance afforded by an extended set of ties. This is not yet the generalized case in the Middle East. The family remains important not only economically but emotionally, even for highly educated Middle Eastern women. But their range of choices regarding family formation, duration, and size has quite definitely expanded.

Notes

1. Sylvia Walby, *Theorizing Patriarchy* (Oxford: Blackwell, 1990); and Sylvia Walby, "The 'Declining Significance' or the 'Changing Forms' of Patriarchy?" in V. M. Moghadam, ed., *Patriarchy and Development: Women's Positions at the End of the Twentieth Century* (Oxford: Clarendon Press, 1996). For a discussion of the status of women in connection with modes of production, see John Lie, "From Agrarian Patriarchy to Patriarchal Capitalism: Gendered Capitalist Industrialization in Korea," in Moghadam, *Patriarchy and Development,* pp. 34–55.

2. On patriarchy in the Middle East, see Hisham Sharabi, *Neopatriarchy: A Theory of Distorted Change in Arab Society* (New York: Oxford University Press, 1988). My approach has been inspired by Deniz Kandiyoti, especially "Bargaining with Patriarchy," *Gender and Society* 2 (3) (September 1988): 274–290; and "Islam and Patriarchy: A Comparative Perspective," in Nikki R. Keddie and Beth Baron, eds., *Women in Middle Eastern History: Shifting Boundaries in Sex and Gender* (New Haven: Yale University Press, 1991), pp. 23–42.

3. Kingsley Davis, ed., *Contemporary Marriage* (New York: Basic Books, 1986); and Anastasia Posadskaya, "Changes in Gender Discourses and Policies," in Valentine M. Moghadam, ed., *Democratic Reforms and the Position of Women in Transnational Economies* (Oxford: Clarendon, 1993), pp. 162–179.

4. Barbara Hanawalt, cited in John Boswell, *The Kindness of Strangers: The Abandonment of Children in Western Europe from Late Antiquity to the Renaissance* (London: Penguin, 1988), p. 410.

5. David Levine, "Punctuated Equilibrium: The Modernization of the Proletarian Family in the Age of Ascendant Capitalism," *International Labor and Working-Class History* 39 (Spring 1991): 3–20. See also James Vander Zanden, *Sociology: The Core* (St. Louis: McGraw-Hill, 1990), p. 254.

6. See, for example, Linda Gordon, *Heroes of Their Own Lives: The Politics and History of Family Violence* (London: Virago, 1989). See also Boswell, *The Kindness of Strangers.* Boswell's study locates the phenomenon of child abandonment in *patria potestas,* the Roman-derived paternal authority. Gordon's study of wife and child abuses in Boston is highly critical of the patriarchal family and the prerogatives of the father. Both studies recognize extra-family causes of abandonment and abuse, such as food scarcity, disease, poverty, and unemployment.

7. See John C. Caldwell, *Theory of Fertility Decline* (London: Academic Press, 1982), pp. 166–169; Teodor Shanin, "A Peasant Household: Russia at the Turn of the Century," in Teodor Shanin, ed., *Peasants and Peasant Societies,* 2nd ed. (London: Blackwell, 1987), pp. 21–34; Amartya Sen, "Gender and Cooperative Conflicts," and Hanna Papanek, "To Each Less Than She Needs, from Each More Than She Can Do: Allocations, Entitlements, and Value," both in Irene Tinker, ed., *Persistent Inequali-*

ties: Women and World Development (New York: Oxford University Press, 1990), pp. 123–148 and 162–183.

8. Stephanie Coontz, *The Way We Never Were: American Families and the Nostalgia Trap* (New York: Basic Books, 1992); and Stephanie Coontz, *Time After Time: Recurring Family Myths, Changing Family Realities* (Minneapolis: National Council on Family Relations, 2000).

9. Barbara Einhorn, "Democratization and Women's Movements in Central and Eastern Europe: Concepts of Women's Rights," in V. M. Moghadam, ed., *Democratic Reform*, pp. 48–73. See also Posadskaya, "Changes in Gender Discourses and Policies"; Valentina Bodrova, "Women, Work, and Family in the Mirror of Public Opinion"; and Sharon Wolchik, "Women and the Politics of Transition in Central and Eastern Europe," in Moghadam, pp. 29–47, 162–179, and 180–195.

10. Rebecca Klatch, "Coalition and Conflict Among Women of the New Right," *Signs* 4 (1988): 671–694; quotes appear on pp. 675–676.

11. Murteza Mutahhari, *Sexual Ethics in Islam and in the Western World,* trans. Muhammad Khurshid Ali (Tehran: Bonyad Be'that Foreign Department, 1982), pp. 7, 31, 58. Note the swipe at the presumed lack of family values in the West.

12. See Youssef M. Choueiri, *Islamic Fundamentalism* (London: Pinter, 1990), pp. 127–128.

13. Fereshteh Hashemi, "Women in an Islamic Versus Women in a Muslim View," *Zan-e Rouz* 22 (March 1981), translated and reprinted in Azar Tabari and Nahid Yeganeh, eds., *In the Shadow of Islam: The Women's Movement in Iran* (London: Zed Books, 1982), p. 180. "Companionship" and "courtship" are euphemisms for sexual services.

14. Research Group for Muslim Women's Studies, *The Social Status of Iranian Women Before and After the Victory of the Islamic Revolution* (Tehran: Cultural Studies and Research Institute, Ministry of Culture and Higher Education, 1990), p. 33.

15. See especially Eli Zaretsky, *Capitalism, the Family, and Personal Life* (New York: Harper, 1976); and Jane Humphries, "Class Struggle and the Persistence of the Working Class Family," *Cambridge Journal of Economics* 1 (1977): 241–258. For a more critical view, see Wally Seccombe, "Patriarchy Stabilized: The Construction of the Male Breadwinner Wage Norm in Nineteenth-Century Britain," *Social History* 11 (1) (1986).

16. Jason Fields and Lynne M. Casper, "America's Families and Living Arrangements: Population Characteristics 2000," U.S. Census Bureau, Current Population Reports, June 2001. Via www.census.gov, accessed October 2002.

17. See Val Moghadam, "The Fourth World Conference on Women: Dissension and Consensus," *Indian Journal of Gender Studies* 3 (1) (1996): 93–102; Colum Lynch, "Islamic Bloc, Christian Right Team Up to Lobby U.N.," *Washington Post,* June 17, 2002, p. A1; and Jennifer Butler, "Alarmed by Global Progress on Reproductive Rights, the Religious Right Storms the United Nations," *Religious Consultation Report* 6 (1) (2002): 5, 11.

18. This discussion draws on Kandiyoti, "Bargaining with Patriarchy"; Ellen Meiksins Wood, "Capitalism and Human Emancipation," *New Left Review* 167 (January–February 1988): 1–21; Gayle Rubin, "The Traffic in Women: Notes on a Political Economy of Sex," in Rayna Rapp, ed., *Toward an Anthropology of Women* (New York: Monthly Review Press, 1975), pp. 157–210; Raphael Patai, *Women in the Modern World* (New York: Free Press, 1967); Julian Pitt-Rivers, *The Fate of Shechem or the Politics of Sex: Essays in the Anthropology of the Mediterranean* (Cambridge: Cambridge University Press, 1977), esp. chap. 1; Germaine Tillion, *The Republic of Cousins: Women's Oppression in Mediterranean Society* (London: Al-Saqi Books,

1983), esp. chap. 6; and Renée Hirschon, "Introduction: Property, Power and Gender Relations," in Renée Hirschon, ed., *Women and Property: Women as Property* (New York: St. Martin's Press, 1984), pp. 1–22.

19. J. G. Peristiany, "Honour and Shame in a Cypriot Highland Village," in J. G. Peristiany, ed., *Honour and Shame: The Values of Mediterranean Society* (University of Chicago Press, 1966), pp. 171–190; quote appears on p. 182. See also Pierre Bourdieu, "The Sentiment of Honour in Kabyle Society," in Peristiany, *Honour and Shame,* pp. 191–242. Honor killing is the name given to a customary practice whereby women and girls are killed by members of their family on suspicion of having had or having aspired to pre- or extramarital relations—because such sexual transgressions presumably violate the integrity and honor of the family.

20. Frederick Engels, *The Origins of the Family, Private Property, and the State* (New York: Pathfinder Press, 1972; originally published in 1884); Gerda Lerner, *The Creation of Patriarchy* (New York: Oxford University Press, 1986); and Michael Mann, "A Crisis in Stratification Theory?" in Rosemary Crompton and Michael Mann, eds., *Gender and Stratification* (Cambridge, UK: Polity Press, 1986), pp. 40–56.

21. Boswell, *The Kindness of Strangers.* It is worth pointing out that in Boswell's brief chapter on Islam, Muslim practices vis-à-vis children are found to be more humane than Roman-derived early Christian practices.

22. Louise A. Tilly and Joan W. Scott, *Women, Work, and Family* (London: Routledge, 1978).

23. On the connection between modernity and the rise of women's rights and feminist movements, see Kumari Jayawardena, *Feminism and Nationalism in the Third World* (London: Zed Books, 1986); and Janet Saltzman Chafetz and Gary Dworkin, *Female Revolt: Women's Movements in World and Historical Perspective* (Totowa, N.J.: Rowman and Allanheld, 1986).

24. Eleanor Doumato, "Hearing Other Voices: Christian Women and the Coming of Islam," *International Journal of Middle East Studies* 23 (2) (May 1991): 177–199. See also Germaine Tillion, *The Republic of Cousins.*

25. Jamal J. Nasir, *The Status of Women Under Islamic Law* (London: Graham & Trotman, 1990), pp. 122–126.

26. Alya Baffoun, "Women and Social Change in the Muslim Arab World," *Women's Studies International Forum* 5 (2) (1982): 227–242.

27. Mounira Charrad, "State and Gender in the Maghrib," *Middle East Report* 163 (March–April 1990): 19–24; quotes appear on pp. 20–21.

28. Nikki R. Keddie, "The Past and Present of Women in the Muslim World," *Journal of World History* 1 (1) (1990): 77–108; quotes appear on pp. 81–82. In addition to the sources in endnotes 2 and 18 above, see Peter McDonald, "Social Organization and Nuptiality in Developing Societies," in John Cleland and John Hobcraft, eds., *Reproductive Change in Developing Countries: Insights from the World Fertility Survey* (New York: Oxford University Press, 1985), pp. 87–114; Hisham Sharabi, "The Dialectics of Patriarchy in Arab Society," in Samih K. Farsoun, ed., *Arab Society: Continuity and Change* (London: Croom Helm, 1985), pp. 83–104; Claude Lévi-Strauss, *Elementary Structures of Kinship* (Boston: Beacon Press, 1969); and Jack Goody, *The Oriental, the Ancient, and the Primitive: Systems of Marriage and the Family in the Pre-Industrial Societies of Eurasia* (Cambridge: Cambridge University Press, 1990). On family honor and *fitna* in the Middle East, see Fatna A. Sabbah, *Woman in the Muslim Unconscious,* trans. Mary Jo Lakeland (New York: Pergamon Press, 1984); Mai Ghoussoub, "Feminism—or the Eternal Masculine—in the Arab World," *New Left Review* 161 (January–February 1987): 3–13; and Fatima Mernissi,

Beyond the Veil: Male-Female Dynamics in Modern Muslim Society, rev. ed. (Bloomington: Indiana University Press, 1987).

29. Erika Friedl, "The Dynamics of Women's Spheres of Action in Rural Iran," in Keddie and Baron, *Women in Middle Eastern History,* pp. 195–214; quote appears on p. 197. Alean al-Krenawi, "Bedouin-Arab Women in the Negev," mimeo, Center for Bedouin Studies and Development, Ben Gurion University of the Negev, Israel, 1999. See also Alean al-Krenawi and John R. Graham, "The Story of Bedouin-Arab Women in a Polygamous Marriage," *Women's Studies International Forum* 22 (5) (1999): 497–509.

30. David Mandelbaum, *Women's Seclusion and Men's Honor: Sex Roles in North India, Bangladesh, and Pakistan* (Tucson: University of Arizona Press, 1988), p. 19; and Naila Kabeer, "Subordination and Struggle: Women in Bangladesh," *New Left Review* 168 (March–April 1988), p. 95.

31. On South Asia, see especially Papanek, "To Each Less Than She Needs"; Mead Cain, "The Material Consequences of Reproductive Failure in Rural South Asia," in Daisy Dwyer and Judith Bruce, eds., *A Home Divided: Women and Income in the Third World* (Stanford: Stanford University Press, 1988), pp. 20–38; Amartya Sen and Sunil Sengupta, "Malnutrition of Rural Children and the Sex Bias," *Economic and Political Weekly* 18 (1983): 855–863; and Jean Drèze and Amartya Sen, *Hunger and Public Action* (Oxford: Clarendon Press, 1989), esp. chap. 4, "Society, Class, and Gender."

32. Cited in Soheir A. Morsy, "Rural Women, Work, and Gender Ideology: A Study in Egyptian Political Economic Transformation," in Seteney Shami et al., *Women in Arab Society: Work Patterns and Gender Relations in Egypt, Jordan, and Sudan* (Providence: Berg/UNESCO, 1990), p. 138. On Turkey see Deniz Kandiyoti, *Women in Rural Production Systems: Problems and Policies* (Paris: UNESCO, 1985); and Armelle Braun, "Slow Death for Turkish Patriarchalism," *Ceres/The FAO Review no. 117,* 20 (3) (May–June 1987): 37–41.

33. Quoted in Cheryl Rubenberg, *Palestinian Women: Patriarchy and Resistance in the West Bank* (Boulder: Lynne Rienner, 2001), p. 1.

34. Nahla Abdo-Zubi, *Family, Women, and Social Change in the Middle East: The Palestinian Case* (Toronto: Canadian Scholars' Press, 1987), pp. 29–30; and Rubenberg, *Palestinian Women,* p. 13.

35. Caldwell, *Theory of Fertility Decline,* p. 162; and Goody, *The Oriental, the Ancient, and the Primitive,* p. 372. See also Carla Makhlouf Obermeyer, "Islam, Women, and Politics: The Demography of Arab Countries," *Population and Development Review* 18 (1) (March 1992): 33–60.

36. Goody, *The Oriental, the Ancient, and the Primitive.* See also Kandiyoti, "Islam and Patriarchy," p. 14.

37. Goody, *The Oriental, the Ancient, and the Primitive,* pp. 375–376.

38. Morsy, "Rural Women, Work, and Gender Ideology."

39. Ibid., p. 114.

40. Nancy Tapper, "Causes and Consequences of the Abolition of Brideprice in Afghanistan," in Nazif Shahrani and Robert Canfield, eds., *Revolutions and Rebellions in Afghanistan* (Berkeley: University of California International Studies Institute, 1984), pp. 291–305; Goody, *The Oriental, the Ancient, and the Primitive,* p. 378; and Nasir, *The Status of Women Under Islamic Law,* pp. 8–9.

41. Kandiyoti, *Women in Rural Production Systems,* p. 88. See also Nermin Abadan-Unat, "Social Change and Turkish Women," in Nermin Abadan-Unat, ed., *Women in Turkish Society* (Leiden: E. J. Brill, 1981), esp. pp. 20–27; and June Starr,

"The Legal and Social Transformation of Rural Women in Aegean Turkey," in Renée Hirschon, ed., *Women and Property: Women as Property* (New York: St. Martin's Press, 1984), p. 100.

42. V. M. Moghadam, *Women, Work, and Economic Reform in the Middle East and North Africa* (Boulder: Lynne Rienner, 1998); and Kandiyoti, "Bargaining with Patriarchy."

43. John L. Esposito, *Women in Muslim Family Law* (Syracuse, N.Y.: Syracuse University Press, 1982), pp. 11, 15, 23. It should be noted that when Islam spread outward from Arabia, it grafted itself onto existing customs and rules—hence differences in family structure, law, and the mobility of women between Arab countries, Southeast Asia, and sub-Saharan Africa.

44. Annelise Moors, "Debating Islamic Family Law: Legal Texts and Social Practices," in Margaret L. Meriwether and Judith E. Tucker, eds., *A Social History of Women and Gender in the Middle East* (Boulder: Westview Press, 1999), pp. 141–176.

45. Amira Sonbol, "Muslim Women and Legal Reform in Egypt, Jordan, and Palestine," paper presented at the thirty-fifth annual MESA conference, San Francisco, November 18–20, 2001.

46. Nasir, *The Status of Women Under Islamic Law,* pp. 7–8.

47. Ghoussoub, "Feminism"; Marie-Aimée Hélie-Lucas, "Women Facing Muslim Personal Laws as the Preferential Symbol for Islamic Identity," in V. M. Moghadam, ed., *Identity Politics and Women: Cultural Reassertions and Feminisms in International Perspective* (Boulder: Westview Press, 1994), pp. 391–407; and Sana al-Khayyat, *Honour and Shame: Women in Modern Iraq* (London: Saqi Books, 1990).

48. Gregory Massell, *The Surrogate Proletariat* (Princeton: Princeton University Press, 1974). See also Jayawardena, *Feminism and Nationalism in the Third World;* Maxine Molyneux, "Socialist Societies: Progress Toward Women's Emancipation?" *Monthly Review* 34 (3) (July–August 1982): 56–100; Sonia Kruks, Rayna Rapp, and Marilyn Young, eds., *Promissory Notes: Women in the Transition to Socialism* (New York: Monthly Review Press, 1989); and Val Moghadam, "Development and Women's Emancipation: Is There a Connection?" *Development and Change* 23 (3) (July 1992): 215–255.

49. Suad Joseph, "Elite Strategies for State-Building: Women, Family, Religion, and the State in Iraq and Lebanon," in Deniz Kandiyoti, ed., *Women, Islam, and the State* (London: Macmillan, 1991), pp. 176–200.

50. Lamia Shehadeh, "The Legal Status of Married Women in Lebanon," *International Journal of Middle East Studies* 30 (4) (1998): 501–519; and Lynn Welchman, "Capacity, Consent, and Under-Age Marriage in Muslim Family Law," in *The International Survey of Family Law* (Cambridge: Cambridge University Press, 2001).

51. Charrad, "State and Gender in the Maghrib," p. 20. See also Mounira Charrad, *States and Women's Rights: The Making of Postcolonial Tunisia, Algeria, and Morocco* (Berkeley: University of California Press, 2001).

52. Sharabi, *Neopatriarchy,* p. 145.

53. Cain, "The Material Consequences of Reproductive Failure."

54. See Bina Agarwal, ed., *Structures of Patriarchy* (London: Zed Books, 1988); and Val Moghadam, "Patriarchy and the Politics of Gender in Modernizing Societies: Afghanistan, Iran, Pakistan," *International Sociology* 7 (1) (March 1992): 35–53.

55. Dilek Cindoglu, "Virginity Tests and Artificial Virginity in Modern Turkish Medicine," *Women's Studies International Forum* 20 (2) (1997): 253–261; and Meltem Muftuler-Bac, "Turkish Women's Predicament," *Women's Studies International Forum* 22 (3) (1999): 303–315.

56. Karl Marx, *The Eighteenth Brumaire of Louis Bonaparte* (Peking: Foreign Language Press, 1978).

57. Levine, "Punctuated Equilibrium," p. 4. See also C. C. Harris, *The Family and Industrial Society* (London: George Allen & Unwin, 1983), esp. chap. 7.

58. Tilly and Scott, *Women, Work, and Family,* pp. 89–90; and Caldwell, *Theory of Fertility Decline,* pp. 176, 221.

59. Tilly and Scott, *Women, Work, and Family,* pp. 91–93. Obviously age at marriage in rural England and France prior to the demographic transition was higher than it has been in rural third world countries.

60. Rodolfo A. Bulatao, introduction to Rodolfo A. Bulatao and John B. Casterline, eds., *Global Fertility Transition* (New York: Population Council, 2001), pp. 2–3.

61. John Caldwell, "The Globalization of Fertility Behavior," in ibid., pp. 93–115.

62. Karen Oppenheim Mason, "Gender and Family Systems in the Fertility Transition," in Bulatao and Casterline, *Global Fertility Transition,* pp. 160–176.

63. Susan Greenhalgh, "Toward a Political Economy of Fertility: Anthropological Contributions," *Population and Development Review* 16 (1) (March 1990): 85–106. The cost-of-children approach is offered by Kingsley Davis, "The World Demographic Transition," *Annals of the American Academy of Political and Social Science* 237 (1955): 1–11. See also John C. Caldwell and Lado Ruzicka, "Demographic Levels and Trends," in John Cleland and Chris Scott, eds., *The World Fertility Survey: An Assessment* (New York: International Statistical Institute, Oxford University Press, 1987), pp. 742–772. The status-of-women approach may be found in Cain, "The Material Consequences of Reproductive Failure." See also Tim Dyson and Mick Moore, "On Kinship Structure, Female Anatomy, and Demographic Behavior," *Population and Development Review* 9 (1) (1983): 35–60.

64. *World Fertility Survey: Major Findings and Implications* (Voorburg, Netherlands: International Statistical Institute, 1984), p. 49. See also Caldwell, *Theory of Fertility Decline,* p. 158.

65. Galal el Din (1977), cited in Caldwell, *Theory of Fertility Decline,* p. 364.

66. Farzaneh Roudy, "Population Trends and Challenges in the Middle East and North Africa," Population Reference Bureau policy brief, October 2001.

67. *World Fertility Survey,* p. 13; Caldwell and Ruzicka, "Demographic Levels and Trends," p. 749; and McDonald, "Social Organization and Nuptiality in Developing Societies," p. 110.

68. *World Fertility Survey,* p. 17; *The Syrian Fertility Survey* (Voorburg, Netherlands: International Statistical Institute, 1984), pp. 5, 9, 12; *The Turkish Fertility Survey* (Voorburg, Netherlands: International Statistical Institute, 1984), p. 7.

69. The Demographic and Health Surveys were carried out by Macro International, Inc., with funding from the U.S. Agency for International Development. Final reports and other publications for the countries surveyed may be found on the DHS website at www.measuredhs.com.

70. Mernissi, *Beyond the Veil,* p. xxv.

71. Caldwell, *Theory of Fertility Decline,* p. 219.

72. Ibid., p. 322.

73. Mernissi, *Beyond the Veil,* pp. xxiii–xxiv.

74. Hind A. Khattab and Syeda Greiss el-Daeiff, "Female Education in Egypt: Changing Attitudes Over a Span of 100 Years," in Freda Hussein, ed., *Muslim Women* (London: Croom Helm, 1984), pp. 169–197. The authors of the study found, however, that their respondents still distinguished between "suitable" and "unsuitable" jobs for

women. Appropriate careers were teaching, social work, and, in medicine, pediatrics and gynecology (p. 183).

75. See, for example, Jennifer Olmsted, "Women 'Manufacture' Economic Spaces in Bethlehem," *World Development* 24 (12) (1996): 1829–1840.

76. United Nations, *The World's Women 2000: Trends and Statistics* (New York: United Nations, 2000).

77. Mernissi, *Beyond the Veil,* p. xxiv.

78. Mona Khalaf, "Employment, Breadwinning, and Women's Status: The Case of Lebanon," paper presented at the Conference on Women and Gender in the Middle East: A Multidisciplinary Assessment of the State of Theory and Research, Bellagio, Italy, August 27–31, 2001, p. 12.

79. See CAWTAR, *Globalization and Gender: Economic Participation of Arab Women* (Tunis: CAWTAR and UNDP, 2001), tab. A/34, p. 231.

80. Chafetz and Dworkin, *Female Revolt.*

81. Mernissi, *Beyond the Veil,* p. xxvii.

82. Saad Eddin Ibrahim, "Anatomy of Egypt's Militant Islamic Groups," *International Journal of Middle East Studies* 12 (4) (1980): 423–453.

83. Tahire Erman, "The Impact of Migration on Turkish Rural Women: Four Emergent Patterns," *Gender and Society* 12 (2) (April 1998): 146–167; quote appears on p. 152.

84. Mansoor Moaddel et al., "Religion, Gender, and Politics in Egypt, Jordan, and Iran: Findings of Comparative National Surveys," report to the NSF (June 2002), kindly made available to me by Moaddel, August 2002.

85. Mann, "A Crisis in Stratification Theory?" p. 52.

86. Kingsley Davis and P. van Den Oever, cited in Levine, "Punctuated Equilibrium," p. 7.

5

Islamist Movements and Women's Responses

How can God's victory prevail when women adorn themselves openly and mix with men, and when defiance of God's law continues day and night?
—Al-Ribat, *Islamist newspaper in Jordan, 1991*

If fundamentalists are calling for the return to the veil, it must be because women have been taking off the veil.
—Fatima Mernissi

The nebulous transnational network Al-Qaida, the Palestinian suicide bomber, the strangely medieval Taliban of Afghanistan—since the late 1990s, these have been the symbols of political Islam in the Western imagination. But what is the larger context in which they arose? Social changes and international relations alike have given rise to an ideological movement of a specific type—known as Islamic fundamentalism, political Islam, or Islamism—advocating reconstruction of the moral order that has been disrupted or changed. Islamist movements have arisen in the context of socioeconomic crisis, a crisis of legitimacy of the state and political order, and the weakening of the patriarchal family structure. In this context, gender has become increasingly problematized and politicized. Community morality and the status of women are central concerns of Islamist movements. Gender identity is linked to group identity—the group here being the radicalized Muslim community, which has a twofold raison d'être. First, it has been under attack by internal and external enemies and must reassert itself. Second, it sees itself as the solution to the country's cultural, political, and economic malaise and to the crisis of national identity. Islamization measures include the banning of alcohol; the imposition of veiling; and the restoration or strengthening of Shari'a law. Islamists are especially critical of Western influences on gender relations. Thus Islamism and feminism have become implacable foes. At the same time, Islamist movements have their own women supporters. A women's movement certainly exists in the Muslim world, with roots in the late nineteenth century, but it is clearly bifurcated along class and ideological lines. This chapter will examine the causes of Islamist movements, their complex gender implications, and women's varied responses to them.

Causes and Social Bases of Islamist Movements

As we have seen in Chapter 3, feminist scholarship has shown that during periods of rapid social change, gender assumes a paramount position in discourses and political programs. Historical studies, too, have found that at times of abrupt change, many people have adhered to religious interpretations that can be regarded as fundamentalist in the sense of emphasizing what are held to be basic religious values, with their accompanying cultural practices often anchored in the past.[1] This type of fundamentalism often focuses on what is perceived to be a better or more moral past as an alternative to new values and ideas that are perceived to be threatening. This perception has often implied a return to traditional social roles. As women are seen as the main transmitters of societal values, the changing role of women is associated with changes in values and behaviors that are felt to be at odds with religious or moral beliefs. As a result, efforts are made to try to reimpose traditional behaviors for women as a remedy for crisis and destabilization.[2]

In summary form, anomie, cultural introspection, identity creation, and Islamist movements in the Middle East have emerged in the wake of three processes: (1) social and economic crisis, including the uneven distribution of socioeconomic advantage within societies and the economic downturn since the late 1980s; (2) a crisis of political legitimacy, with a decline in popular support for existing state systems, widely viewed as authoritarian, corrupt, or ineffectual; and (3) changes in the patriarchal system, with the growing visibility and public participation of women. Below I present a set of propositions regarding the causes and characteristics of Islamist movements.

• Islamist movements emerged in the context of an economic crisis in the Middle East and North Africa, which affected oil economies and non-oil economies alike. Modernization had been very lopsided because it was the result of a single, highly prized commodity.[3] Rising indebtedness, unemployment, and problems arising from austerity measures and economic restructuring in the 1980s added to tensions in the region. These were linked to global restructuring and recession, or what world-systems theorists refer to as the B-phase downturn of the Kondratieff wave; the falling price of oil on the world market had an adverse effect on development and on living standards in the region.

• Islamist movements also arose in the context of the demographic transition, which has been occurring more rapidly in MENA than it occurred in Europe, as we saw in Chapter 4. The result has been accelerated population growth. Also in contrast to Western European countries, in the developing countries the onset of rapid population increase occurred before the start of modern economic development, compounding the burden of a larger and more youthful—and thus more dependent—population.[4] In Algeria in the 1990s, three-quarters of the population was under the age of thirty. In a context of chronic unemployment and economic crisis, this large youthful population found itself without secure prospects, and became willing recruits to Islamism.

• Politically, the region is characterized by neopatriarchal state systems that have silenced left-wing and liberal forces while fostering religious institutions in their search for legitimacy. The growth of left-wing movements in the late 1960s and 1970s led many Middle Eastern regimes to encourage the Islamic tide in hopes of neutralizing the left. This was the basic strategy of President Anwar Sadat, who released the Muslim Brothers from prison in an attempt to counter the Egyptian left in his campaign of de-Nasserization. Iran's Shah Mohammad Reza Pahlavi followed the same strategy in the early 1970s, as did Turkish authorities after the 1980 military coup. Indeed, in the latter case, as the generals' overriding objective was to rid Turkish society of Marxist ideology and parties, they encouraged Islamic ideas and education as an antidote. Thus in 1982 the military regime made the teaching of Islam compulsory in schools; since 1967 it had been optional.[5]

• In the Middle East and North Africa, as in many developing areas, capitalist and precapitalist modes of production coexisted, with corresponding social and ideological forms as well as types of consciousness. There was an uneasy coexistence of modern and traditional social classes, such as the Westernized upper middle class on the one hand and the traditional petty bourgeoisie organized around the bazaar and the mosque on the other. The urban centers all have large numbers of people outside the formal wage market and among the ranks of the urban poor and uneducated.

• Female education and employment, while still limited, had been increasing, thanks to economic development and the expanding state apparatus. This trend challenged and slowly weakened the system of patriarchal gender relations, creating status inconsistency and anxiety on the part of the men of the petty bourgeoisie. Changes in gender relations, the structure of the family, and the position of women resulted in contestation between modern and traditional social groups over the nature and direction of cultural institutions and legal frameworks. A kind of gender conflict emerged, although this conflict has class dimensions as well.

• The experience with European colonialism left deep and abiding tensions and grievances. The nonresolution of the Israeli-Palestinian problem and a pervasive sense of injustice caused by Israeli and U.S. actions have continued to engender Islamist movements. The failure of the secular-democratic project of the PLO has encouraged the Islamist alternative among Palestinians and throughout the region.

• In the absence of fully developed and articulated movements, institutions, and discourses of liberalism or socialism, Islam became the discursive universe, and Islamist movements spread the message that "Islam is the solution." For some Muslims, the new Islamic ideology reduces anxiety because it is able to offer a new form of assurance, and the movement provides new forms of collective solidarity and support.

• In the context of economic, political, and ideological crisis, and in the absence of fully developed, socially rooted, and credible secular alternatives, the vacuum was filled by Islamist-populist leaders and discourses. Most of the Islamist movements that appeared in the 1980s and 1990s could be called populist by virtue of their social base (multiclass but mainly petty bourgeois) and their discourses (articulation of "the people," exhortations against foreigners, and vague notions of social justice). Islamist movements are political projects and are concerned with power.

• In the new ideological formation, tradition was exalted—and frequently invented. Although there are traditional forms of veiling throughout the region, the typical Islamist hijab is a novel contemporary ensemble, deployed as a uniform. A recurrent theme was that Islamic identity was in danger; Muslims had to return to a fixed tradition; identity was incumbent upon women's behavior, dress, appearance; and Muslim personal laws were necessary at the level of the state (in the case of majority Muslim societies) or in the community (in the case of minority Muslim groups, as in India).

• Historically, the Middle East has not experienced a complete bourgeois revolution or an Enlightenment; neither has Islam completed a process similar to the Christian Reformation. Modernizing and reformist movements have been part of Islamic/Middle Eastern history, but they have not succeeded in the way such movements did in Christian/European history.[6] Some scholars, however, have suggested parallels between Protestantism/Calvinism in the fifteenth century and Islamic revivalism in the twentieth century.[7] Islamist movements are a product of the contradictions of transition and modernization; they also result from the north-south contention. What is unclear is whether they impede or accelerate the transition to modernity.

• Thus, culture, religion, and identity act both as defense mechanisms and as means by which the new order is to be shaped. These movements must therefore be seen as both reactive and proactive.

The record since the late 1970s shows that Islamic fundamentalism has been neither a purely religious or expressive phenomenon nor a purely economic and political phenomenon, but rather a complex combination with different movements emphasizing different issues or objectives. Some movements seek to acquire political power (oppositional Islamist movements) while others are fostered by neopatriarchal states seeking to maintain or legitimate political power (state-sponsored fundamentalism). Examples of the first type are the Iranian Islamist movement of the late 1970s, which succeeded in assuming state power in 1979; the U.S.-supported Afghan Mujahidin who ruled (badly) between 1992 and 1996; and the Algerian Front Islamique du Salut (FIS; Islamic Salvation Front), which turned to armed violence in 1992 when its attempt to assume political power was thwarted. Examples of the second type are state-sponsored Islamism under President Zia ul-Haq of Pakistan and General Ershad of Bangladesh. Somewhere in between are neopatriarchal states that manipulate religious or cultural sentiments in order to reinforce their power. For example, during the 1980s war with Iran and since the Gulf wars of the 1990s, President Saddam Hussein of Iraq has sought to put himself in the role of defender of Islam. Islamist movements are also distinguished by their means and methods. Some use extreme forms of violence to attain power or exert authority (e.g., the Afghan Mujahidin and Taliban, the FIS and the Group Islamique Armée in Algeria; Islamists in Egypt who attacked foreign tourists and Copts and assassinated the intellectual Fouad Farag).[8] Others—such as Egypt's Muslim Brothers—have extended their influence through grassroots recruitment or involvement in social and political institutions such as professional associations, unions, and the media. Islamists in Israel gained control over Islamic institutions such as charitable endowments and Shari'a courts, and they battled for control of Nazareth, a city that had long been governed by a secular and left-wing municipal authority and had once had a large Christian population.[9]

Although factors internal to the Middle East and to Islam are key to any analysis or explanation of Islamist movements, mention should be made of another factor in the growth of these movements in MENA and elsewhere. Saudi Arabia, and to a lesser extent Kuwait, have been major funders of Islamist movements not only in the Middle East and Afghanistan but also in Africa and South and Southeast Asia. Moreover, Israel initially encouraged the Hamas as a way of undermining the PLO's exclusive authority among Palestinians. And the United States armed and funded the Afghan Mujahidin in their joint crusade/jihad against communism during the 1980s. Various authors have commented on the circulation of funds linked to Muslim private capital, the involvement of states in fostering fundamentalist movements, and fundamentalist groups operating locally, nationally, and regionally.[10] John Cooley writes about "the course and consequences of a strange love affair which went disastrously wrong: the alliance, during the second half of the twentieth century, between the United States of America and some of the most conservative and fanatical followers of Islam."[11] This is not to say that the Islamist movements would not otherwise emerge, but to highlight the interconnectedness of internal and external factors and to suggest the salience of international relations, in particular self-interested state actions and wrongheaded foreign policy objectives.

As is to be expected of movements fueled by socioeconomic disadvantages and grievances, support for Islamist movements has been found among the urban poor. The involvement of recently urbanized people in Islamist movements was clear in the cases of Lebanon, Iran, Egypt, Algeria, and Tunisia. In Lebanon, the impoverishment of rural areas and the gradual abandonment of agriculture following the outbreak of civil war sparked a rural exodus to Beirut. There, Imam Musa Sadr became the spokesman of Shi'a discontent, and the poor Shi'a community, *mahrumin,* embraced Khomeini-style fundamentalism. In Iran, Khomeini had considerable support among the urban poor, whom he referred to as the *mostazafin*—the oppressed or the wretched.[12] The impoverished Gaza Strip, under Israeli military occupation, produced the first Palestinian Islamist movement—and a challenge to the PLO. In Algeria the locus of rebellion and violence in 1991–1992 was the *bidonvilles* of Bab-el-Oued—the shantytowns of Algiers, as reported at the time in the Algerian newspaper *El Moudjahid.* Support for Islamist movements was also found among the traditional petty bourgeoisie, artisans, shopkeepers, and bazaaris. In Iran, for example, bazaaris and clerics have had long-standing cultural and political ties. Indeed, the bazaar-mosque alliance was crucial to the success of the revolution against the Shah.

One of the striking features of Islamist movements has been the extent to which young and educated people are attracted to them. Indeed, the intellectual leaders of most Islamist movements are trained in the sciences, engineering, and medicine. University and high school students have challenged their parents to follow a more "genuinely" Islamic order, and have gone on to constitute a cadre of Islamist young professionals. There is some evidence that this educated middle class—whose support for Islamist movements was the big surprise of the 1980s—is a first-generation urban and educated stratum. Saad Eddin Ibrahim's in-depth study of the family background and social mobility of thirty-four Egyptian Islamic militants showed that nearly all came out of the middle class or lower middle class, were from rural areas or provincial towns, and were products of the country's university or secondary school system. In Sudan the newly educated urban middle class called for cultural nationalism and formed the recruiting base for the National Islamic Front and the Muslim Brotherhood.[13] Educated people from the upper middle class, bourgeoisie, and landed gentry generally do not join Islamist movements, tending to be found instead in liberal or left-wing parties or associations. In his study of Morocco's political culture, John Entelis showed that the relatively small progressive political subculture of both liberals and leftists was composed almost exclusively of members of the elite.[14]

At first glance, these class-based political affiliations appear the same as those of Germany in the 1930s. Many writers have suggested that Hitler's backers were mainly from the lower middle class, experiencing marginality, status anxiety, and downward mobility. In this analysis, the Nazis were the

prime beneficiaries of all the evils associated with a modern society: uprootedness, excessive competition, rapid urbanization, breakdown of traditions,
erosion of *Gemeinschaft*. All of these led to alienation, frustration, anxiety,
and anomie, which ultimately could be resolved by casting a vote for the
antimodern Nazis, led by a charismatic figure who promised to restore the
bliss of a bygone era. However, Marxist theorists such as R. Palme Dutt
argued that the crucial support for the Nazis came from the German bourgeoisie and that fascism was a bourgeois solution to the capitalist crisis and
the labor-capital contention. An empirical study of German voting patterns
corroborated this view; Richard Hamilton has shown that there was a disproportionately favorable response to the Nazis among Germany's upper and
upper-middle classes.[15] Thus one must be careful not to stretch the analogy
between Islamism and fascism. Their respective social bases have some similarities but also are different.

Islamist movements may appear to be archaic, but in fact they combine
modern and premodern discourses, means of communication, and even political institutions. Robert Wuthnow notes that the institutionalization of ideological movements involves securing a stable and consistent flow of
resources, especially organizational (leadership, communication, administration, and structural autonomy), financial, and symbolic resources (including
legitimation).[16] The classic example was the Iranian Revolution, where cas-
sette tapes of Khomeini's speeches were smuggled throughout Iran and the
bazaar-mosque network was a crucial focal point for organizing and mobilizing against the Shah. In Algeria the FIS used electoral means to try to attain
power. In the 1990s, Islamist parties in Egypt, Jordan, Morocco, and Turkey
sought a more conciliatory stance, leading to a kind of parliamentary accom-
modationism in these countries. In all cases, Islamists use modern means,
including elections and the media, for their purposes. The phenomenon of
Islamic revival is thus both proactive and reactive. It is reactive in the sense
that it seeks to maintain the authenticity of Islamic institutions and traditions
and rejects what is borrowed and external. Islamic fundamentalists, like their
Christian counterparts in the West, insist on a conservative, literal interpretation of the scriptures and do not admit the wider spectrum of theological interpretation that has characterized the development of Islam. But Islamic revival
is also proactive in the sense that many Islamic reformers seek to be modernists, to borrow from the West selectively and enter the advanced technological age with its benefits but with their religion intact. Such contradictory
impulses are similarly found in the movements' approaches to gender and
women's status.

An example of an Islamist movement with a modern approach is that of
Turkey. As described by Binnaz Toprak, the Turkish movement represented a
response of the marginalized sectors of society to rapid industrial growth and
the concomitant structural and cultural transformation. This marginality, in

the Turkish context, was social as well as economic. High-status groups of Turkish republican society consistently excluded Islamic traditionalists from their ranks. In the 1980s, Islamic traditionalists began to bid for social status, intellectual respectability, and political power. They largely succeeded in entrenching themselves within the state and party bureaucracies, in commercial and industrial firms, and in intellectual circles. In short, they became a counter-elite. The women within the ranks of the Islamist movement have been part of the marginals' larger search for respectability and a redefinition of status. The so-called turban and the long coat—the novel Turkish hijab—are cultural markers and uniforms that serve the same function that blue jeans served in Western leftist and countercultural movements. The Islamist search for status entailed possibilities for upward social mobility, which some within the movement ultimately achieved. Toprak concludes that Islamist identity politics are at the same time network politics. They build a web of intragroup relations that become instrumental in terms of acquiring political power, economic wealth, intellectual prominence, and social respectability in Turkey.[17] It should be noted that in Turkey, unlike Algeria, the military's decision to dissolve a coalition government and the Islamist party that was part of it did not lead to violence and terrorism. The Turkish Welfare Party (Refah) regrouped itself as the Virtue Party, one of whose spokespersons, member of parliament Merve Kavakci (who insisted on her right to wear the headscarf during parliamentary sessions), once asserted, "We do not want another Iran" and "in our opinion, secularism and freedom of religion go hand in hand." In 2002 the Turkish Islamic party Justice and Development (AK) joined other political parties in promoting human rights and entry into the European Union.[18]

Clearly, Islamist movements differ across countries and sometimes even within a country. It is also clear that the causes of Islamist movements are complex—political, economic, demographic, and cultural, with social and class conflict an essential feature—and that their goals are not only cultural but also political. That is to say, juridical changes, upward social mobility, political influence, and the acquisition of state power are among the objectives of many Islamist groups.

Gharbzadegi: Problematics of Class and Gender

Islamist movements frequently claim that Westernization has deculturated Muslims and that the return to Islam—to the Shari'a, to Muslim family law, to the hijab—will defeat the crisis and strengthen cultural identity and integrity. It is useful to examine this discourse, and to deconstruct it for its gender and class elements. The Iranian concept of *gharbzadegi*—so prevalent in the 1970s and 1980s—provides rich material for such an investigation. Variously translated as "Westoxication," "Westitis," "Euromania," and "Occidentosis," *gharbzadegi* denotes an illness, a virus, a "plague from the West," a phenomenon of excessive Westernization that renders members of the community (usually those with a Western education) alienated from their own culture. Through those members who are struck by the West, imperialism can penetrate the society and wreak havoc on the culture. It is believed that those members of the community most vulnerable to *gharbzadegi* are women. The claim is made that by depriving women of chastity, modesty, and honor through notions of autonomy, sex appeal, and so on, colonialists and imperialists have been able to weaken cultures. This is said to have happened in Algeria under French colonialism and in Iran during the rule of the pro-U.S. Shah. It follows that the main antidote to the virus of *gharbzadegi* is hijab. Furthermore, veiling must be compulsory in order to protect the cultural identity and integrity of the group and of its female members.[19]

In Iran, this antidote was not delivered to working-class women, peasant women, or the women of the urban poor. For the Islamists, the main targets were upper-middle-class educated women, principally those who had had a Western-style education, whether in high schools or in university. The stereotypical Westoxicated woman was a middle-class individual with no productive contributions or reproductive responsibilities. If she worked at all, she was a secretary, and her work was largely decorative and dispensable. Her access to money was considered a waste, because it was used to cover the cost of her own clothing, cosmetics, and imported consumer goods. She was preoccupied with her physical appearance and wore miniskirts and excessive makeup. She would mingle freely with men, smoke, drink, and laugh in public. If she read at all, she read a romantic novel; she picked her role models from among Hollywood stars, American soap operas, and pop singers. Her lightheadedness and lack of interest in politics and national issues made her easy prey for commercialization and contamination by the West.[20] The term *gharbzadeh* was also used loosely to refer to any "Westernized" woman who appeared to have shed the symbols of tradition and "authenticity," such as religiosity or veiling. It should be noted that many Iranian "Westernized" women became politically active, and they could be seen in the ranks of the Iranian student movement in Europe and North America. But as far as Islamists were concerned, these women had cast off their authentic cultural identity and assumed that of a Westerner, complete with ideas about liberalism, socialism, Marxism, feminism, and sexual equality.

These ideas and practices were anathema to the Islamist paradigm, and women were the persons who quite literally embodied them. Such women were derided as *gharbzadeh*—decadent, bourgeois traitors who were "struck by the West." Thus, when Ayatollah Khomeini and his associates assumed control of the state following violent battles with liberals, the left-Islamic group the Mujahidin, and socialists, the victorious traditional petty bourgeoisie enacted repressive legislation that was both an attack on women (gender conflict) and an attack on the upper middle class (class conflict). Compulsory veiling was a kind of punishment, a form of discipline. The losers were the women of the upper middle class. By contrast, the women of the lower middle class, those from traditional and religious families, found validation in the new system, as well as new educational and employment opportunities.[21]

The veil, in its various permutations, has become the distinguishing mark of the Islamist woman but also of nonpoliticized Muslim women throughout the world. It is the line of demarcation between the Islamist/Islamic community and other communities, a shield against the slings and arrows of imperialists and against the male gaze. But compulsory veiling in countries like Iran, Saudi Arabia, and Afghanistan under the Mujahidin and Taliban also has been a mechanism of social control: the regulation of women. Moreover, it symbolizes the lack of choice in the selection of identity. Identity and "morality," in the form of hijab, are imposed. In Iran, even non-Muslim citizens—Christians, Jews, and Zoroastrians—have had to veil.

A similar construct of the Westernized Algerian woman was described by Cherifa Bouatta and Doria Cherifati-Merabtine, who studied the discourse on women in the FIS magazine *El Mounquid.* Bouatta and Cherifati-Merabtine analyzed forty-two articles and letters in the magazine to discern images of womanhood and of Islamist women's self-representation. A critical theme running through the texts was that there was no need to address the woman question in terms of new rights because Islam established these rights fourteen centuries ago. Moreover, to raise the issue of women's rights is to imitate the West; another line of argument was that feminism is a Marxist or Jewish plot. In the fundamentalist discourse of the FIS, it was claimed that women have rights equal to those of men—the right to education and to religious instruction; the right to respect; the right to vote; the right to employment; the right to struggle. There were also prohibitions, however. A woman cannot be a political ruler, nor can she be a judge. Women should refuse mixed gatherings, should always appear in hijab, should not use cosmetics or perfume or clothes that reveal the female form. The maternal function is exalted, and salaried work is deemed inappropriate. In the Islamist discourse of *El Mounquid,* these rights, obligations, and proscriptions are based on divine precepts and biological and psychological differences between the sexes.[22]

Bouatta and Cherifati-Merabtine also found two antimodels of the non-Islamist woman in the pages of *El Mounquid.* First, the Western woman: she is depicted as a mere sexual object, a commodity, an exhibitionist, subjugated to male desires, sexually and socially exploited. The second representation was that of the Westernized Algerian woman. She is both a traitor and deformed: neither a Muslim woman nor a Western woman, she is a caricature, an alien by way of dress, language, outlook. And what do these women want? They want to subvert women's natural and sacred tasks; to dominate men; to marry when they want and divorce when they want; to go out and return as they wish; to travel without a chaperon or guardian; to reject male authority; to demand the abrogation of the family law, the sole juridical text based on the Shari'a; to create *fitna* (conflict) between men and women. The rights these women want are described by the writers in *El Mounquid* as unacceptable, inconceivable, and illusory.

Bouatta and Cherifati-Merabtine argued that the feminine model projected by the Algerian *intégristes* diverged from that of the state because the official state discourse combined notions of tradition and modernity, whereas the discourse of the FIS, in its construction of a new tradition, eliminated and refused modernity in any form. The authors argued that the FIS adopted a homogeneous discourse and presented ideal types of women to the detriment of real, actually existing women.

States and Islamist Movements

States have dealt with the Islamist threat in various ways, sometimes by accommodating fundamentalist demands and sometimes by confronting the organizations head-on. Early on, the Tunisian government confronted the An-Nahda movement and banned it; the Syrian government put down its growing Islamist movement rather violently though effectively. Accommodation was initially the response of the governments of Egypt and Algeria, who conceded women's rights to the Islamist movements as a way of placating them. This concession took the form of reinforcing the patriarchal principles of Muslim family law. Only when the Islamists took up arms against the governments, sought to overthrow them, or used violence and terror in a way that threatened the power and authority of the state, did the Egyptian and Algerian states turn on the Islamist movements, their leaders, and their members. Nonetheless, several decades of "quiet encroachment" on the part of Egyptian Islamists have given them pervasive influence in social institutions such as education, religion, media, and the judiciary, and in such professions as law, medicine, and engineering. In Morocco, a (nonviolent) conflict emerged between the social-democratic Youssefi government and feminists on one side and Moroccan fundamentalists on the other. The point of contention was a proposed national development plan for the advancement of women, which was bitterly opposed by Islamic fundamentalists. The Moroccan government sought support for the plan through "national dialogue," but continued Islamist opposition led the government to postpone implementation of the plan in 2002.

Similarities and differences in state approaches to Islamism are illustrated by Alya Baffoun's comparative study of Tunisia and Algeria. In both countries, she argued, the causes and roots of fundamentalism were (1) a state system based on single-party rule and external dependence, (2) the cultural dual-ity of the (petty bourgeois) elite, which drew from both modern and traditional culture to legitimate its authority, and (3) failures of political development and economic modernization, and the economic crisis encompassing the region. Tunisia (along with Morocco) had suffered economic losses, especially in export revenue, when Spain and Portugal joined the European Community in 1986. In Tunisia in November 1987, after a summer of mounting tension during which hundreds of supporters of the Mouvement de la Tendance Islamique were arrested and two were executed on terrorism charges, Zine el Abiddine Ben Ali replaced Habib Bourguiba as head of state. In Algeria in 1990, 70 percent of the country's export earnings went to service the country's crushing debt, compared with 30 percent in 1986. Official statistics acknowledged a 22 percent unemployment rate. As a result of Algeria's galloping birthrate, nearly three-quarters of its population was under thirty.[23]

The differences in each state's initial approach are instructive. In Tunisia, the state was fiercely opposed to *intégrisme* and denied it any legitimacy or legality. Within civil society, too, many groups and associations—particularly the women's organizations—took strong positions against the Islamists and sided with the government. The National Union of Tunisian Women, for example, issued "an appeal to all citizens, and foremost to Tunisian women, to show vigilance especially at this time . . . and to mobilize themselves even more around our President."[24] Other Tunisian women's organizations that gained legality in 1989 joined a new consensus opposing Islamism with the slogan "No democracy for the enemies of democracy."[25] The Tunisian state had long been secular and associated with women's rights, and when the Iranian Revolution took place and Ayatollah Khomeini took power in 1979, support among Tunisians was at best tepid.[26] Thus an environment existed that was conducive to the prohibition of *intégrisme* in Tunisia. In Algeria, on the other hand, the rise of Islamism had its origins in a state system whose ideology included Islamic precepts, whose legal system adopted Islamic family law, and whose economy had suffered from chronically high rates of unemployment. Moreover, the Algerian state, ruling party, and media were enthusiasts of the Iranian Revolution and of Ayatollah Khomeini.

Personal Status Laws and the Control of Women

Since the 1980s, Muslim family law, or personal status *(ahwal shakhsiya)* codes, have been at the center of Muslim identities, Islamist demands, and feminist claims. These family laws are derived from the Shari'a and govern marriage, divorce, maintenance, child custody, inheritance, and *iddat* (a period of abstinence during which the wife remains unmarried after the dissolution of marriage by divorce or death, usually to determine pregnancy and paternity). Personal status laws vary from country to country; many do not, for example, allow divorce of a wife by simple repudiation.[27] Still, the restoration or strengthening of personal laws in Iran and Algeria in the 1980s was interpreted by feminists as an expression of the fundamentalists' power and the collusion of neopatriarchal states with Islamist movements. As the Egyptian feminist and writer Nawal el-Saadawi noted, Shari'a-derived personal status laws contravene the spirit and letter of the United Nations Convention on the Elimination of All Forms of Discrimination Against Women. Islamic feminists argue that they are based on patriarchal interpretations of Islam and contravene the spirit if not the letter of the Quran and the intentions of the Prophet Muhammad.[28]

Though regimes may resist the Islamist agenda on other points, family affairs and women's subordination are generally recognized as the reflection of Islamist movements' definition of identity, and laws have been passed or modified in order to meet their demands. In Egypt a 1979 presidential decree liberalizing the personal status laws came to be known as "Jehan's law" for its prime proponent, the wife of President Anwar Sadat. So overwhelming was conservative male reaction that in 1985 the state rescinded the law, only to restore it in diminished form. Still, Egyptian women lost the right to remain in the marital home after a divorce, a right they had previously won following a decade-long battle. Algeria's first family code, passed in 1984, twenty-two years after independence, restored certain patriarchal norms. It stipulated that Algerian women be given in marriage by a *wali* (a matrimonial tutor) and deprived a woman of the right to divorce except in specific cases, restoring divorce as a male prerogative. Men were permitted polygamy and the right to repudiate their wives. With respect to child custody, the children of divorced parents could stay with the mother until the age of six for boys and ten for girls, provided the ex-husband was satisfied with her method of child-rearing; otherwise he could claim them, as the father was made the official guardian. Mothers could not remarry without losing their children; they had to live close enough to their ex-husbands to enable them to exercise their right to control the children's education. Women were to be given just half of a man's share of inheritance.

These developments alarmed many Muslim women. One result was the formation of an international solidarity network called Women Living Under Muslim Laws. In July 1984 the members of the first action committee of this network defined themselves as "women whose lives are shaped, conditioned and governed by laws, both written and unwritten, drawn from interpretations of the Koran tied up with local traditions." The action committee's position was that "men and the State use these laws against women, and have done so under various political regimes." This network continues to monitor laws affecting the status of women in Muslim countries and communities around the world and publicizes gender-related acts of violence or oppression.

Areas outside the Middle East similarly have seen the politicization of gender and the restoration of patriarchal family codes, often in the context of growing fundamentalist and communalist agitation. In 1985 the government of India acquiesced to fundamentalist demands in the famous Shah Bano case and exempted Muslims from maintenance following divorce. In 1986 Sri Lanka appointed a commission to reform Muslim personal law in a way that feminists found to be unfavorable to women. In 1987 and 1989 the socialist and secular government of Mauritius accepted the project pushed forward by the Muslim main opposition party to reintroduce Shari'a law for the Muslim community. Shari'a law was adopted in provinces in Nigeria and Malaysia, and made law of the land in Sudan, Pakistan, and Bangladesh. In countries of emigration, such as Britain, France, and the Caribbean, Muslims have demanded that personal laws be introduced. Islamic organizations in Europe asserted a "human right" to communal authority to apply Shari'a law to their family and personal matters. In France, migrants from Muslim communities even demanded constitutional change from secularism to a multireligious state in order to allow for veiling in schools and the right to polygamy, among other demands.

These and similar developments have led Women Living Under Muslim Laws to stress the international dimension of Islamism. Marie-Aimée Hélie-Lucas has noted that after the Shah Bano case in India, the Sri Lankan government invited an Indian scholar to serve as adviser to its Commission to Reform Muslim Law.[29] In Mauritius the main opposition party, the Muslim Party, proposed the Indian Muslim personal law as a model for the Mauritius Muslim personal law and brought in an Indian adviser. Elsewhere, Saudi, Pakistani, or Iranian advisers have been invited. The implementation and expansion of Muslim personal laws is an integral part of the Islamist agenda, and groups, governments, and communities have advised each other on the matter.

Although Islamist movements share an interest in the restoration or enforcement of Muslim personal law, they differ in other aspects of their political agendas and strategies. Some Islamist movements have sought state power (Iran, Afghanistan, Algeria); elsewhere (Egypt, Jordan) they have mostly exerted pressure on the state to reassert traditional patriarchal controls, such as stricter application of the Shari'a, veiling, segregation, or Muslim personal laws. In some countries, the state itself is the manager of patriarchal Islam (the Islamic Republic of Iran, Pakistan under Zia ul-Haq and since, Bangladesh under General Ershad, the Mujahidin and Taliban rulers in Afghanistan, Sudan since the National Islamic Front [NIF] came to power, Saudi Arabia since its inception). In some of these cases, Islamist movements have arisen in the wake of socioeconomic crisis and win support by identifying a concern—morality, values, cultural identity—and reassuring people that something is being done. In the case of Turkey, the Islamist movement and its journals have sought to create or increase Islamic consciousness—particularly among women—through the development of an alternative culture of Islam and at times in opposition to norms of the secular culture. In all cases Islamist movements are engaged in cultural as well as political contestation.

In the new ideological construction of Islamist movements, women are presented as symbols and repositories of religious, national, and cultural identity. In the context of fear and loss of economic and social status, the link between the honor of the family and the honor of the community leads men to attempt to control "their" women. What is more, the loss of their women is seen as a direct threat to manhood, community, and family. It therefore becomes essential to ensure patriarchal controls over the labor, mobility, and sexuality of women. Benedict Anderson pointed out that nationalism describes its object in the language of kinship or the home, both of which denote something natural and given. Similarly, cultural authenticity in Islamist movements is linked to an image of women unsullied by Western education and the modern world. Islamist movements frequently exhibit a reductionist ideology of gender that places a high premium on motherhood and domesticity, as earlier right-wing movements did in Europe. Alya Baffoun found that movement leaders in these two distinct historical settings argued that housework is more suited to female biology and psychology than is professional work; mortality rates are higher among employed women than among women who stay at home; employed women are less moral; juvenile delinquency reflects the breakdown of the family; and female employment causes male unemployment.[30]

But as we shall see, not all Islamist movements call for domestication of women. In many movements, the official Islamist pronouncements concerning women's social positions are ambiguous and contradictory. Apart from a clear stand on Shari'a, they express varying views on women's educational attainment and labor force participation, ranging from misogynistic (as with the Mujahidin and Taliban in Afghanistan) to fairly tolerant (e.g., Islamists in Turkey and in Iran since the 1990s).

What is striking is the range of women's responses to these movements. There are, of course, secular feminists who are unalterably opposed to Islamist movements, to Shari'a law, and to veiling as a form of social control; in Algeria, Tunisia, Egypt, Iran, and Turkey, such women are actively involved in feminist and democratic movements. Then there are the Islamist women themselves and the surprising activism many display. They accept that men and women are physiologically and psychologically different and thus require different roles. They staunchly defend the veil as liberation from a preoccupation with beauty, call for the education of women in order that they be more competent in raising "committed Muslims," and argue that Shari'a and women's emancipation are compatible. In Morocco, Nadia Yassine, the daughter of Shaikh Abdessalaam Yassine, the leader of the Islamist organization Justice and Spirituality and herself a prominent figure, mobilized against the reform of the Moroccan family law, for which Moroccan secular women have struggled. In her opinion, the reform of the family law is a concept from the developed North, which "has no right to dictate to us what to do and what not to do."[31]

For some women, being designated as the carrier of culture and tradition is an onerous burden, one they would just as soon not assume, especially as it is predicated upon control and conformity. But for Islamist women, it is an honor and a privilege to be elevated to such a lofty and responsible position. Therefore, all fundamentalist movements have women supporters as well as women opponents, and feminism itself has female detractors. As we know, this situation is not limited to fundamentalist movements or the Islamic world. In the United States, feminism has its female opponents, not limited to the formidable Phyllis Schlafly. The participation of women in the U.S. anti-abortion movement, as with female support for Islamist movements in the Middle East and North Africa, certainly reflects religious values, but it may also reflect deep-seated fears among women, especially economically dependent women. Anti-feminist women may be responding to the perceived normlessness of contemporary society and wish to avoid the increased pressures and demands on women. In the case of the Islamist movement, women seem to find value and purpose in the movement's endorsement and exaltation of their domestic activities and nature. Writing about the Islamist movement in Turkey, Feride Acar has stated that "women have been exposed to contradictory, dissonant messages and practices, filled with false expectations and aspirations. This has rendered them vulnerable and receptive to an ideology that simplifies reality and promises escape from role conflict and ambiguity."[32]

Islamist movements promise women security and meaning in what, from a conservative point of view, is a world gone mad. There are some similarities with the Orthodox Jewish women in the United States studied by Debra Kaufman. The latter claim to be psychologically alienated from sexual liberation, individualism, and the secular worldview. They have decided that their personal needs are better met in the religious community. As with Islamist women, these Jewish women fear the loss of boundaries; they celebrate gender differences and extol separatism. Islamist women also bear some similarities to the social conservative American women of the new right studied by Rebecca Klatch. They tend to see everything in religious terms and place the family firmly at the center. They fear the breakdown of the moral universe and blame feminists for it; narcissism and the degradation of housework are said to be the result of the women's movement. Such religious women of the new right also fear the masculinization of the world through the blurring of gender roles. At the same time, they evince a distrust of men for being noncommittal and support measures, such as a ban on pornography, that would "hold back man's animal nature."[33]

As mentioned above, one of the surprises of Islamist movements since the 1980s has been their appeal among university and educated women. One reason for this appeal—apart from that provided by Acar—is that some Islamist movements exhibit a degree of flexibility in their position on women. They encourage education for women, mainly so that women can be more informed mothers but also so they can provide teaching and medical services for other women, thus avoiding the problem of excessive male-female interaction. In an interesting twist to the preoccupation with culture and identity, pragmatism can work its way through ideology to encourage female labor force participation during wartime or periods of labor scarcity, as occurred in Iran.[34] Thus the Islamist discourse on gender combines traditional and conservative ideas about "women's place," vague longings for a mythical, bygone golden age, and acceptance of the needs of a modern economy.

Women from traditional families in the lower middle class also support these movements because the movements and the veil provide space for them. Women from this class can legitimately study, work, and act politically and publicly, with their honor and modesty protected within the confines of the Islamist movement. Veiling becomes not only a cultural symbol and an assertion of identity but a matter of convenience and a form of opportunity—it allows women physical mobility in public spaces, free from the gaze and harassment of men and the disapproval of family members.

All of these trends reflect the weakening of classic patriarchy and the resultant "sexual anomie" that Fatima Mernissi analyzed. Men are frustrated and humiliated at being unable to fulfill their traditional role—because of, inter alia, chronic unemployment—and at the threat posed by women's increasing spatial mobility and access to paid employment. Deniz Kandiyoti adds that this breakdown of classic patriarchy is equally threatening to women, "who often resist the process of change because they see the old normative order slipping away from them without any empowering alternatives." The response of some women who have to work for wages in this context may be an intensification of traditional modesty markers, such as veiling. Often, through no choice of their own, they are working outside the home and thus "exposed"; they must now use every symbolic means at their disposal to signify that they continue to be worthy of protection. Fadwa el-Guindy, Homa Hoodfar, and Arlene Macleod all suggest that the veiling of working women in Egypt since the 1980s represents concern with retaining respectability, although this seems to be a class-specific response, as Macleod showed for lower-middle-class women in Cairo.[35]

There is some evidence that voluntary veiling is not always an expression of affiliation with or support for an Islamist political movement; paradoxically, it sometimes represents rejection of parental and patriarchal authority among rebellious young women. Some young women from nontraditional families who adhere to hijab aspire to personal autonomy and a more serious mien, especially at coeducational colleges. For example, an American Fulbright scholar in Algiers described a scene at a lecture on thermodynamics at the University of Science and Technology. According to his account, the hijab-wearing Muslim sisters arrived early, occupied the entire two front rows of the lecture hall, and for nearly two hours sat in rapt attention, scribbling down notes furiously. Several rows back, most of the young men chatted and smoked away their boredom. "I don't know what to think about this hijab business," confided the professor after class, "but I sure like their attitude. I wish all my students were as disciplined and hardworking." One of them, an aspiring civil engineer, said: "I don't have to behave like a European or American to be a scientist. I can very well be an eminent scientist or engineer and wear my hijab." They also expressed their irritation at the efforts of many Algerian men to veil their women by force and abuse them into submission. "I think it's scandalous how men dominate women in Algeria!" And: "Listen, if I'm able to take on the hijab against the wishes of my father, another woman is also able to decide *not* to wear it, despite the wishes of her father. No woman should let herself be intimidated by a slap, a whack of the belt, or blackmail. A woman must stand up for her rights." When asked if they envied the freedoms enjoyed by their European and American counterparts, the response was uniform: aside from scientific and technical know-how, the West had nothing to offer. They expressed the view that Western societies are materialistic, exploitative, and racist, and that Western women are even more exploited economically, politically, and especially sexually—yet they have no source of spiritual comfort. This image of Western women had apparently been "reinforced by a small but steady diet of old US sitcoms and TV movies."[36]

Women and Islamist Movements: Some Cases

The following sections are case studies of Islamist movements and women's responses—in Algeria, Egypt, Iran, Palestine, Turkey, and Sudan. These cases illustrate the differences among Islamist movements, their gender discourses, and their encounter with different feminisms. The cases also raise questions about Islamist women: Are they patriarchal women or Islamic feminists?

Algeria

Shortly after the death of long-standing leader Colonel Houari Boumedienne, the Algerian state under Chadli Bendjedid initiated economic and political restructuring, and Islamists first made a bid for power. A leftist student was murdered at Algiers University in 1982 by Islamists and a crackdown ensued, but it was not until the late 1980s that Islamists formed a major movement. In the meantime, the Bendjedid government began to make major legal, economic, and political change. One was the announcement of a commission to draft a Family Code; the members' identity was kept secret. On March 8, 1979, a group of 200 university women held an open meeting at the industrial workers' union headquarters in Algiers to express their concerns and demands. The next year, when the Bendjedid government prohibited Algerian women from leaving the country unless accompanied by a male guardian, the embryonic women's movement quickly organized a protest march. On January 21, 1982, women protesters issued a six-point demand, calling for monogamy; the unconditional right of women to seek employment; the equal division of family property; the same age of majority for women and men; identical conditions of divorce for men and women; and effective protection of abandoned children. The government ignored these demands, however, and in 1984 adopted the controversial and conservative Family Code with no public notice or debate.[37]

The Bendjedid government was pursuing market reforms in addition to its adoption of a conservative family law. Falling oil prices, austerity measures, and political frustration directed at the FLN led to protests and riots in October 1988, in which young people, women, trade unionists, and other democratic forces played a prominent role. The riots in turn ushered in a brief period of political liberalization. In 1989 a new constitution was adopted, which allowed for political parties, elections, and a free press. This period also saw the increasing popularity of the organization that would call itself the Islamic Salvation Front. The FIS was allowed to operate politically even though the new constitution had banned political parties formed on the basis of religion. Leaflets distributed by the FIS during its campaign in 1990–1992 bring to mind early Iranian Islamist documents on law, women, and the economy. On solutions to Algeria's massive economic problems the FIS was vague and populist, promising to "make the poor rich without making the rich poor." Despite some radical rhetoric against free-market economics, the Algerian debt, and the IMF, the FIS had no economic strategy and focused more on political and cultural (mainly gender) issues and most stridently on public morality.

Taking advantage of the political opening, Islamists organized a campaign of threats and harassment against women whose lifestyles were considered inappropriate. Khalida Messaoudi, a high school math teacher and one of the leading feminist and anti-Islamist activists at the time, described this campaign in testimony before the Tribunal on Violence Against Women at the United Nations Conference on Human Rights, Vienna, in 1993.[38] Algerian feminists were alarmed by statements emanating from Islamist leaders such as Ali Belhadj, who declared that "the natural place for a woman is at home" and that "the woman is the reproducer of men. She does not produce material goods, but this essential thing that is a Muslim." Leaflets claimed that women were under attack from "pernicious Westernization" and that "a woman is above all a mother, a sister, a wife or a daughter." When Algerian feminists protested against *intégrisme* and state collusion, the president of the FIS,

Abassi Madani, issued statements condemning them. As reported in Agence France Presse and cited in various publications, Madani stated: "Recent demonstrations of women against violence and intolerance are one of the greatest dangers threatening the destiny of Algeria. . . . [T]hey are defying the conscience of the people and repudiating national values." He branded them "the avant-garde of colonialism and cultural aggression."[39]

The FIS was committed to introducing Shari'a law as the fundamental law, which it claimed was superior to Western-style civil codes. The FIS declared its intention to use democracy to destroy democracy, for it saw democracy as completely contrary to Shari'a law, as FIS leader Ali Belhadj made clear. For women, hijab would also be introduced, ostensibly to free women from the prying eyes of men. The obligation to wear hijab was backed by threats and later by violence. At the University of Algiers, women students were bullied and threatened for being unveiled.

As early as the summer of 1989 Islamists murdered a woman and her seven children (she lived without a man) and a nurse who was deemed to have too much contact with men, as described by Messaoudi. The Islamist intentions for women became even clearer after they won the municipal elections of June 1990 and exercised coercive power in almost half the municipalities. In localities under their control, they harassed and intimidated unveiled women and women without men, and prohibited the celebratory aspect of the Feast of Ramadan.[40] Even the participation of women in sports was seen as immoral and corrupting. When Hassiba Boulmerka won the 1,500-meter track event at the World Athletics Championship in Tokyo in August 1991, becoming only the second Arab woman ever to receive a major sporting title, she was hailed by the Algerian sports minister Madame Leila Aslaouni and by many of her compatriots. But the fundamentalist imams affiliated to the FIS pronounced *kofr,* a public condemnation of her from the nation's mosques, because she had run "half-naked" before the world's eyes—that is, in regulation running shorts and vest.[41]

The fundamentalist discourse and agenda of the FIS were supported by a segment of the female population, and in April 1989 a demonstration of 100,000 women in favor of Islamism and sex segregation shocked anti-fundamentalist Algerian women. But this phenomenon also spawned a network of anti-*intégriste* feminist groups. On January 1, 1992, a mass demonstration of some 300,000 women and men, under the sponsorship of the Front des Forces Socialistes, voiced opposition to *intégrisme,* as well as criticism of FLN policies and failures. One Algerian feminist, who blamed the rise of the FIS on the failures of the "parti unique," also insisted that an FIS government would spell "the death of freedom, of creativity, of women's rights."[42]

Algeria held municipal elections on June 12, 1990, and national legislative elections in December 1991. The FIS won the first round of elections, but in January 1992 the military stepped in to cancel the second round, dissolve the National Assembly (where the FIS had many supporters), and force President Chadli Bendjedid to resign. In a court case, the FIS was dissolved, appealed, and lost. When an Algerian court decided to ban the FIS in March 1992, the court ruling was read by Judge Ziani, a woman judge who could not have held her position under an FIS government or, for that matter, in a majority of Middle Eastern countries still inspired by Shari'a.[43] In June 1992 the new president, Boudiaf, was assassinated, and the wave of violence escalated. The Islamists unleashed a violent civil conflict that engulfed Algeria for most of the decade. They targeted feminists and unveiled women, journalists, foreigners, ordinary villagers, and of course the state.

The FIS leadership along with its official armed group, the Armée Islamique du Salut (AIS; Islamic Salvation Army), and the Group Islamique Armée (GIA; Armed Islamic Group), encouraged and carried out most of the terror. After shooting to death one young woman in April 1993 and decapitating a mother and a grandmother in separate incidents early the next year, the GIA issued a statement in March 1994 classifying all unveiled women who appeared in public as potential military targets—and promptly gunned down three teenaged girls. The violence against women escalated during that year, and included kidnappings and rapes. Women were denounced in mosques by imams, who pronounced fatwas that condemned activist or unveiled women to death. Lists of women to be killed were pinned up at the entrance to mosques. March 1995 saw an escalating number of deaths of women and girls.

The violent rhetoric and actions of the FIS led many Algerian women to form new organizations in the defense of democracy and women's rights, and against the Islamist insurgency. These included the Rassemblement Algérien des Femmes Démocrates (RAFD), formed in 1993. Members of the feminist groups and their many supporters took to the streets to protest the sexual violence and the threats against unveiled women, as well as the military government's inability to protect women. After one public protest in the spring of 1994, the independent newspaper *Al Watan* noted: "Tens of thousands of women were out to give an authoritative lesson on bravery and spirit to men paralyzed by fear, reduced to silence. . . . The so-called weaker sex . . . refused to be intimidated by the threats advanced by 'the sect of assassins.'" Every year on March 8, the RAFD held a public hearing or march that protested fundamentalism, and in 1995 the RAFD organized a public hearing in the form of a tribunal to condemn the Islamist leadership, including Madani, Belhadj, and Haddam.

The Islamists responded by continuing their threats and attacks. Feminist leader Khalida Messaoudi was officially condemned to death by one of the early armed groups associated and generated by the FIS leadership and was forced to live underground.[44] Nabila Diahnine, an architect and president of the feminist group Cri de Femmes, was assassinated in February 1995 while on her way to work in the northern city of Tizi Ouzou. Zazi Sadou, who had founded the RAFD in 1993 and was its main speaker and audacious representative, took public positions against theocracy and authoritarianism. In the face of Islamist threats, she too lived underground even as she continued to speak out.

The broader objectives of the Algerian women's rights organizations were: the abolition of the Family Code; full citizenship for women; enactment of civil laws guaranteeing equality between men and women in areas such as employment and marriage and divorce; abolition of polygamy and unilateral male divorce; and equality in division of marital property. These goals were anathema to the fundamentalists. In addition, many Algerian feminists also took (and take to this day) a hard line on the fundamentalist organizations, and adopted the slogan "No dialogue with the fundamentalists." As a result of their beliefs and their insistent opposition to fundamentalism, they were targeted by the men of the FIS, AIS, and GIA.

It has been argued by some that the violent civil conflict would have been avoided had the government, ruling party, and military not "cheated" the FIS out of its electoral victory. While there may be an element of truth to this claim, it cannot be denied that the FIS showed its true colors before the elections, when it established a record of intimidation, and after the elections, when it waged its war. Algeria went through a long and unbelievably violent civil conflict pitting the state against the Islamists, and Islamists against feminists. In the process, the Islamists lost power, influence, legitimacy, and supporters. While the Algerian state remained unpopular, Algerian feminists emerged as a strong political constituency and major social force.

Feminists and Islamists in Egypt

Feminism and Islamism have been in competition with each other since Huda Shaarawi dramatically discarded her veil and became a feminist activist in Egypt and internationally. In the 1930s the Islamic right responded to the growth of a feminist and mainly secular consciousness in Egypt with the creation of the Society of Muslim Sisters (later called the Muslim Sisters when it became attached to the Muslim Brotherhood). During Nasser's time, women were encouraged to take on a wider array of roles; free education also enabled social mobility and access to the public sphere. Many urban women responded enthusiastically. The feminist movement of the first half of the twentieth century and Nasser's program of Arab socialism allowed women to make important advances socially and politically.

In the shift away from Arab socialism following Sadat's arrival to power, Islam was used as a counter-ideology that fed the rise of social conservatism. Margot Badran argues that as the second Islamist wave accelerated in the 1970s and reached a peak in the 1980s, previous gender trends in society, most notably the growing presence of women in the public sphere, were reversed. The Islamist wave idealized women's family and domestic role, reassigning women to the home and urging them out of the workplace, where they had become entrenched. A discourse of modesty, articulated mainly by men, further endangered women's public roles. Segregation of the sexes and a return to the home were part of this rising discourse of modesty articulated in the name of Islam. The contemporary debate over the proper role for women in Egypt has focused on clothing, the most obvious symbol of identifying oneself as either Islamic and modest or secular-Western and, presumably, immodest. The movement to re-veil has thus set some Muslim women apart in a political as well as religious statement. At the same time, the call to (re)veil reflected and reinforced concepts of women's vulnerability. Thus, some women argued that hijab protected them and facilitated their presence in public. Islamic forms of dress provided a way for the educated, professional woman to participate in public life and be both modern and Islamic. Islamic dress was thus enthusiastically adopted by urban women students and working women. In Egypt, hijab encompasses a range of dress from wrist- and ankle-length clothing with head covering to the more extreme use of the face veil and gloves so as not to reveal any portion of the female body.[45]

Some Egyptian Islamist women insisted on playing active roles in society, thereby promoting a vision somewhat different from that of the conservative male agenda. However, they continued to extol women's family roles. Certain women in Egypt's Islamist movement, such as Ni'mat Sidqi, articulated the position that women's rights are fully ordained in Islam. Aisha Abd al-Rahman, a noted Quranic scholar and university professor, affirmed the principle of male authority over women and criticized what she saw as the degrading and dehumanizing aspects of modernity. But she also argued against the "men from our nation who want to eliminate our humanity in the name of Islam" as well as decried "the other men from our nation who, in the name of civilization, want to tear off every covering, material and spiritual." The "truly Islamic" and the "truly feminist" option, she said, was neither immodest dress and identical roles for the sexes in the name of modernity nor sexual segregation and the seclusion of women in the name of Islam. The right path combined modesty, responsibility, and integration into public life with the Quranic and naturally enjoined distinctions between the sexes.[46]

The Egyptian constitution of 1971 stated that women are equal to men in every respect that does not contradict Islamic Shari'a. But the nature of that equality has been subject to current interpretations of women's role in society. While these interpretations have not been as illiberal as in Saudi Arabia, they do emphasize women's family role and disapprove of the nonveiled woman in public. As Badran noted, for the middle-class woman who does not have to work outside of the home for wages, the conservative Islamic ideal of confinement provides the perfect rationale for remaining out of the work force. For those women who work out of economic necessity, a compromise is reached whereby they don a headscarf and loose clothing. For its part, the state provided extended parental leave for women (two years without pay) and supported the use of women in part-time work at reduced hourly wages—although this changed in the late 1990s.[47]

Badran writes that coincident with the ascendancy of second-wave conservative Islam was the rise of second-wave feminism associated with Nawal el-Saadawi, whose writings took feminism in a new direction. Hers was a socialist-feminism calling for social, economic, and cultural revolution. A medical doctor, el-Saadawi published *Al-Mar'a wa al-Jins* (Woman and Sex) in 1972, focusing on physical and psychological disease resulting from sexual oppression of women and attacking the sexual double standard. She enlightened many women and helped raise the consciousness of a whole generation of women students in the democratic movement of the time, although she came to be reviled by the Islamist movement, jailed by Sadat, and harassed by Islamic lawyers. Nonetheless, she is credited with helping to revive organized feminism with the creation of the Arab Women's Solidarity Association (AWSA) in the early 1980s. A less formal but equally committed attempt at collective feminist activism surfaced at the same time, when young women who had belonged to the students' democratic movement of the 1970s came together in a study group in 1984, called the New Woman group. They investigated the history of the feminist movement in Egypt. In the face of the growing Islamist movement, they wanted to recover some of the gains of the Nasser period. In 1986 this group issued the journal *Al-Mar'a al-Jadida* (the New Woman group) as a means of reaching out to other women. Meanwhile, in 1982 in Mansura, a town in the delta, a group of women who had organized with others in public protest over the Israeli invasion of Lebanon came together to form Jam'iyyat Bint al-'Ard, the Society of the Daughters of the Land. They sought to continue activism along feminist lines, encouraging girls in the town and surrounding rural areas to develop their minds and take part in the life of their societies. Like the previously mentioned group, they also wished to connect with other women, and they, too, started a magazine, called *Bint al-'Ard*, in 1984. The first issue discussed the problem of calls for female domesticity.

In 1985 the rescission of the 1979 personal status law provoked the formation of the Committee for the Defense of the Rights of the Woman and the Family. It succeeded in obtaining the reinstatement of the law, albeit in truncated form, after disagreements among feminists split the united front. The membership in the AWSA grew around the time of the crisis, though it later declined. But the organization developed as a forum for feminist debate and outreach through its publications (including a quarterly magazine, *Nun*), international conferences (in 1986, 1988, and 1990), and periodic seminars. Uneasy about AWSA feminism, the government prevented publication of the fourth issue of *Nun,* which thereafter appeared as an internal organ. Saadawi took a strong position against the Gulf War, despite Egypt's support for the Anglo-American war effort. For all these reasons, the government banned the organization in the summer of 1991.[48]

The AWSA regrouped later, and along with the New Woman and other feminist groups continues to respond to conservative Islamist calls for women to retreat to the home. Egyptian feminists and Islamist women remain ideological adversaries. For feminists religion is primarily an individual and personal matter. They do not advocate an Islamic government and they have a pluralist attitude toward society. For Islamists the goal of an Islamic state and society is basic. Well-known Islamist women activists in Egypt such as Zainab al-Ghazali and Safinaz Kazim are hostile to secular and Westernized feminism and extol women's roles as wives and mothers. But they also stress the importance for women to work in society, including *da'wa* (proselytizing) in the society and within one's profession. They believe in and preach the message of liberation of women within Islam and its laws.

Islamism and Feminism in Iran

As we saw in Chapter 3, the Islamic revolution was initially supported by countless urban women, who marched in the streets wearing the *chador,* the traditional veil, as a sign of protest against the Pahlavi monarchy. This act backfired, however, when the Khomeini regime took it as a mandate to impose compulsory veiling. One section of the urban population of women— largely women of the upper middle class—was unalterably opposed to veiling, the application of Islamic laws, and the ideology of domesticity instituted by the new regime. But another section of urban women, in particular the women of the lower middle class and from conservative families, welcomed the transformation of Iranian society and saw themselves as duty-bound to uphold the new ideology and emergent norms. As one woman remarked:

> Iran adopted the worst of the West, including the exploitation of women's bodies to sell modern merchandise. Because we didn't tackle the real feminist issues, we just went from being sex objects Oriental style to being sex objects Occidental style. Worse yet, we often got squeezed in between. Under such circumstances the *chador* could be a tool for reasserting a woman's human dignity by forcing people to respond to her talents and personality rather than to her body alone.[49]

Iranian feminists who took part in or supported the revolution but later became exiles, refugees or asylees, as well as other anti-fundamentalist feminists, have written extensively on Islamization in Iran and the devastating effects it had on women and the society. Janet Afary, Mahnaz Afkhami, Haleh Afshar, Haleh Esfandiari, Haideh Moghissi, Afsaneh Najmabadi, Parvin Paidar, Maryam Poya, Eliz Sanassarian, Nayereh Tohidi, and myself, among other scholars, have produced a rich literature that elucidates the gender causes and consequences of the revolution, the gender dynamics of fundamentalism, the varied meanings of veiling, the implications of the Islamization of family law and the penal code, and forms of women's resistance. Secular feminists who stayed in Iran, such as the lawyer Mehrangiz Kaar, analyzed and explicated the new Islamic laws and their gender meanings. But Iranian women were divided in their approach to Islamization and the gender policies of the Islamic Republic. Whereas secular Iranian feminists pointed to women's second-class citizenship, the harsh enforcement of compulsory veiling, sex segregation in public institutions, and the brutal treatment of women political prisoners, many Islamist women insisted that a kind of paradise had been achieved in Iran. For example, one research group confidently declared:

> As the blessed founder of the Islamic Revolution puts it, "If women change, the society changes." With this in mind, let's hope that a day will come when the degree of true changes and the splendid rate of progress of the community of Iranian Muslim women will be known all over the world. So that the women in the Islamic Republic of Iran might be the example to be followed by all women in the Islamic nations.[50]

Women supporters of the state and the Islamist agenda included such Islamist intellectuals, parliamentarians, and spokespersons as Zahra Rahnavard, Azzam Taleghani, Monireh Gorji, Zahra Mostazafi, Maryam Behrouz, Fereshteh Hashemi, and Marzieh Sediqi. The support of these and other Islamist women has been vital to the legitimacy of the Islamic Republic. Also important, at least in terms of security and public morality, were the Baseej Women and the Zeinab Sisters. The Baseej Women numbered about 4,000 and were organized in 1984 as an arm of the Islamic state. They were a volunteer force that underwent military training and were assigned to guard government ministries and banks. The Zeinab Sisters helped to enforce public morality, including the correct wearing of hijab. On one level, entrusting women with such public responsibility was inconsistent with the earlier decisions of the Islamic Republic to remove women from the ranks of public officialdom, as in 1979–1980 when women holding judgeships and top government posts were forced to resign and, in at least one case, executed. However, the regime understood the need to reward Islamic women for their support in the revolution against the Shah. Moreover, the mobilization of women was a necessary part of strengthening the Islamic state and implementing its policies, including gender policies. Thus it never banned women from politics or employment, although it established strict religious and ideological criteria for higher education, employment, and political participation. Those women who adhered to the model of Islamic womanhood and participated in the revolution as Khomeini supporters became symbols of the transformation of society, thus gaining status as bearers and maintainers of cultural heritage and

religious values. Khomeini himself frequently praised those women by calling them "the real teachers of men in the noble movement of Islam" and "the
symbol of the actualization of Islamic ideals." Their religiosity, veiling, and
loyalty to the Islamic project endowed them with the "cultural capital" that
they were later to deploy to their advantage.

Participation in politics and the social sphere both during and after the
revolution was a turning point in the lives of those women, most of whom had
a traditional middle-class background. Nevertheless, the very politicization of
women and their continuous exposure to ideological and political challenges
undermined efforts to redomesticate and privatize them. Having gained status,
legitimacy, and respect, these women began to feel empowered and self-
confident. Tohidi points out that they appropriated the political purpose of the
veil to their own advantage by arguing that in an Islamic society regulated and
sanctified by clerics and immunized against Westoxication by hijab, women's
public role could no longer be a source of *fitna*.[51] Because these women were
"ideologically correct," they could not be accused of *gharbzadegi;* rather,
they were taken seriously by the authorities in Iran.

Thus, an unintended consequence of Islamization in Iran was the emer-
gence of Islamic feminism, now much debated by expatriate Iranian feminist
scholars.[52] The inevitable tensions arose between women and men in the
Islamist movement. For example, Zahra Rahnavard, wife of the Islamic
Republic's first prime minister and a fierce defender of hijab and of
Islamization, eventually criticized official and vigilante attacks on *bad-
hijabi—mal-*veiling (such as wearing bright colors or showing some hair).
Islamist women began to contest men's rights to polygamy and easy divorce,
their monopoly of political decisionmaking, and employment discrimination
that women faced. The inevitable gender contradictions led them to question
many of the laws and norms of Iranian-style Islamism and to deem it a form
of patriarchy. Their exposure to global feminism—including participation in
the UN conferences of the 1990s—their experiences as second-class citizens, and their belief in an emancipatory and egalitarian Islam led them to a
distinctively different standpoint—an indigenous feminism that sought
equality and empowerment in Islam's "true spirit" as revealed in the Quran
rather than in patriarchal applications of Islamic law. They formed study
groups, associations, publications, and an exegesis and interpretation of the
Quran that gradually generated a new woman-oriented, or Islamic feminist,
discourse.[53]

And how did non-Islamist middle-class Iranian women view their roles
and status in postrevolutionary Iran? A survey conducted by sociologist
Shahin Gerami in the summer of 1989 found that although middle-class Iranian women accepted the idea of "complementarity of roles" and endorsed
"feminine" occupations, they rejected notions of men's intellectual superiority, supported advanced education for women as well as men, and insisted

upon gender equality within the household. In particular, they rejected sex segregation.[54]

Palestinian Uprisings, Hijab, and Feminist Dilemmas

The emergence of Islamism among the Palestinians closely follows the pattern of causes and consequences delineated above. The failure of the PLO to win its goal of a democratic and secular state, whether as a substitute for Jewish Israel or as part of the two-state solution (that is, a separate Palestinian state on the West Bank), is one cause of the rise of Islamism among Palestinians. Ziad Abu Amer, a political science professor at Bir Zeit University, stated, "People resort to cultural references, like the veil, especially when they perceive their whole national existence is threatened."[55] The indignity of the Israeli occupation of the West Bank and the awful living conditions in the refugee camps of Gaza provide fertile ground for the rise of militant Islamism. Before the second intifada, or uprising, began in late September 2000, the daily migration into Israel of more than half the work force had profound effects on Palestinian society, especially in impoverished Gaza. Drug abuse and alcoholism were perceived as major problems related to the experiences of Gazan workers in Israel. Elements of the left had initially tried to stop workers from going into Israel, where they were a superexploited labor force, but this only created resentment, because the left could provide no practical alternatives.

An Islamist group called Mujama emerged in Gaza during the 1980s and proposed a practical solution: a return to the moral social code as embodied in their interpretation of Islam. Mujama activists also turned their attention to women's appearance, at first encouraging, then pressuring women to cover their heads. Graffiti on walls would exhort women to wear hijab; in May 1988 religious youths broke into classrooms and demanded that schoolgirls wear hijab. Gaza is where hijab first proliferated and where non-Islamist women were harassed, threatened, even assaulted. Rema Hammami has explained that Palestinian women of peasant background have always worn a version of hijab, partly as a sign of their rural origins and partly because their socioeconomic status did not permit the wearing of "modern dress." But hijab became politicized to the point where by December 1988, one year after the first intifada erupted, "it was almost impossible for women to walk around Gaza without wearing some form of headcover." Islamist vigilantes also took to denouncing coeducational institutes, such as the French Cultural Center and the British Council in Gaza, and attacked what they perceived to be "gambling houses and dance halls."[56]

The politicization of gender and the preoccupation with women's bodies therefore occurred in the context of economic dependency and malaise and the crisis of the existing political ideologies of secular nationalism. In Gaza as elsewhere, Islamists put liberals and nationalists on the defensive by raising the sensitive issue of women's bodies and women's liberation. Thus, when the Unified National Leadership of the Uprising (UNLU) finally issued a statement denouncing the harassment of women, the first point it made was: "We are against excessive vanity in personal dress and use of cosmetics during these times. This is applied to the same degree for men and women." According to the statement, such vanity is "foreign to our traditions and Islamic religion." Some felt that the PLO nationalists took a defensive and apologetic stance vis-à-vis the religious trend and more specifically toward Hamas, the Islamist movement.[57]

Nahla Abdo interviewed women activists in Gaza and found that they were not docile in the face of Islamist male aggression. They resented the imposition of the veil, blamed the Palestinian leadership for not taking a strong enough stand in defense of women, and stressed the irrelevance of the issue of hijab to the intifada. They also were cognizant of the salience of class in the matter of hijab, for it was the women in the streets, in the fields, and doing public work, as Abdo noted, who were being harassed. Upper-class women in Gaza did not appear to be bothered. As one woman put it: "They hide in their big cars and no one attacks them or throws stones at them."[58]

In the wake of growing Islamism and the fundamentalists' intimidation of women, many Palestinian women activists began to call on the Palestinian nationalist movement to link the struggle for an independent state to a broad program of democratization and sociocultural modernization, especially on issues of women's rights. But as observed by West Bank feminists Rita Giacaman and Penny Johnson, this effort faced fierce constraints, including high unemployment and a large population living below the poverty line. As early as 1991 they pointed out: "A new apartheid-like pass system bans West Bank residents from entering Israel (including Arab East Jerusalem) and cuts the West Bank in two. Residents need permits to exit from Gaza and yet another permit to be in the West Bank. Under such conditions, the effort to initiate a democratic debate is a very difficult ordeal indeed."[59] These conditions did not improve significantly enough in the post-Oslo peace process of the latter part of the 1990s, and by the end of the decade, Israeli refusal to halt the building of Jewish settlements fueled the anger of young Palestinian men with no prospects, hopes, or dignity. When the second uprising erupted, it was religiously oriented and far more violent than the first—which had famously produced an array of autonomous organizations, including many women's groups, that could have formed the basis of a vibrant and democratic civil society. This time, Hamas and Islamic Jihad were the main organizations behind the Al-Aqsa intifada and of course behind the wave of suicide bombings in Israel. The continued nonresolution of the Palestinian question put a brake on the growth of Palestinian feminism and in particular its links with Israeli feminists and peace activists.

Before the eruption of the second intifada, and despite Islamist challenges, Palestinian feminists made important interventions in the national dialogue on the basic law, family law, social policies, and women's rights, and formed a number of organizations. The Women's Affairs Technical Committee, which grew out of the first intifada and included some remarkable women, sought to influence the process of constitution building and lawmaking. In early 1991 an audacious feminist group, El Fanar (The Lighthouse) was formed with the explicit aim of establishing an independent women's movement outside the confines of political parties in order to more effectively push for women's rights. According to a founder, "It is our conviction that women must organize themselves in an autonomous feminist context. . . . [T]he existing political parties refuse to confront the patriarchal traditions which oppress women."[60] In March 1998 Palestinian feminists convened the Model Parliament to discuss personal status laws, but they were met by a nasty campaign orchestrated by Hamas that denounced them as tools of imperialism, Zionism, and so on. Hamas seemed especially exercised by the fact that the renowned Palestinian lawyer Asma Khader, a Christian, had spoken about family law from a national perspective. At the time, the Palestine Authority came to the defense of the Model Parliament, but this and other feminist initiatives were shelved in 2000, when the second intifada and Israeli military actions began.[61] The Jerusalem Link is an organization formed through an alliance between Bat Shalom, the Israeli women's peace group, and the Jerusalem Center for Women, a Palestinian women's peace organization that counts Hanan Ashrawi as a founding member.[62] But though some joint actions were taken to promote an end to the Israeli occupation and a peaceful resolution of the Palestinian question, cooperation "has not been easy," according to Salwa Qannam, one of its Palestinian members.[63]

The Turban Movement in Turkey

Although it defends the conservative view that women's primary capacities should be as mothers and housewives, the Islamist movement in Turkey has nevertheless come to accept a more active public role for Muslim women. In the past, Islamic groups were ambivalent and indecisive about mobilizing women for their political cause. The neo-Islamic National Salvation Party of the 1970s, for example, had a strong youth organization but was hesitant to establish affiliated women's associations. Once the Iranian Revolution showed the power that militant Muslim women could wield, Islamic groups in Turkey began to profess active participation of women within the movement.[64] But in 1980 the military government led by General Kenan Evren, which had already cracked down on the Marxist left, also banned the wearing of Islamic dress at universities.

The most visible example of this new role assigned to Turkish Muslim women was their confrontation with state authorities over the question of covering their heads while attending the university. This "Turban Movement" started as a protest against the legal prohibition of the Islamic headscarf for women students; gradually it became an issue of militant Muslim politics. The students wearing the turban claimed to do so because their faith demanded it and argued that their freedom of conscience was under constitutional guarantee. But what originally started as sporadic and unorganized demands for freedom of entry into universities soon turned into organized sit-ins and demonstrations. Interestingly, the Turban Movement and the participation of women in it became instrumental in radicalizing the Islamist cause.

The education of Muslim women is a second example of the new understanding concerning women's role within the movement. The Islamists viewed the education of women as important primarily in terms of women's crucial duty of raising and socializing children; after all, educated women are better equipped to raise healthy children and ensure a good education for them. A major Islamic magazine for women regularly published articles on modern methods of childcare, suggestions for healthy living, advice on medical problems, and the like, obviously addressing women with some degree of education. But more important, the Islamic movement came to realize that it needed its own educated women in certain professions, such as gynecology.

Feride Acar's study of Islamist magazines found that one magazine contained many articles on medicine and health, sections on literature and history, and items on dress patterns, food recipes, and consumer tips. Acar described the magazine's target group of readers as middle-class women of cities and towns. As relatively educated women, they had been subjected to the contradictory messages of gender equality and freedom on the one hand and the centrality of marriage and motherhood on the other. As such they were likely to experience role conflict, have problems of identity definition, and suffer from unfulfilled expectations. The magazine's Islamist message identified Westernization as the source of all problems and offered reassurance and an alternative. Another magazine contained radical and uncompromising articles on veiling and sex segregation that could be seen as an attempt to enhance women's security by minimizing competition with men. This same magazine also expressed an approval of an equitable division of labor between spouses at home.[65]

In a separate study of a major Islamist magazine for women, Yesim Arat argued that for the women who made up the majority of editors and correspondents contributing to its pages, the work experience provided the opportunity to choose alternative lifestyles. Instead of being confined by the conservative backgrounds from which they came, work with the journal allowed for the emergence of more varied and less community-defined identities. Arat has also studied the Welfare Party's women's wing, called Ladies Commissions, which "allowed marginal women to assert themselves and be integrated into society."[66] Nilufer Göle's study of veiled Turkish women showed that the sociological significance of the movement rested not on an understanding of the ideological orientation and religious beliefs of these women but on an analysis of their social practices. She pointed out that on the one hand, women with the turban refer to the basic foundation of Muslim society through the symbol of the veil, a reminder of the role assigned to women in the private sphere and of the segregation of the sexes. On the other hand, through their claim to university education, they are already leaving this private sphere and developing individual strategies. Göle notes the paradox of these ambiguous traditional and modern identities.[67]

The limitations of Islamist women's involvement in their movement and its political parties cannot be denied. For example, Arat has explained that the Ladies Commissions restricted how far women could seek empowerment through political life. The women in the commissions curbed their aspirations for higher office, while the religious teachings and morality the women endorsed helped legitimize the "hierarchical and patriarchal structure of the party organization."[68]

Until the 1980s, Turkey had prided itself on the women's emancipation that the Kemalists had delivered. But after the coup, and parallel with the emergence of the Islamist movement and its women's wing, an autonomous feminist movement arose that became critical of the Turkish version of modernity and nationalism. This new wave of "radical feminists" distanced themselves from those who considered themselves Kemalist feminists and identified with the nation-state. They developed a language of individualism and autonomy and took up issues such as domestic violence, sexual harassment, and rape. Arat concludes that women from different corners of Turkish civil society—Islamist, Kemalist, and radical feminist—have challenged the patriarchal underpinnings of the Turkish state and its monopoly over the public realm, helped to promote liberalism, democratization, and secularism, and advanced the rights and autonomy of women.[69] It should be noted that secular feminists and Islamists have not clashed in Turkey to the extent that they have in other countries. The comparison with Algeria is indicative of the role played by political culture. In contrast to the record of Turkish Islamists, Algerian Islamists were aggressive in their dealings with (unveiled) women and openly denigrated democracy and secularism, which led Algerian feminists to support the suppression of FIS. Turkish feminists, however, did not call for the suppression of Islamic parties, in part because Islamists did not challenge Turkish secularism or women's rights. Arat has explained that Turkish feminists "were a younger generation of women who had taken Kemalist secularism in a Muslim society for granted, [and] they had more confidence in the rootedness of secular institutions in their polity. For the feminists, political liberalization of the authoritarian state and the flourishing of civil society was a higher priority than the suppression of the Islamists."[70]

Gender and Islam in Sudan

Sudanese women won the right to vote in 1965, and later secured equal pay for equal work. The 1973 constitution guaranteed women a number of civil rights and gender-related protections. But in 1983 Islamization began, along with the attempt to enforce Shari'a. Islamic law gained precedence over civil and customary law, leaving women in a contradictory position. On the one hand, some rights were guaranteed; on the other hand, changes in criminal and civil law by the ruling National Islamic Front discriminated against women. There was a national debate over women in medicine, with the NIF attempting to bar them from such "inappropriate" areas as surgery and obstetrics and channel them into child and mother health, public health, and general medicine. A debate also took place on the appropriateness of work performed by (lower-class) women in the informal sector—that is, as vendors of local brew, prostitutes, and some types of entertainers. In November 1991 the Sudanese government ordered all working women and students to adhere to Islamic dress—not the traditional Sudanese *tobe,* a sari-like wraparound, but a novel ensemble modeled after the Islamist uniforms of Tehran and Cairo. Committees were set up to enforce hijab and public morality in Khartoum's streets, offices, and schools. Following the Iranian example of the early 1980s, the Sudanese authorities also spoke out against the use of cosmetics and perfume outside the home.[71]

As in Iran, Sudanese women were divided in support of and against the Islamists. There were Sudanese women who joined the NIF and became the staunch supporters of Islamization; opponents of Islamization were mainly to be found in the Sudanese Women's Union. Sondra Hale's study of gender politics in Sudan and her interviews with NIF women and university students elucidated the degree to which the Islamic ideal of women and the family had permeated the urban middle class, the contradictions and inconsistencies in the Islamist discourse on gender, and the enthusiasm and activism of Islamist women. Women of the NIF agreed wholeheartedly with the goal of strengthening Islam and enforcing Shari'a in Sudan—something I witnessed firsthand at various UN conferences where Sudanese women officials extolled their government and Shari'a law.[72] To an NIF woman activist, Hale explained, there was no distinction between politics and religion, between public and private life. Women were among the most active and visible organizers of the NIF, which had considerable support at the university.

Hale found that women were not only participating in the formation of the NIF's "modern Islamic woman" but were in fact central to the effort. NIF women said that they were activists because of equal rights in Shari'a. At the same time, Islamist women had internalized the biological argument that men and women are fundamentally different by nature, thereby necessitating different roles and responsibilities. Some even saw women as essentially weak, emotional, and sentimental, with a primary duty in the domestic sphere. NIF women were aware of the importance of their roles in the movement. Devotion and commitment to the NIF followed from the NIF's receptivity to an enhanced role for women in the movement. But why should the NIF be thus? Hale argued that states and political movements alike must maintain gender ideology while balancing labor needs. Within the NIF, the imperatives of organizational strategies required utilization of available human resources. Despite some ideological prohibitions, women were needed in large numbers by the NIF for many political tasks.[73]

Conclusion: Women's Responses to Islamist Movements

In the 1980s and 1990s, some well-meaning Westerners tried to argue that Islamist movements were legitimately concerned with cultural integrity, that they were not antidemocratic, and that they did not threaten Western interests.[74] The first claim is only partially true, for Islamists are also concerned with power. The second claim is false, as Islamists in power have demonstrated. The third claim is true; Islamist movements do not threaten Western interests and can coexist with various types of economic systems, especially capitalism. But the Islamist record on gender politics is clearer. In Algeria, unveiled women, women living alone, and feminist activists were harassed, intimidated, and killed by Islamists. In Afghanistan, women suffered indignities under the Mujahidin and received even worse treatment by the Taliban (see Chapter 7). Feminist scholars of the Middle East as well as transnational feminist networks such as Women Living Under Muslim Laws have documented the adverse effects on women of the gender policies of Islamist regimes in Iran and Afghanistan, and of the Islamist opposition in Algeria.

Islamist movements arose in the context of economic failure, political authoritarianism, and changes in the patriarchal system, with the growing visibility of educated and employed women. As Bassam Tibi has put it, the function of Islamist movements, on the positive side, is to bridge change and absorb disappointment. Its negative side is that "Islam does not offer any concrete future structural perspectives and therefore cannot contribute to the solution of urgent social and economic problems of the Middle East."[75] Tibi wrote these words in 1983, and years later the record has shown that Islamist states have evinced a marked incapacity to tackle economic issues. Neither the Islamic regime in Iran, nor the Zia ul-Haq regime in Pakistan, nor the Islamists of Sudan have been able to adequately address poverty, unemployment, economic stagnation, and income inequalities. Rather, they have focused their attention on the spheres of law and culture, most significantly on gender and the position of women.

Islamization draws on distinct gender and class patterns prevailing in society. Women's responses to Islamist movements generally have followed from class and social positions, and range from participation in the fundamentalist movement to advocacy of reform within the frame of Islam to pursuit of a secular state and secular laws. Hélie-Lucas argues that many Muslim women have accepted the notion of an external monolithic enemy and the fear of betraying their identity. To a large extent, "they also accept tradition not as a living history that informs the present and future but as a dead body, inextricably linked to the group identity, to be revived."[76] Internalizing the notion that Islam or the community is in danger, Hélie-Lucas has argued, results in an ordering of priorities established by the male leadership and an indefinite postponement of issues of equality and empowerment.

In many Middle Eastern countries, especially where Islamist movements are strong, women who try to defend their rights are frequently accused of being Westernized. As was the left before them, they are accused of importing a foreign ideology. But whereas the left's response was to point to universal values of social justice, women initially found it difficult to argue for women's rights as human rights or as universal values of social justice. To be sure, women's equality and autonomy, gender roles, and the family are more sensitive issues than is the position of labor, for example. Consequently, many women have tried to demonstrate that they are genuinely rooted in their own culture rather than in "foreign" ideologies, that they are not alienated, that they do not side with external enemies, and that they are different from "Western feminists." Many women's groups in Muslim countries and communities devote time to research their feminist ancestors, not only to recover their own history but also to seek legitimacy and stop accusations of Westernization by Islamists and rightists.

In this general context, Hélie-Lucas has identified three main strategies in the women's movement. In one strategy, "entryism," women join fundamentalist groups. This strategy avoids challenging identity and frees women from the fear of betrayal; moreover, fundamentalist groups have both the will and the funds to offer their members various gratifications and advantages, such as grants to study, free medical care, and loans without interest. Women followers also benefit from social and parental recognition and the ability to choose a husband within the group instead of going through an arranged marriage. In this context, hijab makes possible women's entry into and activity within the public spaces dominated by men. A second strategy is that of women working for change from within the frame of Islam, both at the level of religion and at the level of culture. Some women theologians try to promote a liberation theology by reviving the tradition of reinterpreting the Quran. Similarly, women historians attempt to track and recapture Islamic women's history. Even if

"Islamic feminism" is seen as threatening by fundamentalists, it does not cut women off from the masses, and allows them to "frame" women's rights in indigenous and culturally familiar ways. The third strategy is for women to fight for secularism and laws that reflect the contemporary global understanding of human rights. To these women, hijab is a form of social control and a patriarchal legacy, and they reject it, as they do Muslim personal laws.

One must conclude, therefore, that in Middle Eastern and Muslim countries there are three strands of the women's movement—one secular and liberal/left in orientation, another that may be called Islamic feminist, and the third more conventionally Islamist. Of the three, secular feminism and Islamic feminism hold the greatest promise, as well as the potential for cooperation. Secular feminism is a rational and universalist discourse vital to any political project of democratization and civil society. Islamic feminism is a reformist movement within Islam, a response to patriarchal fundamentalism, and a component of global feminism. In the case of Iran, the 1990s brought about possibilities for dialogue between secular and Islamic feminists and strategies for issue-oriented coalitions. Elsewhere, too, literacy, education, employment, family planning, and maternal health are issues that could unite both groups of women's rights activists. What once constituted a dividing line—hijab and Shari'a law—seems to have become blurred by the convergence over modernization of family laws.

Middle Eastern feminists have walked a tightrope between reclaiming a national identity and reaffirming progressive elements of the indigenous culture on the one hand and rejecting regressive traditions by subscribing to women's liberation and gender equality on the other. This balancing act, while difficult, has enabled them to contribute significantly to the process of modernity and democratization in the Middle East. It may be that there are different cultural and political paths to gender equality and women's empowerment. One possible outcome—certainly a surprising one—of Islamist movements, of the politicization of gender, and of women's activism for and against these movements could very well be the subversion of the patriarchal order and its rapid demise. In tandem with mass female education and the entry of women into the formal work force, the expanded activities of women's organizations will be the strongest challenge to patriarchy, the neopatriarchal state, and the Islamist agenda. As Hisham Sharabi has put it, "The women's movement . . . is the detonator which will explode the neopatriarchal society from within. If allowed to grow and come into its own, it will become the permanent shield against patriarchal regression, the cornerstone of future modernity."[77]

Notes

The opening quote from *Al-Ribat* is cited in Lisa Taraki, "Islam Is the Solution: Jordanian Islamists and the Dilemma of the 'Modern Woman,'" *British Journal of Soci-*

ology 46 (4) (December 1995): 643–661; quote appears on p. 660. *Al-Ribat* is the newspaper of the Ikhwan Muslemin (Muslim Brothers) of Jordan. The full quote is as follows: "This is a vicious, many-sided battle we are waging (against the Jews and Hebrew civilization), and you, my sister, must rise to the occasion. . . . This is a war . . . being waged against a nation *(umma)*—whose women look up to Khadija, Aisha, Fatima and Asma as models. . . . My sister, if you avoid the path of God you will contribute to the success of the conspiracy, and you will be an obstacle to the liberation of Palestine. . . . How can God's victory prevail when women adorn themselves openly and mix with men, and when defiance of God's law continues day and night? The enemy relies on you, my sister, to strike at this nation from within, as if the stabs we receive from the outside were not enough. We do not presume that you would accept this."

1. Eric Hobsbawm, *Primitive Rebels* (New York: W. W. Norton, 1959); Michael Walzer, *The Revolution of the Saints* (Cambridge: Harvard University Press, 1965); Christopher Hill, *The World Turned Upside Down* (Harmondsworth: Penguin, 1975); and Craig Calhoun, *The Question of Class Struggle: Social Foundations of Popular Radicalism During the Industrial Revolution* (Chicago: University of Chicago Press, 1982).

2. Yvonne Y. Haddad, "Islam, Women, and Revolution in Twentieth Century Arab Thought," in Yvonne Y. Haddad and Elison Banks Finlay, eds., *Women, Religion, and Social Change* (Albany: State University of New York Press, 1985), pp. 275–306; Division for the Advancement of Women (John Mathiason), "Religious Standards of Equality and Religious Freedom: Implications for the Status of Women," in V. M. Moghadam, ed., *Identity Politics and Women: Cultural Reassertions and Feminisms in International Perspective* (Boulder: Westview Press, 1994), pp. 425–438.

3. On "pseudo-modernism" and the weakness of an oil economy, see Homa Katouzian, *The Political Economy of Modern Iran, 1926–1978* (New York: New York University Press, 1981).

4. Basheer K. Nijim, "Spatial Aspects of Demographic Change in the Arab World," in Sami G. Hajjar, ed., *The Middle East: From Transition to Development* (Leiden: E. J. Brill, 1985), p. 39.

5. R. Hrair Dekmejian, "Fundamentalist Islam: Theories, Typologies, and Trends," *Middle East Review* (Summer 1985): 28–33, esp. p. 30; and Dilip Hiro, "The Islamic Wave Hits Turkey," *The Nation,* June 28, 1986, pp. 882–886.

6. Philip Hitti, *A History of the Arabs* (Princeton: Princeton University Press, 1971).

7. Ellis Goldberg, "Smashing Idols and the State: The Protestant Ethic and Egyptian Sunni Radicalism," *Comparative Studies in Society and History* 33 (1) (January 1991): 3–35.

8. On Egyptian violence toward Christians, see Alberto M. Fernandez, "In the Year of the Martyrs: Anti-Coptic Violence in Egypt, 1988–1993," paper presented at the annual meeting of the Middle East Studies Association, San Francisco, November 18–20, 2001.

9. On Egypt, see Salwa Ismail, "The Paradox of Islamist Politics," *Middle East Report* no. 221 (Winter 2001): 34–39. On Palestine, see Graham Usher, "Seeking Sanctuary: The 'Church' vs. 'Mosque' Dispute in Nazareth," *Middle East Report* no. 214 (Spring 2000): 2–4; and Alisa Rubin Peled, "Toward Autonomy? The Islamist Movement's Quest for Control of Islamic Institutions in Israel," *Middle East Journal* no. 3 (Summer 2001): 393–402.

10. On the "Islamist International," see Marie-Aimée Hélie-Lucas, "Women Facing Muslim Personal Laws as the Preferential Symbol for Islamic Identity," in

Moghadam, *Identity Politics and Women,* pp. 391–407; and Eqbal Ahmed, "Jihad International Inc.," in *Women Living Under Muslim Laws Dossier 22* (Montpelier: WLUML, 1999), pp. 114–118. See also Georges Corm, *Fragmentation of the Middle East: The Last Thirty Years* (London: Hutchinson, 1988), esp. p. 90.

11. John Cooley, *Unholy Wars: Afghanistan, America, and International Terrorism* (London: Pluto Press, 2000), p. 1.

12. For an elaboration of this and similar terms in the Iranian Islamist lexicon, see V. M. Moghadam, "Rhetorics and Rights of Identity in Islamic Movements," *Journal of World History* 4 (2) (Fall 1993): 243–266.

13. Saad Eddin Ibrahim, "Anatomy of Egypt's Militant Islamic Groups," *International Journal of Middle East Studies* 12 (4) (1980): 423–453; Goldberg, "Smashing Idols and the State," pp. 19–20; and Yvonne Y. Haddad, "Middle East Area Studies: Current Concerns and Future Directions," Presidential Address 1990, *MESA Bulletin* 25 (1) (July 1991): 1–12.

14. John Entelis, *Culture and Counterculture in Moroccan Politics* (Boulder: Westview Press, 1989).

15. Richard Hamilton, *Who Voted for Hitler?* (Princeton: Princeton University Press, 1982).

16. Robert Wuthnow, *Meaning and the Moral Order: Explorations in Cultural Analysis* (Princeton: Princeton University Press, 1987).

17. Binnaz Toprak, "Women and Fundamentalism: The Case of Turkey," in Moghadam, *Identity Politics and Women,* pp. 293–306.

18. See "Interview with Turkish M.P. Merve S. Kavakci," *Muslim Democrat* 2 (3) (November 2000): 8, www.islam-democracy.org. See also *Turkish Times,* various issues, especially August 2002, www.theturkishtimes.com.

19. Nayereh Tohidi, "Modernity, Islamization, and Women in Iran," in V. M. Moghadam, *Gender and National Identity: Women and Politics in Muslim Societies* (London: Zed Books, 1994), pp. 110–147. See also Afsaneh Najmabadi, "Hazards of Modernity and Morality: Women, State, and Ideology in Contemporary Iran," in Deniz Kandiyoti, ed., *Women, Islam, and the State* (London: Macmillan, 1991), pp. 48–76.

20. Nayereh Tohidi, "Modernity, Islamization, and Women in Iran," in Moghadam, *Gender and National Identity,* pp. 110–147.

21. One outcome of the regime's gender policies was the loss of employment— and thus income—by working-class women who previously had been employed in factories. See V. M. Moghadam, "Women, Work, and Ideology in the Islamic Republic," *International Journal of Middle East Studies* 20 (2) (May 1988): 221–243.

22. Cherifa Bouatta and Doria Cherifati-Merabtine, "The Social Representation of Women in the Islamic Movement," in Moghadam, *Identity Politics and Women,* pp. 183–201.

23. Alya Baffoun, "Feminism and Fundamentalism: The Tunisian and Algerian Cases," in Moghadam, *Identity Politics and Women,* pp. 167–182. On North Africa's economic crisis, see David Seddon, "Austerity Protests in Response to Economic Liberalization in the Middle East," in Tim Niblock and Emma Murphy, eds., *Economic and Political Liberalization in the Middle East* (London: British Academic Press, 1993), pp. 88–112; Dirk Vandewalle, "Breaking with Socialism: Economic Liberalization and Privatization in Algeria," in Ilya Harik and Denis J. Sullivan, eds., *Privatization and Liberalization in the Middle East* (Bloomington: Indiana University Press, 1992), pp. 189–208; and V. M. Moghadam, *Women, Work, and Economic Reform in the Middle East and North Africa* (Boulder: Lynne Rienner, 1998), chap. 8.

24. Cited in Mounira Charrad, "Policy Shifts: State, Islam, and Gender in Tunisia, 1930s–1990s," *Social Politics* 4 (2) (Summer 1997): 284–319; quote appears on p. 300.

25. Lilia Labidi, "Women, Politics and Islam: The Case of Tunisia," paper presented at the Woodrow Wilson International Center for Scholars, Washington, D.C., 2002, p. 34.

26. Baffoun, "Feminism and Fundamentalism," pp. 167–182, esp. 175.

27. Jamal J. Nasir, *The Status of Women Under Islamic Law* (London: Graham & Trotman, 1990).

28. See Nawal el-Saadawi, "The Political Challenges Facing Arab Women at the End of the Twentieth Century," in Nahid Toubia, ed., *Women of the Arab World: The Coming Challenge* (London: Zed Books, 1988), p. 11. On the Islamist feminist position, see Freda Hussein's introduction to her edited book, *Muslim Women* (London: Croom Helm, 1984); Leila Ahmed, "Early Islam and the Position of Women: The Problem of Interpretation," in Nikki R. Keddie and Beth Baron, eds., *Women in Middle Eastern History: Shifting Boundaries in Sex and Gender* (New Haven: Yale University Press, 1991), pp. 58–73; Riffat Hassan, "Rights of Women Within Islamic Communities," in John Witte Jr. and Johan D. van der Vyver, eds., *Religious Human Rights in Global Perspective: Religious Perspectives* (The Hague: Martinus Nijhoff, 1996); Azizah al-Hibri, "Islam, Law, and Custom: Redefining Muslim Women's Rights," *American University Journal of International Law and Policy* 12 (1) (1997): 1–43; and Asma Barlas, *Believing Women in Islam: Unreading Patriarchal Interpretations of the Qur'an* (Austin: University of Texas Press, 2002).

29. Ishtiaq Ahmed, "Communal Autonomy and the Application of Islamic Law," *ISIM Newsletter* (Leiden) no. 10 (July 2002): 32. See also Hélie-Lucas, "Women Facing Muslim Personal Laws," p. 397; and Chibli Mallat and Jane Connors, eds., *Islamic Family Law* (London: Graham & Trotman, 1990), esp. pt. 2 on Europe and pt. 3 on South Asia, Southeast Asia, and China.

30. Benedict Anderson, *Imagined Communities* (London: Verso, 1983); and Baffoun, "Feminism and Fundamentalism." The emphasis on male-female differences, on the desirability and necessity of distinctive sex roles, and on separate male and female natures is hardly unique to Islam or to the Middle East. Cynthia Epstein has shown how pervasive were explanations of biological determinism in U.S. academic disciplines and social science research, explanations that attributed psychological and social characteristics of men and women to physiological causes. See Cynthia Fuchs Epstein, *Deceptive Distinctions: Sex, Gender, and the Social Order* (New Haven: Yale University Press, 1988).

31. Cited in Renate Kreile, "Alliances Between Secular and Islamist Women Activists: Conditions and Perspectives," paper distributed at the Conference on Women, Peace, and Change in the Euro-Mediterranean, Bruno Kriesky Forum, Vienna, January 2000.

32. Feride Acar, "Women in the Ideology of Islamic Revivalism in Turkey: Three Islamic Women's Journals," paper presented at the workshop on Islam in Turkey, at the School of Oriental and African Studies, University of London, May 1988.

33. Debra Kaufman, "Paradoxical Politics: Gender Politics Among New Orthodox Jewish Women," and Rebecca E. Klatch, "Women of the New Right in the U.S.: Family, Feminism, and Politics," both in Moghadam, *Identity Politics and Women,* pp. 349–366 and 367–389.

34. Moghadam, "Women, Work, and Ideology in the Islamic Republic"; and Maryam Poya, *Women, Work, and Islamism: Ideology and Resistance in Iran* (London: Zed Books, 1999).

35. Deniz Kandiyoti, "Islam and Patriarchy: A Comparative Perspective," in Keddie and Baron, *Shifting Boundaries,* p. 37; Fadwa el-Guindy, "Veiling *Intifah* with Muslim Ethic: Egypt's Contemporary Islamic Movement," *Social Problems* 8 (1981): 465–485; Homa Hoodfar, "Return to the Veil: Personal Strategy and Public Participation in Egypt," in Nanneke Redclift and M. Thea Sinclair, eds., *Working Women: International Perspectives on Labour and Gender Ideology* (London: Routledge, 1991), pp. 104–124; and Arlene Elowe Macleod, *Accommodating Protest: Working Women, the New Veiling, and Change in Cairo* (New York: Columbia University Press, 1991).

36. Jim Coffman, "Choosing the Veil," *Mother Jones,* November–December 1991, pp. 23–24.

37. See Peter Knauss, The Persistence of Patriarchy: Class, Gender, and Ideology in Twentieth Century Algeria (New York: Praeger, 1987).

38. This is described in Khalida Messaoudi and Elisabeth Schemla, *Unbowed: An Algerian Woman Confronts Islamic Fundamentalism* (Philadelphia: University of Pennsylvania Press, 1998).

39. See the following sources: George Joffe, "Hidden Strength of God's Party," *The Guardian* (UK), January 15, 1992, p. 3; Faika Medgahed, "Algeria: Fundamental Betrayals," *Ms.,* March–April 1992, p. 13; and Mahl, "Ordinary Fascism, Fundamentalism, and Femicide," via Internet from WLUML, July 31, 2001. For political histories of the Islamist challenge, see Michael Willis, *The Islamist Challenge in Algeria: A Political History* (New York: New York University Press, 1996); and Martin Stone, *The Agony of Algeria* (New York: Columbia University Press, 1997).

40. See Messaoudi and Schemla, *Unbowed,* p. 14–15.

41. Pat Butcher, "Running On Through the Veil of Tears," *The Guardian,* January 11, 1992, p. 15. This episode brings to mind a controversy in Israel in 1986, when Orthodox militants burned bus shelters displaying advertisements showing women in swimsuits. Secular Zionists countered by daubing swastikas on synagogues. See Thomas L. Friedman, "Israeli's Uneasy Mix of Religion and State," *New York Times,* June 22, 1986, p. E3.

42. Personal communication from Algiers, January 26, 1992.

43. This is indicative of Algeria's highly contradictory gender system, wherein women constitute under 10 percent of the measured labor force and have been exhorted to accept the joys of domesticity, as we have seen in Chapters 2 and 3, and yet has women judges in the civil courts.

44. See Messaoudi and Schemla, *Unbowed,* pp. 165–166.

45. Margot Badran, "Gender Activism: Feminists and Islamists in Egypt," in Moghadam, *Identity Politics and Women,* pp. 202–227.

46. Valerie Hoffman-Ladd, "Polemics on the Modesty and Segregation of Women in Contemporary Egypt," *International Journal of Middle East Studies* 19 (1) (February 1987): 36.

47. This generous pronatalist leave policy was rescinded in the late 1990s due to economic restructuring and the worsening of Egypt's unemployment and fiscal crisis. For details, see Moghadam, *Women, Work, and Economic Reform,* chap. 5.

48. For details, see "Egypt Moves to Dissolve Arab Women's Solidarity Association," *Association for Women in Development Newsletter* 6 (2) (April 1992): 1.

49. Naila Minai, quoted in Hoffman-Ladd, "Polemics on the Modesty and Segregation of Women," p. 24.

50. Research Group for Muslim Women's Studies, Tehran, 1990.

51. Tohidi, "Modernity, Islamization, and Women in Iran," in Moghadam, *Gender and National Identity,* pp. 110–147.

52. For a review of the debate, see Valentine M. Moghadam, "Islamic Feminism and its Discontents: Toward a Resolution of the Debate," *Signs* 27 (4) (Summer 2002): 1135–1171.

53. For more on Islamic feminism in Iran, see Haleh Afshar, "Islam and Feminism: An Analysis of Political Strategies," and Ziba Mir-Hosseini, "Stretching the Limits: A Feminist Reading of the Sharia in Post-Khomeini Iran," both in Mai Yamani, ed., *Feminism and Islam: Legal and Literary Perspectives* (New York University Press, 1996), pp. 197–216 and 285–319; Nayereh Tohidi, "'Islamic Feminism': A Democratic Challenge or a Theocratic Reaction?" (in Persian) *Kankash* 13 (1997): 106–116; Afsaneh Najmabadi, "Feminism in an Islamic Republic: 'Years of Hardship, Years of Growth,'" in Yvonne Y. Haddad and John Esposito, eds., *Women, Gender, and Social Change in the Muslim World* (New York: Oxford University Press, 1998), pp. 59–84; and Elaheh Rostami Poya, "Feminist Contestations of Institutional Domains in Iran," *Feminist Review* no. 69 (Winter 2001): 44–72.

54. Shahin Gerami, "The Role, Place, and Power of Middle Class Women in the Islamic Republic," in Moghadam, *Identity Politics and Women*, pp. 329–348.

55. Sabra Chartrand, "The Veiled Look: It's Enforced with a Vengeance," *New York Times*, August 22, 1991.

56. *Tehran Times*, September 3, 1991, p. 15.

57. Quotes from Rema Hammami, "Women, the Hijab, and the Intifada," *Middle East Report*, May–August 1990.

58. Nahla Abdo, "Nationalism and Feminism, Palestinian Women and the Intifada: No Going Back?" in Moghadam, *Gender and National Identity*, p. 167.

59. Rita Giacaman and Penny Johnson, "Mid-East Women Work Toward Democracy," *Ms.*, September–October 1991, p. 14.

60. Mana Hassan, cited in *Women's International Network News* 18 (1) (Winter 1992): 53.

61. For a discussion of the Model Parliament and other matters facing the women's movement, see Rema Hammami and Penny Johnson, "Equality with a Difference: Gender and Citizenship in Transition Palestine," *Social Politics* 6 (3) (Fall 1999): 314–343.

62. For more information on Hanan Ashrawi's views on women's rights and cooperation with Israeli feminists and peace activists, see "The Feminist Behind the Spokeswoman: A Candid Talk with Hanan Ashrawi," *Ms.*, March–April 1992, pp. 14–17. The interview was conducted by Rabab Hadi, a cofounder of the Union of Palestinian Women's Associations in North America.

63. Salwa Hdeib Qannam, in a conversation with the author, Istanbul, September 19, 2002. Salwa is head of the Association of Women's Committees for Social Work in Jerusalem, head of the board for Trustees for the Jerusalem Center for Women (Jerusalem Link), a member of the Women's Affairs Technical Committee, and a member of the Higher Committee of Fateh.

64. See Binnaz Toprak, "Women and Fundamentalism: The Case of Turkey," in Moghadam, *Identity Politics and Women*, pp. 293–306.

65. Acar, "Women in the Ideology of Islamic Revivalism."

66. Yesim Arat, "Women in Turkish Politics: The Islamist Alternative," paper prepared for the conference "Women and Gender in the Middle East: The State of Theory and Research," Bellagio, Italy, August 27–31, 2001.

67. Yesim Arat, "Feminists, Islamists, and Political Change in Turkey," *Political Psychology* 19 (1) (March 1998): 117–132; and Nilufer Göle, *The Forbidden Modern: Civilization and Veiling* (Ann Arbor: University of Michigan Press, 1996).

68. Yesim Arat, *Political Islam in Turkey and Women's Organizations* (Istanbul: TESEV, 1999), p. 61.

69. Yesim Arat, "From Emancipation to Liberation: The Changing Role of Women in Turkey's Public Realm," *Journal of International Affairs* 54 (1) (Fall 2000): 107–123; and Yesim Arat, "Democracy and Women in Turkey: In Defense of Liberalism," *Social Politics* 6 (3) (Fall 1999): 370–387.

70. Yesim Arat, "Toward a Democratic Society: The Women's Movement in Turkey in the 1980s," *Women Studies International Forum* 17 (2–3) (1994): 241–248; quote appears on p. 246.

71. Carolyn Fleuhr-Lobban, "Islamization in Sudan: A Critical Assessment," *Middle East Journal* 44 (4) (Autumn 1990): 610–623.

72. For example, at the preparatory meeting in advance of the Beijing conference, organized by the UN's Economic and Social Commission for West Asia (ESCWA) in Amman, Jordan, November 1994, members of the Sudanese delegation took objection to proposals endorsing "human rights" and "women's rights," which they claimed were Western and were inferior to rights in Shari'a law.

73. Sondra Hale, "Gender, Religious Identity, and Political Mobilization," in Moghadam, *Identity Politics and Women,* pp. 145–166. See also Sondra Hale, *Gender Politics in Sudan: Islamism, Socialism, and the State* (Boulder: Westview Press, 1996), esp. chap. 6.

74. In so doing, these Westerners were naively echoing the arguments of Islamists themselves, who were trying to garner international support in the wake of domestic state repression, especially in Algeria and Tunisia. See, for example, the cover story of *Time* magazine, June 15, 1992.

75. Bassam Tibi, "The Renewed Role of Islam in the Political and Social Development of the Middle East," *Middle East Journal* 37 (1) (Winter 1983): 3–13, esp. p. 13.

76. Hélie-Lucas, "Women Facing Muslim Personal Laws," p. 392.

77. Hisham Sharabi, *Neopatriarchy: A Theory of Distorted Change in Arab Society* (New York: Oxford University Press, 1988), p. 154.

6

Iran: From Islamization to Islamic Feminism—and Beyond?

The most important negative impact of Islamization on women after the 1979 revolution was the reversal of the family law. This reform was so important that we have gone back to it and are using many parts of it now under the Islamic state. Women's demand for change is a movement that will not stop and will carry on, that is why I feel that the future is bright.
—Shahla Sherkat, 2001

How have women fared in the Islamic Republic of Iran since the Iranian Revolution of 1979? How have their legal status and social positions changed? And to what can this be attributed? This chapter elucidates the changing and contradictory status of Iranian women over the past two decades through an examination of the gender discourses of the Islamist political elite, the Islamic state's gender policies, and the outcomes for women in the 1980s in terms of fertility, literacy and education, employment, and political participation. The changing environment in the 1990s and its implications for women, as well as the emergence of a women's rights movement constituted by secular and Islamic feminists, also are discussed.

Gender Ideology and Policies

The gender ideology of the postrevolutionary Islamic Republic rested on several premises and claims. One was that women in prerevolutionary Iran had lived objectionable lives and had been subject to alien ideas, images, and practices. A related claim was that the Islamic state would restore Iranian women to their rightful place and give them the dignity they had lost under the Pahlavi state. Another premise was that because women were both vulnerable to non- and anti-Islamic influences and a potential source of moral decay, they would have to conform to strict rules regarding dress, comportment, and access to the public space. The emphasis on women's domesticity, difference, and danger is illustrative of the extraordinary ideological pressures

193

faced by Iranian women—especially modernized middle-class women—after the revolution. One was the pressure of family attachment, domesticity, marriage, and motherhood. The National Union of Women, affiliated with the Marxist organization Fedayan-e Khalq, bitterly complained in December 1979:

> The women who made history by their equal participation with men in the struggle for life and death gained nothing but a return to the rotten old household of ignorance and silence. Once again, instead of politically conscious hearts and minds, the regime asks for women's motherly protection for a "warm family center."[1]

The Islamic Republic's ideal of women's domesticity was closely tied to the notion of gender difference, whereby the physical, physiological, and biological differences between men and women are translated into universal and immutable differences in their social and intellectual capacities. Because of physiological and psychological differences, husbands and wives in the family, and men and women in the society, were to have different roles and expectations. Islamic thinkers frequently extolled these as "complementary" sex roles that were divinely ordained. But in their separate essays on the writings of Yahya Nuri, Ruhollah Khomeini, and Morteza Mutahhari—ideologues and leaders of Islamization in Iran—Nahid Yeganeh and Haleh Afshar concluded that these Iranian Shia clerics were deeply convinced of the natural inferiority of women, in part because of women's presumed emotionality and deficiency of rational judgment.[2]

The themes of gender difference (in fact, gender inequality) and the need for female domesticity were linked to another theme: the danger inherent in the female nature. Fatna Sabbah's study examined those Islamic writings that harp on the spurious theme of female sexuality (or omnisexuality) and enticement. It is the considered opinion of many Islamic ideologues that men are eminently susceptible to female lures; the mere presence of women is said to undermine men's better judgment, their sanity, and their rationality.[3] For example, the late Ayatollah Mutahhari wrote: "Where would a man be more productive, where he is studying in all-male institutions or where he is sitting next to a girl whose skirt reveals her thighs? Which man can do more work, he who is constantly exposed to arousing and exciting faces of made-up women in the street, bazaar, office, or factory, or he who does not have to face such sights?" Mutahhari went on to declare:

> The truth is that the disgraceful lack of the modest dress in Iran (before the Revolution) whereby we were even moving ahead of America, is a product of the corrupt Western capitalist societies. It is one of the results of the worship of money and the pursuance of sexual fulfillment that is prevalent in Western capitalism. It is one of the means they use to manipulate human society and stimulate them by this force to become consumers of their prod-

ucts. If an Iranian woman only wants to put on makeup for her legal husband or only wants to get dressed up for gatherings with women, she will not be a consumer of Western products. She will not be obliged to unconsciously corrupt the morals of young boys and girls, to weaken them so that they are no longer active members of society which is to the benefit of the exploiters.[4]

Another important factor in the formulation of the new gender policies was the notion of the excessively Westernized woman and the cultural danger she represented. As we saw in Chapter 5, women were regarded as having been most vulnerable to *gharbzadegi,* to deculturation and imperialist culture. The solution to this vulnerability to the slings and arrows of the imperialists was compulsory veiling.

In the early years of the Islamic Republic, the three dimensions of the gender ideology found their material expression in legislation and policy. The 1979 Islamic constitution had several clauses that pertained to the status and social positions of women. The preamble emphasized the significance of the family: "The family is the fundamental unit of society and the main center of growth and transcendence for humanity." It stressed women's primary role as mother: "A woman . . . will no longer be regarded as a 'thing' or a tool serving consumerism and exploitation. In regaining her important duty and most respectful role of mother in the nourishing of human beings who belong to the school of thought, as a pioneer along with men, as a warrior in the active living battlefields, the result will be her accepting a more serious responsibility. In the views of Islam, she will assume higher values and beneficence." In addition to institutionalizing domesticity, the constitution established Shari'a as the law of the land. Article 4 read: "All the laws and regulations concerning civil, criminal, financial, economic, administrative, cultural [and] military affairs must be based on the Islamic standards. This principle will be applied to all the articles of the Constitution and all other laws and regulations."[5]

The constitution of the Islamic Republic was put to a referendum in early December 1979 and was approved by the populace. Confident of their success, the Islamic authorities had taken steps in the months before to institute their new gender policy, steps that alarmed educated, non-Islamist women of the upper middle class. These women mounted the first serious challenge to the authority and legitimacy of the new leadership. In early March 1979, several thousand Iranian women demonstrated against the new sexual politics, especially Khomeini's statements that women should appear in public in hijab. Women staged a sit-in at the Ministry of Justice and carried placards that read: "In the dawn of freedom there is no freedom." There was a week of meetings, rallies, and demonstrations, during which non-Islamist women expressed their outrage and anxiety over the issue of hijab. As Azar Tabari relates it, Prime Minister Bazargan announced that Khomeini's statement had been misunderstood by some genuine women militants and consciously manipulated by left-wing troublemakers. Bazargan said there would be no compulsory veiling in government offices and that it was the view of the imam that women should be guided, not forced, to accept the veil.[6] In fact, hijab was legislated the following year, when the Islamists' position strengthened. In the meantime, other steps were taken to redefine and regulate gender. The Ministry of Education banned coeducation, and the Ministry of Justice declared it would not recognize women judges. Childcare centers at factories and government agencies began to be closed down. Several Caspian Sea resort towns instituted sex-segregated beaches.

Women's responses to the new gender codes varied by class and political/ ideological orientation, ranging from enthusiastic support to acquiescence to outright hostility. Some Islamist women—influenced as they were by the reformist trend in Iranian Islam that had been initiated by the late Ali Shariati—criticized some of the changes, in particular compulsory veiling, which they felt was wrong and would alienate many supporters of the Islamic revolution. Fereshteh Hashemi pointed out that veiling is meant to be undertaken voluntarily by believers, saying, "Not only have we made the religious dress a job requirement for believing women and even for non-believers (of the religious minorities, the Christians and Jews), we are even specifying form and color of dresses—something that is not obligatory in Islam. . . . And if the Islamic system wants to establish Islamic norms in society in order to combat Westoxication, why is this done only to women?"[7] Another critical view of compulsory veiling from Islamist women was expressed at a July 1980 seminar by Azam Taleghani, Zahra Rahnavard, Shahin Etezad Tabatabai, and Ansieh Mofidi. They suggested that "instead of imposition of hijab on women, public decency—meaning modest dressing and not using makeup—should be considered all over the country and lack of its observance punished," though only by the authorities, rather than by vigilantes. As an example of punishment, they offered the case of Algeria, where "this was done by painting the legs of women in short skirts."[8] A more incisive view of compulsory veiling was expressed by the communist Fada'i Khalq (Majority) organization: "The Islamic Republic of Iran claims that the imposition on women of the Islamic veil is a step towards the 'moral cleansing' of society and eradication of the degenerate culture of the monarchical order. Without smashing the social and economic foundations of contemporary capitalism upon which the monarchical order was based, however, cultural degeneration cannot be uprooted. Furthermore, the veil is totally irrelevant to the uplifting or degeneration of culture."[9]

In fact, the veil was far from irrelevant to the regime. The model of womanhood the Islamists sought to impose on the population was an integral part of the political-cultural project of Islamization. The transformation of Iran was seen as incumbent upon the transformation of women. (Re)definitions of gender are frequently central to political and cultural change, as we have seen in earlier chapters.

It should be noted that although the gender system in the Islamic Republic introduced many novel policies, accompanied by a powerful religious ideology, some of its features were legacies of the past, inherited from the previous regime, or reflective of cultural practices. Female physical mobility was not extensive in prerevolutionary Iran, and there were many legal and customary restrictions on women. They could not travel, obtain jobs, or rent apartments without the permission of their father or husband. Moreover, male sexist attitudes and behavior were notorious, making it difficult for women even to stand for taxis or go shopping. The beneficiaries of Pahlavi-style modernization were primarily middle-class and upper-class women, while the majority of women from working-class and peasant households remained illiterate and poor. Western-style dress abounded, but the *chador* was characteristically worn by working-class, traditional/lower-middle-class, and urban poor women. Most secondary schools (the exceptions being the international schools where the language of instruction was a European one) were gender-segregated; universities and workplaces, however, were not. Men could be taught by female instructors (for example, I taught English at the Air Force Language School in the early 1970s), but the matter of appropriate dress was always raised. Thus, after the revolution there were some continuities, and some breaks, in the gender system.

The New Gender Policies

In the first two years of the Islamic Republic, policies were enacted that adversely affected women and curtailed their participation in the public sphere. These policies resulted, in the first instance, in the loss of employment by elite women, who were the main target of the regime's policies. Women's participation in the legal profession was the first and most seriously affected area. A new law barred women from acting as judges; women judges who had been appointed during the Pahlavi era were dismissed. This action was followed by the removal of many women from top-level government posts; they were forced either to accept lower-level jobs or to retire completely. In the summer of 1980 veiling was made compulsory and henceforth was strictly enforced. Many women in high posts resigned or retired rather than endure the hijab. Women were not permitted to wear cosmetics or perfume in public. Women's voices were banned from radio and female singers barred from television. Only those foreign films in which actresses had hair coverings were imported. The Family Protection Act of 1967 (amended in 1973) of the Pahlavi era, which enhanced women's rights within the family, was abrogated. It was replaced by a patriarchal Shari'a-based family law and civil code that denied women the right to initiate divorce and reinstated men's unilateral right to divorce and polygamy. The Islamic Republic assumed a pronatalist stance, banning abortions and distribution of contraceptives, extolling the

Muslim family, and lowering the age of marriage to puberty for girls. A number of laws were passed to encourage women to return to the home and ensure that they remained there. Various retirement programs allowed women who had worked as little as fifteen years to retire without loss of entitlements. Later, another law was passed allowing working couples to enjoy the full benefit of the wife's salary if she decided to stay at home. Women with working husbands were told to forgo employment to open up positions for males.

In 1980 the "Islamic cultural revolution" was launched, and it entailed the closing of universities and some high schools for two years, during which time faculty were purged, new curricula prepared, and ideological criteria established for students and faculty. All coeducational schools were converted into single-sex institutions; Islamic dress codes were introduced; Arabic replaced English as a second language; private schools and international schools were eliminated; and textbooks were rewritten. When the universities were reopened in 1982 and the *konkour,* or national entrance examinations, were held, the government had eliminated some programs of study it considered unnecessary, such as music and counseling. Women were barred from a number of fields of study, such as veterinary sciences and some engineering programs, and gender quotas were established. The general criteria for all applicants were (1) believing in Islam or one of the religions recognized by the constitution (Christianity, Judaism, Zoroastrianism), and (2) having no organizational connection with or advocacy of political parties, antigovernment groups, or atheistic groups. Male applicants also had to meet very strict requirements of military service based on the war with Iraq.[10] All women students had to appear in strict regulation hijab.

Abolishing the Pahlavi state's secular (if harsh) penal code, the Islamic regime instituted a Shari'a-based penal code called *Qessass,* or the Law of Retribution. Among other things, the law allowed victims' families to demand and receive monetary compensation ("blood money") from the family of the perpetrator, but it also established values on the victims based on gender and religion. Accordingly, the worth of a woman (and a non-Muslim) was half of that of a man (and a Muslim). In the case of murder, for example, the family of the Muslim male victim would receive higher compensation than that of a Muslim female victim or a non-Muslim male or female. The law was regarded by much of Iranian society as hopelessly retrograde and a throwback to tribal times, but it was instituted nonetheless.

The regime's attitude toward women was, in one sense, part of a broad political/cultural/class project directed against the Westernized modern middle class. For all men, ties and short-sleeved shirts in public were banned. The outward signs of an Islamist man were a beard and a tieless shirt buttoned at the neck. But beyond this, the new public policies reflected a reinforcement of patriarchy and its Islamic variant, whose defining feature is gender segregation. Women had become second-class citizens at best.

The fate of Iranian women immediately following the establishment of the Islamic Republic is not historically unprecedented, nor is it unique to Islam (or the Iranian Shi'a variant), as we have seen in Chapter 3. Some studies have noted the connection between authoritarian regimes and the control of women. As feminist historian Joan Scott has written:

> Whether at a crucial moment for Jacobin hegemony in the French Revolution, at the point of Stalin's bid for controlling authority, during the implementation of Nazi policy in Germany, or with the triumph in Iran of the Ayatollah Khomeini, domination, strength, central authority, and ruling power have been legitimized as masculine . . . and that coding has been literalized in laws (forbidding women's political participation, outlawing abortion, prohibiting wage-earning by mothers, imposing female dress codes) that put women in their place.[11]

Contradictions of the Islamist Discourse

The Islamic discourse was a patriarchal one, but its ambiguities and contradictions provided room for maneuver for Islamic women who could "bargain with patriarchy." On the one hand, the message was that the rights and responsibilities of men and women were not equal, women's role was as wife and mother, and the breadwinners and fighters were the men. On the other hand, public pronouncements of the new political elite and passages in the constitution could be read as supportive of equal citizenship and rights—although they were always qualified by or subject to "Islamic criteria." For example, Article 20 stipulated: "Every individual citizen, whether male or female, will have equal protection of the law and all human, political, economic, social and cultural rights will be based upon Islamic precepts." Article 21 guaranteed women's rights "according to Islamic criteria," but again emphasized wives, mothers, widows, the family, and children. Article 28 stated: "Every person has the right to pursue the occupation of his or her choice, insofar as this is not contrary to Islam, the public interest or the rights of others."

Public pronouncements by the Islamic authorities frequently showed an awareness of women's modern susceptibilities and their desire for equal treatment, as well as an insistence that Islam elevated women's status. Ayatollah Khomeini was quoted as saying that Shi'a Islam not only does not exclude women from social life but actually "elevates them to a platform where they belong, a higher platform."[12] He declared that "to wear the hijab does not imply suppression or seclusion" and referred "with pride" to women's right under Islam to own property as an indication of their economic independence.[13] In an address to a group of women in Qum on March 6, 1979, Khomeini praised Iranian women, saying, "I take pride in all the courageous deeds accomplished by the women of Iran . . . for you have been in the vanguard of our triumph and have encouraged the men." Elsewhere he stated,

"Islam made women equal with men; in fact, it shows a concern for women that it does not show for men." Finally he asserted, "In our revolutionary movement, women have likewise earned more credit than men, for it was the women who not only displayed courage themselves, but also had reared men of courage. Like the Noble Quran itself, women have the function of rearing and training true men. If nations were deprived of courageous women to rear true men, they would decline and collapse."[14]

Although working-class women were the most adversely affected by the early employment policies, there was always a small contingent who continued to work in factories, whether out of their own need and aspirations, or because the employers could not find men to replace them. These women contradicted the ideal of full-time motherhood and notions of the inappropriateness of factory work for women.

One inconsistency in the Islamist ideology and discourse was that, notwithstanding hijab and Shari'a, and despite sentiments on the part of certain Islamic ideologues against female participation in politics, women were not formally banned from the public sphere. Indeed, the regime rewarded Islamist women by allowing them to run for parliament and giving them jobs in the civil service. As early as the IRI's first parliament in 1980, there were four women members. Nor were women barred from higher education, although a quota system was established. Moreover, due to the chronic shortage of medical personnel and in the interest of maintaining gender-segregated medical care, women were encouraged to study medicine. Contrary to earlier speeches and policies designed to reduce their presence in government offices and the like, there *were* working mothers. Women also received military training; the "Zeinab Sisters"—female paramilitary enforcers—patrolled the streets for violations of Islamic dress codes and other offenses. Despite the regime's pronatalist policies banning abortion and discouraging contraception, World Bank data indicated that in 1983, some 23 percent of married women of childbearing age used contraceptives.[15] This can be regarded as a form of resistance to official impositions.

Throughout the 1980s the authorities criticized women who resisted hijab by dressing "inappropriately" in public. The Persian word is *bad-hijabi,* which usually meant wearing bright colors; stockings that were not dark or thick enough; fashionable trousers, shoes, or bags; and/or revealing some hair beneath the headscarf. But the authorities also issued warnings against *hezbollahi,* the self-styled "partisans of God" who occasionally took it upon themselves to enforce the code on hijab. These and other officials of the Islamic Republic claimed that women's status had been elevated after the revolution and that it would be further enhanced following the cessation of the war with Iraq and as economic conditions stabilized. Indeed, in referring to the relative decline of female economic participation, Ali Akbar Hashemi Rafsanjani, who was then Speaker of the Majlis, or Iran's parliament, said: "When the war is over and the economy improves and expands, you will see that we will have a shortage of manpower, and then the need for women will be greater. . . . In the universities we have a shortage of women professors. In medicine we need women specialists."[16] Rafsanjani also urged men to "forget about virginity" and marry war widows; in addition, he encouraged women to propose to men, citing Khadijeh's proposal to the Prophet Muhammad as justification.[17] He even criticized such "extremism" as partitioning classrooms in grade school and enforcing the *chador* in all-girls schools. He was quoted as saying: "Who can cite a Quranic verse stating that there should only be four women members in the Majlis?"[18] And although Rafsanjani approved of a segregated labor market with women working in "appropriate" occupations, he once noted, "Our wives are basically the kind of people who in the past did not enter the social arena. . . . But our daughters are not like this. They go to university and get jobs and work. Right now the Imam's daughter works in the cultural and educational sector. My daughters do too, as does the wife of the Prime Minister [referring to Zahra Rahnavard]."[19]

The ambiguities in the Islamist discourse as well as the legitimacy accorded to Islamic women allowed the new female elite room for maneuver within the gender system of the Islamic Republic, as well as the right to raise criticisms of and objections to barriers and restrictions. Women Majlis deputies charged in newspaper and magazine interviews that the suppression of women's rights was "un-Islamic" and "prejudicial." Maryam Behrouzi once complained to a leading women's magazine, "Women are never selected to chair committees; the Majlis merely reflects the male chauvinism that is rampant in our society."[20] Zahra Rahnavard—a well-known writer, university lecturer, and author of a book that presented a radical-populist Islamic perspective on social classes and inequality—told a reporter, "Women have been active and present, at times in larger numbers than men, in all our public demonstrations. But when it comes to political appointments, they are pushed aside."[21] She said:

> In our country there is a complex understanding about women . . . which produces a culture of inequality. . . . This culture is a far cry from the true Muhammadan Islam. Thus, although women have shown their political support fully and at all social levels, in the past ten years they have not been allowed to play their part properly in the economic and social construction of our country.
> Some of the activities that result in belittling women and lowering their status are conducted in the name of Islam. But these only have a religious cover and not a religious content. If we follow the true Muhammadan religion of Islam, then women would have no problems.[22]

Statements such as those by Zahra Rahnavard and Maryam Behrouz presaged the emergence of a quiet revolt by Islamic women and the emergence of an "Islamic feminism" that questioned patriarchal interpretations of Islamic law and the spirit of the Quran. This movement emerged in the 1990s, and it was at least partly a response to the failure of the Islamic Republic to elevate the legal status and social positions of Iranian women, as the next section shows.

The Decline of Women's Status in the 1980s

In 1986 the Islamic Republic carried out its first national census on population and housing (Iran's fourth since 1956), and the preliminary results were made available two years later. It revealed a dire sociodemographic situation and very poor indicators on literacy, education, employment, and income. In particular, the gender gaps were enormous.[23]

In the 1970s and 1980s, Iran was among several countries in which males still had a higher life expectancy than females, the others being Bangladesh, Bhutan, India, the Maldives, Nepal, and Pakistan.[24] Moreover, there was a sex ratio that favored men; that is, the male population was larger than the female population. (This was apparently also true for Afghanistan until the late 1980s, when the escalation of the civil war resulted in more male deaths than female.)[25] An adverse sex ratio indicates the low status of girls and women, which in a patriarchal context and relative poverty would mean more nutritional deficiencies by females than males, and therefore higher rates of mortality among girls and women. Female mortality is also linked to high fertility and poor access to healthcare services during pregnancy, childbirth, and illness. During the years 1980–1987, the maternal mortality rate in Iran was 120 per 100,000. This may be compared to the low rates of Cuba (31) and Kuwait (18) and the high rates of Zaire (800) and Peru (310).[26]

In 1976 the population numbered 33.7 million, but by 1986 it had increased to nearly 49 million. This represented an annual rate of population increase of 3.9 percent fueled by a high fertility rate. Iranian women had been having more than five children each, placing Iran among the countries with the highest growth rates.[27] The lowering of the age of marriage, the high rate of marriage, the promotion of childbearing, the absence of family planning services, the large number of women in their reproductive years, and the marginalization of women from the work force kept the birthrate high in postrevolutionary Iran. Accordingly, in 1986 almost half the population was under the age of fifteen.[28]

The 1986 census showed that over 7 million Iranian men and women, mostly in the provinces, did not speak or understand Persian, the official language of Iran.[29] Of that figure, 57 percent, or over 4 million, were women (17 percent of the female population). These women resided mostly in East and West Azerbaijan, Zanjan, Khuzestan, and Kurdestan. How did this compare with the male population? The number of men who did not know Persian was 2.9 million, or 11 percent of the male population. The male-female disparity in knowledge of Persian may be explained by educational and employment disparities.

The 1986 census revealed that universal primary schooling had yet to be achieved, especially for girls. Both absolutely and proportionally, more males than females were receiving education at both the grade school and postsecondary school levels. The gap was narrowest at the primary school level (where boys constituted 55 percent of the student population and girls 44 percent) and began to widen at the intermediate ("guidance") school level, where the male and female shares were 60 percent and 40 percent, respectively. At the tertiary level, the gender disparity was greater. Out of nearly 182,000 students receiving higher education in 1986, just 56,000 (or 31 percent) were female. The *Statistical Yearbook 1367* (March 1988–March 1989) listed forty universities, including one all-male seminary and one all-female seminary. The only institutions in which women's enrollment equaled or exceeded that of men's were the country's public health and medical schools, a reflection of the prevalent view that medicine is an appropriate field of study and profession for women—mainly so that they can provide medical services to women and thus avoid excessive male-female contact.

And what were women studying? Nineteen academic disciplines were listed in the census. Women were represented in all of them, including engineering (2,259), but the largest numbers of women university students were in health and medicine, teacher training, humanities, and the natural sciences. Engineering was the most popular field for male students. Of 4,178 law students in academic year 1367–1368 (1988–1989), there were only 485 women.[30]

Although there had been restrictions on women's admissions prior to the revolution (for example, the study of mining was off-limits to women; some nursing schools admitted only single women or widows without children), the restrictions following the cultural revolution were more extensive. Mojab's study revealed that the program of mathematical and technical sciences offered eighty-four majors, of which fifty-five (65 percent) did not admit women. In the field of experimental sciences, forty majors were offered, of which seven (17 percent) did not admit women: veterinary technician, animal science, agrarian affairs, geology, disease control, veterinary science, and natural resources. There were, of course, fields of study that were considered more appropriate for women, but even so, a ceiling was placed on female enrollments so that men's enrollments were guaranteed. The following twelve majors set quotas of 40–50 percent for women applicants: medicine, dentistry, optometry, radiology, speech therapy, audiometry, lab sciences, anesthesia, operating-room technician, oral and dental hygiene, and physiotherapy. A far lower limit of 20 percent female was established for pharmacology, environmental hygiene, and artificial limbs. Two majors, midwifery and family hygiene, accepted women only. A significant change occurred in nursing, which set a quota of 50 percent male students, an apparent attempt at training male nurses to serve male patients. Thirty-five majors were offered in the humanities, of which seven set a maximum for females: theology and Islamic learning, 50 percent; law, 25 percent (female graduates could not become lawyers or judges); archaeology and art history, 40 percent; physical education and sports, 40 percent. Art offered ten majors, of which design, sewing, and technical instructor for sewing and commercial sewing accepted women only. For women to be eligible for government scholarships to study abroad, they had to be married and accompanied by their husbands.

Labor Force Marginalization

The caveats on labor force data mentioned in Chapter 2 pertain to Iran as well. To sum up, figures for urban areas are more reliable than they are for rural areas; but in either case, dealing with large informal sectors, seasonal employment, migrant workers, unstable work arrangements, and part-time employment makes enumeration very difficult. Refugee populations (in Iran's case, large numbers of Afghan economic refugees work as domestics or construction workers) could also complicate enumeration. And then there is the notorious undercounting of women; rural women in particular are frequently left out of the tabulations or are assumed to be "homemakers." All of the Iranian censuses have overlooked large numbers of women, most of them rural. The 1986 census categorized fully 11 million Iranian women as "homemakers." Consequently, there was a huge disparity in the activity rates of men and women, and only a tiny percentage of Iranian women were calculated as part of the labor force. Last but not least, the census data do not capture the extent of urban women's informal economic activities. In any event, characteristics of the employed female population according to the 1986 census included the following:

- The female share of the total labor force and of salaried employment was very small, at under 10 percent (down from 13.8 percent of the salaried work force in 1976).
- Most women in the work force were wage and salary workers in the government sector, mainly as teachers and health workers employed by the Ministries of Health and Education, working in the state schools and universities and in the public health centers; these women enjoyed social insurance, including pensions, healthcare, maternity leave, and other benefits.
- In contrast, large numbers of "employed" women in the private sector were not receiving a wage for their work. Indeed, the proportion

of women in the private sector receiving a wage or salary was only 19 percent.

- Apart from carpet weaving and traditional craftwork, women's role in modern industrial production was limited—only 14 percent of the manufacturing labor force, and mostly unwaged (that is, home-based workers).
- An extreme form of occupational sex-segregation existed.
- Women were almost nonexistent in decisionmaking positions.
- Women's role in agriculture was deemed marginal; the majority of rural women were designated "housewives" in the census. There were few female agricultural extension agents; this resulted from discriminatory education and training policies that barred women from agrarian affairs and veterinary science.
- The unemployment rate of women was very high: 25.5 percent; for the urban areas, it was 29 percent.

Another characteristic was that during the 1980s, the Iranian female labor force was a very youthful one. For such occupations as scientific/technical workers and teachers, the largest numbers of women were in the age groups 20–29 and 30–39. In agricultural occupations they were far younger; the largest numbers of women were in the age group 10–19, followed by the age group 20–29. And in the "industrial" occupations, such as rug weaving, the largest numbers of women workers were in the 10–19 age group.[31]

Compared with other developing countries, not to mention developed countries, the female share of salaried employment in Iran—a mere 10 percent—was extremely small. By contrast, women's labor force shares in 1990 were about 18 percent in Turkey and Tunisia, 28 percent in Mexico, 35–38 percent in Cuba, Malaysia, and Korea, and 47 percent in Bulgaria, according to ILO data. Even so, Iranian women's presence in the work force contradicted strict Islamist and patriarchal views of women's place. What explained their continued labor force participation?

One reason had to do with the war effort. From 1980 to 1988, large segments of the male population over the age of fifteen were mobilized in the war with Iraq; hundreds of thousands were killed or disabled. Employers and government agencies turned to women to compensate for the loss of vast numbers of males on the labor market. It will be recalled that in other countries during wartime—such as the United States and England during World War II— women crowded the expanded payrolls of factories, offices, and retailers that had traditionally employed females as well as those of heavy industries and war-related agencies. In Iran, as in the United States and England, wartime labor shortages created employment opportunities for women throughout the expanding state apparatus. Maryam Poya's research on women and work in the Islamic Republic confirmed this. According to a nurse interviewed by Poya: "Initially during the early years of the war, the injured Islamic soldiers objected to being treated by female nurses. Later, however, they had no choice as there was a real shortage of nurses and very few men wanted to become nurses." Even women secretaries returned: "Male secretaries were not as good as female secretaries. So female secretaries returned to work."[32] Poya's interviews also showed the importance of the urban informal sector for women who either could not obtain gainful employment or needed to augment their low salaries with additional income. According to Poya, women even took part in the underground economy, whereby they bought rationed food cheaply and sold it on the black market at higher prices.

In summary form, the following factors explain why women were found in the modern sector and the informal sector of the economy during the 1980s: (1) the ambiguities in the discourse and policies of the Islamic political elite and the conflicting cultural images of women, allowing women some room to maneuver within the confines of the Islamic system; (2) the imperatives of the war effort and expansion of the state apparatus, which created a demand, albeit limited, for female labor; and (3) economic need on the part of some

Although hijab is compulsory in Iran, the way women cover themselves reflects class, occupation, and ideological orientation. The author (second from left) with two chemists (in white coats) and two government employees, Tehran, 1994. Photo courtesy of Daroupakhsh Pharmaceuticals.

women and the resistance to total subjection on the part of others, including educated women with prior work experience.

After Khomeini: Economic Versus Ideological Imperatives

The war with Iraq ended in 1988 and Ayatollah Khomeini died in 1989. The death of the charismatic revolutionary and religious leader, the cessation of hostilities with Iraq, and the realization of the enormous task ahead of reconstruction and socioeconomic development led the Islamic Republic under President Rafsanjani in a new direction. The 1986 census had revealed absolute poverty, inequality, and declining standards of living and quality of life; moreover, the government had been unable to create jobs, meet basic needs, and invest in industry and agriculture.[33] The end of the long and expensive war with Iraq had plunged Iran into an economic crisis that could only be worsened by the fast-growing population. A new and more rational strategy was needed.

In 1990 Iran began to borrow heavily on international markets as a way of tackling the crisis, but it more than tripled the total foreign debt (from $6.5 billion in 1989 to $22.3 billion in 1995). The bulk of this long-term debt was owed or guaranteed by the government and it swelled from a low of 4.8 percent of GNP in 1980 to 30 percent of GNP in 1995.[34] This created pressures on the government to implement a long-term national development strategy to curb spending (especially on imports), to focus on raising the quality of human resources, to encourage domestic savings, and to attract domestic and foreign investments in economic sectors that might increase foreign exchange earnings, such as export manufacturing and tourism. In this context, the government lifted any remaining restrictions on women's education and employment, while also advocating family planning.

Spiraling population growth at a time of depleting fiscal resources and increasing pockets of poverty throughout the country led authorities to dramatically reverse the pronatalism of the postrevolutionary period to an official policy of family planning. In June 1989 the government formally lifted the ban on contraceptives at state hospitals and clinics. (Still prohibited by law, however, was abortion.) In January 1990 a seminar on population control convened in Tehran, with the result that the government now openly favored and encouraging family planning and the use of birth control devices—a marked departure from the early pronatalist position. The government was determined to reduce the population growth rate to 2.3 percent per annum. In July 1991 the Iranian cabinet approved a proposal by the Ministry of Health whereby any children born to families already having three would be deprived of the government's family allowances. Tehran University signed an agreement with the United Nations Fund for Population Activities to conduct population research and design a population policy.

In the summer of 1989 the quotas for women at the universities were removed from many disciplines, and Zahra Rahnavard was credited with having negotiated removal of these barriers. The Rafsanjani presidency provided a more conducive opportunity structure for women's education and employment, and during the 1990s women's enrollments in the educational institutions began to increase. Rafsanjani officially inaugurated the 1991–1992 academic year with a visit to a boys school and to a girls school, and in the latter he expressed his satisfaction with the rising number of girl students. According to a newspaper account, he also "called on the female population to strive to take their 50 percent share in the country's educational programmes and institutions." Rafsanjani also stressed that not only should women further their activities in all social fields but also that "even housewives should further their academic studies."[35]

One instance of a shift in gender ideology guided by pragmatic consideration was on the question of women and law. As mentioned previously, women in law, notably all judges, were purged from their positions immediately after the revolution. Women were discouraged from studying law because they were deemed to be by nature too emotional, although a few continued their studies. At the end of the decade, the field of law became more open to women. Unless they were designated anti-revolutionary, even those women who had been purged in the early 1980s were asked to come back to work, though not necessarily to their previous positions. Former judges could now work as inspectors or assistants in certain courts. Thus, after a decade of barring women from law, the Iranian state reversed itself and deemed it advantageous to draw on women with legal experience and education, including those who had acquired their expertise in the period before the revolution. Speaker of the Majlis Hojatoleslam Mehdi Karrubi in September 1991 called on women to compete for key posts in the government and to enter the Majlis in greater numbers. In an address to a group of Islamist women, Karrubi said that women must find their way into the cabinet and take up posts such as vice president.[36]

Another example of a shift in gender policy pertained to women and agriculture. As stated above, the 1986 Iranian census seriously undercounted rural women. Furthermore, there were hardly any female agricultural extension agents in postrevolutionary Iran. But in 1991, the minister of agriculture, Issa Kalantari, announced that agricultural training centers for women would be established "to better utilize the female work force in the sector." The Ministry of Agriculture had apparently counted more women in agriculture than the Statistical Center of Iran had, for the minister said that 40 percent of the farm work in Iran was performed by women. According to a newspaper account, he "regretted that there still exist restrictions preventing women from enrolling in certain academic fields, and that there were certain difficulties in training female farmers." But he said that arrangements would be made to train women alongside men in agricultural fields. Interestingly, he also called on other government agencies to "further employ women and trust them with more key posts."[37] These changes should be understood in the context of the Rafsanjani government's attention to economic issues, a shift from the Khomeini regime's earlier focus on cultural, political, and moral issues. The authorities were cognizant that economic growth and development could not take place in a situation of unbridled population growth and the underutilization of the female resource base.

Interestingly enough, as the Islamic Republic of Iran was making the transition from theocracy and patriarchal Islamism to parliamentarianism and a more liberal Islamic environment in which feminist voices were beginning to be heard, there remained some Islamist women who continued to defend the record of the Islamic Republic even in the face of overwhelming evidence of women's second-class citizenship. A report on the social status of Iranian women before and after "the victory of the Islamist Revolution," authored by the Research Group for Muslim Women's Studies, illustrates the defensive stance of such Islamist women, and is worth quoting at length:

The social state of women like other strata has undergone various changes after the victory of the Islamic revolution, revealing the noble and true value of the Muslim women. Hence, the women who under the impact of foreign culture had lost their identity and had come to view freedom merely as a quantitative equality with men, as a consequence of the glorious Islamic revolution, opened their minds to their own supreme identity. Besides, under the enlightened acceptance of and following the commands of the Supreme Being, women gained independence of thought and true freedom, and realized that in an Islamic system a woman is no longer a mindless consuming agent of the foreign products and no longer is misused under the disguise of equality.

The general policy of the capitalist West is based on shaking the foundation of the family institution and placing men and women in an apparently equal position in spite of their natural differences. In the teachings of Islam although men and women as human beings are considered equal, yet regarding human nature, they have been ascribed different tasks. In general, Islam has assigned real equal rights to all humanity, and the result of such equality in the view of social injustice in Islam is that everyone should come to realize his own true rights as well as divine rights.

Islam regards men and women equal as far as their choice of securing their livelihood is concerned. Therefore, women, like men, can manage their lives independently, and keep the product of their own labor. Hence men and women are equal in Islam, according to the verses of the Holy Quran, which is the voice of God. Mankind has accepted that these rights are divine in nature, rather than man-made.

Obviously, the apparent and quantitative equality is not the only goal of socio-cultural advancement of women. After the Islamic revolution in Iran, the attempt to obtain quantitative equality of women with men in educational centers, offices, and factories, in and of itself, is no longer the criterion of progress. That is why in so-called developed countries though Imperialist propaganda states that men and women are of equal proportion in most areas and occupations, the reality is that the rate of dissatisfaction of these women has increased due to lack of freedom and inequality, and their struggle for gaining equal rights is still continuing.

Iranian women and men, throughout the Islamic revolution and after its victory, have participated in many tasks. Their valuable contributions at home and behind the war fronts, cannot be evaluated by material standards. Therefore, the rate of their advancement or backwardness after the Islamic revolution and at the present situation cannot be examined and judged by sheer international standards. A full knowledge of the social patterns and a reinterpretation of the concepts that represent the value system of the society are the essential prerequisites for such judgments.

Considering that the true role of women in the advancement of society after the revolution can only be appreciated with qualitative standards, it is not quite just to measure the social progress of women of different strata by mere quantitative standards, i.e., presenting the number of females in occupational, education, and professional categories. However, after the revolution, the Iranian women, adopting religious standards, have been able to gain a considerable amount of success, even quantitatively speaking, through participating in various social, educational, and professional activities, and hence regaining their true social status and esteem.[38]

Liberalization and Policy Shifts in the 1990s

The 1990s were characterized by the following: (1) liberalization, development planning, and shifts in gender policy under President Rafsanjani; (2) the growing visibility of Islamic feminists, legal strategies for women's rights by state and independent feminists, and the proliferation of a dynamic feminist press; and (3) the emergence of a movement for reform of the Islamic Republic's cultural practices and political system, which led to the presidency of Mohammad Khatami in 1997 and again in 2001.

In 1992 the High Council of the Cultural Revolution adopted a set of employment policies for women, which, while reiterating the importance of family roles and continuing to rule out certain occupations and professions as Islamically inappropriate, encouraged the integration of women in the labor force and attention to their interests and needs. Women were encouraged to enter certain scientific and technical fields such as gynecology, pharmacology, midwifery, and laboratory work. The government also changed its policy on women and the legal profession, and during the 1990s the field of law became more open to women. "Women legal consultants" as well as assistant judges were permitted in the Special Civil Courts.[39] There was a steady increase in women's share of government employment, perhaps as much a reflection of the deterioration of government wages and the increasing participation of men in the private sector as it was an indicator of progress in the attenuation of gender inequality. By 1995, about 33 percent of public-sector employees were women, most of whom worked in the Ministries of Education and Health and about 35 percent of whom had university degrees.[40]

Especially striking was the complete reversal of the Islamic Republic's position on family planning, the implementation of an aggressive campaign to spread the message of the benefits of small families, and the resulting dramatic decline in the fertility rate. As noted in Chapter 4, the country's total fertility rate declined from 5.6 births per woman in 1985 to 2.0 births in 2000. That same year, fully 74 percent of married women practiced family planning. Clearly Iranian women—both urban and rural—enthusiastically welcomed the idea of family planning and made effective use of the free seminars and contraceptive devices provided by the government's family health workers. What is more, there was a change in marriage patterns that also affected fertility: Women's average age at first marriage increased from 19.7 in 1976 to 22.4 in 1996.[41]

In the realm of politics, the increasing visibility of women was a gradual but noticeable trend. During the 1995 parliamentary elections, nine women were elected to the Majlis, including the outspoken Faezeh Hashemi. The parliamentary elections in 2000 resulted not only in more women members of parliament but also the emergence of several articulate and reform-minded advocates. Speeches by the women parliamentarians attested to changing and more assertive attitudes, with language that was less specifically Islamic and more compatible with the kind of global feminist discourse found in the UN's Beijing Platform for Action. Women's affairs offices were established in each ministry and government agency, and a number of nongovernmental organizations dealing with women's concerns were formed. A lively women's press emerged, with books, magazines, and women's studies journals taking on important political, cultural, religious, and social issues. The educational attainment of Iranian women increased, with the majority completing secondary school. And in the academic year 2002–2003, women's tertiary enrollments exceeded those of men for the first time since universities were established in Iran.

Women in the Labor Force: Still Marginalized

The picture of women in the labor force that was revealed by the Islamic Republic's second ten-year census, which was completed in November 1996, was not so positive. In summary: women's share of the total economically active population was just 12.7 percent; of the urban economically active population, 11.7 percent; of the urban employed population, 11.2 percent; of total public-sector wage earners, 16.4 percent (a slight increase over 1986). Thus women's labor force shares were still under 20 percent and therefore still low by international standards, although they were higher than in 1986. Women's unemployment rate was 12.5 percent—considerably lower than in 1986, but still higher than men's (8.3 percent in 1996).[42]

Who were the unemployed women? Of the 271,565 unemployed women, 53 percent were urban and 47 percent rural. Some 38 percent of the rural unemployed women had completed primary education; 51 percent of urban unemployed women had a high school education and 12 percent had higher education. These figures showed that urban and rural women alike were seeking jobs but were facing barriers to gainful employment. The figures also showed that a higher proportion of educated women found themselves without employment compared with educated men. Of the urban unemployed men, 27 percent had a high school degree (compared to 51 percent for women) and only 4.7 percent of them had higher education (compared to 12 percent of the unemployed women). The figures on women's unemployment were also revealing of the social changes in the country, and especially in the rural areas. Rural women's educational attainment had increased, and with it came the desire for employment, although economic need was very likely an additional factor.

The 1996 labor force data also showed that professional women continued to work in the public sector. Working-class and peasant women in the manufacturing sector were not involved in modern production; their work remained overwhelmingly rural and traditional, whereas men were involved in urban and modern manufacturing. Outside of agriculture (where women's participation continued to be undercounted) and manufacturing (where women's work was largely rural), Iranian women were overrepresented in urban professional jobs (primarily in education and health) and underrepresented in all other occupational categories (such as sales and services). Figures 6.1–6.3 illustrate these patterns not only for 1996, but also over time.

The salient characteristics of Iranian women's employment at the dawn of the twenty-first century may be delineated as follows:

- Although most of the female labor force (55 percent) was engaged in the private sector (compared with 39.5 percent in the public sector), the vast majority of women private-sector workers (86.4 percent) were in the rural areas. By contract, the majority of women public-sector workers (63.3 percent) were urban.
- Most economically active women (28 percent) were working in professional fields; in the urban areas, 46 percent of employed women were in professional fields.
- Women's share of the field of education was 44 percent for the total country, but it was much higher in the urban areas (48.6 percent) than in the rural areas (22 percent).
- Women's share of health services was 39.3 percent for the total country, though it was higher in urban areas (40.4 percent) than in the rural areas (33 percent).

**Figure 6.1   Female Share of Economically Active and Nonactive
Population (10 years and older), Iran, 1956–1996**

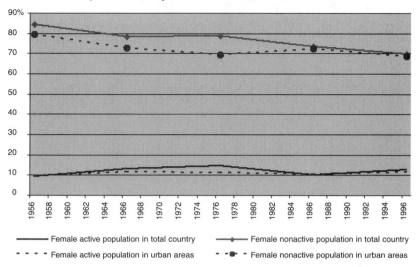

Source: *Statistical Yearbook of Iran 1375/1996* (Tehran: IRI, 1997), tab. 3-1, p. 70.

**Figure 6.2   Female Employees (10 years and older), Share of Major Occupations,
Iran, November 1996**

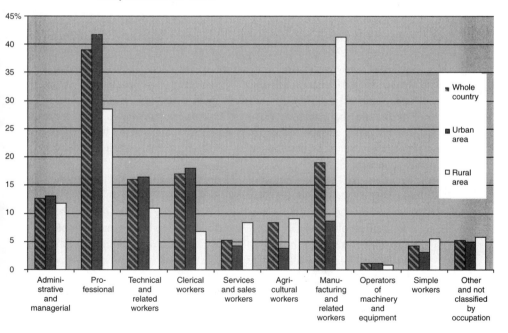

Source: *Statistical Yearbook of Iran 1375/1996* (Tehran: IRI, 1997), tab. 3-8, p. 80.

Figure 6.3   Share of Employed Population (10 years and older) by Gender, Iran, 1956–1996

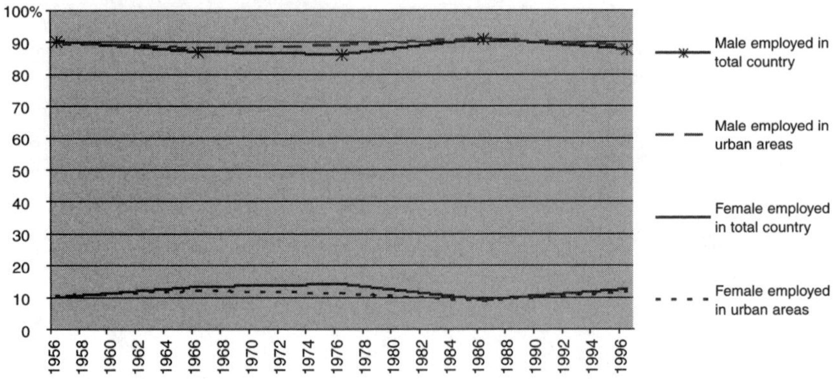

Source: Statistical Yearbook of Iran 1375/1996 (Tehran: IRI, 1997), tab. 3-1, p. 70.

- Some 21.6 percent of working women were in manufacturing— higher than in 1986, but mostly in the rural areas, where they were nonwage earners.[43] Their share of manufacturing was 22.8 percent for the total country—but fully 45.2 percent for rural areas.
- Women were still underrepresented in such occupations as administration and management, technical and related jobs, clerical work, service and sales work, and agriculture.[44] They were also underrepresented in agriculture, *urban* manufacturing, wholesale and retail trade, finance, and real estate/business services.
- The female share of total private-sector employment was 10 percent (mainly rural) and the share of private-sector wage earners was 7.6 percent. By contrast, women's share of public-sector wage earners was 16.4 percent.[45]
- Women's civil service employment had increased to 38.6 percent of all civil service employees covered by social security. (Their share of total public-sector employment was lower, however, because of their marginal involvement in state-owned industries, hotels, etc.) Women were concentrated in the Ministries of Education (44 percent female) and Health (43 percent female). In the Ministry of Justice, women made up about 27 percent of employees.
- Ministries with relatively low female involvement, given their mandates, included Culture and Higher Education (20 percent female), Labor and Social Security (11.3 percent), Agriculture (7.2 percent),

Development and Housing (13.7 percent), Commerce (12 percent), and Culture and Islamic Guidance (17.8 percent).

The above analysis is indicative of the slow rate of progress for women's economic participation and involvement in the formal labor force in the 1990s. Of course, the figures above do not reflect women's nonformal economic participation, and anecdotal evidence suggests that most Iranian women are involved in some form of economic activity (e.g., sewing; making jams and jewelry at home for sale; desktop publishing; providing beauty services; tutoring; offering driving services). Still, many hoped that the situation would improve, especially in the wake of the presidential elections of May 1997 and the appointment of several women to high-ranking offices. After newly elected president Mohammad Khatami named Massoumeh Ebtekar, a U.S.-educated lecturer and editor of a women's studies journal, as a vice president in charge of environmental affairs, Culture Minister Ayatollah Mohajerani appointed Azam Nouri as deputy culture minister for legal and parliamentary affairs. Interior Minister Abdollah Nouri followed by naming Zahra Shojai, a professor at Al-Zahra University in Tehran and a member of the Interior Ministry's Women's Commission, as Iran's first director-general for women's affairs.[46] In her new position, Ms. Shojai would be in charge of issues such as social policies pertaining to women and violence against women. These were the first women to serve in top government posts and decisionmaking positions since the 1979 revolution, and they signaled a new era for women. There were expectations that these women would assist in the modernization of family law and the expansion of women's social rights. Their work for women was, however, stymied by a conservative parliament until the parliamentary elections of February 2000 brought in a majority of reformists, including a number of women's rights activists. In turn, the reformist parliament saw its efforts blocked by the conservative Council of Guardians—a body created in 1980 to ensure that legislation is consistent with Islamic law and the constitution—and by the Islamist judiciary, which continued to adhere to an orthodox and patriarchal interpretation of Islamic law.

The Emergence of Islamic Feminism

In the latter part of the 1990s, a new trend emerged in Iran: a broad-based social movement for reform of the Islamic Republic. The reform movement—composed largely of students, intellectuals, and women—called for civil liberties, political freedoms, women's rights, and a relaxation of cultural and social controls. This was the movement behind the proliferation of a dynamic press (which was, however, constantly subjected to harassment), the 1997 presidential election of liberal cleric Mohammad Khatami, and the outcome of the parliamentary elections of February 2000, in which reformists made sweeping gains. The reform movement, however, faced the hostility of the conservative Islamist forces that opposed any change. Intellectuals issued open letters and penned articles, but when the judiciary or Islamist vigilantes deemed them seditious, several prominent writers and dissidents were jailed or murdered. In a bold move in July 1999, university students protested against state repression and called for an acceleration of President Khatami's appeals for civil society and democracy in Iran, only to be met by violent assaults by Islamist vigilantes, the Ansar-e Hezbollah. The stalemate between reformists and conservatives continued through 2002.[47]

Even before the emergence of the reform movement, disappointment with the outcomes of the Islamic gender policies of the 1980s had led prominent Islamic women to dissent and to agitate for improvements in the status of women. Secular lawyer Mehranguiz Kaar distinguishes between "feminists" and "Muslim women activists," but she observed that the Islamic women had greater access to the institutions of the government than did the secular women, and "they used their position to appeal directly to the public and to higher authorities for justice."[48] I have already referred to the activities of Zahra Rahnavard during the latter part of the 1980s. Azam Taleghani—a well-known activist and member of parliament—published *Payam-e Hajar*, or Hagar's Message. One issue carried an article on family planning, calling it "a basic human right." Remarkably, the article stated that "the right of a woman to control her body and thus her own fertility is central to any discussion of human rights." A sidebar stated, "There is, I believe, great wisdom in the immortal words of Abdul Ibn Badis, the Algerian Muslim reformist, 'Educate a boy and you educate one person, educate a girl and you educate a nation.'"[49] Another prominent Islamic woman, Maryam Behrouzi, similarly promoted women's rights, sometimes in audacious ways.

Born in 1945 to a religious family in Tehran, Behrouzi studied theology in university and was involved in political campaigns against the Pahlavi state. Upon completing her studies in theology, philosophy, and law, she helped organize the Iranian Women's Islamic Association in ten districts in Tehran. In 1975 she was prohibited from pursuing her political activities but continued to do so clandestinely until she was jailed in 1978. Released after the revolutionary uprising, Behrouzi became part of the new Islamist feminine elite, and a member of parliament in 1980. By the end of the decade, Behrouzi became more of an advocate for women's rights. In a 1991 newspaper interview, she said that she regarded it as her role as a woman deputy to upgrade the status of women in Iran's Islamic society. Her tactics included criticizing existing discriminatory laws against women, such as the law that prohibited unmarried women students from receiving government scholarships to study abroad. In the same interview she emphasized the importance of women's presence in the public and private sectors and pointed out that, unlike men, women shoulder the responsibility of childcare and housework. Behrouzi helped draft a bill to offer scholarship entitlements to unmarried women, another bill that would allow women to retire with pensions after twenty years of employment irrespective of their age, and yet a third bill to ease restrictions on recruitment to the Islamic Revolutionary Guards Corps. She was also in favor of marriage reform to strengthen women's position in the family and before the law. One bill on which she worked would provide a widow and her children with some form of insurance. In the 1991 interview, she noted that although Islam allows a man up to four wives, in the Islamic Republic "marital status is based on monogamous rules."[50] In a 1994 interview in the women's magazine *Zan-e Rouz,* she stated, "We don't believe that every social change is harmful. Cultural refinement of some traditions, such as patriarchy *[mardsalari],* anti-woman attitudes *[zan-setizi],* and humiliation of women *[tahghir-e zanan]* must disappear. These have been fed to our people in the name of Islam."

An even more outspoken advocate for women's rights was Faezeh Hashemi, the younger daughter of former president Rafsanjani who wore blue jeans under her Islamic coat, promoted the right of women and girls to engage in athletics, and publicly rode a bicycle, much to the consternation of conservatives. In 1995 she ran for parliament; an extremely popular candidate, she garnered 1 million votes. (She lost her seat in the February 2000 elections.) In a remarkable act, she marched in solidarity with students during the July 1999 protests. She appeared in filmmaker Rakhshan Bani-Etemad's film-within-a-film *(The May Lady),* where she boldly stated that the problems of women in Iran resulted from the fact that all the judges were men. In a 1997 interview she stated, "We generally agree that the role of women on the Iranian political scene has improved in the last years but still there are some basic problems such as an Iranian female official cannot leave the country without her husband's permission. Is this not a basic obstacle to the basic right of a woman, whether official or non-official?" In response to a question about national reconciliation, she was adamant that all Iranians regardless of political views had a place in the country and its system: "I think the Iranian people belong to Iran and live in Iran and tolerated all the problems in the last 17 years and even went to the war-fronts. Even though they might not have even been a Muslim or a Hezbollah, they might have only done that due to their national sentiments and due to their love for their country."[51]

On the issue of veiling, she revealed strong, if contradictory, views. Referring to Turkey, she said: "I think that unfortunately in some countries Western norms are imposed on women. Hijab is an indisputable symbol for Muslim women. Muslim women should not be deprived. Although Turkey is an Islamic country, women are thrown out of universities because of Hijab."[52]

Here she made no reference to the fact that in Iran, veiling is compulsory rather than a freely chosen mode of dress or expression of identity. Subsequently, Hashemi changed her views on veiling. In the run-up to the parliamentary elections of February 2000, she declared that hijab should be voluntary and not mandatory. That was the boldest challenge yet to religious orthodoxy, state policy, and patriarchal norms.

Indeed, a paradoxical outcome of Islamization in Iran has been the emergence of what may be called a feminist pre-movement with at least two strands, Islamic and secular. Liberalization during the Rafsanjani years helped, and organized expressions of women's aspirations developed in tandem with the broader reform movement for political and cultural change. Secular women who had long opposed hijab were now joined by countless young women who clearly disliked compulsory hijab and engaged in numerous informal and spontaneous individual acts of resistance (though not yet organized protests) against it. The women's press grew and included newspapers, magazines, and women's studies journals such as *Zan, Zanan, Jens-e Dovvom, Farzaneh,* and *Hoghough-e Zanan,* as well as Roshangaran Press. Articles published in the women's press criticized the subordinate status of women in the Islamic Republic and called for the modernization of family law. In addition, the women's press translates classic feminist essays (e.g., Mary Wollstonecraft, Virginia Woolf, Alison Jagger) as well as more recent articles appearing in Western feminist publications. Secular and Islamic feminist leaders in Iran began to become known internationally. Apart from the well-known Faezeh Hashemi, these include women who have formed or otherwise helped to sustain women's publishing collectives (for example, Shahla Lahiji, Shahla Sherkat, Mahboubeh Abbas-Gholizadeh, Noushin Ahmadi-Khorassani); filmmakers (Rakhshan Bani-Etemad, Tahmineh Milani, Marzieh Meshkini); practicing lawyers or legal experts who explain and critique the legal constraints on women's rights and equality (Mehranguiz Kaar and Shirin Ebadi); believing women whose questions about the status of women in Islam and in the Islamic Republic launched the field of Islamic feminism (especially Shahla Sherkat, editor of *Zanan*); and academics who tried to form women's studies courses or programs at their universities or wrote on women's topics in the women's press (such as Jaleh Shaditalab and Nahid Motiee). A coalition of secular and Islamic feminists, including the women who became members of parliament in 2000, began to work with reformist male parliamentarians to contest the codified and institutionalized privileges of men over women.

Feminists in Iran have framed their grievances and demands in Islamic terms and have drawn from the cultural stock to press for women's rights and equality. For example, a group of women parliamentarians petitioned Islamic clerics in October 2002 to demand that compensation paid to the family of a woman victim in a murder case ("blood money" according to the *Qessass* law) be the same as that paid for a man. Fatemeh Rakai, head of the parliament's committee on women's issues, justified the proposed change on the grounds that women were now working and supporting their families. (Still left untouched was the inequality of non-Muslims in the penal code.) As a result of a "huge lobbying effort by women activists" to improve conditions of divorced women, Iranian women were granted *ujrat-e mesel,* or the right to wages for housework carried out during the marital years.[53] Feminists also have used secular language and pointed to international conventions and standards, thus challenging the dominant political and ideological framework. Iran's women's rights advocates have engaged in a feminist rereading of the Quran, in which they highlight its emancipatory content and dispute patriarchal interpretations and codifications; they have pointed to the discrepancy between the Islamic Republic's claim of having liberated women versus the fact of male privilege in areas such as divorce and child custody; they have called for the adoption of international conventions and standards such as the UN's Convention on the Elimination of All Forms of Discrimination Against Women and the Beijing Platform for Action; they have participated in international forums such as the Beijing Plus Five deliberations in June 2000; they have formed links (albeit limited) with global feminists outside Iran; and they have received various kinds of support from Iranian expatriate feminists and from other feminist organizations and networks around the world.

Despite the lack of feminist organizations and overt forms of collective action, Islamic and secular feminists alike have discussed, debated, and exchanged ideas through the media, especially in the lively and prodigious women's press. Shahla Sherkat, Azzam Taleghani, Faezeh Hashemi, Mahboubeh Ummi (Abbas-Gholizadeh), and Marzieh Mortazi (elected member of a local council), along with Shirin Ebadi, Mehranguiz Kaar, Shahla Lahiji, and Noushin Ahmadi-Khorasani, have converged and collaborated around issues such as the modernization of family law, the need for more political participation by women, and support for the reform movement and for President Khatami. This coalition building is considered to be an important step in the promotion of women's rights, and a correction of past mistakes. Ummi, the editor of *Farzaneh,* was quoted as saying, "Although secular women do not share our convictions, we can collaborate because we all work to promote women's status. We [Islamist women] no longer consider ourselves to be the sole heirs of the revolution. We have realized that our sectarian views of the first post-revolutionary years led to the isolation of many competent seculars, which was to the detriment of all women. We now hope to compensate [for] our errors."[54] According to Shahla Sherkat, the editor of *Zanan:*

> *Zanan* magazine has pioneered the debate between secular and Muslim feminists over the issue of women's rights. Women's rights issues in Iran are so complicated that we must start from somewhere that we could agree with each other and work through until we arrive at areas of disagreement. Not to

forget that beside secular women we also have religious minorities and national minorities where the issue of feminism could mean different things for different women.[55]

And how do Iranian feminists—state feminists or Islamic feminists—define feminism? According to Faezeh Hashemi:

Feminism is about defending women's rights and fighting for equal rights for women and men. In this context I do believe that I have been involved in defending women's rights. There are issues which affect all of us. Even in the parliament, we may disagree on political issues but most women members are agreeing on most issues in relation to family law, women's education and employment. This is very encouraging, especially as I see this on a global level, where there is a global women's movement that is unstoppable, like a stream.[56]

Shahla Sherkat explained her preference for the term "indigenous feminism" rather than "Islamic feminism":

I prefer to use the term *feminizm boomi* [indigenous feminism], because it relates women's rights to the social and cultural specifics of Iran. For example, at present, we may not be able to raise the issue of abortion in our society. But we could raise the issue of women's rights to have control over their sexuality and fertility. This is a very important issue in a society where the traditional interpretation of the Islamic law gives a man the right to have sexual relations with his wife and decide when and how many children he may want to have, and the wife has to obey his wishes. Therefore, the demand for a woman to have control over her sexuality and fertility challenges the patriarchal rights of men within Sharia law.

For her part, secular lawyer Mehranguiz Kaar said:

I support those who may call themselves Muslim feminists. But, in principle, I disagree with them. I write for *Zanan* magazine because this is an opportunity for me to express my views and I admire them for facilitating this opportunity for me. Similarly, as a lawyer I do not agree with the Constitution but within my work I struggle to change the Islamic law and hopefully the Constitution. I believe that with the existing Constitution it is impossible to talk about the equal rights of women and men and the rights of citizens. But until we achieve the separation of politics from religion, we need to overcome obstacles and in this way I welcome cooperation with Muslim feminists and I hope that in the long run they will come closer to us.[57]

The passages above by Iranian secular and Islamic feminists show the extent to which change has occurred in Iranian society, notwithstanding resistance from elements of the Islamic state.

Conclusion: Religious State, Secular Society?

In the first years of the Islamic Republic, the rhetoric and the policies were intended to segregate the sexes and domesticate the women, based on the notion of fundamental gender difference. Educated, Western-oriented, upper-middle-class women bore the brunt of the regime's most retrograde policies, though almost all women faced an extremely untoward cultural/ideological milieu. The effects of the Islamic Republic's preoccupation with cultural and ideological issues and with the definition of women's place were considerable. The full range of their social impact—which came to light when the results of the 1986 national census of population and housing were analyzed—included increasing fertility and population growth; a decline in female labor force participation, particularly in the industrial sector; lack of progress in literacy and educational attainment; and a sex ratio that favored males. Clearly, Islamist politics had resulted in an extremely disadvantaged position for women; it had reinforced male domination; it had compromised women's autonomy; and it had created a set of gender relations characterized by profound inequality. Inasmuch as this had occurred, it signaled that the intentions and policies of the Islamic Republic had succeeded.

However, a number of factors came to undermine several of the most egregious policies of the Islamic Republic and reverse rather dramatically its program on women, family, and gender relations. The changes occurred after the death of Ayatollah Khomeini and during the presidency of Hashemi Rafsanjani, in the context of a program for economic liberalization and integration into the global economy. Further changes occurred during the presidency of Mohammad Khatami, particularly in terms of the growth and vitality of Iranian civil society, a movement for political and cultural reform, and a movement for women's rights.

That women continued to participate in public life during the repressive years of the 1980s suggests resilience and resistance to domination. In turn, women's continued participation in the public sphere helped undermine the theocratic and male-dominated society. It subverted the notion of clearly defined gender roles and a rigid, gender-based social division of labor. Further educational attainment and employment of women could challenge patriarchal practices and authoritarian structures as a whole, with implications not only for women's economic independence and personal freedom but also for wider social change in Iran. This proposition may be confirmed by considering a recent sociological survey showing that public attitudes have changed dramatically and are at odds with either orthodox interpretations of Islam or the objectives of the conservative forces within the Islamic state.

Mansoor Moaddel's 1999 survey of value orientations in Egypt, Iran, and Jordan found that Iranians, despite living under a theocratic regime, placed less emphasis on religion and more emphasis on nationalism than did Egyptians and Jordanians. Likewise, in terms of the significance of religion in life, spiritual needs, and participation in religious services, Iranians appeared to be less religious than Egyptians or Jordanians, even though a majority still indicated that religious faith was important to them. Iranians were also less concerned about "Western cultural invasion" than were Egyptians and Jordanians. And although there is strong support for marriage, fully 17 percent of the Iranian respondents agreed with the statement that "the institution of marriage is outdated." Forty percent of Iranians—compared with 23 percent of Jordanians and just 19 percent of Egyptians—agreed that a working mother could develop intimate relationships with her children much as a nonworking mother could. The overwhelming majority of Iranians disagreed with the institution of polygamy. And only 24 percent of Iranians strongly agreed with the statement that a wife must always obey her husband—compared to 42 percent of Jordanians and 47 percent of Egyptians. Moaddel concludes that these responses are the result of "the experience of having lived for more than two decades under an Islamic fundamentalist regime."[58]

Notes

1. Message of the National Union of Women (NUW), published in the NUW's organ, *Zan dar Mobarezeh* (Women in Struggle), cited in Azar Tabari and Nahid Yeganeh, eds., *In the Shadow of Islam: The Women's Movement in Iran* (London: Zed Books, 1982), p. 154. Other early works detailing the adverse outcomes for women are: Guity Nashat, "Women in the Ideology of the Islamic Republic," in Guity Nashat, ed., *Women and Revolution in Iran* (Boulder: Westview Press, 1983), pp. 195–216, quoted from p. 195; Farah Azari, ed., *Women of Iran* (London: Ithaca Press, 1983); Eliz Sanasarian, *The Women's Rights Movement in Iran: Mutiny, Appeasement, and Repression from 1900 to Khomeini* (New York: Praeger, 1982); Mahnaz Afkhami, "Iran: A Future in the Past—The 'Prerevolutionary' Women's Movement," in Robin Morgan, ed., *Sisterhood Is Global* (New York: Anchor Books, 1984), pp. 330–338; amd Haleh Afshar, "Women, State, and Ideology in Iran," *Third World Quarterly* 7 (2) (April 1985): 256–278.

2. Nahid Yeganeh, "Women's Struggles in the Islamic Republic of Iran," and Haleh Afshar, "Khomeini's Teachings and Their Implications for Iranian Women," both in Tabari and Yeganeh, *In the Shadow of Islam*, pp. 26–74 and 75–90. Afshar's essay deals with Ayatollah Ruhollah Khomeini's book *A Clarification of Problems,* trans. Hamid Algar (Berkeley: Mizan Press, 1982). Mutahhari's critique of Western relations and his essentially functionalist arguments in favor of polygamy and temporary marriage were serialized in the popular women's magazine *Zan-e Rouz* in the years before the revolution. See also Murteza Mutahhari, *Sexual Ethics in Islam and in the Western World* (Tehran: Bonyad-e Be'that, Foreign Department, 1981).

3. See Fatna A. Sabbah, *Woman in the Muslim Unconscious* (New York: Praeger, 1984).

4. Murteza Mutahhari, *On the Islamic Hijab* (Tehran: Islamic Propagation Organization, 1987), pp. 21–22.

5. Constitution of the Islamic Republic of Iran, Tehran, 1984, pp. 14–15.

6. Azar Tabari, "Islam and the Struggle for Emancipation of Iranian Women," in Tabari and Yeganeh, *In the Shadow of Islam,* pp. 5–25.

7. Fereshteh Hashemi, "Discrimination and the Imposition of the Veil," in Tabari and Yeganeh, *In the Shadow of Islam,* p. 193.

8. Azam Taleghani et al., "Instead of Compulsory Veiling, Public Decency for All Should Be Compulsory," in Tabari and Yeganeh, *In the Shadow of Islam,* p. 194.

9. Fedayeen-Khalq, "Women's Rights and Islamic Hijab," in *In the Shadow of Islam,* p. 136.

10. Shahrzad Mojab, "The Islamic Government's Policy on Women's Access to Higher Education and Its Impact on the Socio-Economic Status of Women," Office of Women in International Development, Working Paper no. 156, Michigan State University, December 1987.

11. Joan Scott, "Gender: A Useful Category of Historical Analysis," *American Historical Review* 91 (5) (December 1986).

12. Quoted in Nashat, "Women in the Ideology of the Islamic Republic," p. 200.

13. Adele Ferdows, "Shariati and Khomeini on Women," in Nikkie Keddie and Eric Hooglund, eds., *The Iranian Revolution and the Islamic Republic* (Washington, D.C.: Middle East Institute, 1982), p. 78.

14. Ayatollah Khomeini, "Address to a Group of Women in Qum," March 6, 1979, in *Islam and Revolution: Writings and Declarations of Imam Khomeini,* trans. and ed. Hamid Algar (Berkeley: Mizan Press, 1981), p. 263. Ayatollah Khomeini was not as conservative as other religious leaders and interpreters of the Quran on the question of women. When Ayatollah Kho'i was in Najaf, both were asked whether women could meet with men to discuss political questions. Kho'i issued a *fatwa* saying that under no circumstances, except for Friday prayers, could men and women who were not married gather together. Khomeini, on the other hand, permitted it in his *fatwa.*

15. World Bank, *World Development Report 1985* (New York: Oxford University Press, 1985), tab. 20, p. 213.

16. *Iran Times,* March 28, 1986, p. 5.

17. *Iran Times,* October 19, 1984.

18. Quoted in Haleh Afshar, "Women and Work: Ideology Not Adjustment at Work in Iran," in Haleh Afshar, ed., *Structural Adjustment and Women* (London: Macmillan, 1991), p. 206.

19. Ibid., p. 215.

20. Ibid., p. 206.

21. Ibid.

22. Ibid., p. 214.

23. For an empirical discussion of gender inequality in the IRI, see V. M. Moghadam, "The Reproduction of Gender Inequality in the Islamic Republic: A Case Study of Iran in the 1980s," *World Development* 19 (10) (1991): 1335–1350. The section on women and work draws partly on V. M. Moghadam, "Women, Work, and Ideology in the Islamic Republic," *International Journal of Middle East Studies* 20 (2) (May 1988): 221–243.

24. John R. Weeks, "The Demography of Islamic Nations," *Population Bulletin* 43 (4) (December 1988). In a personal communication (Helsinki, July 1991), Amartya Sen told me that nearly all Middle Eastern countries had an adverse sex ratio. An examination of demographic data compiled by the United Nations confirmed this.

25. Interview with Dr. Azizullah Saidali, Indira Gandhi Children's Hospital, Kabul, February 9, 1989. See also *UN Statistical Yearbook 1983/4* (New York: United Nations, 1986), tab. 18, p. 65.

26. UNICEF, *State of the World's Children 1989* (New York: UNICEF, 1989), tab. 3, pp. 98–99.

27. Ibid., tab. E, pp. 88–89; World Bank, *World Development Report 1984,* p. 166; and *Selected Statistics* 5 (24) (Tehran: Central Statistical Office, Bahman 1368 [February 1990]), p. 14.

28. *National Census of Population and Housing 1365/1986* (Tehran: Central Statistical Office, 1988), p. 2; and Akbar Aghajanian, "Post-Revolutionary Demographic Trends in Iran," in Hooshang Amirahmadi and Manoucher Parvin, eds., *Post-Revolutionary Iran* (Boulder: Westview Press, 1988). See also Yasmin Mossavar-Rahmani, "Family Planning in Post-Revolutionary Iran," in Nashat, *Women and Revolution in Iran,* pp. 253–262.

29. *National Census of Population and Housing,* November 1986 (Total Country) (Tehran: Central Statistical Office, 1989), tab. 6.1, p. 86.

30. *Statistical Yearbook of Iran 1367/1988* (Tehran: IRI, February 1990), tab. 5.46, p. 124.

31. 1986 Census, tab. 22, pp. 160–161.

32. Maryam Poya, *Women, Work, and Islamism: Ideology and Resistance in Iran* (London: Zed Books, 1999), p. 82.

33. See Hooshang Amirahmadi, *Revolution and Economic Transition: The Iranian Experience* (Albany: State University of New York Press, 1990), esp. chap. 3.

34. Kamran Dadkhah, "Iran and Global Financial Markets: Foreign Investment vs. Borrowing," *Middle East Executive Reports,* August 1996, pp. 8–13.

35. *Tehran Times,* September 24, 1991, p. 1.

36. "Majlis Speaker Says Women Should Aim Higher," *Tehran Times,* September 26, 1991, p. 3.

37. "Centers for Training of Women Will Be Set Up," *Tehran Times,* December 31, 1991, p. 3.

38. Research Group for Muslim Women's Studies, *The Social Status of Iranian Women Before and After the Victory of the Islamic Republic* (Tehran: Cultural Studies and Research Institute, Ministry of Culture and Higher Education, 1990), pp. 1–4.

39. Islamic Republic of Iran, *Zan va Towse-eh: Ahamm-e Eqdamat-e Anjam-Shodeh dar Khosus-e Banovan pas az Pirouzi-ye Enqelab-e Eslami* (Tehran: Shura-ye Hamhangi-ye Tablighat-e Eslami, 1994), p. 15.

40. *National Report on Women in the Islamic Republic of Iran: Prepared for the Fourth World Conference on Women* (Tehran: Bureau of Women's Affairs, 1995), pp. 45–46. See also Moghadam, *Women, Work, and Economic Reform in the Middle East and North Africa* (Boulder: Lynne Rienner, 1998), chap. 7.

41. Farzaneh Roudy-Fahimi, "Iran's Family Planning Program: Responding to a Nation's Need," MENA Policy Brief (Washington, D.C.: Population Reference Bureau, June 2002).

42. Data from *Statistical Yearbook of Iran 1375/1996* (Tehran: IRI, 1997), tab. 3-1, p. 70.

43. Ibid., tab. 3-4, p. 74.

44. Ibid., tab. 3-8, p. 80.

45. Ibid., tab. 3-9, p. 81.

46. Associated Press, "Woman Named Iran Culture Deputy," August 31, 1997, via Internet; "Women's Activist Gets Iranian Post," September 2, 1997, via Internet; Agence France Presse, "Iranian President Names Woman as Advisor," October 18, 1997, via Internet.

47. For an elaboration of the July 1999 protests by university students and of the reform movement in Iran, see the special issues of the *Journal of Iranian Research and Analysis* (Zanganeh 1999, 2000, 2002).

48. Homa Hoodfar, "Women and Personal Status Law in Iran: An Interview with Mehranguiz Kaar," *Middle East Report* no. 198 (January–February 1996): 36–38; quote by Ms. Kaar appears on p. 37.

49. *Payam-e Hajar* (Tehran) 1 (1) (Autumn 1370/1991).

50. "Veteran Female Deputy Specializes on Women's Rights," *Tehran Times,* July 15, 1991, p. 5.

51. "Interview with Faezeh Hashemi," *ASAHI Shimbun* (Tokyo), February 6, 1997, available at www.zan.org/lit2.html.

52. Faezeh Hashemi, quoted in ibid.

53. Mehranguiz Kaar, cited in Hoodfar, "Women and Personal Status Law in Iran," p. 37.

54. Cited in Azadeh Kian, "Women and Politics in Post-Islamist Iran: The Gender Conscious Drive to Change," *British Journal of Middle Eastern Studies* 24 (1) (1997): 75–96; quote appears on p. 91. See also Martin van Bruinessen, "Islam, Women's Rights, and Islamic Feminism," *ISIM Newsletter* no. 9 (January 2002), p. 6.

55. See Elaheh Rostami Povey, "Feminist Contestations of Institutional Domains in Iran," *Feminist Review* no. 69 (Winter 2001): 44–72; quote appears on p. 62.

56. Ibid., p. 63.

57. Ibid., p. 65.

58. Mansoor Moaddel et al., "Religion, Gender, and Politics in Egypt, Jordan, and Iran: Findings of Comparative National Surveys," report to the NSF (June 2002) kindly provided to me by Moaddel.

7

Afghanistan: Revolution, Reaction, and Attempted Reconstruction

> *This revolution was made for women!*
> —Afghan teenager and PDPA member

Between 1996 and 2001, the world's attention was fixated on what appeared to be a medieval form of rule in Afghanistan under the Taliban. For feminists in particular, the Taliban's repressive gender regime was especially anachronistic, a seemingly deliberate violation of all the norms of women's rights that had been achieved to date. How could such a regime possibly have come to power? And what were women's lives like before the Taliban? Answering these questions requires a historical perspective, which this chapter provides.

In April 1978 the Democratic Republic of Afghanistan came to power in a revolutionary coup carried out by officers sympathetic to the People's Democratic Party of Afghanistan. It launched a radical social reform program that included land reform and women's rights, but was almost immediately faced by fierce resistance. A critical period ensued and the Soviet Union finally agreed to support the Afghan government militarily. As it happened, the December 1979 Soviet intervention in Afghanistan became a seminal event in the history of the Cold War. It represented the largest Soviet military operation since World War II and the first extension of the Brezhnev Doctrine outside Eastern Europe. The Afghan crisis was also decisively important for the United States. It allowed President Jimmy Carter to shift U.S. policy from détente to Cold War confrontation. In addition to the hostage crisis in Iran, the Afghan crisis may have contributed to Carter's defeat in the 1980 election and the implementation of an even more aggressive foreign policy under Ronald Reagan, whose principal objective was the collapse of the Soviet Union. The military intervention and nine-year-long military engagement became traumatic for the Soviet Union and may have contributed to Gorbachev's "new thinking": glasnost and perestroika internally, a new foreign policy externally.[1] And of course the conflict was especially traumatic for the people of Afghanistan, who experienced an internationalized war and enormous suffer-

ing. For Afghans, devastation and suffering continued after the withdrawal of
the last Soviet troops in early 1989 and the downfall of the left-wing government in late April 1992, during the years of internecine warfare and lawlessness under the Islamist regime of the Mujahidin (1992–1996), during the
repressive years of the Taliban (1996–2001), and during the U.S. bombing
campaigns to drive out the Taliban and capture Osama bin Laden and others
associated with the Al-Qaida network responsible for the September 11, 2001,
tragedies in the United States.

Events in Afghanistan have been studied almost exclusively in geopolitical terms. The study of Afghanistan during the 1980s and 1990s also was
extremely ideologically charged. Many of the published accounts were
explicitly partisan; they favored the Islamist Mujahidin, cast them as heroic
guerrillas, and denounced the left-wing government in Kabul as a Soviet pup-
pet regime espousing alien ideas (such as women's rights!). Geopolitical and
partisan perspectives precluded an understanding of the class, gender, and cultural dynamics of the battles within Afghanistan. In particular they obscured
the importance of the struggle over women's rights, a question that has long
confronted Afghan modernizing elites but whose resolution has been consistently thwarted.

This chapter surveys the struggle for women's rights in modern Afghan
history, from the earliest reforms in the late nineteenth century to 2002. Like
modernization itself, efforts to improve the status of women have been constrained by a social structure characterized by patriarchal gender relations,
tribal feudalism, and a weak central state.

Afghan Social Structure and Its Implications for Women

Historically, the population of Afghanistan has been fragmented into myriad
ethnic, linguistic, religious, kin-based, and regional groupings. The bases of
the social structure are the *qawm* (communal group) and the *qabila* (tribe).
These microlevel social and political affiliations based on primordial ties have
been structural impediments to nation building and economic development. In
this social structure, which may be termed "tribal feudalism," ethnic, religious, and tribal divisions have impeded class formation, maintained provincial patterns of local independence and hostility toward the central government, and perpetuated the use of violence in place of political negotiations.
Afghanistan's rugged physical environment also has served to isolate communities and create microenvironments. Members of the same ethnic group
and tribe who reside in different locations must adapt to separate microenvironments, which may lead different kin-based groups within the same tribe
and ethnic group to use different modes of production. For example, the Durrani Pashtuns that Nancy Tapper studied in the 1970s were primarily agricul-

turalists, while the Sheikhanzai Durrani Pashtuns, who were the subject of Bahram Tavakolian's research, were primarily pastoralists.[2]

The fragmented and stagnant Afghan economy has its origins in the periodic Turkic invasions of the medieval era, which wreaked havoc on town and country alike. Later, when the country became involved in early international trade, it participated not as a producer of commodities but as a facilitator of transit trade. The early trade routes between China, Central Asia, the Arab states, and Turkey, as well as those between Europe, Russia, and India, cut across Afghan territory, giving rise to what are today the major Afghan cities—Kabul, Herat, and Kandahar—and to the emergence of an urban commercial sector geared to servicing caravans and organizing transportation of goods. In contrast to European cities, Afghan towns did not integrate markets, organizing the exchange of indigenously produced commodities among producers as well as between producers and consumers. Without such organization, a true national economy never evolved. In Afghanistan, economic links between the towns were initially as undeveloped as their links with the surrounding rural areas. Competition from the Russians and the British in the nineteenth century inhibited further development. The reorientation of trade toward export production (of agricultural raw materials and carpets) at the end of the nineteenth century reinforced the stagnation of the national industrial sector. Other important factors in Afghanistan's economic and social underdevelopment are its rugged terrain, making transportation hazardous and costly, the absence of central authority and a taxation system, and the persistence of tribalism and pastoral nomadism.[3]

The development planning that began in the 1950s did not reduce the by-then deeply entrenched dichotomies between rural and urban areas and between foreign trade and domestic production. On the eve of the 1978 revolution, the bazaar controlled roughly 50 percent of financial transactions (including money lending and foreign exchange dealings), retail trade, and foreign trade. A public sector had been created, but investment remained low. Private-sector investment was hindered by high interest rates: bazaar interest rates were between 20 percent and 40 percent per annum. The Afghan government relied heavily on foreign aid—as much as 80 percent for its development expenditure.[4] Arable land was in short supply and patterns of ownership were highly inequitable, with a few families (including families of some of the men who would become Mujahidin leaders) owning vast acreages on which peasants sharecropped. Agricultural productivity was low, and the system of food distribution inefficient; thus, food shortages were common.[5]

Afghan nationalism, properly speaking, has been incipient at best, as the concepts of nation-state and national identity are absent from much of the population; nationalism has been promoted primarily by modernizing elites since the nineteenth century.[6] During most of the country's modern history, the fragmented groupings waged war on each other. Battles were fought principally over land and water, sometimes over women and honor, usually over sheer power. Interethnic hostility among Afghans has been widely discussed in the literature. Tapper describes ethnic identity in terms of claims of religiously privileged descent and superiority to all other ethnic groups. Durrani women, for example, were absolutely prohibited from marrying men of a "lower" ethnic status.[7]

One of the few commonalities in this diverse country is Islam. Yet Afghan Islam is a unique combination of practices and precepts from the Shari'a and tribal customs, particularly Pashtunwali, the tribal code of the Pashtuns. Anthropological studies in the 1970s found that the absence of inheritance rights for women (contrary to Islamic law) was integral to the complex web of the tribal exchange system. The practice of usury, banned under Islamic law, was widespread, keeping rural households in almost perpetual indebtedness. Exorbitant expenditure in marriages was another source of the rural household's debt accumulation. The Islamic dower, *mahr,* called *walwar* in Pushtu, was abused in the Afghan tribal-patriarchal context. The *mahr,* a payment due from groom to bride, is an essential part of the Islamic marriage contract. In the Quran the *mahr* is a nominal fee. In many Muslim countries its purpose is to provide a kind of insurance for the wife in the event of divorce or widowhood. But in tribal Afghanistan, *walwar* was understood to be compensation to the bride's father for the loss of his daughter's labor in the household and was part of the groom's ownership claim over his wife. It was, essentially, the price of a girl.[8] As Tapper explained, the heaviest expenses any household had to bear were concerned with marriage. The choice of bride, the agreed brideprice, and the time taken to complete a marriage could plunge a household into debt and poverty.

In his study of reforms of family law in Afghanistan, Mohammad Kamali explained that the link between Islam and tribalism stemmed from "the fundamental fact that Islam itself was revealed in a tribal society."[9] It is true that Islam challenged many of the pre-Islamic tribal traditions of the Arabs and introduced reforms that raised the sociolegal status of women, given the patriarchal customs of the Arabs. Yet Islam left many aspects of the prevailing tribal traditions unchanged, such as male control over female kin. Still, anthropologists have commented on certain non-Islamic practices in Afghanistan. As Olivier Roy explains:

> The tribal code and Muslim law are in opposition. Adultery *(zina)* should, according to the Shari'at, require four witnesses if it is to be proven; for the *Pashtunwali,* hearsay *(peghor)* is sufficient, for what is at stake is honor (one's self-image) and not morality (defined by the Shari'at as what is permitted as opposed to what is not). Women in the tribes are not allowed to inherit property, for that would contradict the principle of strict patrilineage, which is the very basis of the tribal system; while the Qur'an grants to women half the share of the male. The dowry, a sign of prestige, frequently

exceeds the limits set by the Shari'at, while, on the other hand, the repudiation of a wife by her husband, something which, according to the Qur'an, presents no difficulties, is practically impossible in the tribes, for that would be an insult to the wife's family. Vengeance *(badal)* is commended within the tribal code, while the Shari'at attempts to limit the occasions on which it can take place.[10]

Audrey Shalinsky, who in 1976–1977 studied Uzbek and Tajik households in Kunduz, a provincial capital in northern Afghanistan, observed that Quranic rules about women's rights were more in evidence in urban areas:

> Many women sold dairy products such as milk, yogurt, or butter which they obtained from the few animals most households kept. It was not at all unusual for women to have this type of source of supplementary income and to spend their own money on household furnishings or clothing. Though the women were veiled outside the household, recently in this urbanised situation, it had become acceptable for women occasionally to go to the bazaar and buy things themselves while they were veiled.[11]

Afghanistan is one of the few remaining cases of classic patriarchy, a function of its tribal structure and economic underdevelopment. Afghan patriarchy is tied to the prevalence of such forms of subsistence as nomadic pastoralism, herding and farming, and settled agriculture, all organized along patrilineal lines. Historically, Afghan gender roles and women's status have reflected precapitalist property relations. Property includes livestock, land, and houses or tents. Women and children tend to be assimilated into the concept of property and to belong to a male. A bride who was not a virgin on the wedding night could be murdered by her father or brothers. A widow was often remarried to a cousin or a brother of the deceased husband (the custom of levirate). Polygyny was not widespread because it was economically burdensome and tended to be practiced more often by richer men. Yet among some groups polygyny made economic sense and could indeed prove profitable in cases where the woman was skilled and able to earn additional income. According to Kamali, "This is often the case among the Turkomens of northern Afghanistan where polygamy is encountered most frequently because the income of a second wife through rug weaving tends to offset the cost of her support."[12] Also, in a tribal context where strength is lauded and greater value attached to the proliferation of males, polygyny would function as a means of greater reproduction of potential warriors.

Gender segregation and female seclusion existed, though they varied by ethnic group, region, mode of subsistence, social class, and family. There are few accounts of how and to what degree women veiled before veiling was made compulsory by the Mujahidin and then by the Taliban. Formally, women had the right to attend the mosque and participate in pilgrimages, but they seldom did so because of the institution of purdah, which kept men away from women through veiling and through seclusion of women at home or in separate quarters. Similarly, in public areas, women screened themselves with the veil or turned their backs on male strangers. Men also avoided women who were potential mates. Audrey Shalinksy's description of the "women's community"—revolving around relational ties, household work, and life-cycle ceremonies—stressed the bonding and emotional support it provided. But she described a world that was clearly separate from the world of men. In Afghanistan, women who venture outside the home usually have worn the burqa, a tentlike covering with only a net before the eyes that also was worn in the Central Asian republics before unveilings took place in the 1920s and 1930s. The burqa is far more confining than the modern Islamist hijab of headscarf and long coat, or the *shalwar kameez* (trousers and tunic) and light scarf worn in Pakistan.

Writing in the mid-1960s, John Griffiths asserted that "the most strikingly obvious divisions in Afghanistan are between the sexes." For the most part, these divisions have remained intact. In the towns and cities, female seclusion involves the cooperation of men. Boys learn from early childhood to warn women relatives when men approached the compound walls, to respect the privacy of women, and not to enter a compound unless permission was granted. The control over purdah lies largely with the eldest male household member. Strictly speaking, it is he who decides whether a woman can leave the compound or not. He is the one who decides whether the women in the family will attend school or will participate in training and employment.[13]

Griffiths described a conversation with the governor of a district in Kunduz, who explained with some pride

> the way in which the region's beautiful hand-woven carpets were made; how five or six women might work together for four or five months to make a patterned carpet . . . and how a man would pay a very good bride-price for a girl who was an accomplished carpet weaver. When I asked him who got the money for the carpets, he looked at me in astonishment and replied: "Why the man of course, the woman belongs to the man." This is the attitude which is the chief obstacle facing the champions of women's emancipation in Afghanistan.[14]

The combination of preindustrial modes of production and men's social and political control over women's lives creates a cultural matrix in which men exchange women and control their productive and reproductive capacities within the family unit. This authority, which is based on patrilineal and kinship relationships, is not diminished by women's central role in agricultural production. Indeed, in some cases the participation of women in socially productive work may result in what Haleh Afshar called their "enslavement rather than their liberation." What Afshar means is that in such a context, a woman's labor power is controlled and allocated by someone other than herself, the products of her labor are managed by others, and she receives no remuneration for work performed. The partial penetration of capital in rural areas, where, for example, carpet weaving is a commercial enterprise, allows male kin to exploit women's labor without paying any wages. Here, women's ability to contribute substantially to the family income leads directly to intensified subordination and intrahousehold inequality. In many such contexts, as Hanna Papanek noted, women may be seen as "too valuable" to educate, and the money they earn may well finance the men's education or travel. For both economic and ideological reasons, females may not get "release time" for education. In extended patriarchal and patrilineal households, collective (male) interests dictate strict control of female labor deployment throughout a woman's lifetime.[15] In most parts of Afghanistan, the husband or father of a woman decides whether she can attend school or engage in paid work outside the home, and women do not have the right to keep their wages. The money is considered to be at the disposal of the husband or father.

Another pattern of gender relations, apparently less patriarchal, has been described by anthropologist Bahram Tavakolian with respect to the Pushtu-speaking Sheikhanzai nomads of western Azerbaijan. The division of labor of these goat-herding pastoralists was described by the author as entailing complementary roles rather than gender hierarchy. Tavakolian stressed "the considerable respect with which women and women's work are viewed by Sheikhanzai men and the appreciation and happiness shown when a girl is born." He continued:

> A Sheikhanzai household is more hard-pressed economically if there is a shortage of women than if there is a shortage of men. While adolescent boys frequently provide daily labor services to other households, especially through overnight assistance to the shepherd, girls are usually far too valuable within their own household labor supply to be available for more than a few hours at a time. A further indication of the value of women is also to be found in the customary bride-price of 1 to 3 *laks* (ca. $3,500–$7,000) at the time of my field research. . . . Sheikhanzai men acknowledge that their pastoral economy would be impossible without the labors of their womenfolk.[16]

What is not explained, however, given the economic centrality of girls and women, is why Sheikhanzai men marry a second wife if their first wife bears only girls. Tavakolian goes on to argue that Sheikhanzai women have political power, which is expressed in two forms: (1) as power wielders within a household through their direct influence over their husbands, sons, brothers, and even their fathers; and (2) as power brokers through their influence over the relationships their male kin maintain with one another and with other men. But he does concede that "Sheikhanzai men still come out ahead of women in most aspects of official power and certainly with respect to public recognition of their power."[17]

Entrenched patriarchal relations in Afghanistan were challenged several times by various modernizing initiatives. But these invariably resulted in tribal rebellion against government authority. Vartan Gregorian described opposition to the modernizing efforts, including education for girls, of Habibullah Khan (1901–1919) and Amanullah Khan (1919–1929). In the section below, I turn to the existence of a weak modern state in a predominantly patriarchal and tribal society, which has adverse implications for reform and development, as well as for the advancement of women.

A Prototype of the Weak State

Max Weber defined the state as an organization enforcing regulations, at least in part through a monopoly of violence. States vary in the degree to which they actually approach such an ideal type. Bertrand Badie and Pierre Birnbaum suggested:

> The progress of state-building can be measured by the degree of development of certain instrumentalities whose purpose is to make the action of the state effective: bureaucracy, courts, and the military, for example. Clearly, the more complex and highly developed these instrumentalities are, the greater the capacity of the state to act on its environment and to autonomously impose collective goals distinct from the private goals generated within the social system itself. In this situation, the state's autonomy corresponds to a tangible reality.[18]

But the autonomy and capacity of a state cannot be assumed, and not all states can impose their will on social groups. Neither can there be assured outcomes of state engagements with society. Political scientists and sociologists have distinguished between "strong states" and "weak states." Strong states are those with high capabilities to penetrate society, regulate social relationships, extract resources, and appropriate or use resources in determined ways. Weak states are on the low end of a spectrum of capabilities. Many states have encountered difficulties in effecting widespread changes in people's social behavior and overall transformations in social relations. In particular, they have had difficulties achieving their leaders' aims at the local level.[19]

Afghanistan is today, and has been throughout its modern history, a prototypical weak state, inasmuch as the central authorities have been unable to realize their goals, to regulate social relations or use resources in determined ways. The Afghan state is not alone in these shortcomings; other third world governments, especially those of poorer countries, have been stymied in their attempts to transform their environment. Even India, normally considered a strong state, has had persistent social and economic problems, suggesting that the extent of its control is not great. As one political scientist observed, "Three decades of democratically planned development have failed to alleviate India's rural poverty."[20] But the Afghan state's predicament has been especially dire and exemplifies Samuel Huntington's observation over thirty years ago that many "governments simply do not govern."[21] During the twentieth century, although Afghanistan was not immune to the general process of social change enveloping the Middle East, South Asia, and Central Asia, it saw less transformation than did neighboring countries. Its isolation during the previous century was one reason, as Gregorian explained:

> For most of the nineteenth century, Afghanistan remained culturally one of the most isolated and parochial regions of the Muslim world, almost totally cut off from the mainstream of European thought. It did not undergo any direct and intensive experience of European colonial rule; on the contrary, imperialism while impressing upon the Afghans the necessity of technological borrowing, contributed to Afghan political and cultural isolationism.[22]

British attempts to expand the empire's sphere of influence outward from India led to two Anglo-Afghan wars (in 1839 and 1879), which contributed to the growth of a religious nationalism and xenophobia. The struggle strengthened the position of the Afghan tribes and the monarchy's dependence on their military might and reinforced the position of the Afghan religious establishment. Gregorian wrote that in the absence of noteworthy learning institutions, a secular intelligentsia, reformist movements among the Afghan ulama, and the formulation and propagation of the aims of Afghan nationalism and modernism came late. In the first two decades of the twentieth century, a small group of educated Afghans sought to broaden the base of support for political and economic reform. Under the leadership of Amanullah Khan, these "Young Afghans," inspired by the Young Turks nearby, made ambitious plans for the modernization of the country, explicitly including the emancipation of women in their agenda (as was the case in Turkey). Their ultimate failure determined the course and nature of all future reforms and modernization programs in Afghanistan. During Zahir Shah's long reign (1933–1973), the country was spared war and conflict, but very little social development took place outside of Kabul. One analyst has thus concluded that the record of Afghanistan's leaders until 1978 was a pitiful one: they had failed to give the country any of the attributes of the modern centralized state.[23]

One example of state failure was in the area of education. The first secondary school (for boys only) was established in 1904 and was called Habibiyeh College after its patron, Habibullah Khan. In 1913 the Afghan Department of Education was founded. In 1922 Amanullah Khan established Amaniyeh School, later renamed Lycée Esteqlal, and founded Essmat School for girls (later renamed Malalai School), which was closed after his abdication. The foundations of Kabul University were laid in 1932 when its first faculty, the School of Medicine, was established. Malalai School was reopened in the 1930s under Nadir Shah, but according to Gregorian it was promoted as a special school for nurses and midwives so as to soften the opposition of the mullahs and the other traditionalists. It took another two decades for Malalai to become a true secondary school and produce its first graduates. As late as 1954, the total student enrollment in Afghanistan, excluding the students at Kabul University, was 114,266, or about 4.5 percent of the approximately 2.4 million school-age children. At that time there were only thirteen primary schools, one middle school, and two secondary schools for girls, most of them in Kabul, and only an estimated 8,625 girls were receiving any kind of education. There were reportedly no girls in the village schools.[24]

Early Reforms Concerning Women

After modernization began in the mid–nineteenth century, various governments and rulers sought to discourage excessive expenditure not only on brideprice but also on marriage celebrations. The motivation was twofold: to improve the status of women and to reduce the rural population's indebtedness. Improving the status of women was a major goal of Afghan reformist intellectuals such as Mahmud Tarzi (1866–1935).

As a royal adviser and editor of *Siraj al-Akhbar Afghaniyah,* a biweekly paper and forum for the Young Afghans, Tarzi appealed for compulsory education of all children, including girls. According to Gregorian, he was the first Afghan to take a public, positive stand on feminism, dedicating a series of articles to famous women in history that discussed the many abilities of women. A monogamist himself, Tarzi never explicitly attacked polygamy, but he did so implicitly by constantly casting a family in which there was one wife and a few children as the ideal family. In his view the health, welfare, and education of Afghan families was essential to Afghan progress, so he attacked the extravagant expenditures incurred in connection with multiple marriages, which often financially ruined families.

Reforms to improve the status of women had started during the reign of Abdur Rahman Khan, a ruthless ruler who nonetheless abolished slavery in 1895, although Gregorian writes that the edict was probably not enforced. He also abolished a long-standing customary law that, in violation of Islamic law, bound a wife not only to her husband but to his entire family as well. Widows who wanted to remarry had to marry their husband's next of kin, often against their will. Abdur Rahman Khan decreed that the moment a husband died his wife was to be set free. There is no information on the extent to which this law was enforced, but it is likely that enforcement was weak. Among his other measures was a law requiring the registration of marriages *(sabt).* He also modified a law pertaining to child marriages, permitting a girl who had been given in marriage before she had reached the age of puberty to refuse or accept her marriage ties when she attained full age. Still another law allowed women to sue their husbands for alimony or divorce in cases involving cruelty or nonsupport.[25]

Habibullah Khan attempted to limit the burdensome expenses incurred in connection with marriage. Most Afghans had to borrow money to meet these expenses, at times paying as much as 75 percent interest on the loan. In 1911 he placed a ceiling on the amount that could be spent on marriages, urging his people to abandon the customary public celebrations in favor of private parties. The amounts he set varied according to class. Gregorian doubts that the law was strictly enforced but notes that on a few highly publicized occasions the royal family attempted to set an example for the rest of Afghan society in this connection. The emir himself also tried to set an example for the wealthy Afghans who exceeded the legal number of four wives. Officially banning the practice of keeping concubines and female slaves, Habibullah publicly divorced all but four of his wives in 1903. He also established Habibiyeh College, the first secondary school (for boys only). The Department of Education's attempts to improve and standardize the curriculum were not totally successful, however. Gregorian writes that the mullahs, especially those outside Kabul, resented the government's control of education, the teacher-training center, and the teaching of English and modern subjects in general, and they vehemently resisted all further innovation.

Amanullah succeeded his father when Habibullah Khan was assassinated in 1919, and he had the enormous task of convincing the religious establishment that modern secular education and Islam were not incompatible and that the new schools he built did not threaten the sanctity of Islam in Afghanistan. He also was determined to improve the status of women in the face of overwhelming clerical and rural opposition to any measures in that direction. Gregorian calls him the "ill-fated champion of modernization."[26] Amanallah's first step was to decree the abolition of slavery, which freed women from concubinage. Although slavery as an institution had been abolished earlier, a number of female slaves, mostly Hazaras, were still held as concubines *(suratis)* by influential men in Kabul. The Decree of 1920 *(farman-i elgha-i ghulami)* put an end to this practice, giving upper-class males a choice between officially marrying their concubines or freeing them unconditionally.[27] His other audacious acts were to begin a study-abroad program for Afghan students and to open the first schools for girls. By 1928 there were about 800 girls attending schools in Kabul, and there were even a few Afghan women studying abroad, mainly in Turkey, France, and Switzerland. Gregorian notes that Amanullah had plans to build five more schools for girls and intended his planned compulsory education system to apply to girls as well as boys. But both efforts were dropped after his fall in 1929.

The measures to enhance the status of women and girls were introduced under the general rubric of *himayat-i niswan,* the protection of women, which the government argued was in line with the principles of Islam and its interpretation of Islamic social justice. Amanullah himself believed that the keystone of the future structure of a new Afghanistan would be the emancipation of women. The Afghan press, including bulletins of the war office, took part in the emancipation campaign. The reforms pertaining to the emancipation of women were based on the Muslim reformist ideas initiated by Jamal al-Din Afghani and Muhammad Abduh of Egypt in the last part of the nineteenth century and championed also by modernists in Egypt, Ottoman Turkey, India, and other Muslim countries. According to Gregorian, Amanullah's general program to improve the position of women was promoted by his wife, Queen Soraya (who founded the first women's magazine, *Ershad-e Niswan*), the reformer Mahmud Tarzi and his wife, the small intelligentsia, and the modernist and nationalist Young Afghans, who were impressed by developments in Turkey, Iran, and Egypt. It is also possible that the presence in Kabul of a considerable number of unveiled women, especially Turkish women who had abandoned the veil and adopted modern dress, encouraged the efforts of the new Afghan state feminists.

In examining Amanullah's reform program and the organized resistance to it, one discovers striking parallels with the experience of the DRA some fifty years later (as we saw in Chapter 3). The new family law promulgated in 1921 abolished forced marriage, child marriage, and the payment of bridal money. It also established restrictions on polygamy. Child marriages and intermarriage between close kin were outlawed as contrary to Islamic principles. In the new code Amanullah reiterated the ruling that a widow was to be free of the domination of her husband's family. He followed his father's example and placed tight restrictions on wedding expenses, including dowries, and granted wives the right to appeal to the courts if their husbands did not adhere to Quranic tenets regarding marriage. In 1923 he introduced an administrative code, the *Nizam-nameh,* which attempted in part to liberalize the position of women and to permit the government to regulate the various family problems formerly dealt with by the local mullah. In the fall of 1924, Afghan girls were given the right to choose their husbands, a measure that incensed traditionalists. A group of women students was sent to Turkey for higher education in the fall of 1928, and the Association for the Protection of Women's Rights (Anjoman-i Hemayat-i Neswan) was established to help women fight domestic injustice and take a role in public life. The queen herself presided over several committees to strengthen the emancipation campaign. During the final months of his rule, Amanullah made a frontal assault against the institution of purdah, which he argued hid half the Afghan nation. Because of his efforts and the personal example of Queen Soraya, some 100 Afghan women had publicly discarded the veil by October 1928.

By this time Afghan legislation was among the most progressive in the Muslim world. No other country had yet addressed the sensitive issues of child marriage and polygamy. Afghan family law on these issues became the model for similar reforms in Soviet Central Asia in 1926.[28] It is not surprising that the family law of 1921 as well as the *Nizam-nameh* of 1923 constituted the major cause of the uprising instigated by the clergy in 1924. These unprecedented measures violated traditional norms and offended religious leaders and their following, especially in rural areas. Reaction against the campaign for women's emancipation and anger toward creeping centralization were major factors in the outbreak of violent disturbances in November and December 1928.

Traditionalist mullahs inveighed against the new code, asserting that it was contrary to the precepts of Islamic law. Their cause was picked up in 1924 by the Mangal tribe of the Khost region and soon assumed dangerous proportions. By March armed warfare had broken out. The religious and tribal leaders of the revolt were particularly angered by the sections of the code that deprived men of full authority over their wives and daughters, an authority that had been sanctioned by time-honored custom. They were further incensed at the opening of public schools for girls.

The Khost rebellion continued for more than nine months and dramatically illustrated the weakness of the Afghan army. Gregorian writes that Amanullah was forced to fall back on levies from certain tribes and proclaim a jihad before he was able to suppress the revolt. The rebels suffered enormous losses, as did the government side. The cost of the rebellion represented the government's total receipts for two years. As a result the king was forced to postpone various modernization projects and revoke or modify many important sections of the *Nizam-nameh;* the schooling of girls, for example, was limited to those under twelve. In 1928 the Loya Jirga, the traditional Afghan consultative body, rejected Amanullah's proposal to set an age limit on marriage, which the king suggested should be eighteen for girls and twenty for men. They also vehemently opposed modern, Western education for Afghan girls, either in Afghanistan or outside it.

Amanullah's reform program threatened to upset the entire structure of patriarchal relations and property rights. When the king banned the practice of polygamy among government officials it caused an uproar among the religious establishment. A tribal revolt ensued, led by a bandit, Bacheh Saqo, claiming Islamic credentials. As the political situation deteriorated, Amanullah was compelled to cancel most of his social reforms and suspend his controversial administrative measures. The Afghan girls studying in Constantinople were recalled, and the schools for girls closed; women were not to go unveiled or cut their hair; the mullahs were no longer to be required to obtain teaching certificates; compulsory military recruitment was abandoned and the old tribal system reinstated. As a last, desperate concession, the unhappy king agreed to the formation of a council of fifty notables, to be chosen from among "the most respected religious luminaries and tribal chieftains," and promised to abide by their advice and conform to Islamic law as interpreted by the orthodox religious leaders. Any measure the government proposed to enact was to be ratified by this council. But in the end, all of these concessions were to no avail. The rebels attacked Kabul, and Amanullah abdicated in 1929 and left Afghanistan.

Not until the 1950s were reforms attempted again. The Malalai school for girls was opened, but as mentioned above, there were only thirteen primary schools, one middle school, and two secondary schools for girls, mainly in Kabul.[29] The 1949 marriage law again prohibited the practice of *walwar,* limiting payment to the Quranic *mahr,* and banned other ostentatious life-cycle ceremonies. It prohibited many of the expensive aspects of birth, circumcision, marriage, and burial rituals, but was difficult to enforce. The marriage law of 1971 was a further attempt to curb the indebtedness arising from the costs of marriage, which were decreed to be a burden for Afghan society as a whole. When Daoud Khan overthrew his cousin the king and established a republic in 1973, he too attempted marriage reform. The civil law of 1977 abolished child marriage and set sixteen as the age of majority for girls, removing the right of parents and guardians to wed a girl at the onset of puberty, as was customary. But in the absence of any specified sanctions for violators, the law remained weak and was ignored. Furthermore, the law left the husband's right to unilateral divorce, which urban men were practicing, basically untouched.[30]

The historical background presented above suggests the enormous difficulty faced by Afghan modernizers. The Afghan state had been too weak to implement reforms or undertake modernization in an effective way and was constantly confronted by strong religious-tribal forces seeking to prevent any change whatsoever, particularly in their power and influence. During the forty-year reign of Zahir Shah, the country experienced peace, but very little social development took place compared, for example, to neighboring Iran, Turkey, or the Soviet Central Asian republics. In light of the historical record on modernization and social reforms, including reforms to improve the status of women, and the long-standing center-periphery conflict, the revolutionary program that the Taraki government announced in April 1978 was perhaps doomed. Faced with what Gregorian, writing in the late 1960s, frequently referred to as the "staggering socio-economic problems" of the country and the religious-tribal forces that had prevented resolution of these problems, the reformers of 1978 impatiently wished for change and betterment, assisted by their Soviet neighbors. But if Afghan history suggested anything, it was that social change could not come about rapidly and that direct foreign intervention in particular was highly unpopular. Moreover, the state—small and weak as it was—would be incapable of implementing its program in an effective way. At the same time, all social and economic indicators proclaimed the need for change, especially in the areas of literacy, education, health, food production and distribution, infrastructural development, and the status of women.

Characteristics of Afghan Patriarchy

Kamali wrote that in Afghanistan, a man could acquire a wife in any one of the following four ways: he could inherit a widow, gain a bride in marriage, gain a bride in compensation for a crime of which he or his relatives were the victim, or pay a brideprice. The last method was the most usual, the other three being variations of this form. *Walwar* was the sum of money (or commodity) paid by the groom or his family to the head of the bride's household. Wealthier men could more easily afford brides, and as wealthy men usually happened to be more advanced in age, the bride's parents often arranged the marriage of their young daughters to older men.[31] In a combination of pre-Islamic and Islamic customs, men exercised control over women in two crucial ways: by controlling marriage and property, and by barring landowner-ship for women (contrary to Islamic law and the actual practice in many other Muslim countries), especially among the Pashtuns.

The exchange of women in precapitalist agrarian societies organized around kinship structures has been extensively discussed in anthropological and feminist studies. The concept of honor in patriarchal societies has similarly been elaborated, as we saw in Chapter 4. Both are important elements in Pashtunwali, the highly masculinist tribal code of the Pashtuns. Tapper reports that among the Durrani Pashtuns of north-central Afghanistan, "The members of the community discuss control of all resources—especially labor, land, and women—in terms of honor." Purdah is one important component of the honor code, honor being the most desired status symbol of Afghan society. It is a critical component of the cultural codex and ascribed to the family or individual members by the outside world. Families in Afghanistan are nourished by the degree to which honor is bestowed upon the household, and women are crucial in this process. They are seen as the bearers of the honor of the family; the honor of a man is measured by others through the reputation and behavior of his wife and daughters. If they are seen to deviate from the norm by prominent figures in the community, the reputation of the entire household suffers, and the male is regarded as incompetent or unable to control his home affairs. Shame, the single most status-depriving social stigma, is then ascribed to the entire household.[32]

Based on her fieldwork in Afghanistan in the 1970s, Tapper found that marriage, enforced or otherwise, was traditionally a way of ending feuds, cementing a political alliance between families, or increasing a family's prestige. The exchange of women and the conception of women as property were integral to the social organization of Afghan tribal-feudalism. Women were given for brideprice or in compensation for blood to maintain a "status hierarchy" among households. In the exchange system, men were ranked in the first and highest sphere. Direct exchanges between them included the most honorable and manly of all activities, and these activities were prime expressions of status: vengeance and feud, political support and hospitality, and the practice of sanctuary. Women belonged to the second sphere; they were often treated exclusively as reproducers and pawns in economic and political exchanges. There was only one proper conversion between the first two spheres: two or more women could be given in compensation for the killing or injury of one man. Mobility and migration patterns also revolved around the brideprice. Tapper observed that men from one region would travel to another to find inexpensive brides, while other men would travel elsewhere because they could obtain a higher price for their daughters.[33]

Studies on Pashtunwali note that the code of Afghan behavior among the Pashtuns, who compose over half the population, possesses three core elements: hospitality, refuge, and revenge. Other key values are equality, respect, pride, bravery, purdah, pursuit of romantic encounters, worship of God, and devoted love for a friend. These are, once again, male values. Purdah is a key element in protection of the family's pride and honor; Inger Boesen noted a Pashtun saying that "a woman is best either in the house or in the grave." This seclusion from the world outside the family walls is customarily justified by invoking Quranic prescription and by the notion that women are basically licentious and tempt men. Kathleen Howard-Merriam explained that women are regarded as subordinates dependent on their husbands, a relationship exemplified by women's never asking men for their whereabouts or expecting marital fidelity. Women also are expected to give all the meat, choicest food, and best clothing to their husbands, as well as their personal wealth, if so demanded. Censuses and surveys undertaken in 1967, 1972–1974, and 1979 revealed an unusually high ratio of males to females that exceeded even the expected underreporting of females in a conservative Muslim society. Statistical estimates showed that females constituted 48 percent of the whole population. This low figure was in part a result of a high rate of maternal mortality and probably reflected in part sex bias in the provision of food and healthcare to girl children and women.[34] The adverse sex ratio of females to males continued into the 1980s, and two Afghan physicians confirmed high rates of maternal mortality and widespread anemia among women.[35]

In Afghanistan as in other patriarchal societies, a woman's standing is maintained primarily through bearing sons to continue the family; thus she must marry, for only through marriage can one's basic needs be legitimately fulfilled. The choice of husband is made by her family, with its own concerns for lineage maintenance and property gain. As Howard-Merriam noted, the best an Afghan girl can hope for is a handsome and kind cousin or close relative she has known and with whom she has grown up. The worst is an old man from another village whom she has never seen and who is unkind. In either case he is obliged to provide for her materially and, it is to be hoped, father her sons, who will endow her with status in her new home. If the husband treats her unbearably, she does have the option of breaking out and returning to her own family or seeking refuge with another family. This weapon is not used often, however, as a woman's natal family has given up rights to her through the brideprice at the time of marriage.[36]

In 1985, Kamali summed up matrimonial problems in the following way:

> Extravagant marriage ceremonies and the payment of a huge brideprice . . . are included in the issues which have remained unresolved despite legislative efforts during the last sixty years. In a country where the annual per capita income is barely $150 a marriage can cost anything up to $20,000 or more. Marriage, as a result, has become the privilege of the wealthy which not only leads to intolerable discrimination against the poor but also seriously undermines the human dignity of women. Extravagant ceremonies also weaken the financial status of the family and tend to exacerbate poverty. They increase the dependence of the adults on the family resources thereby weakening their position regarding the exercise of their right of consent in marriage and their freedom of choice for a life partner. These excesses often bring about a wide disparity of age between the spouses and lead to resentment and frustration on the part of the married couple. And finally, such extravagant practices contribute to the continuation of the tradition-bound society and impede healthy social change.[37]

On the eve of the Saur (April) Revolution, Afghanistan was among the poorest countries of the world, with low life expectancy, widespread illiteracy, malnutrition, and an unproductive agricultural system. Its economy was largely agricultural, although there was some light industry, mainly in textiles. Seventy-eight percent of the labor force was rural and agricultural. Infrastructure—especially paved roads, railways, and communications—was highly undeveloped. Along with high fertility rates, Afghanistan's infant mortality, under-five mortality, and maternal mortality rates were very high. There was only one doctor for every 3,000 people, with medical facilities available only in the capital and a number of other cities. In 1979 medical services were poor and unevenly distributed; there was provision for only about 25 percent of the population, and facilities were concentrated in urban areas. Fifty percent of children died before the age of five.

Life expectancy was only about forty years for women and forty-two years for men, which made Afghanistan one of the few countries in the world with a higher life expectancy for men than for women. The estimated total fertility rate was seven births per woman. The infant mortality rate was about 190 of 1,000 live births—that is, almost one in five. Children died from infections, malnourishment, and poor hygiene. The most frequent causes of infant death were respiratory infections, tuberculosis, diarrhea, malnutrition, and measles. In 1979 some 80 percent had not yet had any formal schooling, whereas religious education in Quranic schools held in the mosques was widespread, at least for boys. Formal educational facilities were mainly concentrated in urban areas. About 30 percent of the male population above five years of age was estimated to be literate, compared to only about 4 percent of the female population.[38] (See Table 7.1 for social indicators in 1965 and 1975.)

The DRA and Women's Rights

In 1965 a group from the small Afghan intelligentsia formed the People's Democratic Party of Afghanistan. Invoking the Amanullah experiment, the PDPA envisaged a national democratic government to liberate Afghanistan from backwardness. Among its demands were primary education for all children in their mother tongue and the development of the different languages and cultures of the country. Its social demands included guarantees of the right to work, equal treatment for women, a forty-two-hour week, paid sick and maternity leave, and a ban on child labor.[39] That same year six women activists formed the Democratic Organization of Afghan Women, whose main objectives were to eliminate illiteracy among women, forced marriages, and the brideprice. From its inception, however, the DOAW encountered hostility from mullahs and other conservative elements. In the years before the Saur Revolution, the DOAW managed to win the legal right of women to study abroad. Another achievement was winning the right of women to work outside the home, previously the privilege of a few women from elite families. Both the PDPA and the DOAW were eager for more profound, extensive, and permanent changes.[40]

Among the most remarkable and influential of the DOAW activists was Anahita Ratebzad. In the 1950s she studied nursing in the United States, then returned to Kabul as director and instructor of nursing at the Women's Hospital. Nancy Dupree explains that when the faculty for women at Kabul University was established, Ratebzad entered the medical college and became a member of its teaching staff upon graduation in 1963. She joined the PDPA in 1965 and, along with three other women, ran as a candidate for parliament. This was the first time liberals and leftists had openly appeared in the political arena, and they confronted a reaction against female visibility on the part of conservative members of parliament. In 1968 the latter proposed to enact a law prohibiting young women from studying abroad. Hundreds of female students demonstrated in opposition. In 1970 two reactionary mullahs protested such public evidence of female liberation as miniskirts, women teachers, and schoolgirls by shooting at the legs of women in Western dress and splashing them with acid. (Among those who joined in this action was Gulbeddin Hek-

Table 7.1   Social Indicators, Afghanistan, 1965 and 1975

	1965	1975
GNP per capita (current U.S.$)	70	140
Population and vital statistics		
Total population (thousands)	11,115	14,038
Urban population (% of total)	9.0	13.0
Population growth rate (%)		
Total	n.a.	2.4
Urban	n.a.	5.9
Life expectancy at birth (years)	35	37
Population age structure (%)		
0–14 years	43.0	45.0
15–64 years	55.0	53.0
65 and above	3.0	3.0
Crude birthrate (per 1,000)	54	54
Crude death rate (per 1,000)	29	29
Total fertility rate	8	8
Infant mortality rate (per 1,000)	n.a.	190
Child death rate (per 1,000)	39	35
Food, health, and nutrition		
Index for food production per capita (1979–1981 = 100)	102	102
Per capita supply of		
Calories (per day)	2,203	2,206
Proteins (grams per day)	68	69
Access to safe water (% of population)		
Total	n.a.	6.0
Urban	n.a.	20.0
Rural	n.a.	3.0
Labor force		
Total labor force (in thousands)	3,733	4,569
Female (%)	6.0	7.0
Agriculture (%)	69.0	64.0
Industry (%)	11.0	13.0
Participation rate (%)		
Total	31.0	30.0
Male	56.0	54.0
Female	4.0	4.0
Age dependency (%)	83.2	89.6
Education enrollment rates (%)		
Primary		
Total	16.0	26.0
Male	26.0	44.0
Female	5.0	8.0
Secondary		
Total	2.0	8.0
Male	4.0	13.0
Female	1.0	2.0

Source: World Bank, *Social Indicators of Development 1988* (Baltimore: Johns Hopkins University Press, 1988), pp. 10–11.
   Note: n.a. = information not available.

matyar, who went on to be a leading figure in the Mujahidin, the "freedom fighters" hailed by President Reagan.) This time there was a protest demonstration of 5,000 girls.[41]

Modernization, however limited, had created a stratum of men and women eager for further and deeper social change. According to ILO data, Afghanistan in 1979 had a female population of 6.3 million, of whom 313,000 were considered economically active. Of that figure, 85 percent were production-related workers, employed mainly in textiles—home-based workers producing clothing and carpets who typically did not receive a wage directly. The other major category of employed women was "professional, technical, and related workers": 13,000 women, or 4 percent of the economically active female population. These women were mostly teachers, nurses, government employees (all high-status occupations), secretaries, hairdressers, and entertainers (members of the salaried middle class). Four were parliamentarians. The salaried middle class, the modern working class, and the female labor force in Afghanistan were all small, but a part of the social fabric nonetheless. (See Table 7.2 for data on the economically active population in 1979; note the importance of female labor in manufacturing.)

In April 1978 the PDPA, after having seized power in the Saur Revolution, introduced rapid reforms to change the political and social structure of

Table 7.2   Economically Active Population by Industry, Status, and Sex in Afghanistan, 1979

Industry (major divisions)	Total	%	Males	Females
1 Agriculture, hunting, forestry, and fishing	2,369,481	60.1	2,358,821	10,660
2 Mining and quarrying	59,339	1.5	57,492	1,847
3 Manufacturing	423,373	10.7	170,908	252,465
4 Electricity, gas, and water	11,354	0.3	11,078	276
5 Construction	51,086	1.3	50,670	416
6 Wholesale/retail trade, restaurants, and hotels	137,860	3.5	135,242	2,618
7 Transport, storage, and communication	66,243	1.6	65,376	867
8–9 Business, community, social, and personal services	749,345	19.0	716,511	32,834
Unemployed persons not previously employed	77,510	2.0	66,057	11,453
Total	3,945,591	100.0	3,632,155	313,436

Source: ILO, *Yearbook of Labour Statistics 1945–1989: Retrospective Edition on Population Censuses* (Geneva: ILO, 1990), based on data from the June 1979 Afghan census.

Afghan society, including patterns of land tenure and gender relations. Three decrees—nos. 6, 7, and 8—were the main planks of the program of social and economic reform. Decree no. 6 was intended to put an end to land mortgage and indebtedness; no. 7 was designed to stop the payment of brideprice and give women more freedom of choice in marriage; no. 8 consisted of rules and regulations for the appropriation and redistribution of land. The three decrees were complementary, particularly nos. 6 and 7, for, as noted earlier in this chapter, extravagant expenditure on marriage added to or perpetuated rural households' indebtedness. Decree no. 7, however, seems to have been the most controversial, as it was meant to fundamentally change the institution of marriage. The Taraki government issued the decree with the explicit intention of ensuring equal rights for women and removing patriarchal and feudalistic ties within families. On the premise that women were economically exploited in Afghan society, the decree outlawed traditional cultural practices that had financial implications; both the brideprice and dowry were limited. Forced marriages and the practice of levirate were outlawed. A minimum age of marriage was set: sixteen years for women and eighteen years for men. In a speech on November 4, 1978, President Taraki declared: "Through the issuance of decrees No. 6 and 7, the hard-working peasants were freed from bonds of oppressors and money-lenders, ending the sale of girls for good as hereafter nobody would be entitled to sell any girl or woman in this country."[42]

The six articles of Decree no. 7 were as follows:

Article 1. No one shall engage a girl or give her in marriage in exchange for cash or commodities.

Article 2. No one shall compel the bridegroom or his guardians to give holiday presents to the girl or her family.

Article 3. The girl or her guardian shall not take cash or commodities in the name of dower in excess of ten *dirham* [Arabic coinage] according to Shari'at, which is not more than 300 afs. [about $10 at the time] on the basis of the bank rate of silver.

Article 4. Engagements and marriage shall take place with the full consent of the parties involved: (a) No one shall force marriage; (b) No one shall prevent the free marriage of a widow or force her into marriage because of family relationships [the levirate] or patriarchal ties; (c) No one shall prevent legal marriages on the pretext of engagement, forced engagement expenses, or by using force.

Article 5. Engagement and marriages for women under sixteen and men under eighteen are not permissible.

Article 6. (1) Violators shall be liable to imprisonment from six months to three years; (2) Cash or commodities accepted in violation of the provisions of this decree shall be confiscated.

Along with the promulgation of this audacious decree, the DRA embarked upon an aggressive literacy campaign led by the DOAW, whose task was to educate women, bring them out of seclusion, and initiate social programs. Literacy programs were expanded, with the objective of supplying all adult citizens with basic reading and writing skills within a year. Throughout the countryside, PDPA cadres established literacy classes for men, women, and children in villages; by August 1979 the government had established 600 new schools.[43] The PDPA's rationale for pursuing the rural literacy campaign with some zeal was that all previous reformers had made literacy a matter of choice; male guardians had chosen not to allow their females to be educated, and thus 98 percent of all Afghan women were illiterate. It was therefore decided not to allow literacy to remain a matter of (men's) choice but rather make it a matter of principle and law.

This was clearly a bold program for social change, one aimed at the rapid transformation of a patriarchal society and decentralized power structure based on tribal and landlord authority. Revolutionary change, state building, and women's rights subsequently went hand in hand. The emphasis on women's rights on the part of the PDPA reflected (1) the party's socialist/Marxist ideology; (2) its modernizing and egalitarian outlook; (3) its social base and origins—urban middle-class professionals educated in the United States, the USSR, India, and Western and Eastern Europe; and (4) the number and position of women within the PDPA, especially the outspoken and dynamic Anahita Ratebzad.

In 1976 Ratebzad had been elected to the central committee of the PDPA. Following the Saur Revolution, she was elected to the Revolutionary Council of the DRA and appointed minister of social affairs. Other influential PDPA women in the Taraki government (April 1978–September 1979) were Sultana Umayd, director of Kabul Girls' School; Soraya, president of the DOAW; Ruhafza Kamyar, principal of the DOAW's vocational high school; Firouza, director of the Afghan Red Crescent Society (Red Cross); Dilara Mahak, principal of Amana Fidawa School; and Professor R. S. Siddiqui (who was especially outspoken in her criticism of "feudalistic patriarchal relations"). In the Amin government (September–December 1979), the following women headed schools and the women's organization and sat on government subcommittees: Fawjiyah Shahsawari, Dr. Aziza, Shirin Afzal, and Alamat Tolqun. These were the women who were behind the program for women's rights. Their spirit was reflected in an editorial in the *Kabul Times* (May 25, 1978) that asserted: "Privileges which women, by right, must have are equal education, job security, health services, and free time to rear a healthy generation for building the future of this country. Educating and enlightening women is now the subject of close government scrutiny."[44] Their intention was to expand literacy, especially for girls and women, encourage income-generating projects and employment for women, provide health and legal services for women, and eliminate those aspects of Muslim family law that discriminate against women: unilateral male repudiation, father's exclusive rights to child custody, unequal inheritance, and male guardianship over women.

Internationalized Civil Conflict

The Saur Revolution was considered not a socialist revolution—which in any event was inconceivable in a tribal-feudalistic society—but a "national democratic revolution." President Taraki himself, in his first press conference on May 7, 1978, characterized the new regime as reformist, constructive, and tolerant of Islam. Taraki's conciliatory gestures, such as attendance at Friday congregational prayers and assurances that his government's policies would be consistent with Islamic principles, failed to prevent the mobilization of opposition. In response to the decree of July 1978 on agrarian reform, which reduced or canceled all rural debts prior to 1984 and forbade lenders to collect usury in the future, many angry lenders murdered debtors who refused to pay.[45] There was also universal resistance to the new marriage regulations, which, coupled with compulsory education for girls, raised the threat of women refusing to obey and submit to family (male) authority. Believing that women should not appear at public gatherings, villagers often refused to attend literacy classes after the first day. PDPA cadres viewed this attitude as retrograde and thus resorted to different forms of persuasion, including physical force, to make the villagers return to literacy classes. Often PDPA cadres were either kicked out of the village or murdered. In the summer of 1978 refugees began pouring into Pakistan, giving as their major reason the forceful implementation of the literacy program among their women. In Kandahar three literacy workers from the women's organization were killed as symbols of the unwanted revolution. Nancy Dupree reports that two men killed all the women in their families to prevent "dishonor." According to another observer, the reforms "inevitably aroused the opposition of Afghan men, whose male chauvinism is as massive as the mountains of the Hindu Kush."[46]

The content of Decree no. 7 and compulsory schooling for girls were perceived by some as unbearable interference in domestic life. The prohibition of the brideprice also prevented the traditional transactions and compromised the economy of many households that had counted on brideprice as convertible capital for the future. Compulsory education was disliked because the male householder could no longer be in control of the women and their external relations; if women were not in purdah, then the reputation of the household was at risk. These kinds of sentiments against the reforms were behind the early rebellion. Reaction was soon to follow. After the announcement of the decree, serious resistance against the DRA was organized in Paktia and spread rapidly to other areas of eastern Afghanistan.[47] This was almost a repeat performance of the experience with the Amanullah reforms fifty years earlier.

Land reform, cancellation of peasants' debts, and marriage reform threatened vested rural interests and patriarchal structures. The large landowners, the religious establishment, and money lenders were especially appalled at the prospect of social structural transformation. An Islamist opposition began organizing and conducted several armed actions against the government in the spring of 1979. Moreover, the Carter Administration authorized CIA funding of the rebellion in July 1979 (that is, six months before the Soviet intervention). Internal battles within the PDPA and hostility between its two wings, Parcham and Khalq, contributed to the government's difficulties. In September 1979 President Taraki was killed on the orders of his deputy, Hafizullah Amin, a ruthless and ambitious man who imprisoned and executed hundreds of his own comrades and further alienated the population. The Pakistani regime of Zia ul-Haq was opposed to having leftists next door and supported the armed uprising of the Mujahidin. In December 1979 the Soviet army intervened. Amin was killed and succeeded by Babrak Karmal, who initiated what is called "the second phase" *(marhale-i dovvom),* predicated upon a more gradualist approach to change. Even so, the Mujahidin continued their attacks, encouraged by Pakistan, the United States, Saudi Arabia, and China. In turn, Soviet aircraft carried out bombing raids that resulted in considerable destruction as well as further migration.

It should be noted that not everyone in the PDPA and the DOAW was in favor of the pace of the reforms. According to Soraya, many DOAW activists, including herself, were opposed to the fast pace and the compulsory nature of the program for land reform, women's education, and the new family law. As a result of her antagonism toward Hafizullah Amin, Soraya, like many members of the PDPA's Parcham wing, was imprisoned and even endured torture. She, along with the others, was released after the Soviet intervention, the death of Amin, and his replacement by Babrak Karmal.[48]

In 1980 the PDPA slowed down its reform program and announced its intention to eliminate illiteracy in the cities in seven years and in the provinces in ten. In an interview that year Anahita Ratebzad conceded errors, "in particular the compulsory education of women," to which she added, "The reactionary elements immediately made use of these mistakes to spread discontent among the population."[49] Despite the slowing down of reforms (including concessions such as the restoration of Islamic family law),[50] the opposition movement spread, supported militarily and diplomatically by a large number of countries. In contrast to the Iranian state next door, the Afghan state was unable to impose its will through an extensive administrative and military apparatus. As a result, the programs on land redistribution and women's rights faltered. The government's efforts to raise women's status by changing marriage laws were stymied by patriarchal structures highly resistant to change and by an extremely hostile international environment.

From Revolution to Reconciliation

The DOAW was renamed the All-Afghan Women's Council in 1986 and underwent a shift in orientation: it became less radical and more of a service organization providing social and legal assistance to poor Afghan women. During the late 1980s the Women's Council was led by Massouma Esmaty Wardak, an early DOAW member and member of parliament but not a PDPA member.[51] The PDPA's emphasis on the woman question subsided in favor of a concerted effort at "national reconciliation," which began in January 1987. The Democratic Republic of Afghanistan was renamed the Republic of Afghanistan. A new constitution was drafted, and PDPA members and activists from the Women's Council tried to retain an article stipulating the equality of women with men. This measure, however, was opposed by the non-PDPA members of the assembly. As explained by Farid Mazdak, a party member and government official, compromise was reached in the form of another article stating that all Afghan citizens, male and female, had equal rights and obligations before the law. This compromise was reached after PDPA members and delegates from the Women's Council failed in their attempts to include an equal rights clause.[52]

Article 38 of the constitution of the Republic of Afghanistan, ratified in November 1987, stated:

> Citizens of the Republic of Afghanistan, both men and women, have equal rights and duties before the law, irrespective of their national, racial, linguistic, tribal, educational and social status, religion, creed, political conviction, occupation, kinship, wealth, and residence. Designation of any illegal privilege or discrimination against rights and duties of citizens is forbidden.[53]

Mark Urban, a political journalist, was one of the few writers on Afghanistan at the time to assert that "one genuine achievement of the revolution has been the emancipation of (mainly urban) women." He continued: "There is no doubt that thousands of women are committed to the regime, as their prominent participation in Revolutionary Defense Group militias shows. Eyewitnesses stated that militant militiawomen played a key role in defending the besieged town of Urgun in 1983. Four of the seven militia commanders appointed to the Revolutionary Council in January 1986 were women."[54]

Throughout the 1980s activist women continued to be engaged in formal politics and participated in the different ranks of the party and the government, although there were no women in the Council of Ministers. The Loya

Jirga included women delegates, and in 1989 the National Assembly had seven female members. In 1989 women in prominent positions included Massouma Esmaty Wardak, president of the Women's Council; Shafiqeh Razmandeh, vice president of the Women's Council; Soraya, director in the late 1980s of the Afghan Red Crescent Society; Zahereh Dadmal, director of the Kabul Women's Club; and Dr. Soheila Siddiqi, chief surgeon of the military hospital, who also held the rank of general. The central committee of the PDPA had several women members, including Jamila Palwasha and Ruhafza Kamyar. Ruhafza's position exemplified the sort of social mobility afforded women by the PDPA. An alternate member of the central committee of the PDPA, she was also a working-class grandmother and "model worker" at the Kabul Construction Plant, where she did electrical wiring and supervised male workers.

In Kabul in January–February 1989, I saw women employees in all government agencies and social organizations visited. Ariana Airlines employed female as well as male flight attendants. An employee of the Peace, Solidarity, and Friendship Organization remarked that he was thirty-seven and male, yet he had a supervisor who was ten years younger and female. There were female radio announcers, and the evening news (whether in Pashtu or Dari) was read by one male and one female announcer. The female announcer was

Ruhafza Kamyar, foreman of the Kabul Construction Plant. Mrs. Ruhafza was also a "model worker," a party member, and a grandmother. Photo by Val Moghadam.

neither veiled nor wearing a headscarf. There were women technicians and reporters working for radio and television stations, as well as newspapers and magazines. Women workers were present in the binding section of a printing house in Kabul, in the page-setting section of the Higher and Vocational Education press house, at the CREPCA state-run carpet company (where young women wove carpets and received a wage), and at the Kabul Construction Plant (which specialized in housing and prefabricated materials). Like their male counterparts, these women were members of the Central Trade Union. I also saw one woman employee (and several female volunteer soldiers) at Pol-e Charkhi Prison; she was assigned to the women's section, where she oversaw the six remaining female political prisoners, all charged with terrorist acts. I was told that there were women soldiers and officers in the regular armed forces, as well as in the militia and Women's Self-Defense (Defense of the Revolution) units. There were women in security, intelligence, and the police agencies, women involved in logistics in the Ministry of Defense, women parachutists, even women veterinarians—the latter occupation is usually off-limits to women in Muslim countries. In 1989 all women members of the PDPA received military training and arms. These women were prominent at a party rally of some 50,000 held in early February 1989. As a concession to traditionalist elements, schools were now gender segregated above the primary level, and middle school and secondary school girls could only be taught by female teachers. In offices and other workplaces, however, there was no segregation. Neither were buses divided into male and female sections (as they were in Iran). The Kabul government and the ruling party made a number of compromises and concessions to bolster their position. In June 1990 the PDPA held a party congress and voted to change its name to Hezb-e Vatan (Homeland Party) to emphasize nationalism and reconciliation.

Social Organizations and Social Services

One consequence of this political reorganization was the dismantling of a number of quasi-independent "social organizations" *(sazmanha-ye ejtemayee)* that had functioned effectively to mobilize the citizenry, provide social services, increase women's participation and visibility, and constitute an incipient civil society. Apart from the PDPA itself, they included the Council of Trade Unions, the Democratic Youth Organization, the Peace, Solidarity, and Friendship Organization, the Women's Council, and the Red Crescent Society. Only the Women's Council was left intact following the reorganization. A discussion of the social organizations is useful for the historical record but also to suggest the "gender shock" that doubtlessly occurred when the Kabul government fell and the Mujahidin came to power in 1992. It is followed by a description of women's access to health, literacy, and education services in

Afghanistan in the late 1980s, to provide a picture of the efforts of the Afghan government in a situation of poor resource endowment, weak state capabilities, and an internationalized civil war.

The Afghan Women's Council

The most important organization actively involved in women's rights and betterment was the Afghan Women's Council (AWC), a high-profile social organization that in 1989 was run by Massouma Esmaty Wardak and her staff of eight women. Mrs. Wardak (who in 1990 was appointed minister of education) was not a member of the PDPA, though some of her staff were. A graduate of the Academy of Sciences with a degree in sociology and an interest in literature and history, she was the author of *The Position and Role of Afghan Women in Afghan Society: From the Late Eighteenth to the Late Nineteenth Century;* she also wrote the introduction to a book on Mahmud Tarzi. Active in political and social affairs since the 1960s, she told me that she saw no contradiction between her activities and her religious beliefs: "Hekmatyar and some others think that only they are true Muslims. But I am a Muslim, too, and all those Afghan women working and studying in Kabul are also Muslims."[55]

Both Mrs. Wardak and Ms. Soraya (the latter president of the Red Crescent Society and a former president of the Women's Council) explained that the Women's Council was less political and more social and service-oriented than it had been in the past, especially when it was under the direction of Anahita Ratebzad. Soraya's view was that the reform program initiated by the Taraki government and the PDPA in 1978 had been ill conceived, badly implemented, and too dramatic and hasty for the Afghan rural population. "We now have a gradualist approach," she said. The AWC provided social services to women, such as literacy and vocational training in such fields as secretarial work, hairdressing, and sewing (workshops were located in the complex); organized income-generating activities such as handicraft production (mainly rug and carpet weaving, as well as sewing); offered assistance to mothers and widows of "martyrs of the Revolution" in the form of pensions and coupons; and gave legal advice, mainly through a network of female lawyers. Some women had "outwork" arrangements with the AWC; as Mrs. Wardak explained, "They prefer to work at home; they bring their work to us and we pay them." During two trips to the Women's Council, I was able to observe dozens of women, many of them poor and veiled, entering the grounds to attend a class or to seek advice.

An example of the kind of cases and causes the AWC took up was the complaint by twenty-two-year-old Najiba, who had been abandoned by her husband for another woman because she could not give him a child. He had since remarried, but the AWC took up Najiba's case for maintenance rights in accordance with the law. According to Najiba: "Earlier a woman like me

Massouma Esmaty Wardak, director of the Afghan Women's Council, conducting a staff meeting in 1988. Photo by Ellen Ray.

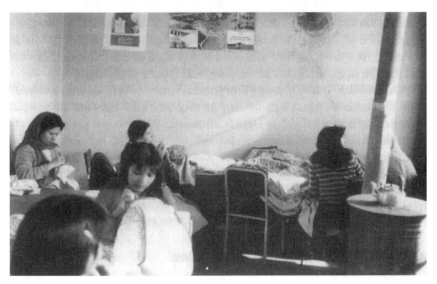

A sewing and embroidery workshop at the Kabul Women's Club. These women earned a salary. The club also offered literacy and other classes. Photo by Val Moghadam.

would have had no prospects. Today I am assured of my rights as an individual, and have also been given a job due to the efforts of the AWC."[56]

Mrs. Wardak told me the AWC had a membership of 150,000, with branches in almost all provinces. The branches organized traditional festivals, which included awards for handicraft pieces, and "peace camps" that provided medical care and distributed garments and relief goods free of charge. The branches also assisted women in income-generating activities such as raising chickens, producing eggs and milk for sale, and sewing and craftwork. The work of the AWC was made possible by generous funding from the government. The principal objectives of the AWC were raising women's social consciousness, making them aware of their rights (particularly their right to literacy and work), and improving women's living conditions and professional skills. Mrs. Wardak stressed equal pay with men and workplace childcare as two important achievements. As Decree no. 7 had been largely ignored by the population and the government had been unable to enforce it, there was an ongoing radio and television campaign "against the buying and selling of girls." The AWC was also trying to change the laws on child custody, based on Muslim family law, that favor the father and his agnates.[57]

Like the AWC, the Kabul Women's Club was located on spacious grounds and held two-hour literacy classes every day. It also offered vocational training and employment workshops where women learned to weave rugs and carpets, sew uniforms, embroider, and produce handicrafts. The work was entirely waged, and childcare and transportation were provided. Courses on house management, health, hairdressing, and typing were offered free of charge. The Women's Club also worked with the Ministry of Public Health on mother-and-child issues such as prevention of diseases, vaccination of children, breast-feeding, and family planning.[58]

The Democratic Youth Organization

Established in 1975, the Democratic Youth Organization (DYO) was the youth wing of the PDPA. According to its director in 1989, Farid Mazdak, more than half of the members of the PDPA came out of the DYO.[59] Youth brigades were assigned to control traffic, dispense coupons and distribute goods at government stores, and ferret out food hoarders. Women DYO members were involved in all the above activities but were especially prominent in learning and dispensing first aid. The DYO also had economic activities, wherein members worked in productive units to help regular workers reach or exceed production targets. Some 12,000 DYO members worked in construction brigades in Kabul and three northern provinces. Mazdak said the construction brigades were the least successful of the DYO activities because— significantly—girls insisted that they take part even though their participation was culturally unacceptable to many men. In the villages, DYO volunteers distributed eggs and chemical fertilizer and worked as assistants to government extension agents. Girls were involved in this kind of work, which, while culturally unacceptable, proved important: Female extension agents could talk to rural women, as well as address health and family planning issues.

On the cultural front, the DYO was involved in the campaign against illiteracy and for the extension of teaching. Mazdak explained that, cognizant of "past mistakes," the campaign used only female teachers for girls, even in Kabul. The country suffered from a serious lack of teachers, 2,000 of whom were killed during the war; others, notably those who were trained abroad, had left Afghanistan, while yet other teachers had become state ministers or assumed other government posts. As a result, DYO members were called up to construct schools (Mazdak said the DYO had built twenty-six schools in Kabul alone) and serve as teachers. The DYO organized literary seminars, cultural festivals, and concerts featuring jazz and Afghan classical and folk music. The organization even put on fashion shows, not only to demonstrate folk and Western styles but also to suggest what was *not* acceptable. (Mazdak singled out leather and chains!)

The Young Pioneers organization, established in 1982, was part of the DYO. Mazdak explained that 100,000 youngsters between the ages of eight and fourteen were members and that its director was a woman. Patterned after the Soviet and Western scout models, the Afghan Young Pioneers attended camp, did artwork, and learned to play musical instruments at Young Pioneer Palaces.

Providing Health and Literacy: Policies and Constraints

After 1981, healthcare and dental care became free for all citizens, and doctors in private practice could not charge above certain amounts. According to Dr. Azizullah Saidali, in 1989 vice president of the Indira Gandhi Children's Hospital, a doctor could not charge more than "the price of an egg." The quality of medical care was not high and the quantity of services insufficient. In 1989, according to official sources, there were 64 hospitals, 5,141 beds, and 98 clinics. Kabul had 14 hospitals and 5 clinics. Total medical personnel numbered 4,400, of which 2,379 were doctors. The monthly salary of the top administrators (both doctors) of a leading hospital in Kabul was 5,000 afghanis in February 1989, the equivalent of $25.[60]

Apart from the military hospital, Indira Gandhi Children's Hospital, built and equipped by India, was considered the nation's most modern hospital, but in 1989 it had an occupancy rate of 120 percent. It also suffered from a shortage of nurses, poor facilities (such as only one properly working ambulance), and chronic supply shortages. According to the hospital's president, Dr. Abdul Salaam Jalali, children frequently came in with malnutrition, infectious diseases, and war injuries. Blood donations came from the army, from members of the social organizations, and from medical personnel. The hospital relied on the army because parents and relatives were frequently unwilling to donate blood for superstitious reasons. Dr. Jalali and Dr. Saidali explained that 60 percent of children under five suffered from malnutrition. Babies typically had low birthweight, generally a function of the poor health of mothers, who often suffered from anemia. The common diet of bread, tea, and some vegetables was not high in nutrition. Research on infant and under-five mortality had shown that vaccination, birth attendants, mother's literacy, poverty, and water supply were major determinants. Because of Afghanistan's poverty and underdevelopment, both infant mortality and maternal mortality were high.

In 1985 the Council of Ministers endorsed a national program called Protection of Mother and Child Health in Afghanistan. Mother-and-child health clinics were established in Kabul, offering, among other things, various birth control methods to limit family size. The government was not averse to family planning, but it did not have a specific program linking changes in family structure and size to broader socioeconomic achievements and changes. Nonetheless, in 1986 some 138,000 women adopted various birth control/family planning techniques, and the birth control pill became the most popular form of contraception among women.[61] Although three maternity clinics were established in Kabul, most women preferred to deliver at home, and thus the training of midwives was also emphasized.

Educating the population had been a key objective of the revolution, but the government faced many obstacles to its realization. There had been periodic literacy drives in Afghanistan in the twentieth century, but as we have seen, the education of girls was always a sensitive issue. A literacy campaign was launched in 1968, but ten years later only 5,000 persons had benefited from it. In the 1980s the DRA's literacy drives were carried out in military units and in factories, and an average of 18,000 persons became literate every year. The magazine *Afghanistan Today* reported in 1988 that in the province of Badghis, "over 210 women are acquiring literacy in 13 literacy courses conducted by members of the Provincial Women's Council." In the province of Kabul, "over 250 housewives of Sorobi district are admitted to 22 literacy courses, taught by volunteer teachers and preachers." The literacy campaign annually convened professional seminars for all the teachers involved in literacy programs. In 1985 Afghanistan was cited by the United Nations Educational, Scientific, and Cultural Organization (UNESCO) for its literacy effort.[62]

To the extent that it could, the national education system continued to function, and some progress was achieved in school enrollments, as can be seen in Table 7.3. Primary school enrollment rates for girls increased steadily—from 5 percent in 1965 to 8 percent in 1975 to 14 percent in 1987—but remained very low. The rates for female attendance at secondary school increased from 1 percent in 1965 to 2 percent in 1975 to 5 percent in 1987. Girls numbered less than half the primary school and secondary school populations, but as can be seen from Table 7.3, their share doubled between 1981

Table 7.3   Enrollment and Educational Data, Afghanistan, 1981–1991

	1981	1982	1983	1991
Primary school pupils, % female	18.6	31.5		33.8
Primary education teachers, % female	20.6	46.7		
Female primary school enrollment, % gross	14.1	9.2	10.6	18.6
Female secondary school enrollment, % gross	4.9	4.8	4.9	9.0
Secondary school pupils, % female				32.2

Source: World Bank, *World Development Indicators 2002* CD-ROM.
Note: Blank cells indicate data not available.

and 1991. School attendance historically had been low, and during the 1980s the civil conflict made education even more precarious. This danger was the reason for the dispatch of students to the Soviet Union—although Western anticommunists criticized this as "Sovietization" and "brainwashing."[63]

Some attention was also directed to vocational schools. With financial and technical assistance from the United Nations, four schools were opened in 1988 to train young people in carpentry, leather work, and tailoring. Higher education continued, and was especially receptive to women students. In 1985 a special program was worked out for rendering financial aid to outstanding students through a joint venture of Kabul University and the Democratic Youth Organization. Students received a stipend of 1,500 afghanis per month to facilitate their studies. Among these recipients of aid were female students in the Faculty of Construction, again a field of study usually off-limits to women in Muslim societies. In 1988 a university was established in Herat. As part of the government's nationalities policy, Uzbeks and others could now learn in their own languages; textbooks in the various languages were provided by the Ministry of Education. According to an AWC survey conducted in 1988, there were 7,133 women in institutions of higher education and 233,000 girls studying in schools. The total number of female professors and teachers was 190 and 22,000, respectively. According to the 1989 UN Report on Afghanistan by the UN's Special Rapporteur, Dr. Felix Ermacora, there were seven higher education institutes in Kabul with a total of 15,319 students of both sexes. The Medical Institute under the Ministry of Public Health had 3,000 students, making a total of over 18,000—compared to a total enrollment of 7,000 in 1977–1978. In 1989, Kabul University had about 7,000 students, of which 65 percent were women.

Women in the Refugee Camps

In contrast to the figures on education in Kabul, the educational situation in the refugee camps of Peshawar was dire, and especially biased against girls.

In Peshawar, 104,600 boys were enrolled in schools, as against 7,800 girls. For boys there were 486 primary schools, 161 middle schools, and 4 high schools. For girls there were 76 primary schools, 2 middle schools, and no high schools.[64] A United Nations Children's Fund (UNICEF) study indicated that there were only 180 Afghan women with high school education in the camps. This was reflective of the highly patriarchal arrangements among the Mujahidin and in Peshawar. Moreover, the schools established in the refugee camps were of questionable value and utility—oriented toward recitation of the Quran, with much propaganda about the jihad and against communism rather than standard instruction in the arts and sciences.

At the end of 1989, the Afghan refugee population in Pakistan was estimated at between 2.5 and 3 million people. Some 350 camplike villages had been established and were administered by the government of Pakistan. War casualties had rendered thousands of women widows. In keeping with the Afghan tradition of the levirate, some widows were remarried to a cousin or a brother of the late husband. For those widows who could not be remarried, a controversial widows' camp was established, which was criticized especially by the Revolutionary Association of Women of Afghanistan (RAWA) as resembling a concentration camp. Although during the 1980s most adult male refugees developed sources of income through employment, most refugee women were barred from income-generating activities and remained secluded behind the compound walls with their children. This was first noted by a 1983 UN report on Afghan refugees in Peshawar. In the section on family organization, the report noted

> the practice of female seclusion, belief in the defense of the honor of women, and a well-developed division of labor within the family on the basis of age and sex. The emphasis on manhood and its association with strength is pervasive and we were told in one camp that even old men were expected to remain out of sight along the women and children. . . . Men assume responsibility for relationships and tasks outside the family compound including purchase and sale of subsistence items from the market (i.e. monetary transactions), agricultural production, house construction, wage labor and maintaining social and political relationships outside the immediate family (including attendance at educational and religious institutions). Where "contact with outsiders" is concerned, there are universal constraints on participation of women . . . puberty defines adulthood for women, and early marriage is common.[65]

The report also explained the difficulty of designing income-generating projects for women:

> The influence of both Islam and traditional codes is pervasive and has many ramifications and implications for our work. Likewise, the role and position of women and the division of work in the household among the different

Afghan tribes, have defined the limits of what is feasible and acceptable for schemes for women refugees.[66]

It is not irrelevant to note that the refugee camps were set up during the Islamization campaign of Pakistan's President Zia ul-Haq. Having assumed power in a military coup and after executing the previous prime minister, Zulfikar Ali Bhutto, Zia ul-Haq and his Jama'at-i Islami Party imposed legislation to segregate the sexes, reinforce Islamic family law, and mete out harsh punishment for prostitution and adultery.[67] This political environment encouraged the intensification of patriarchal arrangements in the Peshawar refugee camps, including an extremely rigid and unequal gender division of labor. A study conducted for the United Nations Research Institute for Social Development described the very different lives led by men and by women and is worth quoting in some detail:

With the exception of fetching water and washing clothes, all tasks outside the home are carried out by men or boys. On the other hand, the women participate in all domestic tasks, including house-building and repair work. The women clearly have the longest working day in most homes, working from five in the morning until nine in the evening, with a number of prayer periods and tea breaks in between. They start the day's work before dawn by making breakfast for the men who are going to work or to seek work, and then feed and milk the animals. It takes a couple of hours to make a dough and bake bread, washing clothes and bathing babies and infants. Midday dinner is then prepared. After the evening meal and the washing up, work continues on the handicrafts. The young women do the heavy housework. For example, they bake the bread, which is a particularly onerous task. They have to sit with their arms in an oven which is about 75 centimetres underground and burning hot. They bake bread on a raised site in the yard, mostly during the hottest time of the day. They also wash clothes and clean the compound and stable, and collect manure, which they dry in the sun and use for fuel. They also fetch water if they do not have big children to do this for them. Women walk either alone or in small groups of five to six to get water. Special pathways are followed to avoid being exposed to the attention of the adult male community.

Men's working hours are usually from seven in the morning to four in the afternoon. Their work in the household rarely takes more than a few hours each day unless they have gainful employment in the home. They spend most of their leisure time out in the local community among other men, with whom they discuss matters of common interest, the resistance work in Afghanistan and tribal affairs. The market belongs to the males. Bargains are made and loans arranged in the tea shops. News as well as rumours and personal affairs are discussed. Weapons are cleaned and tested, the *katcha* buildings under construction providing the targets for practice. Discussion about weapons takes up quite a lot of their energy. Guns and other firearms are bargained for at the bazaars or in individual compounds, especially when the *mujahids* return from Afghanistan. The new equipment and supplies are examined and tested out with absorbed attention. The time for the household is spent on shopping, collecting firewood, collecting aid rations and possibly herding animals. The identity of men is predominantly associated with public life. They obviously enjoy being with other men outside the private compounds, without questioning the inherent seclusion of women. Men also tend to take for granted that women and older girls should serve them at whatever time they may return home. Many apparently spend months away in search of employment or for bargaining purposes, without leaving word as to when they would expect to be back. Men and older boys ensure that *purdah* is observed, which means checking on who enters the compound and which of the younger women leave it for places other than nearby houses and the water source. If other men come visiting, they also ensure that women of childbearing age are hidden from the view of the guests. If a woman in *purdah* has to go the health centre, her husband escorts her there or finds someone else to go with her.[68]

In Peshawar, while women had to observe purdah at its strictest, refugee men enjoyed an unprecedented freedom of movement. Many men found employment in the Pakistani labor market, others became small merchants in the adjacent villages, and still others crossed the border to fight with the resistance. Women, however, were rarely allowed to leave their uncomfortable and unsanitary environments. The only acceptable outing for a refugee woman was to visit a clinic, but not all were allowed to do even that. To some degree the situation for women was similar in prewar Afghanistan, but the restrictions in the camp setting served to isolate them more than ever. Traditional maliks expanded their role to control the lives of single women and widows and to be the guardians of purdah. They also took it upon themselves to prevent women from engaging in "unacceptable occupations," such as productive activities that could help them acquire some economic independence.[69]

Access to food was a persistent problem for single women and widows and infants. The traditional custom of feeding men and boys first continued. Since women did not fight in the so-called jihad, they were perceived as contributing less to the struggle and consequently in less need of sustenance. According to one report, "When supplementary food is available, it is given to the boys and not girls." Women who had a male relative were not allowed to collect their own allocations. As a result, women heads of households often did not receive their fair share of food and had to rely on charity. Although the UN's World Food Program tried to correct this problem, inequity in food distribution caused a high incidence of anemia among the adult female population.[70]

When women become excluded from productive activities, their role in human reproduction becomes exaggerated and fetishized. The control of women's fertility, sexuality, and even mobility becomes a matter of male honor. The honor/shame complex in Peshawar was thus not only a legacy of the traditional patriarchal social structure, but also a feature of the extreme privatization of the domestic sphere to which women had been relegated as a result of uprootedness and war.

Observers repeatedly noted that Afghan refugee women suffered from depression and emotional imbalance. Feelings of loneliness, fear, and guilt over having left relatives and friends behind in Afghanistan were reportedly overwhelming psychological problems created by the refugee situation. According to Howard-Merriam, who conducted extensive interviews with women in the Peshawar refugee camps: "As beings set apart and excluded from the public, women are united in their hostility toward men as 'bad, ugly and cruel.'" Women's low level of expectation, the writer continued, stands in contrast to the "men's higher and often unrealistic ones of world conquest."[71]

Education for girls remained a contested terrain. According to Nancy Dupree, "Even the mere mention of education for girls was anathema and those who advocated it were branded as 'traitors' and 'communists.'"[72] Throughout the 1980s education for girls in the refugee camps in Peshawar, administered by the United Nations High Commissioner for Refugees (UNHCR), remained woefully inadequate. Surprisingly, UN officials acquiesced to Afghan male resistance to teaching girls; most of the UN's camp schools were for boys only. Boys went to school for as many years as possible, while girls left at the age of ten or eleven to weave carpets. In healthcare, too, the UNHCR initially encountered resistance to the extension of services to women. In Peshawar, Afghan men did not allow male medical workers to attend to women, and many were reluctant even to allow women to leave their houses or get treatment from female doctors or assistants. Because of the observance of purdah, many infants with developmental problems or disabilities were overlooked by relief workers and physicians. A French woman doctor once complained to a reporter, "We have to fight with the men to take women to a hospital when necessary."[73] Unfortunately, most of the aid agencies acquiesced to the patriarchal norms established by the Mujahidin, partly because of reluctance to "impose" Western norms about women's rights and human rights, partly because they supported the Mujahidin's war against the "communists." Indeed, many male aid workers in Peshawar showed their support and sympathy by wearing the distinctive Afghan cap.[74]

Unlike liberation, resistance, and guerrilla groups elsewhere, the Afghan Mujahidin never encouraged the active participation of women. Whereas women in Cuba, Algeria, Vietnam, China, Eritrea, Iran, Nicaragua, El Salvador, and Palestine were or are active in the front lines as well as in social services, the Mujahidin threatened women in Peshawar who became too visible or vocal. The group responsible for most of the intimidation of women was the Hizb-e Islami, led by Gulbeddin Hekmatyar, who received substantial military, political, and financial support from the United States, Pakistan, and Saudi Arabia.

The situation in the refugee camps was protested by a few Afghan women, notably an underground group of former Maoists who formed the Revolutionary Association of Women of Afghanistan. In the late 1980s they produced and distributed leaflets strongly criticizing the misogyny of the Mujahidin groups. One communiqué from 1988 denounced the Islamists for the following:

> Killing the innocent men and women, raping, marrying forcefully young girls and widows, and hostility toward women literacy and education, are some customary cruelties committed by the fundamentalists who have made the life inside and outside the country bitter and suffocating.[75]

The communiqué decried the "anti-democratic and anti-woman" activities of the fundamentalists and warned of "fundamentalist fascism." These warnings were well founded, but they fell on deaf ears, for the international community seemed disinterested in Afghan feminist issues. Nor was an alarm raised by international aid workers in Peshawar when in 1990 a group of eighty Afghan mullahs—all from the seven parties that made up the Western-backed Mujahidin "government-in-exile"—issued a *fatwa* (a religious decree) stating that women were not to wear perfume, noisy bangles, or Western clothes. Veils had to cover the body at all times and clothes were not to be made of material that was soft or that rustled. Women were not to walk in the middle of the street or swing their hips; they were not to talk, laugh, or joke with strangers or foreigners. When the Mujahidin assumed control of Kabul in late April 1992, their first step was to ban the sale and consumption of alcohol and to declare that all women would henceforth appear in public veiled. Two months later women television broadcasters were fired. By all accounts, in the summer of 1992 there were fewer women in the streets of Kabul than at any time in the previous decade.[76]

Gender Shock: Life Under Islamist Rule

Almost immediately upon assuming power, the erstwhile Mujahidin allies turned their guns on each other, and for the next two years fierce fighting broke out in Kabul, all but destroying the city and creating a situation of lawlessness and chaos. In addition, kidnapping and rapes of women and girls took place in an apparently unprecedented manner. The security situation was so dire in August 1992 that even the UN staffers had left Kabul, but a group of thirty Afghan women bravely organized a protest against the anarchy and the abuses against women. According to a news report, the women complained that "hundreds of girls had been abducted from their homes by armed mujahideen, held prisoner and in some cases for up to 20 days, and repeatedly raped. One 16-year-old girl protected her honor by committing suicide by leaping from her sixth floor window in order to escape her would-be captors, locals in her housing estate said. They said 3,000 people gathered to protest the assaults on women but mujahideen guards disrupted them by firing their Kalashnikovs."[77]

The combination of Mujahidin infighting and chaos and the Rabbani government's strict Islamist regime resulted in an environment of extreme insecurity for women. Habiba Hasan, president of Amnesty International in Karachi, wrote in 1995 about abuses that had taken place through the summer of 1994. She described how women of a rival faction were taken as "booty," for money or for "forced marriages." Others were sold into prostitution, frequently in Pakistan. Apparently, mothers were forced to watch their young daughters being raped, and girls witnessed their parents being beaten and killed. She concluded that "women's rights [were] violated with impunity." According to Amnesty International, tens of thousands of civilians were killed and numerous girls and women—as well as boys—were kidnapped and raped between 1992 and 1996.[78]

In response to the atrocities of the Mujahidin and the failures of the Rabbani government—which included also the proliferation of narcotics—a group of religious students called the Taliban formed an opposition army, and in September 1996 they captured Kabul after a bloody two-year campaign. Initially, many Afghans welcomed the Taliban as the harbinger of law and order. Ahmed Rashid explains: "All those who gathered around [Mullah Omar, the leader of the Taliban] were the children of the *jihad* but deeply disillusioned with the factionalism and criminal activities of the once idealized Mujahidin leadership." Rashid quotes Omar as follows: "We were fighting against Muslims who had gone wrong. How could we remain quiet when we could see crimes being committed against women and the poor"?[79] Shortly thereafter, the Taliban instituted one of the harshest political and gender regimes known.

The Taliban were Pashtun men, raised in the refugee camps of Peshawar, Pakistan, during the 1980s who later formed an unconventional army and who briefly ruled Afghanistan. They adhered to a particularly orthodox brand of Islam, one that opposed education for girls and employment for women and that called for compulsory, and very heavy, veiling. The Taliban's only education came from poorly equipped religious schools in Peshawar espousing a very conservative doctrine partly inspired by the Wahhabi ideology of Saudi Arabia. They had no conception of modern governance, democratic or participatory rule, human rights, or women's rights. Nonetheless, the Clinton administration was very close to recognizing the Taliban regime, partly because of its disappointment with the Mujahidin's corrupt rule, and partly because of the opportunity for a lucrative oil pipeline deal involving a California-based corporation, Unocal.[80]

As early as February 1996, when the Taliban controlled some parts of Afghanistan, they had decreed that women would be forbidden to work outside their homes, except in hospitals and clinics, and then only to treat women and girls. But given that there were so few Afghan women health workers, and given that the Taliban did not allow male health workers to treat females, women and girls were not receiving medical treatment. In areas under Taliban control, girls had been expelled from schools and young women from colleges; it was announced that, for the time being, education was for males only. Women were also told that if they went shopping in the bazaars, they had to be accompanied by male kinfolk and wear the traditional burqa.

Taliban enforcement of the new rules regarding compulsory veiling was brutal. Women who did not conform—perhaps they showed a little leg, or their burqa wasn't made of heavy enough fabric—were publicly beaten, in a few cases by men wielding chains, and in at least one case in front of the women's crying children.[81] In addition to the disruptions and destruction of services caused by war, many women health workers were too frightened to work. This despite a Taliban ruling that they could work provided they saw only women patients and had no conversations with male doctors except to discuss diagnosis and treatment. Only one woman general practitioner was running her practice in Kabul in October 1996 and most of her patients could not pay her. The lack of running water or adequate heating in Kabul forced people to attend public baths to wash, but a Taliban edict ordered that the women's section had to close, ostensibly to avoid moral corruption.

In March 1997 the Taliban ordered Kabul residents to screen windows in their homes to ensure that women could not be seen from the street. The regulations, announced on Taliban-controlled radio, told householders to paint clear glass in their upper windows or replace it with opaque glass up to a height of six feet from the floor. The Kabul city council rules referred to "second floor windows on both sides of the house, which pose a threat to neighbors as far as the women's dress code is concerned." A Taliban official said that women's faces corrupt men. The Taliban's Office for the Enforcement of Islamic Virtue and the Prevention of Vice implemented and enforced these and other new laws. The power of the Taliban and the harsh manner in which they enforced their brand of Islam and patriarchy made it impossible for all but the most determined women to engage in such basic human endeavors as education, work, and travel. Small groups of such resilient women held classes in their homes for young girls, tried to obtain jobs with international humanitarian agencies in the country, organized income-generating projects for other women, or traveled to Peshawar to make contact with women activists.[82] Apart from the severe oppression of women, the Taliban also practiced ethnic discrimination. They decreed that all men must wear beards; the fact that some Afghan men of Uzbek origin cannot easily grow beards did not prevent the Taliban from punishing those men.

Resistance to the Taliban's gender regime emerged among expatriate Afghan women scholars and activists, such as those involved with the Afghan Women's Council and the Revolutionary Association of Women of

Afghanistan, in Peshawar, and expatriate groups based in North America and Europe, such as the U.S.-based Women's Association for Peace and Human Rights in Afghanistan (WAPHA) and Negar, which was based in France. They worked with feminists in South Asia, North America, and Europe to raise international awareness about the plight of Afghan women. The United Nations and its specialized agencies took note of the plight of Afghan women, and in a marked departure from their stance in the 1980s and early 1990s, issued warnings to the Taliban that they would not conduct operations in Afghanistan if women could not be employed by the agencies. The transnational feminist network Women Living Under Muslim Laws (WLUML) issued numerous action alerts on the plight of Afghan women and produced a compendium of documents. The South Asia branch of WLUML—Shirkat Gah in Lahore, Pakistan—was especially active in publicizing the repressive regime of the Taliban and the violation of Afghan women's human rights.[83] In the United States, the Feminist Majority launched a highly visible "Gender Apartheid" campaign that drew widespread attention to the violation of women's rights in Afghanistan under the Taliban. The transnational feminist campaign in support of women's rights in Afghanistan succeeded in preventing all but three countries from extending diplomatic recognition to the Taliban regime (Saudi Arabia, Pakistan, and the United Arab Emirates) and in preventing the realization of the oil pipeline deal.[84] All this pointed to the emergence of a new international environment, including the influence of global feminism.

Toward Reconstruction, Development, and Women's Rights

Following the tragedy of September 11, 2001, events moved quickly in Afghanistan. The United States began a bombing campaign to "rout out" Osama bin Laden and the Taliban; in this the United States was assisted on the ground by the former Mujahidin, now called the Northern Alliance. The United Nations, the European Union, and the United States then convened a special meeting in Bonn, Germany, in November 2001, to select an interim government. Three of the thirty official representatives were women, although they were part of the delegations of three of the political factions, not representatives of Afghan women's organizations. A six-month interim government was decided upon in Bonn, and two women—the respected surgeon Dr. Soheila Siddiqi (mentioned earlier in this chapter) and the activist Sima Samar, also trained as a physician—were appointed to the posts of health and women's rights, respectively. This was followed by the launching of an electoral process to establish a representative government and begin preparations for the drafting of a new constitution. The process involved the

Soheila Siddiqi, health minister (left), and Sima Samar, women's affairs minister (right), arrive at the swearing-in ceremony of interim prime minister Hamid Karzai on December 22, 2001. Samar lost her post after the Loya Jirga convened in June 2002 but was named head of the new human rights commission. AP/Wide World Photos; photo by Marco Di Lauro.

convening of a Loya Jirga, the traditional Afghan assembly, and it was encouraging that several women, including Soraya (mentioned earlier in this chapter), had been appointed to the Loya Jirga commission, and that the vice chair of the commission was a woman, Mahboubeh Hoghoughmal.[85] It was also an achievement that talented and experienced women such as Siddiqi, Soraya, Samar, and Hoghoughmal had managed to transcend their divergent political backgrounds and past ideological conflicts to work together toward the building of a new Afghanistan.

However, it was felt by some that women's rights and needs had been placed on a back burner, and that funding for Afghanistan's reconstruction was inadequate. For example, less than two weeks after the Taliban's departure from Kabul, permission to hold a women's march through the streets of Kabul was refused. The Afghan women's consultation called for a minimum of 25 percent representation of women in the Loya Jirga, though the final figure was closer to 12 percent, and the interministerial commission for the advancement of women that it recommended had yet to be established. The conference of donors in Tokyo in January 2002 pledged a total of $4.5 billion, including $297 million from the United States and $500 million from the European Union. Other countries pledged funds over a period of years (e.g., Saudi Arabia pledged $220 million over three years). The total of $4.5 billion, it should be noted, was less than the $5 billion that the United States is said to have expended on the Mujahidin during the 1980s.[86] The donors' meeting marginalized women's concerns, and an alert was issued by the U.S.-based feminist group Women's Edge in late January 2002. For some months after the meeting, the pledged funding was held up due to disagreements between the EU donors and Karzai over monetary policy. In late August 2002, of the $1.8 billion promised for the year, fully $1.2 billion was outstanding.[87]

Continued warfare and the lack of security for women remained a major impediment. In April 2002, Sima Samar said she had very limited resources to run the women's affairs ministry *(vezarat-e omour-e zanan),* and that it was hard to coax women out of their homes when there was no real security on the streets. She, like many other concerned Afghans, wanted to see the extension and expansion of the peacekeeping forces beyond Kabul and throughout the country, but the United States opposed this proposal. Northern Alliance forces were accused of abuses, including murder, rape, and extortion, especially against the ethnic Pashtun population, but they were not prosecuted. Clerics denounced the women's ministry and Ms. Samar herself, and she was not invited back to the position of minister for women's rights after the Loya Jirga took place and the second transitional government was formed. Women students returned to Kabul University, but reports indicated that they faced hostility from many of the conservative and religious male students.[88]

The arduous but necessary process of building a modern state and modern civil society in Afghanistan will require that its women leaders and the representatives of the Afghan women's organizations have a voice in decisionmaking. Certainly Afghan women can count on the continued support, solidarity, and technical assistance of the transnational women's movement. At the same time, the welfare and rights of Afghan women depend very much on the success of peacebuilding efforts, the type of government and legal system that are formed, the reconstruction and development of the country's social and physical infrastructure, and the amount and allocation of foreign aid. A separate Afghan Women's Fund would have been a sound idea. As this chapter has shown, Afghan women have suffered oppression, exclusion, and deprivation for a very long time. With a literacy rate estimated (optimistically) at only 20 percent and a life expectancy of only forty-three years, Afghan women will require massive amounts of financial resources and technical assistance from the international donor community, and a serious commitment on the part of the national government to provide health, schooling, and employment opportunities for women and girls. Investing in the women of Afghanistan and ensuring that women's groups participate in negotiations and decisionmaking are necessary steps to bring about development, modernization, and women's rights in Afghanistan. Whether it happens, and when, is perhaps *the* intriguing question.

Conclusion

In 1978 the government of the newly established Democratic Republic of Afghanistan, led by President Noor Mohammad Taraki, enacted legislation to raise women's status through changes in family law, reform of marriage customs, and new policies to encourage female education and employment. The Afghan state was motivated by a modernizing outlook and socialist ideology that linked Afghan backwardness to feudalism, widespread female illiteracy, and the buying and selling of young brides. The leadership resolved that women's rights to education, employment, mobility, and choice of spouse would be major objectives of the national democratic revolution. In this connection the new leadership was simply continuing the tradition of reform and modernization in developing countries. As in other modernizing and socialist experiments, the woman question constituted an essential part of the political project, as we have seen in Chapter 3. But the experiment failed, the victim of internal rivalries, tribal-Islamist opposition, and a hostile international climate.

The attainment of women's rights in Afghanistan has been constrained historically by three factors and forces. The first two are structural: (1) the patriarchal nature of gender and social relations, deeply embedded in tribal community, and (2) the existence of a weak central state, which since at least the beginning of the twentieth century has been unable to fully implement modernizing programs in the face of "tribal feudalism," especially among the Pashtuns. The two are interconnected, for the state's weakness is correlated with a strong (if fragmented) society resistant to state bureaucratic expansion, civil authority, regulation, monopoly of the means of violence, and extraction—the business of modern states. In his study of causes and forms of collective action, Charles Tilly has noted a pattern of reactionary movements by declining or threatened social classes. Contenders who are in danger of losing their place in a polity are especially prone to "reactive" collective action, often taking communal forms.[89] Such reactions have occurred time and again in modern Afghan history, as we have seen. The third factor is opportunistic intervention on the part of neighboring countries and great powers (e.g., Great Britain in the nineteenth century and possibly during Amanullah's rule in the 1920s, the United States in the 1980s and early 1990s), which served to intensify tribal-based conflict, stall or set back development, reinforce Afghan patriarchy, and increase women's insecurity.

These three factors were behind the defeat of the modernizing efforts of King Amanullah in the 1920s, the incapacity of modernizing efforts during the Zahir Shah era, and the defeat of the DRA's attempt to implement a wide-ranging program for land reform, women's rights, and social development in the 1980s. The patriarchal social structure and tribal feudalism also explain the disintegration of the U.S.-backed Mujahidin government and the inability of both the Mujahidin and the Taliban to undertake reconstruction and development, much less women's rights. The persistence of a particularly entrenched form of patriarchy and a tribal-based social structure in which only men have rights, equality, and unlimited access to public space, and the absence or failure of the developmentalist, welfarist state, has meant that apart from a very small (albeit very talented) urban female elite, the vast majority of Afghan women have experienced social exclusion, illiteracy, poor health, and subordination.

This chapter has also sought to underscore the gender dimension of the long Afghan conflict. During periods of change or contestation, women become the sign or marker of political goals and of cultural identity; representations of women are deployed during processes of revolution and state building and when power is being reproduced, linking women either to modernization and progress or to cultural rejuvenation and religious orthodoxy. In Afghanistan's case, the Soviet intervention and world attention to it obscured the very real conflicts between modernizers and traditionalists and between women's emancipation and patriarchy. Not until the latter part of the 1990s did Afghan women's plight come to the attention of the world community, via the transnational feminist movement. But in the meantime, Afghan women paid a very high price indeed for the silence and inattention of the international community.

Notes

The opening quotation is from a conversation I had with the Afghan teenager in Kabul in February 1989.

1. I am grateful to David N. Gibbs for these points.

2. Richard Nyrop and Donald Seekins, *Afghanistan: A Country Study* (Washington, D.C.: American University, Foreign Area Studies, 1986), p. 105.

3. Ibid., pp. 140–185; David Gibbs, "The Peasant as Counterrevolutionary: The Rural Origins of the Afghan Insurgency," *Studies in Comparative International Development* 21 (1): 36–95; Vartan Gregorian, *The Emergence of Modern Afghanistan* (Stanford: Stanford University Press, 1969), esp. pp. 19–24; and Yuri Gankovsky, *A History of Afghanistan* (Moscow: Progress Publishers, 1985), esp. pp. 182–184.

4. John Griffiths, *Afghanistan* (Boulder: Westview Press, 1981), p. 136.

5. This is a matter of dispute among students of Afghanistan. Anthropologist Nazif Shahrani, for example, denies inequality in landownership and therefore the need for land reform. See M. Nazif Shahrani, "Introduction: Marxist 'Revolution' and Islamic Resistance in Afghanistan," in M. Nazif Shahrani and Robert L. Canfield, eds., *Revolutions and Rebellions in Afghanistan* (Berkeley: University of California International Studies Institute, 1984), esp. pp. 10–24.

6. On this issue, see, inter alia, Gregorian, *The Emergence of Modern Afghanistan;* Robert Canfield, "Afghanistan: The Trajectory of Internal Alignments," *Middle East Journal* 42 (4) (Autumn 1989): 635–648; Nyrop and Seekins, *Afghanistan,* pp. 112–113; Ralph Magnus, "The PDPA Regime in Afghanistan: A

Soviet Model for the Future of the Middle East?" in Peter Chelkowski and Robert Pranger, eds., *Ideology and Power in the Middle East* (Durham and London: Duke University Press, 1988); and Anthony Hyman, "Nationalism in Afghanistan," *International Journal of Middle East Studies* 34 (2) (May 2002): 299–315.

7. Nancy Tapper, "Causes and Consequences of the Abolition of Brideprice in Afghanistan," in Shahrani and Canfield, *Revolutions and Rebellions in Afghanistan*, p. 304.

8. On the meaning and function of the brideprice, see Tapper, "Causes and Consequences." My view of the brideprice is more critical.

9. Mohammad Hashim Kamali, *Law in Afghanistan: A Study of the Constitutions, Matrimonial Law, and the Judiciary* (Leiden: E. J. Brill, 1985), p. 8. Kamali argues for the need for Shari'a law reform as well.

10. Olivier Roy, *Islam and Resistance in Afghanistan*, 2nd ed. (Cambridge: Cambridge University Press, 1990), pp. 35–36. On Pashtunwali and its disagreement with Islam, see also Griffiths, *Afghanistan*, pp. 111–112, 122; Beverly Male, *Revolutionary Afghanistan* (New York: St. Martin's Press, 1982); Thomas Hammond, *Red Flag Over Afghanistan* (Boulder: Westview Press, 1984), p. 71; Raja Anwar, *The Tragedy of Afghanistan: A First-Hand Account* (London: Verso, 1988), esp. chap. 11; Mark Urban, *War in Afghanistan* (New York: St. Martin's Press, 1988); Kathleen Howard-Merriam, "Afghan Refugee Women and Their Struggle for Survival," in Grant Farr and John Merrian, eds., *Afghan Resistance: The Politics of Survival* (Boulder: Westview Press, 1987), pp. 103–105; and Inger Boesen, "Conflicts of Solidarity in Pashtun Women's Lives," in Bo Utas, ed., *Women in Islamic Society* (Copenhagen: Scandinavian Institute of Asian Studies, 1983), pp. 104–125.

11. Audrey Shalinsky, "Women's Relationships in Traditional Northern Afghanistan," *Central Asian Survey* 8 (1) (1989): 117–129; quote appears on p. 127.

12. Simone Bailleau Lajoinie, *Conditions de Femmes en Afghanistan* (Paris: Notre Temps/Monde, 1980); Anwar, *The Tragedy of Afghanistan;* Male, *Revolutionary Afghanistan;* Nyrop and Seekins, *Afghanistan,* Tapper, "Causes and Consequences"; and Kamali, *Law in Afghanistan,* pp. 142–143.

13. Hanne Christensen, *The Reconstruction of Afghanistan: A Chance for Rural Afghan Women* (Geneva: United Nations Research Institute for Social Development, 1990), pp. 4–9.

14. Griffiths, *Afghanistan,* p. 78.

15. Haleh Afshar, "The Position of Women in an Iranian Village," in Haleh Afshar, ed., *Women, Work, and Ideology in the Third World* (London: Tavistock, 1985), p. 67; Hanna Papanek, "Class and Gender in Education-Employment Linkages," *Comparative Education Review* 29 (3) (1985): 317–346; and Christensen, *The Reconstruction of Afghanistan,* p. 5.

16. Bahram Tavakolian, "Women and Socioeconomic Change Among Sheikhanzai Nomads of Western Afghanistan," *Middle East Journal* 38 (3) (Summer 1984): 433–453; quotes appear on pp. 439–440.

17. Ibid., p. 449.

18. Bertrand Badie and Pierre Birnbaum, *The Sociology of the State* (Chicago: University of Chicago Press, 1983), p. 35.

19. Joel Migdal, *Strong Societies and Weak States: State-Society Relations and State Capabilities in the Third World* (Princeton: Princeton University Press, 1988), p. 8. See also Peter Evans, Dietrich Rueschemeyer, and Theda Skocpol, eds., *Bringing the State Back In* (New York: Cambridge University Press, 1985).

20. Quoted in Migdal, *Strong Societies and Weak States,* p. 8. Urban, in *War in Afghanistan,* also notes the historical incapacity of the Afghan state (p. 4).

21. Samuel Huntington, *Political Order in Changing Societies* (New Haven: Yale University Press, 1968), p. 2.

22. Gregorian, *The Emergence of Modern Afghanistan,* p. 3.

23. Urban, *War in Afghanistan,* p. 204; and Gregorian, *The Emergence of Modern Afghanistan,* p. 7.

24. Gregorian, *The Emergence of Modern Afghanistan,* pp. 309–356.

25. Ibid., pp. 138–139; and Lajoinie, *Conditions des Femmes en Afghanistan,* p. 61. The discussion that follows draws from Gregorian, *The Emergence of Modern Afghanistan,* pp. 138–264, and Kamali, *Law in Afghanistan,* pp. 111–112.

26. Gregorian, *The Emergence of Modern Afghanistan,* p. 227.

27. Rhea Tally Stewart, *Fire in Afghanistan, 1914–1929* (New York: Doubleday, 1973), p. 370. See also Senzil Nawid, *Religious Response to Social Change in Afghanistan, 1919–29: King Aman-Allah and the Afghan Ulama* (Costa Mesa, Calif.: Mazda, 1999).

28. Gregory J. Massel, *The Surrogate Proletariat: Muslim Women and Revolutionary Strategies in Soviet Central Asia, 1919–1929* (Princeton: Princeton University Press, 1974), p. 219. See also Nawid, *Religious Response to Social Change,* p. 96.

29. Gregorian, *The Emergence of Modern Afghanistan,* p. 356.

30. Tapper, "Causes and Consequences"; and Kamali, *Law in Afghanistan,* pp. 86–87, 196.

31. Kamali, *Law in Afghanistan,* pp. 84–85.

32. Tapper, "Causes and Consequences," p. 304; and Christensen, *The Reconstruction of Afghanistan,* pp. 5–6. See also Boesen, "Conflicts of Solidarity," pp. 104–125; and Nyrop and Seekins, *Afghanistan,* pp. 126–128.

33. Tapper, "Causes and Consequences," p. 304.

34. Nyrop and Seekins, *Afghanistan,* p. 86; Howard-Merriam, "Afghan Refugee Women," p. 114; and Kamali, *Law in Afghanistan,* p. 141; Boesen, "Conflicts of Solidarity," p. 104.

35. Author interviews with Dr. Saidali Jalali and Dr. Azizullah Saidi at Indira Gandhi Hospital in Kabul, February 11, 1989.

36. Howard-Merriam, "Afghan Refugee Women," p. 106.

37. Kamali, *Law in Afghanistan,* p. 142.

38. Christensen, *The Reconstruction of Afghanistan,* pp. 7–8. Statistics by the government of the Democratic Republic of Afghanistan were provided to me in October 1986 by the Office of the Permanent Mission to the UN in New York. See also The Economist, *The World in Figures 1981.*

39. Fred Halliday, "Revolution in Afghanistan," *New Left Review* 112 (November–December 1978), p. 30.

40. Interviews with Soraya, DOAW founding member and past president, Kabul, February 6, 1989, and Helsinki, October 8, 1990. Soraya identified three of the four women parliamentarians: Anahita Ratebzad, Massouma Esmaty Wardak, and Mrs. Saljugi.

41. Nancy Hatch Dupree, "Revolutionary Rhetoric and Afghan Women," in Shahrani and Canfield, *Revolutions and Rebellions in Afghanistan,* p. 310.

42. Quoted in Tapper, "Causes and Consequences," p. 291. On Decrees no. 6 and no. 7, see also Mansoor Akbar, "Revolutionary Changes and Social Resistance in Afghanistan," *Asian Profile* 17 (3) (June 1989): 271–281; Dupree, "Revolutionary Rhetoric and Afghan Women," esp. pp. 322–325; and Hugh Beattie, "Effects of the Saur Revolution in Nahrin," in Shahrani and Canfield, *Revolutions and Rebellions in Afghanistan,* p. 186.

43. Suzanne Jolicoeur Katsikas, *The Arc of Socialist Revolution: Angola to Afghanistan* (Cambridge, Mass.: Schenkman, 1982), p. 231.

44. Quoted in Dupree, "Revolutionary Rhetoric and Afghan Women," p. 316.

45. Henry Bradsher, *Afghanistan and the Soviet Union* (Durham, N.C.: Duke University Press), p. 93. See also Kamali, *Law in Afghanistan,* p. 32.

46. Hammond, *Red Flag Over Afghanistan,* p. 71. See also Dupree, "Revolutionary Rhetoric and Afghan Women," p. 321, and Katzikas, *The Arc of Socialist Revolution,* p. 231.

47. Christensen, *The Reconstruction of Afghanistan,* p. 9. See also Beattie, "Effects of the Saur Revolution in Nahrin." The brief account of the reform of the "dowry system" by Olivier Roy (*Islam and Resistance in Afghanistan,* pp. 94–95) is incorrect on several counts: it was not dowry but brideprice (or dower) that was being reformed; Decree no. 7 was not, strictly speaking, an affront to Islamic law but rather to customary law; Decree no. 7 provided for not only a ceiling on the brideprice but also an end to the levirate, a minimum age of consent, and so on. The reaction to the decree was, as we have seen, far stronger than Roy suggests in his brief commentary.

48. Soraya, in conversations with the author, Kabul, January–February 1989.

49. Dupree, "Revolutionary Rhetoric and Afghan Women," p. 330.

50. The formal reinstatement of Muslim family law did not apply to party members. Author interview with a PDPA official, New York, October 28, 1986.

51. Author interview with Massouma Esmaty Wardak, Kabul, February 1, 1989.

52. Interview with Farid Mazdak, PDPA official, Kabul, February 9, 1989.

53. Constitution of the Republic of Afghanistan, Kabul, 1988.

54. Urban, *War in Afghanistan,* p. 209.

55. Interview with Massouma Esmaty Wardak, Kabul, January 24, 1989.

56. *Afghanistan Today* 5, September–October 1988, p. 22.

57. Interview with Massouma Esmaty Wardak, Kabul, January 24, 1989. Interviews with Soraya, Kabul, February 6, 1989, and Helsinki, October 8, 1990.

58. Interview with Zahereh Dadmal, director of the Kabul Women's Club, Kabul, February 8, 1989.

59. Interview with Farid Mazdak, Kabul, February 9, 1989. The Democratic Youth Organization was dismantled in 1990. Farid Mazdak himself was elected one of the four vice chairs of the newly formed Hezb-e Vatan. The party chair was the president of Afghanistan, Dr. Najibullah.

60. Interview with Dr. Abdul Salaam Jalali and Dr. Azizullah Saidali, Indira Gandhi Children's Hospital, Kabul, February 11, 1989.

61. *Afghanistan Today* 2, March–April 1988, pp. 20–21.

62. Information from *Afghanistan Today* 1, January–February 1988, p. 15; *Kabul Times,* September 22, 1988; and *Afghanistan Today* 5, September–October 1988.

63. This view was expressed in the Helsinki Watch Report of 1984 written by Jeri Laber and Barnett Rubin, and again in their book *A Nation Is Dying* (Evanston, Ill.: Northwestern University Press, 1988). The education provided to boys in the Mujahidin camps in Peshawar (girls hardly received any education at all) emphasized religion, militarism, and Mujahidin values, but this was not criticized by Laber and Rubin.

64. See Henry Kamm, "Afghan Refugee Women Suffering from Isolation Under Islamic Custom," *New York Times,* March 27, 1988, p. A1; and Kamm, "Aid to Afghan Refugees: Donors Bend the Rules," *New York Times,* April 2, 1988, p. A2.

65. ILO and UN High Commissioner for Refugees, *Tradition and Dynamism Among Afghan Refugees* (Geneva: ILO, 1983), p. 19.

66. Ibid., p. 3.

67. Khawar Mumtaz and Farida Shaheed, *Women of Pakistan: Two Steps Forward, One Step Back?* (London: Zed Books, 1987).

68. Christensen, *The Reconstruction of Afghanistan,* pp. 50–53.

69. See Doris Lessing, "A Reporter at Large: The Catastrophe," *The New Yorker,* March 16, 1987.

70. *Issues and Options for Refugee Women in Developing Countries* (Washington, D.C.: Refugee Policy Group, 1986).

71. Howard-Merriam, "Afghan Refugee Women," p. 106.

72. Nancy Hatch Dupree, *Women in Afghanistan: Preliminary Needs Assessment* (New York: UNIFEM, 1989). This paper was prepared for a UNIFEM/UNICEF workshop on Afghan women (February 1989), in which I also participated.

73. Kamm, "Afghan Refugee Women Suffering from Isolation," and Kamm, "Aid to Afghan Refugees." See also Christensen, *The Reconstruction of Afghanistan,* pp. 17–19.

74. For a critique of the work of nongovernmental organizations in Peshawar, see Helga Baitenmann, "NGOs and the Afghan War: The Politicization of Humanitarian Aid," *Third World Quarterly* 12 (1) (January 1990).

75. A copy of the communiqué was kindly given to me by Selig Harrison.

76. See Derek Brown, "New Afghanistan Carries on Grisly Game of the Old," *The Guardian,* May 4, 1992, p. 7; and Brown, "Afghan TV Pulls Plug on Women," *The Guardian,* July 29, 1992, p. 6.

77. "Afghanistan: Fourteen Years of War Takes Toll on Women, Children," Inter Press Service Global Information Network, August 25, 1992 (via Factiva Dow Jones & Reuters).

78. Amnesty International, *Women in Afghanistan: A Human Rights Catastrophe* (New York: Amnesty International, 1995). See also Habiba Hasan, "Women in Afghanistan: A Human Rights Catastrophe," *Pakistan Journal of Women's Studies: Alam-e Niswan* 2 (2) (1995): 105–110.

79. Ahmed Rashid, *Taliban* (New Haven: Yale University Press, 2000), pp. 23, 25.

80. Rashid, *Taliban.*

81. Information above from various news accounts of the time, as well as from Physicians for Human Rights, *The Taliban's War on Women, A Health and Human Rights Crisis in Afghanistan* (Boston: Physicians for Human Rights, 1998); *Women's Health and Human Rights in Afghanistan: A Population-Based Assessment* (Boston: PHR, 2001).

82. Information from the RAWA website www.rawa.org and from discussions with three expatriate Afghan women at a conference at Harvard University, November 2000. See also Physicians for Human Rights (1998, 2001).

83. See various appeals reprinted in the compendium by Women Living Under Muslim Laws, *Women's Situation in Afghanistan/La Situation des Femmes en Afghanistan: Compilation* (Montpelier: WLUML, August 1998).

84. Dan Morgan and David B. Ottaway, "Women's Fury Towards Taliban Stalls Pipeline," *Washington Post,* January 11, 1998.

85. Soraya (now known as Soraya Parlika) was featured in an article in the December 3, 2001, issue of *Newsweek* and described as perhaps the principal feminist leader in Afghanistan. She had bravely stayed on in Kabul during the nightmare years of the Mujahidin and the Taliban (as had Dr. Soheila Siddiqi), and had held classes and meetings at her home for women and girls, in clear defiance of the Taliban.

86. Estimate by Barnett Rubin, *The Fragmentation of Afghanistan* (New Haven: Yale University Press, 1995).

87. Chris Kraul, "Donors Plan New Roads to Aid Afghans," *Chicago Tribune,* August 30, 2002, p. 4; Mark Turner, "Karzai Urges Donors to Fulfil Pledges," *Financial Times,* April 11, 2002; and Judy Dempsey, "EU to Warn Kabul on Monetary Framework" *Financial Times,* April 15, 2002.

88. See BBC World Service, March 7, 2002, citing a recent Human Rights Watch report; Pamela Contable, "Karzai's Cabinet Is Sworn In," *Washington Post,* June 25, 2002, p. A14; and Mary Beth Sheridan, "At Kabul University, Degrees of Change," *Washington Post,* June 17, 2002.

89. Charles Tilly, "Revolutions and Collective Violence," in F. I. Greenstein and N. W. Polsby, eds., *Handbook of Political Science 3: Macropolitical Theory* (Reading, Mass.: Addison-Wesley, 1975).

8

All That Is Solid
Melts into Air . . .

The visibility of women disturbs the patriarchal order and weakens men's position within society.
—Doria Cherifati-Merabtine

The cultural revolution is happening right now, right before our eyes.
—Fatima Mernissi

A specter is haunting the Middle East—the specter of modernity and women's rights.

This book has analyzed the gender dynamics of some of the major social change processes in the Middle East, North Africa, and Afghanistan—economic development and the expansion of wage employment, political and social revolutions, the demographic transition, changes in family structure, the rise and expansion of Islamist movements, civil war and political conflict, and the emergence of feminist discourses. In so doing, I have tried to show that analyses of economic, political, and cultural developments within societies or regions are incomplete without attention to gender and its interaction with class, state, and the world system—which themselves shape institutions, discourses, and movements. In turn, the social relations of gender are influenced by the state, development strategies, and the world system. This is as true of the Middle East as it is of any other region. Gender relations are undergoing profound change in MENA countries. This change in the position of women, in concepts of femininity and masculinity, and in notions of the different rights and obligations of men and women, has been met with the politicization of gender and family law, the preoccupation of Islamist movements with women's appearance and behavior, shifting state policies, and cultural debates about authenticity and Westernization.

This book has been neither a catalog of injustices and discrimination against women nor a celebration of the Middle Eastern Woman. Rather, it has been an attempt to rectify the neglect of Middle Eastern women as a subject of sociological inquiry and their exclusion as participants in the formation of systems of ideas and as actors in social change. My analysis of Afghanistan, in particular, has emphasized the primacy of gender in the conflicts between center and periphery—a critical dimension that has been occluded in standard accounts. In this book I have placed the spotlight on middle-class women to bring into focus the rather pivotal role they have assumed—consciously and unconsciously, as secularists and as Islamic activists—in the social and political changes under way in the Middle East. I viewed these changes through a Marxist-feminist sociological lens.

Women are at the center of change and discourse about change in the Middle East. Whether they be socialist-feminists, women participating in political movements, activists in women's organizations, prominent women such as the Palestinian Hanan Ashrawi and Egypt's audacious Nawal el-Saadawi, Fatima Mernissi and her regionwide network of antifundamentalist activists and intellectuals, or the growing silent minority of women at work in government agencies, universities, and factories—what is uncontestable is that women have come into their own since the latter half of the twentieth century. They are a product of socioeconomic development and change but are themselves spurring development and change. They are formulating ideas about women's rights, governance, and social justice, and ideas are being formulated with middle-class women as the reference point. They are the subject of intense debates among men—state managers, clerics, status-anxious petty bourgeois males—who are convinced that such women need to be put in their place. When complaints are voiced that the family is in danger, that cultural imperialism is taking place through "Westernized women," that women are assuming "inappropriate" forms of employment, that being a wife and mother is the most sacred obligation for a woman—these discourses refer to middle-class women with education and jobs. The fundamentalist backlash was directed at this stratum of women, who collectively symbolize social change in the Middle East.

As Fatima Mernissi pointed out, "It's these women, the teachers and others belonging to the petite bourgeoisie, who are in the process of changing the world around them, because their situation as it is is untenable. There are too many archaic aspects in marriage, in the relations between the sexes, in the work situation. These educated women were nourished with a desire for independence."[1] A Beirut-based Palestinian writer observes, "Here, the question of women lies at the bottom of things and cannot be touched without upsetting the whole order. Can the question of women be separated from religious arguments? Can it be separated from social or cultural ones?"[2] The answer is that it cannot. Accordingly, the 1986 report of the Arab Women's Solidarity Association tied the question of women to political, economic, social, and cultural change. The preamble called on women "to unite, to close ranks and become a political and social force able to effect changes in prevailing systems, laws and legislation that will be beneficial not only for women but for all the people." A recommendation of the political committee was for the "release of general freedoms, particularly the freedoms of expression and organization; for respect of human rights for men and women; for a greater participation by women in political decision-making, and for an equal share with men in the authority exercised both in the state and the family."[3] Rights for women and overall human rights are of a piece.

These are times of opportunity, risk, and challenge for women. The economic crisis in the region has in some ways compromised women's positions in the labor market, but in other ways it has led to greater female labor force participation. Islamist movements have applied enormous pressure on governments to conform to Islamic law and many governments have acquiesced to their demands, but Islamism also has engendered a vibrant women's movement and feminist organizations throughout the region. A movement for democratization has emerged in the region, calling for the expansion of the rights of citizens and for the establishment of a civil society independent of state control. How do women fit into this? Can they stem the tide of reaction while also pushing for more rights, greater democratization, and social development for the benefit of all?

Engendering Citizenship, Feminizing Civil Society

The structural features of the MENA region—neopatriarchal states, oil-based (or "rentier") economies, and the strength of Islamist forces—make the struggle for civil, political, and social rights distinctive and difficult. In particular, the movement for women's citizenship and for the establishment of civil society has had to contend with patriarchal Islamist movements, neopatriarchal states, and religious-based family laws—a rather formidable combination of forces. It is all the more remarkable, therefore, that women's institutionalized second-class citizenship is being challenged by women's organizations throughout the region, using a variety of legal and discursive strategies. In general, feminists and the women's organizations are quietly rebelling against women's location in the private domain and men's control of the public domain. In particular, they are calling for: (1) the modernization of family laws, (2) the criminalization of domestic violence and other forms of violence against women, (3) women's right to retain their own nationality and to pass it on to their children (a demand mainly of Arab women), and (4) greater access to employment and participation in political decisionmaking. They are also pointing out that existing family laws are at odds with the universal standards of equality and nondiscrimination embodied in international instruments such as the Convention on the Elimination of All Forms of Discrimination Against Women. In many of the MENA countries, the struggle for civil, political, and social rights is led by women's organizations, which are composed of highly educated women with employment experience and international connections. What is more, the nature of women's organizations has changed, and their activities have become more deliberate, self-conscious, and political. The fact that these organizations exist at all is a sign of important demographic changes, of women's increasing access to the public sphere, and of the gradual process of political liberalization in the region. What is especially noteworthy is that the women's organizations are working to change the nature of that public sphere, to enhance the rights of women in the private sphere, to advance democratization, and to build civil society.

In a regional context of political liberalization and in a global context of the growing import of women's rights and human rights, the 1990s saw the proliferation of women's organizations—some explicitly feminist—in the region. Whereas the 1950s–1970s saw women involved almost exclusively in either official women's organizations or charitable associations, the period since the third UN world conference on women, in Nairobi in 1985, has seen the expansion of many types of women's organizations. At the same time, increasing state conservatism in some countries forced women's organizations and feminist leaders to assume a more independent stance than they might have had in previous decades. Indeed, one observer has noted the shift from "state feminism to civil society feminism" in the Middle East.[4]

In analyzing the proliferation of women's organizations during the 1990s, seven types of women's organizations may be identified. These are service organizations, professional associations, research centers and women's studies institutes, women's rights or feminist organizations, women-in-development NGOs, worker-based organizations, and official women's organizations (see Table 8.1). All are contributing to the development of civil society in the region, although the feminist organizations are perhaps doing so most consciously—a point also made by other feminist observers.[5] The women-in-development NGOs have an important function in fulfilling the development objectives of civil society: decentralized, participatory, and grassroots use of resources. For example, in countries such as Bahrain, "women's voluntary associations have come to form an integral part of civil society," which is responsible for "initiating all organizations for the handicapped as well as institutions for modern education."[6] In Iran, too, women have formed a large number of NGOs that provide social services as well as education on topics such as the environment. Groups focusing on women workers are few, but are likely to grow as more women enter the work force. One such group, the Palestinian Working Women Society, seeks to improve conditions of women workers and raise their awareness about labor rights and trade unions. Israeli occupation and local patriarchal attitudes, however, create obstacles to advancement.

The women's rights or feminist organizations appear to be the most significant contributors to citizenship and civil society. These organizations

Table 8.1 Women's Organizations in MENA, 1990s

	Service Organization	Professional Association	Research Center and Women's Studies Institute	Women's Rights Organization (or Women's Press)	Women-in-Development NGO	Worker-Based and Grassroots Women's Organization	Official Women's Organization
Algeria	SOS Femmes en Détresse	SEVE (women in business)		Egalité Triomphe Emancipation Rassemblement des Femmes Democratiques			Union Nationale des Femmes Algériennes
Egypt	Red Crescent Society	Women's Committee of the Chamber of Commerce Medical Women's Association	New Woman Research and Study Center Women's Study Center: Together	New Civic Forum New Woman Society Women's Rights Committee EOHR	Association for the Development and Enhancement of Women	ETUF Women Workers Department	National Council for Women
Iran	Red Crescent Society	Women's Society Against Environmental Pollution	Center for Women's Studies and Research (Farzaneh)	Zanan Hoghough-e Zanan Jens-e Dovvom	Market Resource Center for Women's Products	Rural Women's Co-ops	Women's Bureau
Jordan	Noor al-Hussein Foundation	Professional and Business Women's Association	Women's Studies Program of Jordan University	Jordanian Women's Union SIGI/Jordan			General Federation of Jordanian Women
Morocco	Association for Protection of the Family	Federation of Women in Liberal and Commercial Careers	Center for Studies and Research on Women (Fez)	Moroccan Women's Democratic Association	Committee of Moroccan Women for Development		Women's Section of USFP

continues

Table 8.1 continued

	Service Organization	Professional Association	Research Center and Women's Studies Institute	Women's Rights Organization (or Women's Press)	Women-in-Development NGO	Worker-Based and Grassroots Women's Organization	Official Women's Organization
Palestine	Women's Health Program		Women's Studies Program of Birzeit University	Al-Haq Center for Legal Aid and Counseling	Women's Unit, Bisan Research and Development Center	Palestinian Working Women Society	Women's Affairs Technical Committee
Tunisia	Tunisian Mothers Association	National Chamber of Women Heads of Businesses	Center of Research, Documentation, and Information on Women (CREDIF)	Association of Democratic Tunisian Women	General Association for Vocational Training and Productive Families	National Commission on Working Women	Union National des Femmes Tunisiennes
Turkey	Mothers' Association	Association of Turkish Women Lawyers	Women's Research and Education Center Women's Library and Information Center	Purple Roof Women's Shelter Legal Aid Center Flying Broom	Foundation for the Support of Women's Work	Anakultur	Director-General on Status and Problems of Women

target women's subordinate status within family law, women's low participation in formal politics, and violence against women. Members of such organizations, such as the Lebanese League for Women's Rights, often run (successfully or otherwise) for political office.[7] Beirut is home to the Women's Court: The Permanent Arab Court to Resist Violence Against Women, which launched highly visible campaigns in 1995, 1998, and 2000. Women's rights and feminist organizations seem to be most numerous in North Africa, where they formed the Collectif 95 Maghreb Egalité, which was the major organizer behind the "Muslim Women's Parliament" at the NGO Forum that preceded the fourth UN world conference on women, in Beijing in September 1995. In preparing for the post-Beijing follow-up, the Collectif 2000 formulated an alternative "egalitarian family code" and promoted women's political participation. Social rights were also placed on the agenda of women's advancement. In Morocco in 1995, women's groups convened a Roundtable on the Rights of Workers, to explore the ways in which a revised labor code could better address women's conditions, include domestic workers in the definition of wage-workers and the delineation of rights and benefits, set the minimum work age at fifteen, and provide workers on maternity leave with full salary and a job-back guarantee.[8] In 2000 controversy emerged over the proposed national plan for women's development. An ambitious document to extend education, employment, and political participation to Moroccan women, the plan came under attack by conservative Islamic forces. In response, Moroccan feminists took to the streets in support of the plan, while the Youssefi government sought to institute a "social dialogue" to promote the plan. However, in the face of overwhelming opposition from Islamist forces, in 2002 the government put the plan on the back burner.

Tunisian feminists and women's NGOs have been somewhat more successful than women activists elsewhere in working with government agencies to develop and implement a national action plan in accord with the Beijing Platform for Action and to insert the rights of working women into the labor code.[9] Feminists like Esma Ben Hamida have worked at the grassroots level with low-income women in income-generating projects, and the key objectives have been women's empowerment and community transformation.[10] Indeed, more so than in other Arab or Middle Eastern countries, Moroccan and Tunisian feminists have developed a kind of social feminism, one that emphasizes not only the modernization of family laws, but also the rights of women workers. This may be due to the different history and political culture of Morocco and Tunisia, which includes a stronger tradition of trade unionism and socialist and social-democratic parties, as well as higher female labor force participation. Indeed, the women's section of Morocco's Socialist Union of Popular Forces (USFP, which became the ruling party in 1998), is active within the women's section of Socialist International, and hosted a special meeting of the international group in Rabat in July 2000.

Another way that MENA women have been contributing to civil society is through literary efforts, including the publication of books, journals, and films. Morocco's Edition le Fennec has produced numerous books on women's rights issues as well as many literary works by women, while L'Union de l'Action Féminin produces the monthly *8 Mars.* The very lively women's press in Iran—a stand-in for an organized women's movement—includes *Zanan* (Women), *Zan-e Rouz* (Today's Woman), *Hoghough-e Zanan* (Women's Rights), and *Jens-e Dovvom* (Second Sex). Shahla Lahiji's Roshangaran Press has published important feminist works as well as historical studies, while the new Cultural Center of Women organized by Noushin Ahmadi-Khorassani and others produces feminist analyses, calendars, compendiums, and the journal *Jens-e Dovvom.* Feminist newspapers are produced in Turkey, and the Women's Library in Istanbul contains research and documentation on women and gender issues. Mention should also be made of the first Arab Women's Book Fair, held in Cairo in November 1995 and organized by Noor, a women's publishing house in Cairo. *Al-Raida,* a quarterly feminist journal of the Institute for Women's Studies in the Arab World, of the Lebanese American University, has published issues since 1976 on topics such as women in Arab cinema, women and the war in Lebanon, women and work, and violence against women.

Demographic, political, and economic changes are the internal factors behind the growth of women's organizations, but global effects have been important as well. The role of the UN and its world conferences has been especially important. Women's organizations from the Arab countries first met at a regional meeting—sponsored by the UN's regional commission for West Asia as part of UN preparations for the Beijing Conference—which took place in early November 1994 in Amman, Jordan. The two-week deliberations resulted in a document titled "Work Program for the Non-Government Organizations in the Arab Region." That document summarized women's conditions in Arab countries as follows: (1) Women suffer a lack of employment rights and undue burdens caused by economic crisis and structural adjustment policies. (2) The absence of democracy and civil rights harms women especially. (3) There is inequality between men and women in authority and decisionmaking. (4) Women suffer from violence, including "honor crimes." The solutions offered were comprehensive. The document called for the immediate ratification and implementation of the Convention on the Elimination of All Forms of Discrimination Against Women, and a revision of all national laws that discriminate against women. It called for legal literacy and free legal services for women, the promotion of women judges, "revision and modernization of the legislation related to women's status in the family," the insertion of the rights of the wife in the marriage contract, and "the amendment of nationality laws so that children can join their mothers and enjoy their nationalities."[11]

With the exception of the call for nationality rights, these demands are similar to those made by feminists and the women's organizations in Iran and Turkey. Turkish feminists have long made domestic violence and street harassment of women major targets of their collective action; they have also been involved in peace actions.[12] As was discussed in Chapter 6, Iranian secular feminists and Islamic feminists actively promote women's rights both in the women's press and in the intellectual press to which they have contributed. Their primary concern is to enhance women's (civil) rights in the family, particularly with respect to marriage, divorce, and child custody. Azam Taleghani's attempt to run for president in 1997 also raised the important question of political rights for women; in the 2001 presidential elections, some forty women tried to run for the presidency, though all were disqualified. It is not irrelevant to note that the dramatic fertility decline in Iran—now close to two children per woman—frees women's time for participation in public affairs.

Women's engagement with the state is illustrative of an approach that may be called "critical realist." That is, feminists are aware of the neopatriarchal nature of the state and the way that it reinforces their subordinate status; but they are also aware that the state is an unavoidable institutional actor. They therefore make claims on the state for the improvement of their legal status and social positions, or they insist that the state live up to commitments and implement the conventions that it has signed—notably, the Convention on the Elimination of All Forms of Discrimination Against Women.

Women in Movement: Claims and Gains

What are some recent campaigns toward women's full citizenship that have implications for more expanded political rights and for the development of civil society? The modernization of family law and the enhancement of women's rights with respect to marriage, divorce, and child custody have been the principal objectives of feminists in Iran and Egypt (among other countries). In both countries they have succeeded in having reforms adopted that ease the restrictions of women's capacity to divorce and make male unilateral divorce more difficult, and in Iran, more expensive for men. As a result of a well-publicized case in Iran of a girl's death at the hands of her brother and father, Iranian feminist lawyers and activists challenged the automatic granting of child custody to the father in the aftermath of divorce. Reformist and feminist parliamentarians introduced a bill in the summer of 2000 to establish a legal age of marriage of at least fifteen—though they failed because conservatives insisted that Islam allows parents to marry off their daughters at puberty. Reformists and feminists also have introduced bills to equalize women's rights in divorce and in blood money. In 1999, Egyptian feminists secured the reversal of Article 291—which exonerated rapists who married their victims. Feminist lawyer Mona Zulficar and other activists succeeded in introducing a new marriage contract that would stipulate the rights of the wife. Egyptian feminists and public health activists also have formed or worked with coalitions against female circumcision.

In Jordan, the criminalization of honor killings of daughters and sisters has become a major social issue, a preoccupation for feminist lawyer Asma Khader, journalist Rana Husseini, and other activists, as well as some concerned members of the Jordanian royal family. Initially, the state was timid in the face of a tribe- and kin-based social structure, but women's groups and the Royal Commission for Human Rights pushed for legal reforms. In December 2001 the Jordanian cabinet approved several amendments to the Civil Status Law. The legal age for marriage was raised from fifteen for women and sixteen for men to eighteen for both, and Jordanian women were also given legal recourse to divorce. New restrictions on polygamy require a man to inform his first wife of plans to marry again and to submit evidence of his financial ability to support more than one wife. As a result of an amendment to the penal code, perpetrators of honor crimes are no longer exempt from the death penalty (though judges are still allowed to commute the sentences of the convicted).[13] At the same time, women leaders such as Toujan Feisal and Emily Naffa secured a position at the forefront of Jordan's democracy movement.

In Lebanon, feminists formed the Permanent Arab Court to Resist Violence Against Women, and a Feminine Rights Campaign to focus on gender equality in divorce. In a country where communal traditions hold sway, the state is weak, and there are fifteen family codes for the eighteen legally recognized religious sects, many feminists nonetheless are in favor of civil codes that supersede sectarian authority.[14] Secularists, feminists, and democrats in an array of civil society organizations encouraged President Hrawi to propose an optional civil marriage, but it was defeated by entrenched religious forces, especially among the Sunnis.[15]

Lebanese feminists within the Lebanese League for Women's Rights are working to increase women's parliamentary participation—a matter of some importance in Egypt, too, where the National Council for Women provides some funding for women candidates. In Morocco, L'Association Démocratique des Femmes Marocaines (ADFM) prioritizes the identification and removal of obstacles to women's political participation. To that end it formed the Centre pour le Leadership Féminin (CLEF).[16] In Iran, enhancing women's political participation is considered an important objective of secular feminists in and around the women's press and of Islamic feminists in the Office of Women's Participation and in the Majlis (parliament). In addition to running for the 2001 presidency, women set their sights on the Majlis (to which thirteen were elected in 1996 and eleven in the 2000 elections), and on the

1998 elections for the Islamic Republic's first local councils (in which women won 784 out of 107,000 seats throughout the country).

In Yemen, a woman was appointed state minister for human rights in 2001, and a successful campaign was launched against the "house of obedience" law, or the forced return of a woman to the matrimonial home. Yet much remains to be done. Feminists and human rights activists have worked together to try to insert an equality clause into the constitution (it was removed four years after the 1990 unification of the progressive south and the conservative north), to criminalize honor killings (the penal code currently exonerates a husband's killing of his adulterous wife), to decriminalize sexual misconduct by women (90 percent of women prisoners are charged with adultery or similar sexual misconduct), and to change the electoral laws to allow for quotas for women candidates. Yemeni activist Amal Basha has explained that the strategy is to encourage "a progressive, enlightened reading of the Shari'a, one that hopefully is acceptable to religious leaders."[17] Thus feminist and human rights activists seek to show that Yemen's laws on adultery (known as *hodood* law) are in fact patriarchal distortions of genuine Islam.

In Palestine, feminists formed the Women's Affairs Technical Committee, the Legal Aid and Counseling Center in Jerusalem, and a Women's Studies Program offering a master's degree in gender, law, and development at Birzeit University. In the post-Oslo period, they organized a Model Parliament and drew media attention to women's issues, particularly inequality in the family. They succeeded in having more schools established for girls, securing social rights for working mothers in the Labor Law, removing the regulation that a male guardian authorize a woman's request for a passport and travel, ending the requirement that female drivers be accompanied by a male guardian, and producing the first women's newspaper, *Sawt an-Nisssa.*[18] Palestinian feminists have developed sophisticated analyses of gender relations and the problems and prospects of women's citizenship as well as technical reports on questions pertaining to social policy, the family law, the proposed Basic Law, the NGO sector, and the political situation.[19]

Women's organizations are arguably the most institutionalized and "indigenized" in Turkey, where they have become an important part of the political landscape and are credited with having made significant contributions to the process of democratization during the 1980s. In the years immediately following the 1980 military coup, all leftist and radical thought and action were prohibited. Moreover, a law passed in 1982 mandated religious instruction in secondary schools, an anticommunist move that served to embolden Islamists. New-wave feminism emerged in this period, and feminists entered the political arena in the 1980s by waging colorful, sometimes quirky campaigns on women's issues—for example, protesting sexual harassment in the streets by selling large purple needles for women to use against harassers. In 1986

Ankara and Istanbul groups collaborated to launch a petition campaign and urge the government to implement the UN Convention on the Elimination of All Forms of Discrimination Against Women, which Turkey had signed in 1985. Feminist groups organized a temporary Woman's Museum, where everyday utensils women use were displayed as tools that defined women's alienation. Since 1987 the centerpiece of the feminist movement has been a campaign against domestic violence. The emphasis on questions of sexuality and home life initially puzzled older, Kemalist feminists, who continued to connect feminist projects with other political agendas, such as nationalism or socialism. But the new feminists took on political issues as well. In the summer of 1989, a group of feminists demonstrated in support of prisoners who had gone on a hunger strike to protest the conditions in state prisons.

Yesim Arat has argued that radical and socialist feminists alike defied tradition and male authority to uphold a woman's right "to exercise her will, choose her destiny." An important goal of the feminist movement was to enhance women's respectability and rights as individuals, not only as mothers or sisters. She goes on to argue that in the context of the Islamic revival in the 1980s, "the women's movement was a secular front, defending the secular interests of women and arguing for the primacy of a democratic context for the promotion of women's rights." Not surprisingly, women's issues became a visible item on the campaigns and party programs of all the major parties in the 1991 general election.[20]

Since then, Turkish feminists have continued to campaign for equality and empowerment, and protested what they regarded as retrogressive measures and discourses in the late 1990s, when the Islamist Welfare Party joined in the coalition government. Organizations such as the Association to Support Women Candidates (Kader), Flying Broom, the Turkish Women's Union, and the Foundation for the Support of Women's Work, Anakultur (a feminist organization for rural women), as well as many women's professional associations, have lobbied politicians, talked to the media, and demonstrated on the streets. A concerted feminist campaign against mandatory virginity examinations compelled the Ministry of Justice to decree a ban on the tests in 1999, although virginity tests continued to be performed. The feminist campaign to modernize Turkey's family law and to give CEDAW more teeth was more successful. As a result of the decade-long feminist pressure, the Turkish government withdrew its reservations to CEDAW in September 1999. In November 2001 the Turkish parliament adopted an equality clause in its civil code, which also gives women and men equal roles in family matters, including decisionmaking and the division of matrimonial property in case of divorce.[21] The widening political space created by the women's movement and the global environment emboldened Turkey's women trade unionists. In September 2000, some thirty-five women affiliated with the trade union KESK mobilized to send letters to the UN in support of the Women's Global March 2000

Members of the Palestinian delegation at a regional meeting in Amman, 1994. Photo courtesy of ESCWA.

against capitalism and patriarchy, although they were briefly detained by police.[22] Arat concludes:

> The women's movement of the 1980s transformed the state feminism of the Kemalists at the same time that it upheld deep-seated Kemalist ideals. It brought dynamism to Turkish political life during a most repressive period in its history. It practiced liberalism, defended secularism, and sowed the seeds of pluralism at a period when governments that promised liberalism gradually resorted to conservative statism. . . . [The woman's movement] expanded the political space allotted to civil society. In the Turkish context, where the tradition of peaceful association against the strong state was weak, achievements of the women's movement were significant.[23]

As in Turkey, "state feminism" in Tunisia gave women a wider range of rights than in other MENA countries. As we have seen in earlier chapters, the Tunisian personal status code under Bourguiba abolished polygamy, forced marriage, and unilateral repudiation; it established civil marriage, divorce, and child custody rights for women, as well as a law for the adoption of children. For a while, Tunisian women enjoyed the most progressive family law in the MENA region. At the same time, they were aware of social injustices and formed women's organizations, magazines, clubs, and research centers, to study the issues and offer solutions. Lilia Labidi explains that in the 1980s, the recurring themes of Tunisian women's research were the precariousness of the rights of low-income women, mothers deprived of support as family networks disintegrated, the condition of the old and handicapped who were without resources, girls forced to leave school, unequal wages of men and women in rural areas, household violence, and media images of women.[24]

During the 1980s the Taher el Haddad Club became a center for the discussion of social problems and women's rights. Other forums include the Women's Commission of the General Union of Tunisian Workers, the Tunisian Association of Women Democrats, the Tunisian Human Rights League, and of course the National Union of Tunisian Women. In 1985 a bilingual (Arabic and French) feminist magazine called *Nissa* (Woman) appeared, which, according to its opening editorial, would be "a place for personal testimony, information, reflection and debate, open to women and men alike . . . committed to respecting diverse points of view provided that . . . they aim to promote more harmonious and satisfying relations between the sexes and to establish the foundations of a more free and open society."[25] *Nissa's* feature articles over the first year of publication included discussions of the problem of illegitimate children, the personal status laws of Tunisia and Egypt (both under attack that year), the Israeli bombing raid of the PLO headquarters in a suburb of Tunis, the pros and cons of sex-segregated activities, the risks of childbirth, and feminism. The magazine folded in 1987 mainly because of disagreements among its staff members, who then went on to join some of the associations mentioned above.[26] Nonetheless, women intellectuals and "the woman question" alike gained greater visibility. Feminists began to point out the limitations of the family law, such as the fact that women were still unequal in inheritance and that the law prohibited the marriage of a Muslim woman to a non-Muslim man while allowing a Muslim man to marry a Christian or Jewish woman.[27] And they were concerned about the economic crisis and the rise of *intégrisme* in Tunisia and elsewhere in North Africa.

As a result of women's activities—and possibly, too, because of their stated opposition to Islamic fundamentalism—the Tunisian state under President Ben Ali introduced wide-ranging amendments to the family law in 1993. As explained by Labidi, schooling for children of both sexes was made compulsory to the age of fourteen. The amendments stipulated that the mother's consent was required in addition to the father's for the marriage of a minor. A wife's duty of obedience to her husband was replaced by her right to be treated with care and concern. The woman gained the right to participate in the management of the family's affairs (such as children's education, travel, and financial matters). The couple could choose joint or separate financial holdings, to be stipulated in the marriage contract. The 1993 amendments were followed by additional laws that women called for and welcomed. In 1998, a law criminalizing crimes of honor was adopted; what is more, the punishment for domestic violence was made double that of an ordinary offense. In addition, when a child is born out of wedlock and the father is known, the child carries the father's name, has the right to the father's support until reaching adulthood, and inherits the same portion as a daughter.[28] Labidi concludes that the promulgation of the personal status code in the 1950s along with the rise of a women's movement had resulted in "a change in public morality which allowed the State—the first in the Arab world—to provide women with a personal status code that constituted a substantial advance in protecting their rights as citizens equal to men." She also asserts that the legal reforms represented a "recognition of the country's dependence on women."[29]

As we saw in Chapter 5, Algerian feminists have shown a most audacious opposition to Islamism—and to state autocracy as well—in a manner that cost a number of women activists their lives during the wave of Islamist terror in the 1990s. But like Turkish feminists, Algerian feminists saw their movement as simultaneously democratic and feminist. They fought for modernity and individual rights while also holding on to the socialist legacy of equality of citizens. They were critical of past practice, which subsumed the woman question under national liberation and the building of Algerian-style social-ism. The ideological and cultural divide between Islamist and non-Islamist women activists was enormous; feminists distinguished "women of the mod-ernist trend" from the women of the Islamist movement. According to one such activist-theorist, the modernist women's movement was comprised mainly of older university women from the first postindependence generation of intellectuals. Doria Cherifati-Merabtine observed that these women "have learned, at their expense, that no change is possible if the outlook on woman and her place within society does not evolve." And although these modernist women "carry generous ideas and an egalitarian project of society," their experience leads them to "put the recognition of the Woman-Individual on the agenda."[30]

Algerian feminists paid a high price for their stance against Islamism and authoritarianism, but they were rewarded with government positions. Khalida Messaoudi, one of the leaders of the antistate women's campaign in the early 1980s and the anti-fundamentalist women's campaign in the late 1980s and early 1990s, was appointed adviser to President Bouteflika after he assumed office in summer 1999. When he issued an amnesty to several thousands who had been jailed for terrorism, he acquiesced to feminist demands that those Islamists guilty of "crimes or rape" be exempt from the pardon.[31] Moreover, Algerian women's involvement in the judiciary has increased. In 2001, they constituted about 25 percent of judges, and President Bouteflika increased the number of courts headed by women.[32] In 2001 he agreed "to the long and per-

sistent demand of Algerian women's organizations for the need to amend the
Family Status code issued in 1984."[33] Most dramatically, in the summer of
2002, five Algerian women were appointed to ministerial posts—an unprecedented number in the MENA region. They included feminists Khalida Messaoudi and Bouthaina Cheriat.

In some countries women activists take part in national debates and campaigns for democratization and political change, but focus their efforts on the
modernization of family law and ending the most egregious forms of discrimination against women. In other countries, feminists are contributing to
the national dialogues and political debates. Algerian feminists are not only
active in the struggles for modernization of family law and against religious
extremism but also have a considered position on democracy, based on their
experience with the violent Islamist movement of the late 1980s and the
1990s. As one explained:

> If democracy is the predominance of numbers, regardless of quality, I don't
> want to be a democrat, because this can allow extremist groups to take power
> and oppress people, especially women—this is my Algerian experience. . . .
> If democracy is the right to speak out and be heard, as a voice and not just
> as a number, then I am a democrat. But if democracy is the freedom to
> choose between Coca-Cola and Pepsi, Levis or Nike, BBC or CNN,
> McDonald's or Pizza Hut, then I am not a democrat.[34]

The cooperation of women's rights and human rights organizations—
especially in Egypt, Tunisia, Morocco, Algeria, and Palestine—is a fruitful
one, for the expansion of both civil society and citizenship rights. Four examples will illustrate this point. In Egypt, women's organizations, human rights
organizations, and some professional organizations collaborated to protest the
imminent passage of a controversial NGO law. The women's groups included
the Center for Egyptian Women's Legal Assistance, the Egyptian Center for
Women's Rights, and the New Woman Research Center. A hunger strike and
a sit-in were organized, mainly by women activists. They included two
women psychiatrists associated with the El-Nadim Centre for the Rehabilita-
tion of Victims of Violence, a woman lawyer with the Center for Trade Union
and Workers Services, and a writer associated with the Forum for Women's
Development.[35] In a second example, the campaign against female circumcision in Egypt has been conducted by a coalition of women's, human rights,
child welfare, and family planning organizations. Third, demonstrations and
public support for the Youssefi government's proposed Plan of Action for the
Integration of Women in Development, which would include reform of
Morocco's family law as well as greater participation by women in education,
health, and employment, were organized by Moroccan feminist groups and
political parties such as Al Istiqlal and Al Taqaddom wa al Ishtirakiyya.[36]

In the fourth example of collaboration between human rights and women's rights organizations, the First International Conference of the Arab Human Rights Movement took place in Casablanca, Morocco, on April 23–25, 1999. It issued a declaration that called for an end to the practice of torture; the need to respect freedoms of expression, assembly, and association; the realization of economic and social rights; securing citizens' rights to participation, including guaranteeing public oversight of the public revenues of the state; and the recognition of women's rights as an integral part of the human rights system. The declaration asserted that women's enjoyment of human rights is an integrated and comprehensive process that should encompass all facets of life within and outside the family. It is worth quoting from the declaration in some detail, as it shows the promise of such cooperation, as well as the obvious influence that the feminist groups have had within the human rights community:

> Real equality between women and men goes beyond legal equality to encompass changing the conceptions and confronting the stereotypes about women. Thus, it requires not only a comprehensive review of laws, foremost of which are personal status codes, but also the review and upgrading of educational curricula as well as the critical monitoring of the media discourse.
>
> In this respect, the Conference stresses the necessity of engaging women's and human rights NGOs in the process of reviewing current legislations and in upgrading civil and criminal laws, with a view to resolutely confronting all forms of violence and discrimination against women.
>
> The Conference also calls upon the Arab governments that did not ratify [the CEDAW Women's Convention] to do so expeditiously, and those that ratified it to lift their reservations.
>
> It also calls upon women and human rights NGOs to work to refute these reservations, to challenge the culture of discrimination, and to adopt courageous stances in exposing the practice of hiding behind religion to legitimize the subordination of women. These NGOs should also give special attention to the continued monitoring of the compliance by Arab governments to their international commitments concerning women's enjoyment of their rights.
>
> The necessity of considering the possibility of allocating a quota for women in parliaments, representative institutions and public bodies as a temporary measure. This should stand until appropriate frameworks for women's voluntary activity take shape and until the awareness of the necessity of equality and the elimination of all forms of discrimination increases.[37]

Mention should also be made of cooperation between Israeli and Palestinian women peace activists, especially since the second intifada and the Israeli military incursions into the West Bank in the spring of 2002. In December 2001 the Coalition of Women for a Just Peace held a March of Mourning in Jerusalem with banners that read, "The Occupation is Killing Us All."

Among the invited participants was Zahira Kamal, formerly head of the Palestinian Women's Technical Committee, who found a way to outwit the closure in order to reach Jerusalem and address the rally. In April 2002 a joint declaration by Bat Shalom, the Israeli women's peace group, and the Jerusalem Center for Women, a Palestinian women's peace organization—which together compose the Jerusalem Link—decried "the humanitarian crimes" of the Israeli military forces in the West Bank and asked "the international community of states to accept its duty and mandate by international humanitarian law to prevent abuses of an occupying power, by officially intervening to protect the Palestinian people." And on May 7, 2002, the director of Bat Shalom spoke at the UN Security Council in New York and ended by reading a joint declaration with the Jerusalem Center for Women. By intervening in a sphere traditionally regarded as male—that of international relations and military action—Israeli and Palestinian feminist peace activists confound gender stereotypes, push the boundaries of women's political citizenship, offer an alternative model of politics, and strengthen civil society.

I end this section with two final comments concerning feminism and Islamism in North Africa, and the implications for civil society and for gender norms. Feminist organizations in North Africa, and especially in Algeria, have been criticized by some for their strong opposition to fundamentalist movements and the legalization of Islamist organizations—or for their criticism of what some scholars of democratic transitions call "democracy without democrats." And yet, given that a necessary condition of civil society is the "civility" of its constituent organizations, such feminist opposition is understandable. Surely it defeats the purpose of civil society when organizations such as fundamentalist groups that threaten or brutalize citizens, such as unveiled women, are included in its constituency. A related comment is that in Algeria, Morocco, and Tunisia, feminists (and intellectuals) are seen as ramparts against the danger of fundamentalism.[38] Statements by government officials that are reported by the media, and some newspaper editorials, have referred to the feminists' strong opposition to fundamentalism as constituting a major bulwark against the success of Islamists and for modernity and democracy. Such representations of women—in which women are depicted as citizens and political actors and not only as wives and mothers—may herald a transition in gender relations, at least in some countries of the region.

Conclusion

Economic development, universal schooling, mass communications, and legal reforms in Middle Eastern countries have produced a stratum of women whose very existence subverts the patriarchal order and accelerates the transition to modernity. Grounded in socialism, liberalism, feminism, and emancipatory Islam, the "modernizing women" of the Middle East are challenging popular understandings and legal codes regarding the public sphere and the private sphere; they are demanding more access to the public sphere, full and equal participation in the national community, and full and equal rights in the family. These gender-based demands for civil, political, and social rights would not only extend existing rights to women but also, and more profoundly, broaden the political agenda and redefine citizenship in the Middle East and North Africa. Aziz al-Azmeh notes that the struggle for citizenship will complete the transition from communal to civil society, but that, like all historical processes, it is highly conflictual.[39] In the MENA countries, agents of this conflictual historical process include Islamist movements, intransigent or colluding states, and women's organizations. Although states and Islamist movements wield political and economic power, the women's movement may be the specter that haunts them. It is hard to escape the conclusion that in the absence of other progressive social movements, women's struggles in the Middle East—whether around the modernization of family laws, or in the fight against fundamentalism, or around demands for greater employment opportunities and political participation—are the central motor of the drive for citizenship, civil society, and progressive social change.

Notes

The first opening quote, from Doria Cherifati-Merabtine, is from her chapter "Algeria at a Crossroads: National Liberation, Islamization, and Women," in V. M. Moghadam, ed., *Gender and National Identity: Women and Politics in Muslim Societies* (London: Zed Books, 1994). The second quote, from Fatima Mernissi, is from Kevin Dwyer, *Arab Voices: The Human Rights Debate in the Middle East* (Berkeley: University of California Press, 1991), p. 184. The third quote is my variation on a theme by Marx and Engels, from the opening lines of *The Communist Manifesto,* and by Marshall Berman, *All That Is Solid Melts into Air: The Experience of Modernity* (New York: Simon and Schuster, 1982).

1. Fatima Mernissi, quoted in Dwyer, *Arab Voices,* pp. 182–183.

2. Jean Said Makdisi, *Beirut Fragments: A War Memoir* (New York: Persea Books, 1990).

3. The AWSA Final Report and Recommendations is reprinted in Nahid Toubia, ed., *Women of the Arab World: The Coming Challenge* (London: Zed Books, 1988), pp. 148–153.

4. Personal interview with Shaha Riza, head of the Middle East Gender Unit at the World Bank, May 1, 2000.

5. Nadje al-Ali, *Secularism, Gender, and the State: The Egyptian Women's Movement* (Cambridge: Cambridge University Press, 2000); Nemat Guenena and Nadia Wassef, *Unfulfilled Promises: Women's Rights in Egypt* (Cairo: Population Council, 1999); and Fatima Sadiqi, "Aspects of Moroccan Feminism," in Fatima Sadiqi et al., eds., *Mouvements Féministes: Origines et Orientations* (Fes: Centre d'Études et de Recherches sur la Femme, 1999), pp. 195–214.

6. Mounira Fakhro, "Civil Society and Non-Governmental Organizations in the Middle East: Reflections on the Gulf," *Middle East Women's Studies Review* 11 (4) (January 1997): 1–3; quote appears on p. 2. From another vantage point, however, this may be seen in more critical terms as a failure of the state and as a neoliberal solution.

7. In the summer of 2000, nine Lebanese women were running for parliamentary seats in a campaign organized by the National Committee to Follow Up Women's Issues and the Lebanese Women's Council.

8. "Roundtable on the Rights of Female Wage-earners: Need for Joint Action," in *Exaequo,* Information Bulletin published by the Directorate of Multilateral Cooperation, *Rabat* no. 1 (August 1995): 3.

9. See WEDO, *Mapping Progress: Assessing Implementation of the Beijing Platform 1998* (New York: WEDO, 1998).

10. As reported by Esma Ben Hamida at the ERF/MDF3 conference, Cairo, March 8, 2000.

11. The right of women to retain their own nationality after marriage to a foreigner is a right that European women won in stages. Feminists first tried to win nationality rights for women through the League of Nations–sponsored Women's Consultative Committee on Nationality in the 1930s. It should also be noted that Article 9 of the Convention on the Elimination of All Forms of Discrimination Against Women requires states parties to grant women equal rights with respect to their nationality and to the nationality of their children. Many MENA countries that have signed the convention entered reservations to this article.

12. Sirin Tekeli, "Emergence of the Feminist Movement in Turkey," in Drude Dahlerup, ed., *The New Women's Movement: Feminism and Political Power in Europe and the USA* (London: Sage, 1986), pp. 179–199; and Yesim Arat, "Democracy and Women in Turkey: In Defense of Liberalism," *Social Politics: International Studies in Gender, State, and Society* 6 (3) (Fall 1999): 370–387, special issue: *Middle East Politics: Feminist Challenges,* eds. Nitza Berkovitch and Valentine M. Moghadam.

13. Information from the Women's Learning Partnership for Rights, Development, and Peace, via Internet, www.learningpartnership.org, December 31, 2001.

14. Suad Joseph, "Civic Myths, Citizenship, and Gender in Lebanon," in Suad Joseph, ed., *Gender and Citizenship in the Middle East* (Syracuse, N.Y.: Syracuse University Press, 2000), pp. 107–136; Laurie King-Irani, "From Program to Practice: Towards Women's Meaningful and Effective Political Participation in Jordan and Lebanon," paper presented at the Conference on Middle Eastern Women on the Move, Woodrow Wilson International Center for Scholars, Washington, D.C., October 2–3, 2001; and Lamia Shehadeh, "The Legal Status of Married Women in Lebanon," *International Journal of Middle East Studies* 30 (4) (1998): 501–519.

15. Sofia Saadeh, "The Political Repercussions of President Hrawi's Optional Civil Marriage (1998)," paper presented at the thirty-third annual meeting of the Middle East Studies Association, Washington, D.C., November 19–22, 1999.

16. Nouzha Skalli, ADFM vice president, in a talk delivered at the ERF/MDF3 conference, Cairo, March 8, 2000.

17. Amal Basha, Sisters' Arabic Forum for Human Rights, Sana'a, Yemen, in conversations with the author, Chicago, May 22, 2002.

18. Suheir Azzouni, director of the Women's Affairs Technical Committee, Palestine, in a talk delivered at the ERF/MDF3 conference, Cairo, March 8, 2000, and in conversations with the author. Unfortunately, what began as a very promising women's movement appears to have been set back seriously as a result of the second intifada (which began in October 2000), the continued Israeli occupation, and the terrible cycle of violence in 2001–2002.

19. Rema Hammami and Penny Johnson, "Equality with a Difference: Gender and Citizenship in Transitional Palestine," *Social Politics* 6 (3) (Fall 1999): 314–343; and Penny Johnson and Eileen Kuttub, "Where Have All the Women (and Men) Gone? Reflections on Gender and the Second Palestinian Intifada," *Feminist Review* no. 69 (Winter 2001): 21–43.

20. Yesim Arat, "Toward a Democratic Society: The Women's Movement in Turkey in the 1980s," *Women Studies International Forum* 17 (2–3) (1994): 241–248; quotes appear on pp. 245–246.

21. Pinar Ilkkaracan of Women for Women's Human Rights–New Ways, via Internet (AMEWS Listserv), December 19, 2001. See also Associated Press, "Sexual Equality Becomes Law in Turkey," *Washington Post,* November 23, 2001.

22. International Confederation of Free Trade Unions (ICFTU), "Turkey: Annual Survey of Violations of Trade Union Rights, 2001," www.icftu.org, accessed April 10, 2002.

23. Arat, "Toward a Democratic Society," p. 246.

24. Lilia Labidi, "Women, Politics, and Islam: The Case of Tunisia," paper presented at the Woodrow Wilson International Center for Scholars, Washington, D.C., March 6, 2002, p. 24.

25. Dwyer, *Arab Voices,* p. 145.

26. Ibid.

27. Alya Chérif Chamari, *La Femme et la Loi en Tunisie* (Rabat: Edition de Fennec, 1992).

28. Labidi, "Women, Politics, and Islam," pp. 25–26.

29. Ibid., pp. 30, 39.

30. Cherifati-Merabtine, "Algeria at a Crossroads," pp. 59–60.

31. Robert Cornwell, "Algeria to Free 5,000 from Jail," *The Independent* (UK), July 5, 1999.

32. U.S. Department of State, Bureau of Democracy, Human Rights, and Labor, Country Report on Human Rights Practices, "Algeria," March 4, 2002, www.state.gov/hrrpt/2001. In Morocco and Tunisia, too, women constitute 20–25 percent of judges. In other countries, the religiously based prohibition against women judges persists. Egypt has had women ambassadors and cabinet ministers but no women judges. In the Islamic Republic of Iran, after a twenty-year postrevolutionary ban on women judges, women were allowed to become judicial deputies and then full judges—but their judgments and verdicts, however, remain advisory.

33. Machreq/Maghreb Gender Linking and Information Project, March 2001 Regional Monthly Update, www.macmag-glip.org.

34. Nadia Leila Aissaoui, head of the Association for Reflection, Exchange, and Action on Environment and Development, as reported in *International IDEA* (Winter 1999): 19.

35. *Civil Society* 8 (90) (June 1999): 22–23.

36. For an elaboration of the proposed action plan and the opposition to it, see Rania al-Abiad, "A Turbulent Morocco: A Khutta, a Mudawwana, a Reform Movement, and Rivalry Frames," *Al-Raida* 17 (89) (Spring 2000): 30–34.

37. *Civil Society* 8 (91) (July 1999): 20–23.

38. Rabea Naciri, *The Women's Movement and Political Discourse in Morocco,* UNRISD Occasional Paper no. 8 (Geneva: UNRISD, 1998).

39. Aziz al-Azmeh, *Islam and Modernities* (London: Verso, 1993), p. 36.

Acronyms

ADFM	L'Association Démocratique des Femmes Marocaines
AIDS	acquired immune deficiency syndrome
AIS	Armée Islamique du Salut (Islamic Salvation Army, Algeria)
AK	Justice and Development (Turkey) [Islamic party in Turkey]
ALN	Armée de Liberation Nationale (Algeria)
AWC	Afghan Women's Council
AWSA	Arab Women's Solidarity Association
CEDAW	Convention on the Elimination of All Forms of Discrimination Against Women (UN)
CIA	Central Intelligence Agency
CLEF	Centre pour le Leadership Féminin (Morocco)
CUP	Committee of Union and Progress (Turkey)
DHS	Demographic and Health Survey
DOAW	Democratic Organization of Afghan Women
DRA	Democratic Republic of Afghanistan
DYO	Democratic Youth Organization (Afghanistan)
EAP	economically active population
EOI	export-oriented industrialization
EPZ	export processing zone
EU	European Union
FDI	foreign direct investment
FIS	Front Islamique du Salut (Islamic Salvation Front, Algeria)
FLN	Front de Libération Nationale (Algeria)
FWCW	Fourth World Conference on Women (UN)
GAD	gender-and-development
GIA	Group Islamique Armée (Armed Islamic Group, Algeria)
GNP	gross national product

ICPD	International Conference on Population and Development (UN)
ILO	International Labour Organisation
IMF	International Monetary Fund
IRI	Islamic Republic of Iran
ISI	import-substitution industrialization
MENA	Middle East and North Africa
MNC	multinational corporation
MVA	manufacturing value-added
NGO	nongovernmental organization
NIC	newly industrialized country
NIF	National Islamic Front
NUW	National Union of Women
OPEC	Organization of Petroleum-Exporting Countries
PDPA	People's Democratic Party of Afghanistan
PDRY	People's Democratic Republic of Yemen
PLO	Palestine Liberation Organization
PWWS	Palestinian Working Women Society
RAFD	Rassemblement Algérien des Femmes Démocrates
RAWA	Revolutionary Association of Women of Afghanistan
UAE	United Arab Emirates
UK	United Kingdom
UN	United Nations
UNDP	United Nations Development Programme
UNESCO	United Nations Educational, Scientific, and Cultural Organization
UNFA	Union Nationale des Femmes Algériennes
UNFPA	United Nations Fund for Population Activities
UNFT	Union Nationale des Femmes Tunisiennes
UNHCR	United Nations High Commissioner for Refugees
UNICEF	United Nations Children's Fund
UNLU	Unified National Leadership of the Uprising (Palestine)
USFP	Socialist Union of Popular Forces (Morocco)
USSR	Union of Soviet Socialist Republics
WAPHA	Women's Association for Peace and Human Rights in Afghanistan
WFS	World Fertility Survey
WID	women-in-development
WISTAT	Women's Indicator and Statistics Database
WLUML	Women Living Under Muslim Laws (Afghanistan)

Selected Bibliography

Abdo-Zubi, Nahla. 1987. *Family, Women, and Social Change in the Middle East: The Palestinian Case.* Toronto: Canadian Scholars' Press.

Abu Nasr, Julinda, A. Khoury, and H. Azzam, eds. 1985. *Women, Employment, and Development in the Arab World.* The Hague: Mouton/ILO.

Afary, Janet. 1996. *The Iranian Constitutional Revolution, 1906–1911: Grassroots Democracy, Social Democracy, and the Origins of Feminism.* New York: Columbia University Press.

Afkhami, Mahnaz, ed. 1995. *Faith and Freedom: Women's Human Rights in the Muslim World.* Syracuse, N.Y.: Syracuse University Press.

Afkhami, Mahnaz, and Erika Friedl, eds. 1997. *Muslim Women and the Politics of Participation.* Syracuse, N.Y.: Syracuse University Press.

Afshar, Haleh, and Carolyne Dennis, eds. 1992. *Women and Adjustment Policies in the Third World.* London: Macmillan.

Akbar, Mansoor. 1989. "Revolutionary Changes and Social Resistance in Afghanistan." *Asian Profile* 17 (3) (June): 271–281.

al-Ali, Nadje. 2000. *Secularism, Gender, and the State: The Egyptian Women's Movement.* Cambridge: Cambridge University Press.

al-Azmeh, Aziz. 1993. *Islam and Modernities.* London: Verso.

Anker, Richard. 1998. *Gender and Jobs: Sex Segregation of Occupations in the World.* Geneva: ILO.

Anwar, Raja. 1988. *The Tragedy of Afghanistan: A First-Hand Account.* London: Verso.

Arat, Yesim. 2000. "From Emancipation to Liberation: The Changing Role of Women in Turkey's Public Realm." *Journal of International Affairs* 54 (1) (Fall): 107–123.

———. 1997. "The Project of Modernity and Women in Turkey." In S. Bozdogan and R. Kasaba, eds., *Rethinking Modernity and National Identity in Turkey.* Seattle: University of Washington Press, pp. 95–112.

———. 1994. "Toward a Democratic Society: The Women's Movement in Turkey in the 1980s." *Women's Studies International Forum* 17 (2–3): 241–248.

Badran, Margot. 1999. "Toward Islamic Feminisms: A Look at the Middle East." In Asma Afsaruddin, ed., *Hermeneutics of Honor: Negotiating Female "Public"*

Space in Islamic Societies. Cambridge: Center for Middle Eastern Studies, Harvard University, pp. 159–188.

Beck, Lois, and Nikki R. Keddie, eds. 1978. *Women in the Muslim World.* Cambridge: Harvard University Press.

Berkovitch, Nitza. 1999. *From Motherhood to Citizenship: International Organizations and Women's Rights.* Baltimore: Johns Hopkins University Press.

Berkovitch, Nitza, and Valentine M. Moghadam, eds. 1999. *Social Politics: International Studies in Gender, State, and Society* 6 (3) (Fall), special issue: *Middle East Politics: Feminist Challenges.*

Bodman, Herbert, and Nayereh Tohidi, eds. 1998. *Women in Muslim Societies: Diversity Within Unity.* Boulder: Lynne Rienner.

Botman, Selma. 1999. *Engendering Citizenship in Egypt.* New York: Columbia University Press.

Brand, Laurie A. 1998. *Women, the State, and Political Liberalization: Middle Eastern and North African Experiences.* New York: Columbia University Press.

Brynen, Rex, Bahgat Korany, and Paul Noble, eds. 1995. *Political Liberalization and Democratization in the Arab World.* Vol. 1: *Theoretical Perspectives.* Boulder: Lynne Rienner.

Butenschon, Nils A., Uri Davis, and Manuel Hassassian, eds. 2000. *Citizenship and the State in the Middle East: Approaches and Applications.* Syracuse, N.Y.: Syracuse University Press.

Caldwell, John C. 1982. *Theory of Fertility Decline.* London: Academic Press.

Chafetz, Janet Saltzman, and Gary Dworkin. 1986. *Female Revolt: Women's Movements in World and Historical Perspective.* Totowa, N.J.: Rowman and Allanheld.

Charrad, Mounira. 2001. *States and Women's Rights: The Making of Postcolonial Tunisia, Algeria, and Morocco.* Berkeley: University of California Press.

Chirot, Daniel. 1983. *Social Change in the Modern Era.* San Diego: Harcourt Brace Jovanovich.

Cooke, Miriam. 2001. *Women Claim Islam: Creating Islamic Feminism Through Literature.* New York and London: Routledge.

Crompton, Rosemary, and Michael Mann, eds. 1986. *Gender and Stratification.* Cambridge, UK: Polity Press.

el-Sayyid, Mustapha K. 1994. "The Third Wave of Democratization in the Arab World." In Dan Tschirgi, ed., *The Arab World Today.* Boulder: Lynne Rienner, pp. 179–190.

Engels, Frederick. 1972 [1884]. *The Origin of the Family, Private Property, and the State.* Introduction by Evelyn Reed. New York: Pathfinder Press.

Epstein, Cynthia Fuchs. 1988. *Deceptive Distinctions: Sex, Gender, and the Social Order.* New Haven: Yale University Press.

Esposito, John L., with Natana J. DeLong-Bas. 2001. *Women in Muslim Family Law.* Syracuse, N.Y.: Syracuse University Press.

Fathi, Asghar, ed. 1991. *Iranian Refugees and Exiles Since Khomeini.* Costa Mesa, Calif.: Mazda.

Ferree, Myra Marx, Judith Lorber, and Beth Hess, eds. 1999. *Revisioning Gender.* Beverly Hills: Sage.

Goody, Jack. 1990. *The Oriental, the Ancient, and the Primitive: Systems of Marriage and the Family in the Pre-Industrial Societies of Eurasia.* Cambridge: Cambridge University Press.

Gregorian, Vartan. 1969. *The Emergence of Modern Afghanistan.* Stanford: Stanford University Press.

Hiltermann, Joost. 1990. *Behind the Intifada: Labor and Women's Movements in the Occupied Territories.* Princeton: Princeton University Press.

Hitti, Philip. 1971. *A History of the Arabs.* Princeton: Princeton University Press.

Hoffman-Ladd, Valerie. 1987. "Polemics on the Modesty and Segregation of Women in Contemporary Egypt." *International Journal of Middle East Studies* 19 (1) (February): 23–50.

Ibrahim, Saad Eddin. 1992. *The New Arab Social Order: A Study of the Impact of Oil Wealth.* Boulder, CO: Westview Press.

———. 1982. "Islamic Militancy as a Social Movement: The Case of Two Groups in Egypt." In Ali E. Hillal Dessouki, ed., *Islamic Resurgence in the Arab World.* New York: Praeger.

———. 1980. "Anatomy of Egypt's Militant Islamic Groups." *International Journal of Middle East Studies* 12 (4): 423–453.

Jayawardena, Kumari. 1986. *Feminism and Nationalism in the Third World.* London: Zed Books.

Joseph, Suad, ed. 2000. *Gender and Citizenship in the Middle East.* Syracuse, N.Y.: Syracuse University Press.

Kamali, Mohammad Hashim. 1985. *Law in Afghanistan: A Study of the Constitutions, Matrimonial Law, and the Judiciary.* Leiden: E. J. Brill.

Kandiyoti, Deniz, ed. 1991. *Women, Islam, and the State.* London: Macmillan.

Kandiyoti, Deniz, and Ayse Saktanber, eds. *Fragments of Culture: The Everyday of Modern Turkey.* Newark: Rutgers University Press.

Karam, Azza M. 1998. *Women, Islamisms, and the State: Contemporary Feminisms in Egypt.* London: Macmillan.

Keddie, Nikki R. 1990. "The Past and Present of Women in the Muslim World." *Journal of World History* 1 (1): 77–108.

Keddie, Nikki R., and Beth Baron, eds. 1991. *Women in Middle Eastern History: Shifting Boundaries in Sex and Gender.* New Haven: Yale University Press.

Khoury, Nabil F., and Valentine M. Moghadam, eds. 1995. *Gender and Development in the Arab World: Women's Economic Participation, Patterns, and Policies.* London: Zed.

Knauss, Peter. 1987. *The Persistence of Patriarchy: Class, Gender, and Ideology in Twentieth Century Algeria.* New York: Praeger.

Korany, Bahgat, Rex Brynen, and Paul Noble, eds. 1998. *Political Liberalization and Democratization in the Arab World.* Vol. 2: *Comparative Experiences.* Boulder: Lynne Rienner.

Kruks, Sonia, Rayna Rapp, and Marilyn Young, eds. 1989. *Promissory Notes: Women in the Transition to Socialism.* New York: Monthly Review Press.

Lajoinie, Simone Bailleau. 1980. *Conditions des Femmes en Afghanistan.* Paris: Notre Temps/Monde.

Lerner, Gerda. 1986. *The Creation of Patriarchy.* New York: Oxford University Press.

Lister, Ruth. 1997. *Citizenship: Feminist Perspectives.* London: Macmillan.

Lobban, Richard A., ed. 1998. *Middle Eastern Women and the Invisible Economy.* Gainesville: University of Florida Press.

Male, Beverly. 1982. *Revolutionary Afghanistan.* New York: St. Martin's Press.

Mandelbaum, David. 1988. *Women's Seclusion and Men's Honor.* Tucson: University of Arizona Press.

Mayer, Ann Elizabeth. 1995. "Cultural Pluralism as a Bar to Women's Rights: Reflections on the Middle Eastern Experience." In Julie Peters and Andrea Wolper, eds., *Women's Rights, Human Rights: International Perspectives.* New York: Routledge.

Meriwether, Margaret L., and Judith E. Tucker, eds. 1999. *Social History of Women and Gender in the Middle East.* Boulder: Westview Press.

Mernissi, Fatima. 1988. *Doing Daily Battle: Interviews with Moroccan Women.* Trans. Mary Jo Lakeland. London: Women's Press.

———. 1987. *Beyond the Veil: Male-Female Dynamics in Modern Muslim Society.* Rev. ed. Bloomington: Indiana University Press.

Messaoudi, Khalida, and Elisabeth Schemla. 1998. *Unbowed: An Algerian Woman Confronts Islamic Fundamentalism.* Philadelphia: University of Pennsylvania Press. Originally published in French in 1995.

Minces, Juliette. 1982. *The House of Obedience.* London: Zed Books.

Mir-Hosseini, Ziba. 1999. *Islam and Gender: The Religious Debate in Contemporary Iran.* Princeton: Princeton University Press.

Moghadam, V. M. 2001. "Organizing Women: The New Women's Movement in Algeria." *Cultural Dynamics* 13 (2): 131–154.

———. 1999. "Gender and Globalization: Female Labor and Women's Mobilization." *Journal of World-Systems Research* 5 (2) (Spring 1999): 301–314.

———. 1998. *Women, Work, and Economic Reform in the Middle East and North Africa.* Boulder: Lynne Rienner.

———. 1992. "Patriarchy and the Politics of Gender in Modernizing Societies: Afghanistan, Iran, Pakistan." *International Sociology* 7 (1) (March): 35–53.

———. 1988. "Women, Work, and Ideology in the Islamic Republic." *International Journal of Middle East Studies* 20 (2) (May): 221–243.

———, ed. 1996. *Patriarchy and Development: Women's Positions at the End of the Twentieth Century.* Oxford: Clarendon Press.

———, ed. 1994. *Gender and National Identity: Women and Politics in Muslim Societies.* London: Zed Books.

———, ed. 1994. *Identity Politics and Women: Cultural Reassertions and Feminisms in International Perspective.* Boulder: Westview Press.

Motzalfi-Haller, Pnina. 2001. "Scholarship, Identity, and Power: Mizrahi Women in Israel." *Signs: Journal of Women in Culture and Society* 26 (3): 697–734.

Najmabadi, Afsaneh. 1998. *The Story of the Daughters of Quchan: Gender and National Memory in Iranian History.* Syracuse, N.Y.: Syracuse University Press.

Nashat, Guity, ed. 1983. *Women and Revolution in Iran.* Boulder: Westview Press.

Norton, Augustus Richard, ed. 1994, 1995. *Civil Society in the Middle East.* Vols. 1, 2. Leiden: Brill.

Paidar, Parvin. 1995. *Women and the Political Process in Twentieth Century Iran.* Cambridge, UK: Cambridge University Press.

Pitt-Rivers, Julian. 1977. *The Fate of Shechem or the Politics of Sex: Essays in the Anthropology of the Mediterranean.* Cambridge: Cambridge University Press.

Poya, Maryam. 1999. *Women, Work, and Islamism: Ideology and Resistance in Iran.* London: Zed Books.

Rashid, Ahmed. 2000. *Taliban: Militant Islam, Oil, and Fundamentalism in Central Asia.* New Haven: Yale University Press.

Redclift, Nanneke, and M. Thea Sinclair, eds. 1991. *Working Women: International Perspectives on Labour and Gender Ideology.* London: Routledge.

Richards, Alan, and John Waterbury. 1996. *A Political Economy of the Middle East.* 2nd ed. Boulder: Westview Press.

Rubenberg, Cheryl. 2001. *Palestinian Women: Patriarchy and Resistance in the West Bank.* Boulder: Lynne Rienner.

Sabbagh, Suha, ed. 1998. *Palestinian Women of Gaza and the West Bank.* Bloomington: Indiana University Press.

Shahrani, M. Nazif, and Robert Canfield, eds. 1984. *Revolutions and Rebellions in Afghanistan.* Berkeley: University of California International Studies Institute.

Shami, Seteney, L. Taminian, S. Morsy, Z. B. el Bakri, and E. Kameir. 1990. *Women in Arab Society: Work Patterns and Gender Relations in Egypt, Jordan, and Sudan.* Providence: Berg/UNESCO.

Sharabi, Hisham. 1988. *Neopatriarchy: A Theory of Distorted Change in Arab Society.* New York: Oxford University Press.

Sivan, Emmanuel. 1985. *Radical Islam.* New Haven: Yale University Press.

Standing, Guy. 1999. "Global Feminization Through Flexible Labour: A Theme Revisited." *World Development* 27 (3): 583–602.

———. 1989. "Global Feminisation Through Flexible Labour." *World Development* 17 (7): 1077–1096.

Tabari, Azar, and Nahid Yeganeh, eds. 1982. *In the Shadow of Islam: The Women's Movement in Iran.* London: Zed Books.

Tavakoli-Targhi, Mohamad. 2002. *Refashioning Iran: Orientalism, Occidentialism, and Historiography.* London: Palgrave.

Tillion, Germaine. 1983. *The Republic of Cousins: Women's Oppression in Mediterranean Society.* London: Al-Saqi Books.

Tinker, Irene, ed. 1990. *Persistent Inequalities: Women and World Development.* New York: Oxford University Press.

Toubia, Nahid, ed. 1988. *Women of the Arab World: The Coming Challenge.* London: Zed Books.

United Nations. 2000. *The World's Women 2000: Trends and Statistics.* New York: United Nations.

United Nations Development Programme. 2002 [and various years]. *Human Development Report 2002.* New York: Oxford University Press.

Urban, Mark. 1988. *War in Afghanistan.* New York: St. Martin's Press.

Walby, Sylvia. 1994. "Is Citizenship Gendered?" *Sociology* 28 (2) (May): 379–395.

———. 1990. *Theorizing Patriarchy.* Oxford: Blackwell.

Ward, Kathryn, ed. 1990. *Women Workers and Global Restructuring.* Ithaca: ILR Press.

Weeks, John. 1988. "The Demography of Islamic Nations." *Population Bulletin* 43 (4) (December).

Wood, Ellen Meiksins. 1988. "Capitalism and Human Emancipation." *New Left Review* 167 (January–February): 1–21.

World Bank. 2000. *World Development Indicators 2000.* New York: Oxford University Press.

Worsley, Peter. 1986. *The Three Worlds: Culture and World Development.* Chicago: University of Chicago Press.

Yuval-Davis, Nira. 1997. *Gender and Nation.* Thousand Oaks, Calif.: Sage.

Yuval-Davis, Nira, and Floya Anthias, eds. 1989. *Woman-Nation-State.* London: Macmillan.

Index

Abd al-Rahman, Aisha, 173
Abdur Rhaman Khan, 236
Abed, Yamina, 94
Abortion, 14, 117–118, 207
Accommodation as response to Islamism, 161–162
Activism. *See* Feminism; Women's movements
Administrative and managerial employment, 54, 213(table), 214
Adoption of children, 289–290
Adultery laws, 287
Affirmative action, 76(n65), 79
Afghanistan, 14; dower reform, 273(n47); early reforms concerning women, 236–241; effect of modernization on employment, 246–247; emergence of the Taliban, 227–228, 264–267; employment patterns, 246(table), 265–266; employment reforms, 252–253; family law reforms, 127; land ownership and distribution, 271(n5); marriage age and fertility rates, 139; national reconciliation, 251–253; patriarchal characteristics, 241–244; post-revolution state building, 104–107; post-Taliban reforms, 267–270; precapitalist social organization, 123; rise of Islamism, 155; role of widows in family, 117; Saur Revolution, 82, 101–104; social change through revolution, 23; social indicators, 245(table); social organizations and services, 253–259; social structure and

women's status, 228–234; sociodemographic features, 140(table); state weakness, 234–236; tribal structure, 122–123; women in refugee camps, 259–264
Afghan Women's Council, 254–256, 266–267
Afzal, Shirin, 248
Age of Iranian work force, 205
Age of marriage. *See* Marriage age
Agrarian societies and patriarchy, 119
Agricultural economies, 37, 45; Afghanistan's non-integrated economy, 229; agricultural reform in Afghanistan, 249–251; female employment in, 213(table); fertility behavior, 133–134; globalization and, 36; Iran's labor force marginalization, 205; Iran's revised stance on women in, 208–209; statistics on Afghanistan, 43–44
Agro-Poor countries, 39
Aid, international, 263–264, 268
Algeria: Algerian Revolution, 82, 93–95; changes in family law, 128, 138; economic development, 18, 153; female employment, 51(table), 52(table), 62–63; fertility behavior, 134; gender dynamics of revolutions, 107(table); globalization in, 37; hijab as form of rebellion, 167–168; Islamism and education, 141; labor force participation, 50(table); oil-centered industrialization, 43; personal status laws, 163; political economy, 39;

About the Book

Moghadam's influential study of gender dynamics and social processes in the Middle East has been fully updated to reflect a decade of major changes—including shifts in development strategy and population policy, the rise of a reform movement in Iran incorporating both Islamic and secular feminists, the fundamentalist war on feminists in Algeria, and the rise and fall of the Taliban in Afghanistan. New data and analysis of emerging trends make this second edition a welcome successor.

Valentine M. Moghadam is director of women's studies and associate professor of sociology at Illinois State University.